Discontinuous Constituency

Natural Language Processing

6

Mouton de Gruyter
Berlin · New York

Discontinuous Constituency

Edited by
Harry Bunt
Arthur van Horck

Mouton de Gruyter
Berlin · New York 1996

Mouton de Gruyter (formerly Mouton, The Hague)
is a Division of Walter de Gruyter & Co., Berlin.

⊚ Printed on acid-free paper which falls within the guidelines
of the ANSI to ensure permanence and durability.

Library of Congress Cataloging-in-Publication Data

Discontinuous constituency / edited by Harry Bunt, Arthur van Horck.
p. cm. – (Natural language processing ; 6)
Rev. papers of the Conference on Discontinuous Constituency, organized and sponsored by the Institute for Language Technology and Artificial Intelligence (ITK). 1990, at Tilburg University in the Netherlands.
Includes index.
ISBN 3-11-013011-4 (cloth : alk. paper)
1. Grammar. Comparative and general – Syntax – Congresses. 2. Computational linguistics – Congresses. I. Bunt, Harry C. II. Horck, Arthur van, 1954- . III. Conference on Discontinuous Constituency (1990 : Tilburg University) IV. Series.
P291.D56 1996
415–dc20 96-29087
CIP

Die Deutsche Bibliothek – Cataloging-in-Publication Data

Discontiniuous constituency / ed. by Harry Bunt ; Arthur van Horck. – Berlin ; New York : Mouton de Gruyter, 1996
(Natural language processing ; 6)
ISBN 3-11-013011-4
NE: Bunt, Harry [Hrsg.]; GT

Disk conversion with T_EX: Lewis & Leins, Berlin. – Printing: Ratzlow-Druck, Berlin. – Binding: Lüderitz & Bauer GmbH, Berlin.
Printed in Germany

Preface

The present book contains thirteen edited papers presented at the Conference on Discontinuous Constituency, organized in 1990 at the Institute for Language Technology and Artificial Intelligence (ITK) at Tilburg University in the Netherlands.

Discontinuous constituency is a pervasive phenomenon in natural languages that presents problems for its description in formal grammars. A wide variety of syntactic solutions have been suggested in the context of different theoretical and computational frameworks. These vary from the introduction of transformations and metarules to the use of crossing branches and incomplete tree fragments. Like virtually any linguistic phenomenon, discontinuous constituency not only raises syntactic problems, but also gives rise to semantic and pragmatic considerations, and involves issues of processing in generation and understanding. The introductory chapter gives an impression of the pervasive nature of the phenomenon of discontinuous constituency, and presents an overview of the approaches and techniques proposed in this book.

The aim of the Conference on Discontinuous Constituency was to bring together theoretical and computational linguists working in different theoretical frameworks and computational approaches in order to discuss the problems and issues involved in discontinuous constituency. The contributions in this book make it clear to what extent we have succeeded in this. Most of the current mainstream linguistic theories are represented in this book: Categorial Grammar, Head-driven Phrase Structure Grammar, Government & Binding theory, the Barriers framework, Tree Adjoining Grammar; alternative frameworks such as Segment Grammar and Discontinuous Phrase Structure Grammar are also present.

We would like to thank Riny Huijbregts, Erik-Jan van der Linden, Henk van Riemsdijk, Elias Thijsse, and Frans Zwarts for refereing submissions to the conference. Thanks are also due to Digital Equipment bv. and the Institute for Language Technology and Artificial Intelligence (ITK) for their sponsoring of the conference. Our thanks also go the staff of ITK and Tilburg University for their logistic and administrative support for the conference. Most of all, we wish to thank Wietske Sijtsma, who was mainly responsible for setting up and organizing the conference.

The editors,
Tilburg, April 1994

Table of Contents

Discontinuous constituency: Introduction

Harry Bunt

1. Discontinuity and linguistic theory

This book is concerned with the phenomenon of discontinuous constituency, studied from different theoretical perspectives.

Is discontinuous constituency a theory-dependent notion? It might certainly appear that way, since the notion of constituency and the role that constituent structure plays vary from theory to theory. The notion of phrase structure plays a central role in the formulation of many of the best developed grammatical theories, and the assignment of structural descriptions to sentences in terms of constituents is often a major goal, the main differences between theories in this respect being the variety of constituent types they employ and the operations for buiding representations of constituent structure.

Head-driven Phrase Structure Grammar (HPSG) and Categorial Grammar (CG) are somewhat different from more traditional phrase-structure based approaches. Although obviously phrase-structure based, HPSG approaches the relations between constituents in a special way, in that

- the theory focuses on the immediate-dominance aspect of constituent structure and does not use phrase markers representing the dominance- and precedence relations among constituents, but instead encodes dominance relations as part of a sign, the unit of all linguistic information in HPSG;
- linear precedence relations are not represented in signs, and are only considered in separately expressed LP-constraints.

In Categorial Grammar the situation is sometimes claimed to be entirely different from phrase-structure based approaches, since CG does not pursue the derivation of constituent structures of any kind. Still, any categorial analysis of a sentence corresponds to an *implicit* constituent structure being assigned, since the categorial derivation makes decisions on which words and word groups to combine, based on their categories and their linear precedence relations. This is brought out clearly in the contributions by Moortgat and

Bunt in this volume, where CG rules are considered that allow non-adjacent elements to be combined by introducing discontinuity in categories (functors and arguments).

The case of CG illustrates that, more generally, in those linguistic theories that do not aim at assigning explicit descriptions of constituent structures to sentences, the construction of such descriptions does nonetheless occur implicitly and is in fact unavoidable, since semantic interpretation requires decisions on which elements in the sentence are combined. Whenever non-adjacent elements are combined, this requires the description of discontinuity in some way or other.

It therefore seems that the phenomenon of discontinuous constituency is essentially theory-independent, and does not go away when we choose one theory rather than another. There is some variation in the linguistic data that are recognized as manifestations of the phenomenon, because different theories have somewhat different views on what counts as a constituent; still, there is a great deal of consensus about this matter across linguistic theories. As a result, the phenomenon of discontinuous constituency provides a potentially fruitful domain for discussion across the borders between linguistic theories. The present book aims at contributing to this discussion.

2. Empirical facts about discontinuity

When we describe the syntactic organization of a sentence, we group the words at various levels and divide the sentence into noun phrases, verb phrases, relative clauses, adjective phrases, prepositional phrases, amount expressions, and the like. The use of such word groups may be syntactically motivated by the possibility to achieve a higher level of generalization by describing syntactic structure in terms of such groups than in terms of individual words. Semantically, there is the perhaps even stronger motivation formed by the Principle of Compositionality, which requires the decomposition of sentences into meaningful parts in order to systematically derive sentence meanings.

More often then not, the syntactically and semantically meaningful word groups, or 'constituents', are contiguous: they consist of words standing next to one another. But sometimes this is not the case, as in example sentence (1):

(1) *Mary* <u>woke</u> *me* <u>up</u> *at seven-thirty.*

The verb form 'woke up' is split into two non-adjacent parts here, the particle 'up' being separated from 'woke' by 'me', which causes a discontinuity in the verb phrase.

Exactly which discontinuities a particular grammar formalism has to deal with, depends on the general views on constituency that the grammatical theory in question takes. Theories which recognize verb phrases, for instance, have to deal with VP discontinuities. As most theories do assume verb phrases, it is not surprising that VP discontinuities form an important topic of study (see e.g. the contributions to this volume by Hepple, Hoekstra, and Reape).

Noun phrases are not so often discontinuous. But of course, relative clause extraction leads to discontinuous NPs, and so do the VP discontinuities in NP-embedded VPs, as in premodifying relative clauses in Dutch or German. A genuine NP discontinuity is formed by Dutch determiner structures of the form *Wat voor*, as in sentence (2):

(2) Wat *heb jij* voor auto *gekocht?*
(What did you car buy?, meaning *What car did you buy?)*

Such discontinuities are studied by Corver (this volume).

PPs and APs are mostly contiguous, but again, it is certainly not impossible for them to be discontinuous. Examples of discontinuous adjective- and adverbial phrases are presented in (3):

(3) a. *This is a* better *movie* than I expected.
b. *Leo is* harder *gegaan* dan ooit tevoren.
(*Leo has been going faster than ever before.*)

Moreover, virtually any phrase can become discontinuous by the insertion of *metacomments*, such as parentheticals. Some examples:

(4) a. *John* talked *of course* about politics.
b. *Peter bought a house* on, *or almost on,* Angels Beach.
c. *Leo is going* faster, *I would say,* than ever before.
d. *He invited* the vice-chairman, *I think it was*, of the committee.
e. An undergraduate student, *supposedly*, who had witnessed the event *reported it to him.*
f. *This designer is* equally cool, *you know*, as Armani.

(Examples d and e taken from Dowty, this volume.)

Even idiomatic expressions, which one may be inclined to think of as fixed, inseparable, sequences of words *par excellence*, can be discontinuous:

(5) a. Will *John soon* kick the *proverbial* bucket?

b. Le marchand de sable va *bientôt* passer.

(See Abeillé and Schabes, this volume.)

It is thus not an exaggeration to say that discontinuities may arise almost everywhere; discontinuous constituents are by no means rare or exceptional. Still, most grammar formalisms are explicitly or implicitly based on the idea of a constituent as a continuous sequence of words, being primarily designed to describe continuous constituents and having to take recourse to special operations for dealing with discontinuities. This is because concatenation, and therefore the notion of *adjacency*, plays a central role in most grammar formalisms. The description of structures made up of non-adjacent elements therefore in general presents difficulties.

3. Approaches and techniques for handling discontinuity

In this book a wide variety of approaches to the study and treatment of discontinuous constituents is presented, varying from attempts to reduce the problems they pose by re-examining the notion of constituency and minimizing the articulation of syntactic description in constituent structures, to mathematical and computational techniques for dealing effectively with discontinuous constituents in linguistic descriptions and computer programs for interpreting and generating sentences with discontinuities.

Dowty in his contribution *Towards a minimalist theory of syntactic structure* takes a fundamental approach to discontinuous constituency by addressing the more general question what might count as a constituent and for what reasons. Dowty notes that

> "No assumption is more fundamental in the theory (and practice) of syntax than that natural languages should always be described in terms of constituent structure, at least whereever possible."

and goes on to note that, in spite of this,

> "... syntacticians don't usually ask questions ... as to what the nature of evidence for a constituent structure in a particular sentence in a particular language is: we just take whatever structure our favorite syntactic theory would predict as the expected one for the string of words in question - by current X-bar theory, etc. - unless and until that assumption is contradicted by some particular fact. .. I suspect syntacticians today have almost come to think of 'the primary empirical data' of syntactic research as phrase structure trees, so firm are our convictions as to what the right S-structure for most any given sentence is."

Dowty advocates a more skeptical, 'minimalist' approach to syntactic structure which takes the default assumption that a clause or group of words is only a linear structure: a string, and that a hierarchical structure should be assigned only when necessary for getting the data right. By taking linear structure to be the norm, Dowty argues that the description of various discontinuous syntactic phenomena can be simpler. This minimal, string-like syntactic structure Dowty calls the *phenogrammatical* structure, which he contrasts with the *tectogrammatical* structure, thereby making a distinction originally due to Curry (1963). The tectogrammatical structure describes the steps by which a sentence is built up from its parts, but without regard to the form that these combinations of parts take, i.e. without information about the order of words and phrases, whether inflectional morphology marks the syntactic organization or not, and so on. The representation of the latter information is the phenogrammatical structure.

Abeillé and Schabes in their contribution use Tree Adjoining Grammar as their theoretical framework, and argue that the formalism of Lexicalized TAGs, where sets of elementary trees are associated to lexical items, defining linguistic units of *extended domain of locality* that have both syntactic and semantic relevance, offers a natural representation for constituents that may exhibit internal discontinuities. Such constituents follow regular syntactic TAG composition rules, but lack semantic compositionality. This representation considers noncompositional constituents as one semantic unit without having to stipulate any element to be semantically empty, and is thus kept strictly increasing.

Corver's contribution approaches discontinuous constituency within the Barriers framework of Chomsky (1986). Specific attention is given to the discontinuity in Dutch determiner phrases that may occur in structures of the form *wat voor*, as in (2). It is argued that such noun phrases consist of an interrogative quasi-argument *wat*, that functions as the head of the NP, and a predicative PP headed by *voor*, which is conjoined to *wat*. The presence or absence of discontinuity in *wat voor*-phrases in various syntactic environments can be accounted for in terms of the Subjacency Condition and the Empty Category Principle on the basis of the proposed internal structure of the *wat voor*-phrases.

Hoekstra's contribution, that falls within the same theoretical tradition, is concerned not just with discontinuity but more generally with phenomena of movement and binding. Two types of binding relationships are distinguished, the stronger of which is subject to a strict locality requirement. The proposed approach to binding results in analyses that, among other things, account for a recently discovered problem concerning the effect of move-alpha on the binding of negative polarity items.

The contribution by Bunt is concerned with the development of tools for formal description and effective processing of bounded discontinuities. Bunt argues first that articulate syntactic descriptions of hierarchical constituent structure do not necessarily take the form of *trees*. He argues, with McCawley (1982), that syntactic descriptions in general should be allowed to have crossing branches, and that there is nothing objectionable about such structures, which he calls *discontinuous trees* (or *disco-trees*, for short). A precise mathematical definition of these structures is provided. A fairly intriguing matter is the definition of a linear precedence relation among discontinuous trees in a way, useful in the formulation of grammatical rules for combining such trees. The key notion used for this purpose is the *adjacency sequence*, which is defined in such a way that the concatenation of two or more discontinuous trees, forming an adjacency sequence, has the effect that the elements of those trees are interwoven. Complexity-theoretical issues are briefly addressed, as are computational issues concerning their implementation in chart parsers.

The notions introduced by Bunt are theory-neutral in that they can be used in many different grammatical frameworks. In his contribution, Bunt explains their use in phrase-structure grammars in some detail, developing a formalism called *Discontinuous Phrase Structure Grammar* (DPSG), and very briefly considers their possible use in Categorial Grammar. In a categorial framework, their use could be in allowing *discontinuous categories*. A simple example would be that of a discontinuous verb phrase like *'woke Mary up'*, here we could use a category discontinuous category (NP\)[/NP]/PART for the verb (*'woke'*), which concatenates to the right in an adjacency sequence (NP\)[/NP]/PART + NP + PART as follows:

(6) (NP\)[/NP]/PART + NP + PART $\Rightarrow$ (NP\)/NP

The part [/NP] in the discontinuous category indicates that a noun phrase (*'Mary'*) may separate a VP-final particle (*'up'*) from the verbal stem (*'woke'*); the verb and the particle form a discontinuous functor which applies to the separating NP as its right-hand side argument.

Moortgat, in his contribution, goes at great length in studying the consequences and possibilities of discontinuous categories. He considers two *discontinuous type constructors*, intended to capture extraction and infixation operations at a level suitable for linguistic generalization. In the first case, the operator constructs a discontinous category of which the two constituent parts together form a discontinuous functor, applicable to the intervening material; in the other case (infixation) the constructor constructs a discontinuous argument for the functor corresponding to the intervening material. These operators had been introduced before in Moortgat (1988) in an attempt to accomodate Bach's (1981; 1984) work on discontinuity within a categorial type logic approach. In his contribution, Moortgat improves on his earlier proposal by presenting a *complete* logic for extraction and infixation type constructors in terms of the sign-based approach to categorial deduction.

Sanfilippo in his contribution develops the idea that the relevant constraints on discontinuous verb-object dependencies, arising in Italian sentences like *'A Maria, Carlo non gli ha ancora scritto'* ('To Mary, Carlo has not written to-him yet'), can be expressed in terms of access to the thematic domain of a sentence. It is shown how a strong generalization expressed in these terms can be given a precise syntactic, semantic and computational interpretation within the framework of Unification Categorial Grammar augmented with a neo-Davidsonian verb semantics and predicate-argument association. The resulting approach can easily be extended to also provide an empirically motivated account of dislocated subjects, and is thus interesting for the treatment of discontinuous subject-VP dependencies as well.

Hepple's contribution is also in the framework of Categorial Grammar. He presents a novel view of the relation between word order and subcategorization, according to which the canonical word order in any language arises through the interaction of three factors: (i) the 'underlying' order of subcategorization by the verb for its complements corresponding to obliqueness; (ii) the direction (left or right) of subcategorization by the verb of each complement; (iii) a lexical process of 'verb displacement', causing the verb to be displaced from its position relative to its complements according to the underlying subcategorization.

Pollard's contribution is concerned with a detailed study of verb-second and raising phenomena in the framework of Head-driven Phrase Structure Grammar. In Government-Binding theory and associated frameworks it has become standard to regard to occurrence in second position of the finite verb in declarative sentences (in English, Dutch, German, and many other languages) as a case of head movement. The finite verb or auxiliary, on this account, undergoes movement into the COMP position, and some phrasal constituent moves to the left of it. The apparent discontinuity between the finite auxiliary and its VP sister in such sentences might be thought to be problematic for nontransformational theories. Pollard discusses this issue in detail for verb clusters in German, and gives an account of the possibilities and constraints to front parts of such clusters. A satisfactory analysis of these phenoma is proposed within the HPSG framework, with one issue not entirely resolved: the resulting set of combination schemata allow different parses for certain sentences, with no demonstrable linguistic (e.g., pragmatic) differences between the alternative analyses. Exactly how this poblem of spurious ambiguity can be resolved is not entirely clear.

Reape's contribution is also in the framework of HPSG. He argues that surface syntax should be rejected as the basis of word order. Instead, he claims that word order is determined within locally definable 'word order domains', where nonlexical word order domains are composed from smaller word order domains, and where the word order domain of a daughter may be the same as that of the mother. This last stipulation is the basis for allowing discontinuities, as it means, informally, that the elements of the daughters's domain can be interleaved with those of the mother's domain. Technically, Reape introduces an operation called *sequence union* to be able to describe an 'interleaving concatenation' of discontinuous constituents. The sequence union operator applied to two strings *A* and *B* can produce any sequence of elements from *A* and *B* which conserves the relative order among the *A*-elements and that among the *B*-elements. This concept is similar to Bunt's notion of concatenating *adjacency sequences*, the latter being slightly more constraining.

Aarts in his contribution introduces a variant of Bunt's DPSG framework, which he calls *Discontinuous Rewrite Grammar*. He shows how the formalism can describe both bounded and unbounded dependencies in terms of discontinuous trees with crossing branches, and pays particular attention to the design of an elegant and efficient chart parser for this formalism.

De Smedt and Kempen describe a grammar formalism designed for incremental generation of sentences, called *Segment Grammar*. This formalism is somewhat reminiscent of Tree-Adjoining Grammar, but differs in that sister nodes can be incrementally added to an existing (partial) structure. The formalism distinguishes two levels of syntactic description: *f-structures*, which are unordered functional structures, and *c-structures*, which represent left-to-right order of constituents. True discontinuities are viewed as differences between immediate dominance relations in c-structures and those in corresponding f-structures. Constructions that are treated in this way include clause union (including Dutch cross-serial dependencies), right dislocation, and fronting.

Their contribution is concerned with discontinuous constituency not only from a structural viewpoint but also from a processing point of view. They note that several kinds of discontinuities seem to offer advantages for an incremental generation strategy; this is especially true of optional dislocations. Fronting of focused constituents is natural if we assume prominent concepts to be passed on to the grammatical encoder earlier than other parts of the semantic input. Similarly, right dislocation allows the generator to utter constituents which are ready and postpone uttering more complex ('heavy') ones, which are still being processed semantically. In addition, right dislocation allows the incorporation of new semantic input as afterthoughts.

Saint-Dizier's contribution is devoted to new techniques for expressing constraints and relations on discontinuous elements in a structure in a computationally attractive way. To this end, an extension to the logic programming language Prolog is presented, called *Dislog*, especially designed for logic programming with discontinuities. A Dislog clause is a set of definite clauses, possibly sharing common variables, which must co-occur in a parse (or proof) tree. The notion of discontinuity is expressed by the fact that there are no *a priori* restrictions on the locations of these definite clauses in the parse (proof) tree. Saint-Dizier explains the concepts of Dislog and shows how Dislog can be applied to the parsing of discontinuous constituents in natural language.

References

Aarts, E.
1996 Discontinuous Rewrite Grammar, a description of discontinuities by separating recognition and structure assignment. *This volume*, 99–113.

Abeille, A. and Schabes, Y.
1996 Non-compositional discontinuous constituents in Tree Adjoining Grammar. *This Volume*, 113–139.

Bach, E.
1981 Discontinuous constituents in generalized categorial grammar. *NELS XI*, Amherst (MA), 1–12.

Bach, E.
1984 Some generalizations of Categorial Grammars. In: F. Landman and F. Veltman (eds.), *Varieties of Formal Semantics*, 1–23.

Bunt, H.C.
1996 Formal tools for describing and processing discontinuous constituency structure. *This volume*, 63–83.

Chomsky, N.
1986 *Barriers*, MIT Press, Cambridge (MA).

Corver, N.
1996 Discontinuity and the 'wat voor'-construction in Dutch. *This volume*, 165–179.

Dowty, D.R.
1996 Toward a minimalist theory of syntactic structure. *This volume*, 11–62.

Emonds, J.E.
1976 *A transformational approach to English syntax*. Academic Press, New York etc.

Emonds, J.E.
1979 Appositive relatives have no properties. *Linguistic Inquiry*, vol. 10, 211–243.

Hepple, M.
1996 Grammatical relations and the Lambek calculus. *This volume*, 255–277.

Hoekstra, E.
1996 Discontinuity and the Binding theory. *This volume*, 307–322.

McCawley, J.D.
1982 Parentheticals and Discontinuous Constituent Structure. *Linguistic Inquiry*, vol. 13, no. 1, 91–106.

Moortgat, M.
1996 Generalized quantifiers and discontinuous type constructors. *This volume*, 181–207.

Pollard, C.J.
1996 On head non-movement. *This volume*, 279–305.

Reape. M.
1996 Getting things in order. *This volume*, 209–253.

Ross, J.R.
1973 Slifting. In: M. Gross, M. Halle and M.P. Schützenberger (ed.), *The formal analysis of natural language*. Mouton, The Hague.

Saint-Dizier, P.
1996 Expressing discontinuous constituency in DISLOG. *This volume*, 85–98.

Sanfilippo, A.
1996 Thematic accessability in discontinuous dependencies. *This volume*, 323–344.

Smedt, K. De and Kempen, G.
1996 Discontinuous constituency in Segment Grammar. *This volume*, 141–163.

Toward a minimalist theory of syntactic structure

David R. Dowty

1. Introduction

No assumption is more fundamental in the theory (and practice) of syntax than that natural languages should always be described in terms of constituent structure, at least wherever possible. To be sure, certain kinds of cases are well-known where constituent structure of the familiar sort runs into problems, e.g.

(1) a. VSO languages
b. Cases for which "wrapping" operations (Bach 1980: Pollard 1984) have been proposed
c. Free word order and free constituent order languages
d. Various other instances of proposed "flat" structures
e. Clause unions
f. Extrapositions
g. Parenthetical phrases

But even here, the strategy has usually been to accommodate these matters while modifying the received notion of constituent structure as little as possible. Indeed, the most extreme and general theoretical proposal I know of for systematically departing from constituent structure, Zwicky's (1986) *direct liberation* framework, which incidentally was the inspiration for this paper, still takes the familiar hierarchical constituent structure as its point of departure, in an important sense, and derives "flat" structure from these (more on this below).

There are two things that worry me about the situation syntactic theory finds itself in. Since hierarchical syntactic structure is so often assumed, syntacticians don't usually ask questions – at least beyond the elementary syntax coursc – as to what the nature of evidence for a constituent structure in a particular sentence in a particular language is: we just take whatever structure our favorite syntactic theory would predict as the expected one for the string of words in questions – by the current X-bar theory, etc. – unless and until that assumption is contradicted by some particular fact.

My second concern is closely related: I suspect syntacticians today have almost come to think of the "primary empirical data" of syntactic research as phrase structure trees, so firm are our convictions as to what the right S-structure tree for most any given sentence is. But speakers of natural languages do not speak trees, nor do they write trees on paper when they communicate. The primary data for syntax are of course only *strings* of words, and everything in syntactic description beyond that is part of a theory, invented by a linguist.

What I want to do today is describe what I will call a *minimalist theory of syntax*, that is, one in which the default assumption in syntactic description is that a clause or group of words is *only* a string; hierarchical structure is postulated only when there is direct evidence for it or when it is unavoidable in generating the data right. Unlike Zwicky's approach, which is really very similar in the class of phenomena that can be analyzed[1], this theory is deliberately formalized in such a way as to make linear relationships more salient and hierarchical ones less so.

As you might expect from the context in which I am presenting this paper, I am suggesting that this is also a theory which permits the description of various discontinuous syntactic phenomena, in fact descriptions which are simpler, I will argue, by virtue of it's taking linear structure as the norm; in the course of the discussion, I will treat examples of many of the problems in (1).

While not appealing so much to tree structure, I will on the other hand take much advantage of the idea of *Linear Precedence Principles* from GPSG (Gazdar et al. 1985; henceforth GKPS), and also an idea which I think has been too little pursued: that some words and constituents are more tightly bound (or *attached*) to adjacent words than others are. This draws a parallel between syntax in general and the well-studied phenomenon of clitics.

Though the theory as described here is in a very simple and embryonic form, and there are many aspects of the problems under discussion that I cannot yet give a satisfactory treatment of, I hope the reader can get some flavor of the possibilities and constraints from this presentation. One of the main interests that such a theory has for me is the way it challenges us to justify our assumptions about constituent structure at every step of the syntactic description of a natural language.

1.5 Two senses of "constituent"

Now, there is one sense in which I am proposing to do away with much syntactic constituency and one sense in which I am not. I still assume that sentences of a language are described by rules of a recursive grammar which specify how words and phrases of some categories can be combined to form expressions of another category. And I assume that language is interpreted by semantic rules, corresponding one-to-one to these syntactic rules, that specify how the interpretation of a syntactically-derived phrase is determined by the interpretations of the inputs to the rule. All this implies syntactic constituents, in one sense. I am going to introduce a distinction which H. B. Curry drew in 1963 (Curry 1963) and which I have found it useful to appeal to before (Dowty 1982a): the sense of syntactic structure we have just been talking about is *tectogrammatical* structure – the steps by which a sentence is built up from its parts, but without regard to the actual form that these combinations of parts take.

This notion may be best visualized by a Montague-style analysis tree as in (2), which you might imagine as illustrating the generation of a sentence, in an unknown language, meaning "Harold gave Max a mango", with lexical items only glossed:

(2)

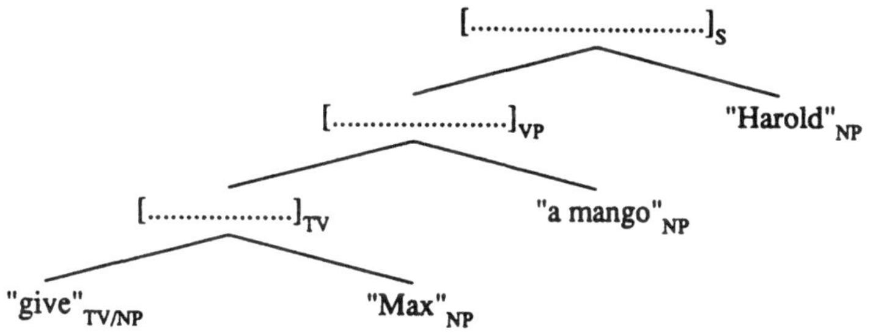

Here we see the lexical expressions involved, the syntactic categories, the steps by which words and phrases are combined, and the implicit form of the compositional semantics. But the complex expressions at the nodes of the tree have been omitted. What is missing is, in Curry's term, the *phenogrammatical* structure: *how* the words and phrases are combined, in what order, whether word order is fixed or free, whether inflectional morphology marks the syntactic organization or not, whether the tectogrammatical groups in (2) come out continuously or discontinuously in the sentence itself, and so on. It is in phenogrammatical structure, not tectogrammatical structure, that I am suggesting natural language may be more string-less, less tree-like, than has been suspected.

One might ask at this point whether it really matters whether phenogrammatical structure is string-like or not, as long as tectogrammatical constituent structure exists; doesn't the latter do everything we want phrase-markers to do anyway? The answer is, it would not matter at all, if all languages had fixed word order and syntactic formation rules that invariably concatenated input expressions as undivided wholes: the phenogrammatical structure of every sentence like (2) would in that case be a straightforward mapping of the tree's leaves into a linear string. The problem, of course, is that languages do not always work this way: they have discontinuous word order, extraposition, and all the other phenomena in (1) that are problematic for the context-free phrase structure model. My claim is therefore that when one gets around to describing such phenomena, one may well find that they are better formulated in terms of syntactic operations applying to strings of words than to phrase markers.[2] Furthermore, I am questioning whether some of the familiar tree-based descriptions of apparently context-free phenomena (in languages like English) are really the best descriptions, so I'm suggesting the class of non-phrase-structural phenomena could be wider than is generally assumed.

The distinction between tectogrammatics and phenogrammatics is an important one if we are to seriously examine the basis for traditional constituent structure. Many arguments and lines of reasoning that are taken to show, inter alia, that surface structures are trees really establish only tectogrammatical constituency, not phenogrammatical constituency.

Here is an example to illustrate. The sentences in (3a)–(3d) would constitute one good traditional argument that the English VP has a hierarchical "nested" VP structure:

(3) a. They said he could have been slicing the spinach, and have been slicing the spinach he could.
b. They said he could have been slicing the spinach, and been slicing the spinach he could have.
c. They said he could have been slicing the spinach, and slicing the spinach he could have been.

This conclusion, in particular, meant that (4) had at least three VP constituents:

(4) He could have been slicing the spinach.

However, (3) and other distributional facts about VPs show only that English has nested VPs tectogrammatically – that rules create various kinds of (fronted) VPs in (3), and that these rules derive all these kinds of VPs sequentially in the process of producing (4): It does not show that (4) itself has a phenogrammatical form that involves nested VP constituents; and I will argue below that the VP in (4) has no such constituent structure.[3]

For a second example consider co-reference conditions involving pronouns and reflexives in English. There is a long tradition that describes these in terms of tree structure. But in what sense is the tree structure necessary? In 1980, Emmon Bach and Barbara Partee (1980) showed how to construct, for a reasonable fragment of English, an analysis of anaphora and pronominal expressions, in terms of the kind of compositional semantic interpretation I am assuming here. It was as adequate as the approach of Reinhart (1983), they argued, and superior in a few respects – namely, where there was an asymmetry in anaphoric behavior that would necessarily be paralleled by some asymmetry in semantic interpretation but was no well-motivated asymmetry in traditional constituent structure. Bach and Partee's compositional semantic interpretation had the same form as the tectogrammatical syntactic structure – as it does by definition in a "rule-to-rule" semantic interpretation. But the actual phenogrammatical form of the English sentences plays no role in their system.

In this paper, I will begin by describing this theoretical framework briefly, then illustrate it, first with a very small corpus of Finnish data, to indicate the treatment of relatively free word order, then turn to English, where I will address the "constituency" of the verb phrase, then turn to extraposition data. English extraposition offers a very interesting challenge to someone who would postulate much less constituent structure but more reliance on LP principles: "extraposed" relative clauses and PPs end up at exactly that place in the clause where English LP principles say that subordinate clauses and PPs should end up anyway: at the right hand margin. The challenge is to see whether the phenomenon of extraposition can in fact be made to follow automatically from these LP rules simply by "loosening" the English constituent structure properly.

2. What would a "minimalist" syntactic theory look like?

The components of the theory I have in mind are as follows:

a. *A Categorial Grammar* with compositional semantics; syntactic operations build up expressions from words to larger expressions.
b. The *"default operation"* for combining two expressions syntactically is to merge their words into a single (unordered) multiset.

c. However, *Linear Precedence Principles*, as in Generalized Phrase Structure Grammar (or GPSG) (GKPS 1985) and Head-Driven Phrase Structure Grammar (or HPSG) (Pollard 1984; Pollard – Sag 1987), which apply to the output of the whole grammar, limit the orders in which expressions may appear relative to others, either partially (leaving some word order variation) or entirely (leaving none). Specifications like "must appear in second position" are to be allowed. But LP principles are actually defaults, not absolute rules, as they can be overridden by rule-particular syntactic operations (Zwicky 1986; Powers 1988); see below.
d. For each language, there is a list of *Bounding Categories*: parts of expressions of these categories cannot mingle with expressions outside the bounding category expression and vice-versa; these are "constituents" in the traditional sense. The list of bounding categories is regarded as a language-specific parameter. For (probably) every language, "Sentence" is a bounding category, since even in very free word order languages, words do not stray outside their own clause. For some languages, NP is a bounding category (so-called "free constituent order languages" are of this type, e.g. Makua (Stucky 1981)), for others it is not (these are so-called "free word order languages"), where an adjective may stray away from its head noun. A language in which all categories were bounded would of course be completely "constituentized," as normal phrase structure theory assumes all languages to be.
e. Constituent-formation *can* be specified as a rule-specific syntactic operation, but a marked one: there are two other kinds of possible syntactic operations besides the default one:
   (i) *ordering* one expression[4] to the left or right (13) of the head[5] of another, and
   (ii) *attaching* one expression to the left or right of the head of another. The difference is that two expressions connected by attachment cannot be subsequently separated by other expressions, while ordering allows this.
f. Finally, since categorial grammar is the basis of this theory, it is important to emphasize that agreement and government morphology would still be treated either as in Bach (1983), or in a unification-based system as in Karttunen (1989) or Zeevat – Klein – Calder (1987); both of these allow one to observe the so-called "Keenan principle" that in a functor-argument pair, agreement morphology is "copied" from the argument to the functor, while the functor determines what government morphology appears on the argument (Keenan 1974).

Needless to say, the details of this proposal are provisional (or absent at present) and might well be modified; some will in fact be modified as we proceed.

3. A simple "free word order" example: Finnish

I will begin with a very brief illustration of how a relatively free word order language would be described in this method. Fortunately, Karttunen (1989) describes a small part of the grammar of Finnish that is just right for my purposes, so I will borrow his data (but not his analysis). First, we will need some notation.

3.1 Basic notation

Since a set is a familiar mathematical construct that has members with no inherent ordering on them, I will use the set notation to represent expressions that have been produced by grammatical operations but not linearly ordered by the LP (Linear Precedence) principles, as for example (5) is:

(5) $\{a, b, c, d\}$

Suppose the language has the LP principles in (6),

(6) $A < B$, $C < D$

which are interpreted as saying that expressions of category A (to which we assume *a* belongs) must precede those of category B (to which *b* belongs), and those of C (etc.) must precede those of D. This will then authorize the following as well-formed linearly ordered sentences of the language:

(7)	*a*	*b*	*c*	*d*	*c*	*d*	*a*	*b*
	a	*c*	*b*	*d*	*c*	*a*	*d*	*b*
	a	*c*	*d*	*b*	*c*	*a*	*b*	*d*

(This is taken over from GPSG, as in Gazdar – Pullum (1981)).

To indicate a bounded constituent, a set "inside" (represented as a member of) an expression will be used. For example, if in the derivation of the expression in (5) the combination of *c* and *d* had been of a bounded category, then the whole expression produced would have been (8):

(8) $\{a, b, \{c, d\}\}$

and since bounded expressions cannot be separated by expressions outside, the linear phrases allowed by the same LP rules would now be only:

(9)
a b c d
a c d b
c d a b

For grammatical rules, I will adopt a Montague-style notation (since phrase-structure rules will obviously not be suitable), and the default combination operation will be represented by set union:

(10) (Default syntactic operation)
S1. If $\alpha \in A/B$, $\beta \in B$, then $F_1(\alpha,\beta) \in A$, where $F_1(\alpha,\beta) = \alpha \cup \beta$.

Lexical items themselves will be singleton sets; therefore all expressions, lexical and complex will be sets, so set union is always well-defined on them.

The two "marked" operations will be symbolized as in (11)

(11) a. $F_2(\alpha,\beta) = \alpha << \beta$ ("α ordered to left of β")
b. $F_3(\alpha,\beta) = \alpha + \beta$ ("β attached to the head of α")

3.2 Finnish data

Karttunen is concerned with four statements about Finnish grammar:

(12) a. In declarative sentences, subjects and objects may occur in any order with respect to the verb and to one another.
b. In yes-no questions and imperatives, the finite verb comes first.
c. The negative auxiliary (*e-*) precedes the temporal one (*ole-*) and both precede the main verb, but the three types of verbs need not be adjacent.
d. Elements of participial and infinitival clauses can be interspersed among the constituents of a superordinate clause (Karttunen 1989: 48).

Assume that Finnish has at least these operations for combining subjects and objects for verbs:[6]

(13) a. If $\alpha \in S/NP$, $\beta \in NP$, then $F_4(\alpha,\beta) \in S$, where $F_4(\alpha,\beta) = \alpha \cup NOM(\beta)$.
b. If $\alpha \in TV$, $\beta \in NP$, then $F_5(\alpha,\beta) \in VP$, where $F_5(\alpha,\beta) = \alpha \cup ACC(\beta)$.

(I give only a very rudimentary treatment of morphology here, merely to point out at what point in the derivation case government is determined; see Bach (1983) or Karttunen (1989) or Zeevat, Klein – Calder (1987) for fully-developed theories.)

And if Finnish has *no* LP principles affecting NPs and verbs, then the following kinds of sentences will be generated, all of which mean "John loved Lisa":

(14) a. Jussi rakasti Liisaa.
b. Jussi Liisaa rakasti.
c. Liisaa Jussi rakasti.
d. Liisaa rakasti Jussi.
e. Rakasti Jussi Liisaa.
f. Rakasti Liisaa Jussi.

For Karttunen's second condition, we need simply a Linear Precedence Condition for Finnish that specifies that certain kinds of words, namely interrogative auxiliaries[7], must be first in their clause.

(15) $\frac{\text{V}}{\text{[+Q]}} < \text{X}$

Here "X" is understood as a variable over categories, i.e. an interrogative verb precedes anything. I assume a syntactic rule derives interrogative verbs from ordinary verbs, by suffixing *-ko*, and performing the necessary semantic operation. This will allow (16a) but not (16b):

(16) a. Rakastiko Jussi Liisaa?
Did John love Lisa?
b. *Jussi rakastiko Liisaa?

Karttunen's third condition, restricting the order of two kinds of auxiliaries and main verb is only a slightly more complicated LP condition,

(17) $$\frac{\overset{\mathrm{V}}{[+\mathrm{Aux}]}}{[+\mathrm{Neg}]} < \frac{\overset{\mathrm{V}}{[+\mathrm{Aux}]}}{[+\mathrm{Tem}]} < \frac{\mathrm{V}}{[-\mathrm{Aux}]}$$

permitting four (but only four) ways of saying that Lisa has not slept. Here, *ei* is the negative auxiliary and *ole* the past auxiliary:

(18) a. Liisa ei ole nukkunut.
Lisa has not slept
b. Ei Liisa ole nukkunut.
c. Ei ole Liisa nukkunut.
d. Ei ole nukkunut Liisa.

The more interesting case, for our concerns, is the fourth one, for Finnish is rather unusual in permitting words from a subordinate infinitive complement to "escape" into a main clause. Below is some data. We will have an infinitive meaning "play tennis in these (clothes)" embedded as complement to the verb "start" (*ruveta*), all of which is then embedded as complement to "intend" (*aikoa*), along with negative and tense auxiliary verbs:

(19) *En minä ole aikonut ruveta pelaamaan näissä tennistä*
not I have intend start play these-in tennis
I did not intend to start to play tennis in these.

(*ruveta* takes infinitive complements with the verb in the 3rd infinitive in the illative case; *aikoa* requires the 1st infinitive.) In this example, of course, the infinitives appear in contiguous groups. But the object *tennistä* and adverbial *näissä* can "scramble" to any of six possible positions in the superordinate clause. Karttunen says that it is not clear that all of the 42 possible "free" word orderings are acceptable, but it is not clear that any are ungrammatical either. Some clearly acceptable ones are in (20), where the "discontinuous constituents" are in boldface:

(20) En **minä näissä** ole **tennistä** aikonut ruveta **pelaamaan**
not I these-in have tennis intend start play
En minä **tennistä näissä** ole aikonut ruveta **pelaamaan**
not I tennis these-in have intend start play
En minä **tennistä** ole aikonut **näissä** ruveta **pelaamaan**
not I tennis have intend these-in start play

In the present theory, Karttunen's property (6d), that elements of an infinitival clause can escape into a superordinate clause, which is responsible for this data, reflects simply that infinitival VP is not a bounding category in Finnish, as it is in many other languages. The syntactic rule combining the verbal subcategory to which *aikoa* ("intend") belongs with its complement is approximately as in (21), morphology again simplified:

(21) If $\alpha \in$ VP/VP, $\beta \in \mathrm{VP}_{[-\mathrm{fin}]}$, then
$F_6(\alpha,\beta)$ e VP, where
$F_6(\alpha,\beta) = \alpha \cup [\text{3rd-Inf}](\beta)$.

And assume a parallel rule for *ruveta* ("start"). The analysis tree responsible for (19)–(20) is then (22):

(22)

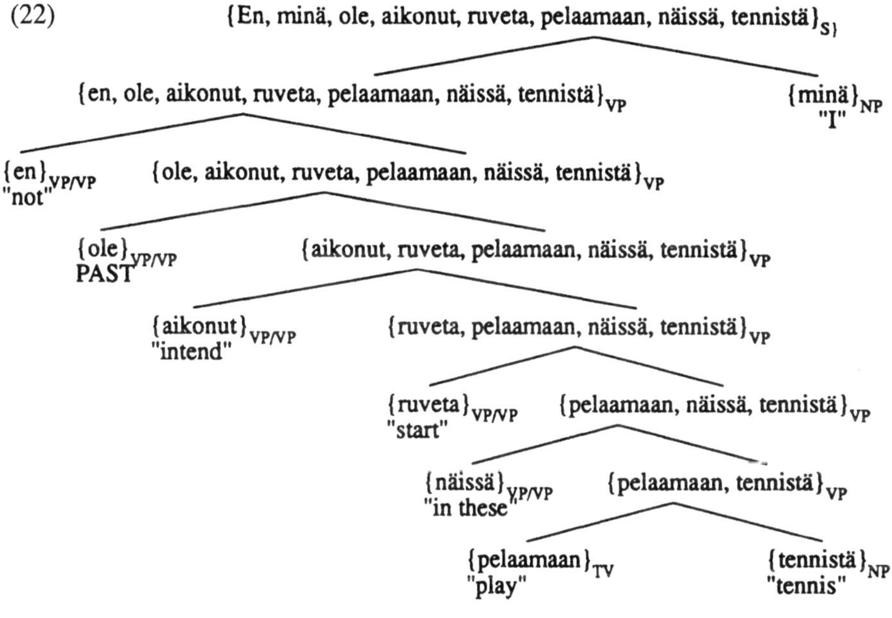

As the only LP principles we have used for Finnish relate to the order of the first two auxiliaries and as VP is not a bounding node, the sentences in (20), and many others, are all permissible linearizations of (22).[8]

With this brief illustration, I turn to a language which is not traditionally thought to have any free word order phenomena of this sort, namely English, and will first discuss verb phrase word order, then turn to extraposition.

4. English: Verb Phrase order and constituency

4.1 English bounding nodes

With regard to bounding categories for English, surely "sentence" is one. One can see this not only from, e.g. the fact that NPs do not float freely from one clause to another but, as will turn out to be very relevant to this paper, from the familiar fact that extrapositions from NP also do not escape the clause of their host NP, the so-called "right roof constraint" (Ross 1967). The bounding status of NP itself is complicated and will be delayed until we talk about extraposition. Is VP a bounding category in English? It seems to me that we have no choice but to treat infinitives as bounding categories, where by "infinitive" I mean a nonfinite VP introduced by *to*. As for other kinds of English VPs, one might think there is a good argument that they too are bounding nodes, from that fact that, as show by Baltin (1982), extraposition seems not to be able to escape from VP in examples like (23), where a VP in fronted position permits us to visibly demonstrate that an extraposed PP (or relative clause) cannot move outside it.

(23) a. They said he would call people from Boston up, and call people from Boston up he did.
b. *They said he would call people from Boston up, and call people up he did from Boston.

However, I believe this not really the correct conclusion to draw from (23). Example (23) is one of a more general class of focus sentences, which include not only VP focus sentences but NP focus sentences such as (24):

(24) a. She said she would hire a good syntactician, and by golly, a good syntactician she hired!
b. We expected him to catch a big one, and a whopper he caught.
c. They said he would pick out a nice one, and a nice one it was.

These of course can include PP or relative clause modifiers, and just as with Baltin's examples, we see that extraposition from the fronted constituent is prohibited (whereas relative classes and PPs can of course be extraposed from non-preposed NPs):

(24′) a. She said she would hire a syntactician with a PhD, and by golly, a syntactician with a PhD she hired!
a′. *She said she would hire a syntactician with a PhD, and by golly, a syntactician she hired with a PhD!
b. We expected him to catch a big one with red scales, and a big one with red scales he caught.
b′. *We expected him to catch a big one with red scales, and a big one he caught with red scales.
c. They said he would pick out a nice one that fit her, and a nice one that fit her it was.
c′ *They said he would pick out a nice one that fit her, and a nice one it was that fit her.[9]

Since the fronted NPs in (24') cannot possibly be dominated by VP, Baltin's constraint cannot apply to them. The more general way to formulate a constraint which covers both kinds of examples is (25):

(25) Elements may not be extraposed out of a focussed constituent (and perhaps not out of any non-WH fronted constituent?)

Here are some further kinds of examples of frontings of various kinds: in some of these the fronted element is a VP (or can be analyzed that way, anyway) and so are not relevant to demonstrating Baltin's conclusion insufficient. But once examples like (24') have done that, these show the generality of the phenomenon. A third sentence is added in each case showing that extraposition is possible in a different structure:

(26) a. A student who excelled at math is what he wanted to become.
b. *A student is what he wanted to become who excelled at math.
c. A student visited us yesterday who excelled at math.
e. A mile from the spring where we got our water there appeared a big cloud of dust.
f. *A mile from the spring there appeared a big cloud of dust where we got out water. (If not *, then not synonymous with (26e).)
g. We rode about a mile from the spring almost every day where we got our water.
h. Under the bed which we put in the attic is a good place to hide.
i. *Under the bed is a good place to hide which we put in the attic.
j. I put it under the bed one day last week which we put in the attic.

Thus I will assume that the syntactic rules for focus and inversion (which I will not treat here) must mark their pre-verbal constituents as bounded, but I believe VPs in general are not bounded.

4.2 Grammatical categories

I will assume at least the following syntactic categories for English, shown with a few exemplary members of each:

(27)	a.	NP	(*John, Mary,* etc.)
	b.	VP (= S/NP)	(*walk, talk*)
	c.	TV(= VP/NP)	(*eat, love*)
	d.	TV/NP	(*ask, give*)
	e.	$\text{TV/PP}_{[\text{to}]}$	(*give, offer*)
	f.	$\text{IV/VP}_{[\text{inf}]}$	(*try, want*)
	g.	$\text{TV/VP}_{[\text{inf}]}$	(*persuade, convince*)
	h.	$(\text{VP/VP}_{[\text{inf}]})\text{/NP}$	(*promise*)
	i.	(VP/VP)	(*slowly, carefully*)
	j.	S/S	(*today, obviously,* – also parenthetical phrases like *on the other hand, she suggested,* etc.)
	k.	PP (= XP/XP)	(*in the garden*, etc.)
	l.	P (= PP/NP)	(*to, for, in*)
	m.	CN	(*dog, cat,* etc.)
	n.	NP/CN	(*a, the, many*)
	n.	$\text{CN/CN}_{[\text{atr}]}$	(*former, imitation, etc.*)
	o.	$\text{CN/CN}_{[\text{prd}]}$	(prd. adjectives, *asleep* etc., PPs *on the sofa,* etc., Relative clauses *who loves Mary*)

This is intended to be a fairly uncontroversial category system for a categorial grammar for English, though of course much detail, especially in morphology, is omitted from the category descriptions in order to save space. Prepositional Phrase is treated as a category schema, XP/XP where X ranges over (at least) VP, S, and CN. One thing to note is parentheticals, which I have assigned to category S/S (to get their compositional semantics right) and of which I will have nothing to say about the internal syntax, though I will return to their external syntax below. Also note that I have divided noun modifiers into attributive adjectives, versus predicative modifiers – the latter including predicating adjectives, prepositional phrases, and relative clauses; I believe this distinction can be justified both syntactically and semantically.

In order for LP principles to work properly, certain further distinctions in category must be introduced beyond the usual categorial ones. VP/VP includes both adverbs and prepositional phrases, but the latter must be distinguished, possibly with a feature, from adverbs. Complement sentences are often treated categorially as NPs, with their complementizer of category NP/S, but their sentential nature must be specified somehow. And so on. For convenience, I will refer to traditional categories like PP below without spelling out any one of the several ways these might be defined with features on the category system above.

4.3 English LP principles

For the purposes of this paper, I will work with the LP principles (28):

(28) V,N,Adj < NP < Prt < PP < $VP_{[inf]}$ < S

These are based loosely on the LP principles worked out in GPSG (Gazdar and Pullum 1981; GKPS 1985). Here, the complement structure of verbs like *persuade* is treated in the now-traditional way for categorial grammar (Bach 1980), in which they combine with their infinitive complements before their NP complements[10]. By the use of LP principles and a "flat" structure, the correct word order (e.g. *persuade Mary to leave*) results without any wrapping operation (in much the same way as in GPSG, though here with a categorial syntax).

One thing that should be noticed about (28) is that it seems to order constituents according to their length. That is, I think it is fairly likely (though I have not attempted a statistical study) that an average English NP is longer than an average verb; that an average PP is longer than an average NP; an average infinitive is longer than an average PP, and an average clause longer than an average infinitive. As is known, and as we shall have occasion to see later on, violations of this ordering are often acceptable when the particular instance of a constituent placed on the right is significantly longer than whatever (28) says should instead be on the right of it. This raises the question whether (28), or part of it, should be replaced by a general rule sensitive to the length of particular phrases and saying "heavier constituents to the right".[11] I don't have an answer to this question, but I think one should keep it in mind.

4.4 The double NP construction and attachment

How should we insure the correct word order when there are two NPs following the verb, as in (29)?

(29) a. Mary gave Harold a book.
b. Richard asked Sue a question.

Here the order of NPs is rigidly fixed, unlike the order of two PPs, which the LP rule (28) correctly predicts to be free (e.g. *talk to Bill about John, talk to John about Bill*). We could, as in the GPSG treatment, introduce via the syntactic combinatory rule a syntactic feature [+F] on the NP that we want to appear to the left, then add the LP principle:

$$NP_{[+F]} < NP_{[-F]}$$

It has been objected that this step is ad hoc and is at odds with the spirit of the LP program. There is, however, a more interesting way to account for this ordering.

It has often been observed (e.g. Postal 1974) that adverbs can intervene almost anywhere in an English VP except between the verb and immediately following NP:

(30) a. I believe very strongly that Tony is honest.
b. *I believe very strongly Tony to be honest. (Postal 1974)
c. I persuaded George quite easily to leave the party.
d. I persuaded George to leave the party quite easily.
e. *I persuaded quite easily George to leave the party.
f. I easily could have been passing the note to her.
g. I could easily have been passing the note to her.
h. I could have easily been passing the note to her.
j. I could have been easily passing the note to her.
k. *I could have been passing easily the note to her.
l. ?I could have been passing the note easily to her.
m. I could have been passing the note to her easily.

With parentheticals (*however, I think, George, on the other hand,* etc.), the same prohibition against separating a verb from its object obtains. This suggests to me that this is one point in the English verb phrase where a tighter connection exists between adjacent elements than at other points, and it is this kind of case for which I included the syntactic operation of *attachment* (cf. (11b) above). Thus, the syntactic rule for combining verb with direct object is to be revised from the default operation to that in (31). (This will be revised slightly below.)

(31) S5. If $\alpha \in$ TV, $\beta \in$ NP, then $F_3(\alpha,\beta) \in$ VP, where $F_3(\alpha,\beta) = \alpha + \beta$. ($\beta$ attached to the head of α)

A derivation of the VP *give a book to Harold*, for example, would proceed as in (32):

(32)

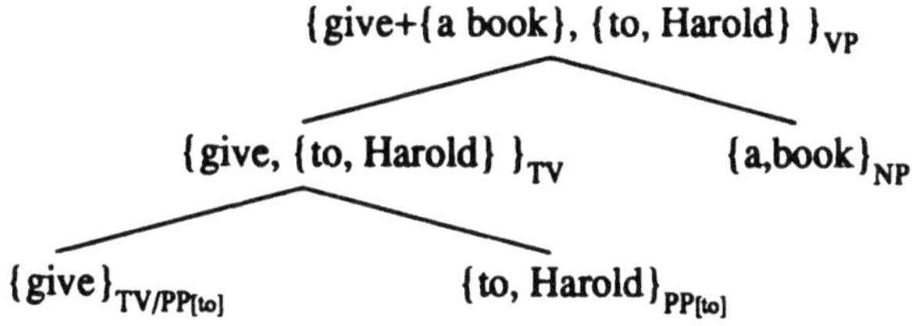

That is, the attachment of the NP *a book* to the verb is by the special "marked" syntactic operation introduced earlier and cannot be interrupted by adverbs. The PP *to Harold*, necessarily follows afterward (but cf. below).

A phenomenon which may correlate with this one in an interesting way is that unstressed personal pronoun objects are unacceptable when they do not appear immediately to the right of their verbs, necessarily preceding even a verb particle (Zwicky 1986):

(33) a. We took in the unhappy little mutt right away.
b. *We took in it right away.
c. We took it in right away.

(34) a. Martha told Noel the plot of *Gravity's Rainbow*.
b. *Martha told Noel it.
c. Martha told it to Noel.

After surveying the range of syntactic environments where unstressed personal pronouns *are* acceptable in English, Zwicky offers the following two-part solution to this problem. Unstressed personal pronouns are *leaners* (in the sense of Zwicky (1982), what have been called *clitics* in other, less fine-grained analyses), and must form a prosodic unit with adjacent material, either preceding or following, in order to be acceptable. (Stressed personal pronouns, on the other hand, have a freer distribution.) The first part of his solution is the Unaccented Pronoun Constraint:

(35) A personal pronoun cannot constitute a prosodic phrase by itself unless it bears accent.

Connection of a subject or possessive pronoun to a following prosodic host is relatively unconstrained. For object cases, Zwicky proposes the constraint (36):

(36) A personal pronoun can form a prosodic phrase with a preceding prosodic host only if:
a. the prosodic host and NP constituted by the pronoun are sisters
c. the prosodic host is a lexical category
d. the prosodic host is a category that governs case marking

The second two conditions generalize the condition from verb + object cases to preposition + object and adjective + object cases (as in *I'm nearer her than you are*).

The interesting question here is whether the cases in which prosodic combination of a pronoun with its functor are "obligatory" are the same as the ones in which, in our framework, the syntactic operation of attachment is motivated. If so, syntactic attachment may offer a way of describing this constraint, or even a motivation for it. Zwicky points out a number of other kinds of cases besides (33)–(34) where the effect can be observed. A subject pronoun can appear after an auxiliary when the latter is inverted (examples below from Zwicky (1986a)), but in this situation it may not be separated from that verb:[12]

(37) a. Was he posing on the couch?
b. *Was apparently he posing on the couch?

(38) a. When did she learn that pigs can't fly?
b. *When did supposedly she learn that pigs can't fly.

(39) a. He isn't dangerous, is he?
b. *He isn't dangerous, is conceivably he?

(40) a. Were she prime minister, she would dissolve parliament.
b. *Were, I suspect, she prime minister, she would dissolve parliament.

(41) a. Not only would he eat the snails, he also enjoyed the brains in black butter.
b. *Not only would, however, he eat the snails, he also enjoyed the brains in black butter.

But in fact this effect is not peculiar to pronouns; *no* NP in these positions can be separated by an adverb from its auxiliary, (in contrast to the its uninverted form of the same sentence):

(37′) *Was apparently Henry Kissinger posing on the couch?
Henry Kissinger apparently was posing on the couch.

(38′) *When did supposedly Aunt Susan learn that pigs can't fly.
Aunt Susan supposedly did learn that pigs can't fly.

(39′) *He isn't dangerous, is conceivably Bad Bart?
He isn't dangerous, is Bad Bart?
Bad Bart conceivably is dangerous, isn't he?

(40′) *Were, I suspect, Mrs. Gardmore prime minister, she would dissolve parliament.
If Mrs. Gardmore, I suspect, were prime minister, she would dissolve parliament.

(41′) *Not only would, however, Henry eat the snails, he also enjoyed the brains in black butter.
Henry, however, would eat the snails, and he even enjoyed the brains in black butter.[13]

To finish out the range of English cases, we note the familiar facts that prepositions cannot be separated from their objects:

(42) *We put the fertilizer on, probably, the table.
*The president of, he remarked, Brazil will be there.

Nor adjectival objects from their adjectives:

(43) *The dog was near, I thought, the vase.

Thus the generalization that is apparently true of English syntax is (44):[14]

(44) Whenever a functor combines with a NP argument to its right in English, they combine via the operation of syntactic attachment.

And the corresponding prosodic principle is (45), giving us an analysis somewhat similar to Zwicky's but stated in terms of attachment rather than tree structure, is (45):

(45) An unstressed personal pronoun which has been combined with its functor by the operation of syntactic attachment is only acceptable if it can form a phonological phrase with the lexical head of that functor.

Note that there is a naturalness about this: a tighter syntactic binding requires, for certain unstressed items, a tighter phonological binding as well. If this is right for English, one would like to know if the combination is found in other languages. Unfortunately, I do not know of any research investigating a possible connection between cliticization conditions and syntactic "intervention constraints" in other languages.

Consider first the verb-particle examples. I assume that verb-particle combinations are single lexical entries which can consist of more than one word; this step is motivated semantically by the fact that many such combinations are not compositional in meaning at all (*egg on, buzz off*, etc.) or are not completely predictable(e.g. *try out, try on*, but not *try in*, *try up*, etc.). I also assume that lexical entries can consist of more than one word; see Dowty (1979) for discussion. In fact, I will propose that verb-particle constructions each have two kinds of lexical entries, one which consists of a verbal functor and a particle complement, as in (46),

(46) Cat TV: {$\text{look}_{TV/Prt}$, up_{Prt}}

and one which consists of the same two words, but in which they are somehow "glued together", either by means of a bound, or by means of attachment: for my purposes here, it doesn't matter:

(47) Cat TV: {{$\text{look}_{TV/Prt}$, up_{Prt}}}

These two forms will result in the familiar two forms of verb-particle VPs, the first in (48) (cf. LP principles above), the second in (49):

(48) {look+{the, answer}, up}

(49) {{look, up}+{the, answer}}

Consider what happens in the case of an object pronoun. For the first kind of lexical entry there is not a problem, as the pronominal argument is syntactically attached to the lexical head of its functor and can form a phonological phrase:

(50) {look+{it}, up}

but in the second the attachment (or bounding) that keeps the particle next to the verbal head keeps the pronoun away from it (and thus violates (45), if we assume with Zwicky that pronouns cannot form phonological phrases with particles, prepositions or parentheticals to the left):

(51) {{look, up}+it}

For the double-NP constructions, I must make it explicit that I am assuming that in a VP *give Harold the oyster*, the verb *give* combines (tectogrammatically) first with its immediately adjacent NP *Harold*, then with the other object *the oyster*: this is not the same order as in most other works dealing with grammatical relations and categorial grammar (e.g. Bach 1980; Dowty 1982a), but grammatical relations can still be defined in terms of the categories of this system, nonetheless, as pointed out in Dowty (1982b).[15] (It would in fact still be possible to treat the pronoun data assuming the NPs to combine the other way, but with a more complicated analysis.[16]) And since the principle (44) clearly applies to both objects of a two-object verb, we must assume that syntactic attachment is used for both objects of a double-object verb to maintain its full generality. And indeed, separation of either object from the verb by an adverb sounds pretty bad, even though the first object separation sounds worse:

(52) a. Harry had undoubtedly slipped Roger the Kiwi sauce.
b. *Harry had slipped undoubtedly Roger the Kiwi sauce.
c. ?*Harry had slipped Roger undoubtedly the Kiwi sauce.
d. Harry had slipped Roger the Kiwi sauce, undoubtedly.

If so, the difference between the acceptable and unacceptable derivations is as in (53) (good) and (54) (bad):

(53)

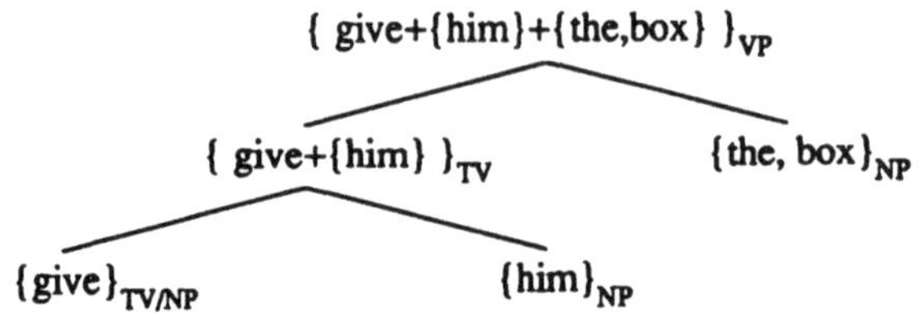

(54)

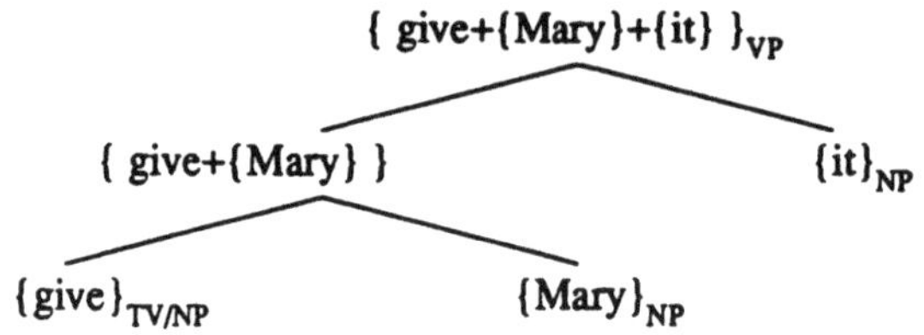

In the latter case, (54), the pronoun cannot form a phonological phrase with the lexical head of its functor, because the attached NP *Mary* intervenes; (53) has no such problem.

4.5 Heavy NP shift

Of course, the English direct object need not always appear adjacent to the verb but can, in a process known traditionally as "Heavy NP Shift", move to the right of the clause if it is long or otherwise lengthy ("heavy"):

(55) Susan gave to Ellen for her birthday a large purple ceramic tureen with lavender handles.

I do not have a great deal to say about this but can suggest two possibilities:

(i) syntactic attachment is optional for the TV + NP rule in the case of "heavy" objects, and the LP principles should be understood in such a way as to allow a very heavy constituent to gravitate to the right of the clause, no matter what its category, or
(ii) an alternative operation for the TV + NP rule is to bound all the words within the TV and order the object NP after it, i.e. if a is the TV and b is the NP, the phrase produced is { {a} << b }.

One interesting argument for both formulations is that they, together with the syntactic category assignment to verbs given earlier, predict the observation (Bach 1980) that Heavy-NP Shift is possible for sentences with *persuade* but not *promise*:

(56) a. I persuaded to go to the game all those nutheads who were afraid of a little rain.
b. *I promised to go to the party all the people who were afraid I would stay home.

This is because Heavy-NP Shift would be tied to the operation for a particular syntactic category, TV, and as sentences with *promise* never involve this category, (56b) would not be produced.

By the same token, the left-most NP in double-object sentences would be predicted not to undergo Heavy-NP shift under either of these analyses,

(57) *I gave a copy of the book everyone I saw today in the office or on the street.

since that NP does not participate in the TV + NP rule. It does predict, however, that the *second* of the two NPs should be shiftable (it *is* combined via the TV + NP rule), and this seems to be so:

(58) I gave Mary yesterday for her birthday the old book I had bought in the used bookstore on 17th Street.

(The configurational analysis of Zwicky (1986) shares these same predictions, incidentally.)

4.6 Ordering of auxiliary verbs

Here, again, I am not so much defending a particular analysis as pointing out various alternatives which exist in a linear-oriented theory. One thing I would like to assume is that a VP with several auxiliary verbs has a flat structure, not a hierarchical one. As is well-known, English auxiliaries appear in one order (Modal, Perfective, Progressive, Main Verb) and in one order only. So we will have derivations roughly like (59):

(59)

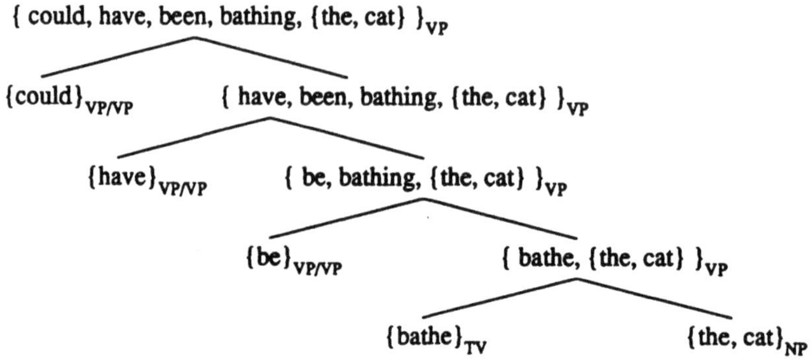

In a flat-structured VP, the most obvious alternative would be to build this into the LP principles:

(60) [+V,+M] < [+V,+Perf] < [+V, +Prog] < [+V, -Aux]

Note that we cannot thereby dispense with a system of subcategorization and agreement features among the auxiliaries, both because of morphology and semantics: having auxiliaries in the proper order would do little good if the wrong interpretation were assigned. There is a bit of redundancy in (60), therefore.

A more interesting method would be to try to order each successive auxiliary verb added in the course of a derivation at the beginning of its phrase, as the LP principle (61):

(61) V < X

might (at first) seem to do, where *X* is a variable over syntactic categories. But this is not enough. In a flat VP containing several auxiliaries, (61) would apply to all such verbs equally, once they have been introduced.

Could one save (61) by adopting a kind of "freezing principle"? That is, LP principles would be applied, as it were, "immediately", not at the end of the derivation, and once two constituents were ordered with respect to each other, their order could not change? The intent would be that the variable *X* above stands for everything already ordered by LP principles, and the *V* for the new auxiliary.

This however is still not inadequate. The previously added auxiliary verbs would still be indistinguishable in syntactic *category* from the newly added one, yet LP principles are traditionally understood as depending only on category.

What one needs is an LP principle that orders the lexical functor of the *current* phrase being produced before the rest of the phrase, something like (62):

(62) VP/X < Y where VP/X is any verbal category, and VP/X is the lexical head of the current phrase.

And this has to be understood in such a way that it can be applied recursively, repeatedly ordering "new" functors before "old" functors.

"Current lexical head" is however a very different notion from the other categories we have used in LP rules: what is current at one stage of the derivation is not current later on, so we are admitting in a roundabout way a feature of tectogrammatical structure – which is hierarchical structure – into the determination of word order, even if the phrase we are building is not to be hierarchical. Is this undesirable? I am not sure. Since both GPSG and HPSG (Pollard – Sag 1987) have found "(lexical) head" to play such an important role, it seems possible that one should admit just this derivational notion without admitting others.

The only other way I can see of handling auxiliary order in a flat structure is to make ordering specific to each auxiliary rule, i.e. all such rules are of the form of (63):

(63) If $\alpha \in VP/VP_{[+aux]}$, $\beta \in VP$, then $F_2(\alpha, \beta) \in VP$, where $F_2(\alpha, \beta) = \alpha << \beta$.

(Note the operation actually orders α only before the head of β.) This is a less general statement.

4.7 Subject-Predicate rule

I really have nothing to say about this, except that I want to assume that it, like the verbal auxiliary rules, does not introduce bounding. Since English otherwise has functors before arguments, I suppose this rule will involve rule-specific ordering of the argument (or at least its head – see below) to the left of the functor.

4.8 Sentence adverbs and parentheticals

As mentioned, I have assumed that both sentence adverbs and parentheticals are of category S/S and are thus sentence modifiers semantically, which is appropriate. I will not deal with how parenthetical expressions such as *I think, on the other hand, if you don't mind, George, please*, etc. are generated. The syntactic operation for combining such an expression with a sentence is the default one[17], i.e. "union", or merging. As there are no LP principles applying to adverbs or parentheticals, an adverb is free to "settle" anywhere as long it

(i) does not cross a bounding category boundary or
(ii) separate attached words.

Since the (finite) VP is not bounded, this predicts such adverbs can appear just about anywhere in the VP, except between a verb or preposition and its object, or in a subordinate VP or S (see examples throughout this paper). This is more or less correct, and it is a natural virtue of this kind of theory to deal with this traditionally knotty problem in this simple way. (See below on adverbs and parentheticals in NPs.)

5. Extraposition and the bounding of NPs

As I said at the beginning, an important attraction of this kind of theory is to be able to describe extraposition by the same LP principles that determine the position of complement S's and PP's in the VP. But in order to determine just how we want to permit NP modifiers to "break away" from NPs and extrapose, and therefore the nature of NP bounding in this theory, we will want to look at some extraposition data.

5.1 What extraposes?

First of all, I will *not* discuss sentences like (64) in this paper:

(64) a. That John is asleep is obvious.
b. It is obvious that John is asleep.

In accord with GKPS (1985), as well as Dowty (1982b), I will assume that the clause *that John is asleep* in (64b) is an argument of the verb itself, with a "dummy" subject being an independent argument, and thus these examples do not involve anything peculiar in word order or constituency.

Here are, instead, the kinds of things I assume to "extrapose":

(65) *Relative clauses from subject and objects*
a. Someone arrived who I have never met before.
b. We met a student yesterday at lunch who only recently arrived in this country.

(66) *Non-Restictive relative clauses*
a. The President appeared shortly at the party, who had just come from an important meeting.

(67) *Prepositional phrases from subjects and objects*
a. Two people were there from Alaska.
b. I called some doctors up with late office hours.

(68) *Prepositional phrases from nominalizations*
a. My appointment was at 2 PM with Dr. Smith.
b. She gave me a picture at that time of Mr. Howard.

(69) *Predicative Adjectives*
a. I want to see someone at every window armed and alert.
b. Nothing ever shows up on her table even remotely palatable. (Both examples from Stucky 1987: 388.)

(70) *Infinitival relative clauses*
The person didn't arrive to fix the plumbing?

5.2 How are NPs bounded?

Were the above examples the extent of the extraposed phrases (and these are certainly the majority), the generalization would be clear: onc can extrapose a predicative modifier (i.e. a $CN/CN_{[+prd]}$) from a NP. It is even observable that non-predicative adjectives (which appear exclusively in pre-nominal position in a NP) cannot extrapose:

(71) a. *I saw some senators at the party former and future.

b. *It appear I have given the assignment to a fool after all complete and utter. (Stucky)

At this point, let's consider how the NP bounding might be described. Since extraposable phrases appear both within their "host" NP and in separated position, I assume NPs will have to have two syntactic analyses, one in which these phrases are somehow connected to the rest of the NP, and one in which they are not (and therefore appear at the end of the clause in accord with LP principles).

If one followed Bach and Cooper (1978) in treating restrictive relative clauses (and, shall we suppose, all the above predicative modifiers as well) as of category NP/NP, then a simple analysis of NP bounding is at hand. In the Bach-Cooper analysis, there are two expressions of category NP whenever there is such a modifier, an "inner" and an "outer" one, as in (72):

(72) $\{\ \{\text{someone}\}_{NP}\ \{\text{whom I have never met}\}_{NP/NP}\ \}_{NP}$

If we stipulate that in such cases *either* one *or* the other of these NPs can be bounded, but not both, we have the result we need: if the bound is taken to be the outermost NP, the relative clause remains immediately adjacent to the head noun of the NP (as in (73a); but if the bound is taken to be the inner NP, and if subject-predicate and verb-object operations order (or attach) only the *head* of the NP, then the remaining parts, namely the modifying relative clause, will, like all other parts of the clause not specifically attached, appear in whatever position the LP rules specify. In the case of a clausal constituent, this is clause-final position, as in (73b):

(73) a. $\{\{\text{someone}\}_{NP}\ \{\text{whom I have never met}\}_{NP/NP}\ \}_{NP}\ \text{arrived}\}$
b. $\{\{\text{someone}\}_{NP}\ \text{arrived}\ \{\text{whom I have never met}\}_{NP/NP}\}$

However, the NP/NP analysis of restrictive relative clauses is not the most semantically appropriate one. If instead the more familiar CN/CN analysis is chosen, then some way must be found of making all CN/CN modifiers of the CN within a NP "optionally free" from the bound part of the NP at the point at which the NP combines with its functor.

For example, one might propose that anything to the right of the CN in a NP is extraposable, anything to the left is not, regardless of category.

One interesting argument (or a possible argument) that the distinction between CN/CN and other NP constituents is the right one to invoke here comes from a fact noticed by Ross (1967): when a PP modifiers a CN, the object of the preposition can be extracted if the PP remains adjacent to its head (74a), but not if the PP has been extraposed (74b):

(74) a. Who did Bill give Harry a picture of yesterday?
b. *Who did Bill give Harry a picture yesterday of? (cf. Bill gave Harry a picture yesterday of his brother wearing a rabbit suit.)
c. Who did you witness the arrest of at the station?
d. *Who did you witness the arrest at the station of? (cf. I witnessed the arrest at the station of the entire group of demonstrators that had gathered there.)

I argued in Dowty (1989) that prepositional NPs attached to nominals should be analyzed as modifiers rather than arguments; even if not as widely true as suggested there, I believe it is sometimes valid. On the other hand, these PPs are in some respects like arguments. It has been suggested a number of times in various theoretical frameworks that a fundamental difference in extractability exists between arguments and adjuncts (or modifiers): one can extract from arguments but not from adjuncts. (Different theories have different ways of capturing such a constraint of course; compare for example Kaplan – Zaenen (1989) with Steedman (1985a; 1985b.))

Thus, if the PPs accompanying event-nominals and picture-nominals are in principle either adjuncts or arguments of the nominals ambiguously, but if they are only extraposable on their adjunct (i.e. NP/NP) analysis, not when they are arguments then the difference in extractability Ross observed will follow.

5.3 More kinds of extraposition

However, there are still more kinds of extraposition we have not yet considered:

(75) *Noun-complements*
a. Sue denied the charge vehemently <u>that she had been in the study at midnight</u>.
b. The idea appalled Bill <u>that anyone would have considered him appropriate</u>.

(76) *<u>Too-</u> and <u>enough</u> infinitival complements*
a. Mary was too tired after all that work <u>to take another step</u>.

b. His examples were clear enough to everyone to make it obvious that he had researched the subject.

(77) *Comparative than- clauses*
She was wiser when it was all over than anyone would have expected her to be.

(78) *So and too result clauses*
a. So many people came to the lecture that I couldn't find a place to sit down.
b. He put too much chlorine in the pool for us to swim in it without our eyes burning.

Now I can imagine a CN/CN (or NP/NP) analysis being given to the noun complement clauses in (75), though it is not the first analysis that comes to mind. But I cannot envision any modifier analysis at all for the complements of *too* and *enough* in (76) or for the *than*-clauses in (77). But I cannot say such analyses are impossible, either. (I will return to (78) later.) Pending the development of such modifier analyses, I will tentatively conclude that the distinction between extraposable and non-extraposable complements on the basis of predicative modifier status is to be ruled out. (In addition, there are extrapositions which are not from NPs at all: see below.)

The alternative I will pursue here is to see if there is evidence that the rest of the NP – the (pre-) determiner, adjective(s) and CN – might all be syntactically attached. And in fact, it seems that such constituents are not separable by parentheticals:

(79) a. *The, however, big Dalmatian may take the prize.
b. *The judge picked several, he said, collies that were quite impressive.
c. *We looked at some large, in any event, dark houses.
d. *I talked to almost, apparently, all the students.
e. *A very, in my opinion, absurd judgment was rendered.
f. *We drank too, possibly, much wine to give a reliable judgment.
g. *We drank too much, possibly, wine to give a reliable judgment.

Is there a contrast with the post-noun modifiers as to interruptability? While not all examples below are totally felicitous, I think there is a clear difference between those of (79) and those of (80), where something intervenes between the CN and a non-extraposed post-nominal modifier:

(80) a. He invited the vice-chairman, I think it was, of the nominating committee to come to the party.
b. An undergraduate student, supposedly, who had witnessed the event reported it to him.
c. ?Someone, apparently, asleep at the wheel must have caused the accident.
d. They dismissed the suggestion, she said, that anyone would protest the action as unrealistic.
e. A taller person, if that's possible, than they had ever encountered was coming up the walk.
f. Too much wine, possibly, to permit a reliable judgment was consumed on that occasion.

This indicates that even where these phrases are *not* extraposed, some sort of syntactic difference exists between them and the pre-CN constituents of the NP.[18]

Though the other alternatives should perhaps not be completely ruled out, I will adopt at present the hypothesis that an attributive adjective is syntactically attached to its CN and that a determiner is syntactically attached to its following material (i.e. lexical or phrasal CN) – as one might expect it to be, in this approach, because of the phonological status of determiners as clitics dependent on following material. We have thus motivated this situation:

(81) The pre-CN elements of a NP are syntactically attached to each other and to the CN; the post-CN elements (both CN-modifiers and others) are not syntactically attached.

Because of this linking of the pre-CN elements, the group will inevitably behave like a traditional "constituent", whether the category NP itself is a bounded category or not.[19]

This makes possible a straightforward treatment of the bounding problem for NP and therefore for extraposition (from NP):

(82) The category NP in English is optionally bounded: both derivations in which NP expressions are treated as bounded and those in which they are treated as unbounded are well-formed.

If a NP is taken to be bounded, an unextraposed sentence is derived; if the NP is taken to be unbounded, the extraposed version is produced, and produced automatically.[20] Since the VP, as I have tried to show above, with which a subject NP combines is not bounded, the unattached modifying PP, AdjP or relative clause of the NP become "constituents" of the clause itself by the default "union" operation, as in (83):

(83)

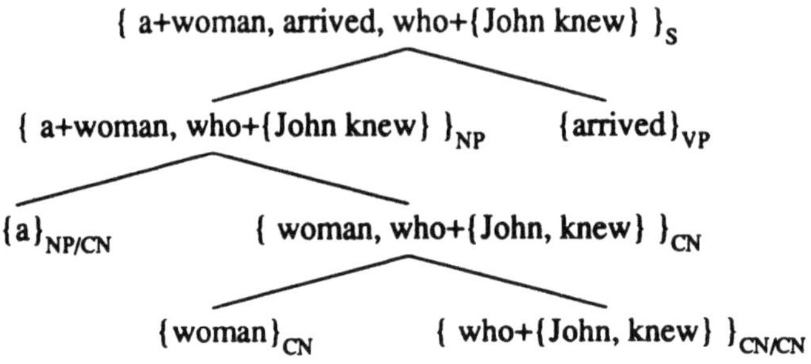

Consequently, the LP principles which order the rest of the clause will also be responsible for the linear order of the "extraposed" relative clause, PP or AdjP: in general, these will be at or near the end of the clause.

Since direct objects are not part of a bounded TV constituent in English, nor are objects of prepositions so confined (I assume a preposition is united to its NP object via syntactic attachment), choosing the unbounded option for these NPs will likewise free their post-nominal constituents to be positioned within the clause as a whole by the LP principles.

It's time to make revisions to bring a couple of formal definitions up to date. Above, I have mentioned the category NP as if it were always a bounded category, when discussing attachment, ordering and LP principles. The syntactic operation of attachment has already been defined so that when an unbounded functor attaches to an argument, it is actually the head of the functor that "attaches" (becomes linearly inseparable). Now we must do the same thing for the argument:

(84) Attachment (redefined): the operation $\alpha + \beta$ is defined as specifying that the expression α (if α is bounded), or the lexical head of α (if α is unbounded), or α and any material already attached to α, is ordered to the left of, and is subsequently inseparable from, β (if β is bounded) or the head of β, or β and any material already attached to β.

A parallel change must be made in the syntactic ordering operation "<<" to linearly order only the lexical heads of unbounded expressions (without thereby ordering their attachments), as well as ordering bounded expressions in the way already described.

A similar change must be made in the interpretation of LP principles:

(85) If an LP principle mentions a category A, and A is not a bounded category, then the interpretation of the principle is that only the head of an expressions of category A, together with any material syntactically attached, is to be ordered as the LP principle specifies for A itself.

Two final comments for this section: extraposition also occurs from adjective phrases, for example:

(86) a. I am anxious to meet someone from there right away.
b. I am anxious to meet someone right away from there.

As far as I can see, these can be treated satisfactorily just by making the category adjective phrase, as well as NP, optionally bounded.

The second comment is that at least one class of potentially extraposable complements exists which does not extrapose: the complements of prenominal "tough"-adjectives:

(87) a. He seemed to be an easy person to talk to when I met him.
b. ?*He seemed to be an easy person when I met him to talk to.

Yet the complement seems quite interruptible by parentheticals:

(88) a. He was an easy person, I thought, to talk to.

Possibly the difference relates to the fact that here the extraposed phrase is a complement to an attributive adjective, not to the CN itself. Yet *too* Adj and Adj *enough* complements and comparative *than*-clauses are arguably complements of attributive adjectives, and they extrapose. I have no solution to propose to this at the moment.

6. Where do extraposed phrases end up?

The matter of the resulting position of extraposed phrases is the main point of comparison I want to make between the present theory and other linguistic theories of extraposition.

First of all, however, notice that in this theory one cannot raise the question whether an extraposed phrase is (phrase-structurally) attached to the VP node or the S node of a clause, though this is a matter which has been much disputed in the literature. If the category VP is not bounded, as I have argued, membership in the VP *is* membership in the S and vice-versa. (I personally suspect this particular simplification of theoretical options is a fortunate one.)

Second, note that the "upward boundedness" of extraposition (Ross 1967) is captured, since we obviously need for S to be a bounded category in English for various reasons.[21]

6.1 Multiple extrapositions

Extraposition of multiple modifiers from the same NP is possible (Stucky 1987, 390–395), though such examples are usually awkward. If one is a PP and the other a relative clause, usually only the extraposed order PP–S is acceptable:

(89) a. And then, a man suddenly appeared at the door from the CIA who I had seen the previous week.
b. ??And then, a man suddenly appeared at the door who I had seen the previous week from the CIA .

(90) a. Surprisingly enough, several books have appeared over the years by that author that had fewer that 300 pages.
b. ??Surprisingly enough, several books have appeared over the years that had fewer than 300 pages by that author. *[NB: avoid irrelevant reading where author writes less than whole book].*

(91) a. Can you give me the names of any newcomers as soon as possible from Finland who may have programming experience?
b. *Can you give me the names of any newcomers as soon as possible who may have programming experience from Finland? (examples from Stucky 1987: 391–392)

The appeal to LP rules in describing extraposition predicts this, as English has the LP rule PP < S.

It is not clear to me how a "landing site" theory of extraposition (Baltin 1982) or other movement theory could predict this effect. Note that an appeal to a preference for nesting in multiple dependencies is not possible: if these modifiers were adjacent to their head NPs, their order would likewise be PP before relative clause, so the hypothesized relationships between "fillers" and "gaps" in such a movement analysis would have to be the unnested ones, not the nested ones, for the acceptable examples.

If however the PP is made especially long or "heavy", then the ordering in which the PP is on the right can be acceptable:

(92) a. And then a man suddenly appeared at the door whom I had seen last week from that organization that we all know but which will go unnamed here.
b. Surprisingly enough, several books have appeared over the years that had fewer than 300 pages by that author whom we all know to be especially long-winded.
c. Can you give me the names of any newcomers as soon as possible who know LISP from any of the countries on our list of overseas development targets?

But this too is just the effect one finds in PPs and S's that originate in the VP:

(93) a. We announced to the students that the exam was over.
b. ?We announced that the exam was over to the students.
c. We announced that the treaty had been signed to all the dignitaries and reporters who were waiting in the outer hall.

The point is not to delve into the well-known but mysterious trade-off between grammatical category and length ("heaviness") in the ordering principles for the English VP. I don't know the solution to this problem, whether there is a "basic" versus "heavy" order, nor even whether there are actually any order principles based on categories, but it doesn't matter here. The point is rather that whatever solution is found to this problem, this theory will allow us to describe the ordering of extraposed complements by the same principles as those for VP-original clause elements, which looks as if it is the right thing to do.

6.2 Multiple extrapositions and nesting

As Stucky (1987: 393) points out, extrapositions from two different noun phrases in the same clause are awkward at best and then only acceptable when they are

(i) in a "nested" relationship to their hosts[22], and
(ii) preferably of different categories. Her nested example, (modified to remove an ambiguity she did not intend) is (94):

(94) Improbable as it may seem, an impeccably dressed man struck up a conversation with me on the plane last month about 'Situations and Attitudes' *who was going to Missoula, Montana.* [PP, Relative clause]

Example (95) (from Stucky, likewise modified), is the same except for "unnested" host-modifier relationships;

(95) *Improbable as in may seem, an impeccably dressed man struck up a conversation with me on the plane last month *who was going to Missoula, Montana* about 'Situations and Attitudes'. [Relative clause, PP]

it is worse, and for me, completely ungrammatical.

The following, adapted from Stucky's example, is about the best I can construct with extraposed relative clauses from different NPs (nested order):

(96) ??Improbable as in may seem, an impeccably dressed man struck up a conversation with me on the plane last month that was about 'Situations and Attitudes' *who was going to Missoula, Montana.*

Why relative clause extrapositions from two NPs should be impossible while two extrapositions from the same NP are at least marginally acceptable, I have no idea, unless this is entirely due to parsing difficulties; there is no obvious way to block the former at all in this approach.

6.3 Extraposition and VP constituents

Stucky also offers, from Henry Thompson and Mark Liberman, an example in which the extraposed relative clause does not make it all the way to the end of the clause, appearing instead before a (very heavy) PP that modifiers the verb:

(97) A man arrived that I had been expecting *at the time he had said he would come.* (Relative, PP)

This particular example is dubious, as the phrase *at the time ...* can be parsed as an S-modifier as well as a VP-modifiers (cf. *The man's arrival occurred at the time he had said ...*) and therefore not necessarily an element of the clause. But because of the theoretical significance of this kind of example (cf. below) it is relevant to try to construct others: (For clarity, the first extraposed phrase is underlined, the second marked in italics.)

(98) a. Some guy was hired that Sue knows *to fix the plumbing and the air conditioning.* [Relative clause, infinitival purpose clause]
b. George actually convinced somebody this morning who neither of us had ever seen before *to buy 600 shares of stock in our new company for* $5 *a share.* [Relative, subcategorized infinitival]
c. Lois told a woman today from Finland *about the great weather in Central Ohio.* [PP, subcategorized PP]
d. This event is harder right now than anyone would have imagined *for him to just accept as if nothing had happened.* [*than*-S, *tough*-complement]

(99) By the way, that fellow cabled headquarters whom none of us had ever met *that he would be arriving in Paris on Tuesday.* (Stucky 1987: 396, from Stuart Shieber.) [Relative, subcategorized *that*-clause]

I find such examples to be of *reduced* acceptability, but definitely *not* ungrammatical. But there is a good reason for this reduced acceptability: these are examples of a kind of double dependencies. Though there is no second instance of a "filler-gap dependency" in the traditional sense here, the meaning of the verb (or adjective) would, in the categorial analysis, have to combine compositionally with that of the italicized complement before the whole verbal meaning combined with the meaning of the subject (or object), but the latter must have combined with its italicized modifying phrase before it does this. To the extent that one can categorize, the dependency is "nested" in (98b,c) and "unnested" in (98a,d) and (99). I suspect it is because the categories of the two nested pairs are different from each other here that their unacceptability here is not as great as that of (96) above or the more familiar unnested double leftward NP extractions examples, where the parser has to fight ambiguity as well.

These examples, even with their reduced acceptability, are significant for theories which postulate a fixed site for extraposition to move to, and particularly for those that assume extraposed clauses from subject position (as (97) and (98a) are) are attached to S; in these examples, constituents which cannot possibly be dominated by S follow the extraposed element. Again, if extraposed elements are free among VP and S constituents to be ordered only by their heaviness and/or category, such examples are just what we expect to find.

One possible objection to such examples is that here the constituent to the right of the extraposed one has been moved there by some kind of Heavy Constituent Shift. This is not an option of course in accounts that claim that subject relatives are attached to S and Heavy Shift keeps elements within the VP. But it is implausible in any movement theory because the putatively shifted constituent need not really be heavier than what it moves over:

(98c′) Lois told a woman today from Finland *about the news.*

Still, this possibility deserves more study.

6.4 So ... that ... Result Clause constructions

All that has been said above about nesting and multiple extrapositions is apparently contradicted by combinations of relative clause extraposition with (what I will call) *so ... that ...* Result Clause constructions, exemplified in this much-discussed example of Williams' (1974):

(100) Everybody is so strange whom I like that I can't go out in public with them.

First of all, there seem to be two extraposed clauses, originating from different hosts, yet the sentence has none of the awkwardness of the multiple clausal extrapositions we saw earlier (94, 98d, 99). More striking, the order of the extraposed clauses in (97) is the unnested order (the "host" of the WH-clause is the subject, that of the *that*-clause is *so*); the opposite, "properly nested" order is abysmally bad:

(100′) *Everybody is so strange that I can't go out in public with them whom I like.

This then is a considerable problem for the hypothesis that extraposition in English can be viewed as a consequence of LP-principles, unbounded NPs, and "flat" clausal structure.

Gueron – May (1984) have studied the *so* ... *that* ... result clause construction in detail and have observed several properties relevant to us (among other properties). First, pronouns in the main clause can have their antecedents in the *that*-result clause (101a), while this is not possible in a superficially similar extraposed relative clause (101b):

(101) a. I told *her*$_i$ that so many people attended last year's concert that I made *Mary*$_i$ nervous.
b. *I told *her*$_i$ that many people attended last year's concert who made *Mary*$_i$ nervous. (Gueron – May, 1984: 14)

Second, it has been known since Ross (1967) that extraposition is upward-bounded by S (cf. 102b); this appears not to be the case for the *that*-result clause in (102a): In fact, the result-clause has "moved" out of a syntactic island here:

(102) a. Critics who have reviewed so many books were at the party that I didn't have time to speak to them all.
b. *Critics who have reviewed many books were at the party which I've enjoyed reading. (Gueron – May 1984: 18).

Third, and perhaps most revealing for our purposes, it has been noted by a number of investigators (Hankamer – Sag 1975; Andrews 1975; Libermann 1974; Baltin 1982), result clause can have more than one antecedent *so*-phrase in the host clause:

(103) So many people liked so many paintings at the gallery that the exhibition was held over for two weeks.

And the number of *so*-phrases need not stop at two; the following is fanciful but in no way ungrammatical or uninterpretable:

(104) So many football fans brought so much beer and so much popcorn in so many knapsacks with so many rips in them in such drunken stupors that a bulldozer had to be brought in to clear the parking lot.

Consider the semantics of such examples, e.g. (105):

(105) John ate so much caviar in 10 minutes that he got sick.

They express a causal relationship, but not a causal relationship that can be described as holding between the host NP's referent and the event described in the result clause: (105) doesn't really say that some quantity of caviar made John sick, or even that his eating that quantity made him sick, but rather it was his eating it in this period of time that made him sick. In other words, the quantity of caviar such that John ate it in ten minutes caused, or brought it about, that he became sick. The causal relation is between the extent(s) to which something or other obtained *in the event described by the first clause*, and the event described by the second. (Note on the other hand that the compositional semantic effect of a relative clause on its matrix clause is, in a sense, confined to the denotation of its host NP.)

Consider a double-host example like (103): not only can the causal relation *not* be described without reference to the event reported in the entire first clause, the relevant extents cannot be separated from one another: (103) does not assert that the number of people that liked many paintings caused the exhibition to be held over, nor that the number of paintings liked by many people caused this; rather the *combined* extents x and y such that x people liked y paintings caused the extension.[23]

What this indicates, briefly, is that a compositional semantics must involve multiple variable-binding over the first clause, then a causal relation between this and the (event expressed by) the second clause is asserted. Thus (following a series of predecessors) I claim that no "extraposition" in the sense of this paper is involved in *that*-result clauses.

The analysis I am proposing actually has much in common with Gueron and May's (1984) (but see note 22), though as it is proposed within a very different theory, it looks superficially quite unlike it. The idea, basically is that *so*-phrases have unbound variables in them which must be bound at a higher level, specifically a sentential level. The result clause rule then takes a first clause with one or more of these variables, binds it/them semantically, combines it syntactically with a result clause, and semantically has the interpretation that there is a causal relation between the two events.

Assuming we don't want to just permit the result-clause rule to apply vacuously, i.e. when there are no *so*'s in the first clause as well as when there are,[24] we will need something like a feature [+*so*] to be passed up from the *so*-phrase to the sentence containing it; I will assume some mechanism of this sort. The syntactic rule is then (106):

(106) *So* ... *That* ... Result Clause Rule
If $\phi \in S_{[+so]}$, then $F_i(\phi) \in S/S_{[that]}$, where $F_i(\phi) = \phi$

That is, the initial clause in a result construction becomes a subordinate clause, though one that takes a *that*-clause as its argument to form a complete sentence.[25] Also, I will assume a lexical expression *so*, probably a determiner modifier, i.e. of category Det/Det (but with restrictions I won't attempt to go into here), and a translation involving a variable x_i over "extents".

I will indicate the semantic interpretation rule informally:

(107) If ϕ translates into ϕ' then $F_{10}(\phi)$ translates into that function on sentence meanings ψ such that:
the extent x_0 and ... and the extent x_n to which ϕ' causes it to be the case that ψ'.

Now, let us return to the properties of result clauses observed by Gueron and May. The fact that the rule permits multiple *so*-phrases is of course captured by introducing *so*-phrases independently of the result-clause in the syntax; the right interpretation is derived because it is the result-clause rule which binds the (one or more) variables and supplies the causal relationship.

The observed fact that result-clauses "escape" syntactic islands and fail to be upward bounded follows here because there is no "movement" of result clauses at all (as in a traditional analysis), hence no movement out of syntactic islands. Rather, only the binding of variables connects the result-clause with its *so*-phrase(s), so there is nothing to prohibit the *so*-variable from being inside an island. Ordinary extraposed relative clauses, by contrast, are generated as part of their "host" NP, and cannot appear any farther away from that NP than the clause the NP belongs to.

Third, the antecedent of an (definite) embedded pronoun can appear in a result clause in (101a), repeated here,

(101) a. I told *her* that so many people attended last year's concert that I made *Mary* nervous.
b. *I told *her* that many people attended last year's concert who made *Mary* nervous. (Gueron – May, 1984)

because if the result clause construction is generated by (106), the first clause becomes a kind of subordinate clause to the second, and as the pronoun is in the familiar precede-and-command position that permits coreference, just as it is in *Because I told her that so many people attended the concert, I made Mary nervous.*

Finally, this analysis, which I have now tried to motivate on other counts, explains why extraposed relative clauses must appear before result clauses, as in Williams's example, repeated here:

(100) Everybody is so strange whom I like that I can't go out in public with them.

(100′) *Everybody is so strange that I can't go out in public with them whom I like.

The result "clause" is indeed an independent clause, outside the bound of the clause in which the *so*-phrase originates. As the relative clause on the other hand is not independent of its host's clause and cannot cross its boundary, the relative clause appears first. As result clauses are not extrapositions, it is not surprising that they should not be subject to the same limits on multiple extrapositions as are ordinary extrapositions.

Of course, this analysis predicts that *that*-result clauses should never appear adjacent to their hosts, since they do not "originate" there; in fact, the absence of sentences where they *do* appear there (or just past the CN anyway):

(108) a. So many books have been published lately that I haven't been able to read them all.
b. *So many books that I haven't been able to read them all have been published lately.
c. I persuaded so many students to come to the lecture that we couldn't all fit in the lecture hall.
d. *I persuaded so many students that we couldn't all fit in the lecture hall to come to the lecture.

has in fact traditionally been viewed as an embarrassment for the extraposition analysis (Stucky 1987: 388). I find these quite clearly bad, but some may accept them and find them only awkward; Stucky accepts the second sentence in (108).[26]

This analysis also appears to predict that result constructions could be nested by reapplying the result rule, binding one *so*-phrase the first time, another the second. Though it is often said in the literature said such examples do not exist, the following kind of example has been pointed out too.

Everyone finds it somewhat awkward, and a few claim it isn't possible at all, though I find it not very bad:

(109) So many mothers complained that their children ate so much of the candy that they got sick that the manufacturers took it off the market.

(Note the relationship of *so*-phrases here, which contrasts with the "multiply-headed" result clauses discussed earlier: the outer result clause is a quantification of the sentence *x complained that x's child ate so much of the candy that it got sick* which contains an internal result clause that is semantically independent of the outer one.)

7. Conclusions

It is hard to convincingly present and motivate a new theory and a novel analysis of a well-known language in a single paper, and I won't pretend I have done so. But I hope I have shown there might be some interest in exploring the idea that a familiar language could have much less constituent structure than supposed, if one simultaneously admits the possibility that some words and phrases could be more tightly connected than others, and that LP-principles apply across a language in GPSG fashion. Of more interest to me than persuading linguists of all this, however, is to getting linguists to question our automatic assumptions about constituents and our basis for assuming as a methodological principle that languages must always have a phenogrammatical syntactic structure describable by phrase structure trees.

Notes

1. Beyond differences of how the two formulations affect the methodology of the linguist, there are only two differences between Zwicky's formulations and mine that I can see:

   (i) my description of bounding requires one to list the "bounding categories" for the whole language; these then are treated as bounded by all rules (though, at present, I also allow additional rule-specific bounding as a marked option).

Bounding (for which his corresponding concept is "concatenated daughter", as opposed to "liberated daughter") can be specified by Zwicky only rule by rule, so he cannot, e.g., directly describe a generalization (assuming there is such) that all rules of some language mentioning NP must treat it as bounded.

(ii) Zwicky does not employ anything corresponding to syntactic "attachment" (see below).

2. This might appear to have much in common with early transformational grammar, in which a context-free phrase-structural component generated strings which are operated on, in a purely string-based way, by transformations. Many differences exist, however, in the question of which phenomena are to be described by string-based operations (e.g. I assume here that Passive, Raising, etc. are not), differences in the restriction on how "structural descriptions" are stated, the ways "movement" is determined (e.g. here by LP and other general principles, etc.), the fact that here string-based operations are either tied to particular syntactic formative operations (i.e. like generalized transformations) or not a consequence of any one rule at all (LP principles). (WH-extraction is not treated in the present paper, but both a functional-composition analysis like that of Steedman (1985a, 1985b) and the "feature-passing" analysis of GKPS (1985) are compatible with my proposals.)
3. Zwicky, coincidentally, uses the same example to illustrate his system of direct generation, noting that phonological phrasing does not motivate the nested VP structure in English (Zwicky 1986: 67). One reason that I prefer the present formulation to Zwicky's is that his system does not clearly distinguish between phenogrammatical and tectogrammatical structure, as it comes from a tradition that presumes these are the same: the phrase markers his rules generate are, presumably, phenogrammatical, and if there are any "flattened nodes" (corresponding to my tectogrammatical constituents which are not phenogrammatical ones), these do not appear in his trees at all and are like "phantom categories" in early GPSG (though they must be "reconstructed", in effect, in the compositional semantic interpretation). An auxiliary notation might be added to his system to remedy this, but I prefer one based on tectogrammatical analysis trees, permiting phenogrammatical trees (in bracketed form) as well, when needed.
4. I assume for the moment that ordering one expression before (after) the head of another is only meaningful if the first is bounded. Thus, options the theory could take at this point are (i) that such ordering is only to be well-defined for bounded expressions, and (ii) that if the first expression is not bounded, this operation has the effect of ordering the head of the first before (after) the head of the second. The latter will be adopted below: cf. (81), (82).
5. I assume head is defined as more or less customary in categorial grammar: in a complex expression formed from one expression of category A/B and a second of category B, where A =/ B, the first is the head; if A = B, then the second is the head (i.e. the functor A/A is a modifier). Below, we will have occasion to refer to the lexical head of an expression, the simplest definition of which is that it is both a head and a lexical expression (i.e. is not a syntactically derived phrase). Some

expressions would not have a lexical head by this definition, of course. If it turns out that we are to assume lexical heads for all expressions, the intuitive way to proceed is by a recursive definition: one seeks the (non-modifier) functor of the expression, and if that head is not lexical, then one seeks the head of the head, and so on. However, the problem with this kind of definition is that it indirectly makes reference to the derivational history of an expression and therefore to its tectogrammatical "constituent structure", thereby defeating my goal of avoiding reference to constituency in syntactic operations. But the data treated in this paper do not suffice to determine what sort of notion of "head" is needed; the experience of Pollard (1984) and Pollard and Sag (1987) should be relevant, but I am not sure how to apply it here. Cases of attachment in this paper involve attachment to a (first-order) lexical head, or attachment to a group of attached words, of which the group is the (first-order) head and which also includes the (ultimate) lexical head.

6. Since under the convention we have adopted β is here a set, "NOM(β)" would be more properly understood as applying the nominative morphological operation to the expression in the set β; the same applies to attachment and rule-specified precedence in the rules below. The unification-based treatment of Karttunen 1989, or Bach's (1983) "lexical implementation", is actually preferable here, since we do not want to take rules like (a) and (b) to imply that a syntactically analysed version of the phrase β is necessary at this point (to apply the morphological operation correctly to the appropriate words within β), but only that a derivation of a nominative (or accusative, etc.) phrase β is well-defined elsewhere by the grammar.
7. To save time, I will ignore the other ways of forming questions that Karttunen mentions, namely by suffixing -ko to a NP or by using a WH-word such as keta. Thus the LP principle should order any word with some feature corresponding to -ko at the beginning of the sentence. The syntax and semantics of deriving these other questions is more complex.
8. Actually, this grammar may be inadequate for this or slightly larger fragments of Finnish because it permits the order of complement-taking verbs to be too unrestricted (once the morphological restrictions on these particular complement verb forms no longer disambiguate); if so, restrictions like those suggested below for English auxiliaries might be needed, which order the head of a VP before (for Finnish, non-NP) elements of the VP.
9. This sentence actually has a grammatical reading, but not one that is synonymous with (25c); it is rather a focussed version of the cleft sentence *It was a nice one that fit her.*
10. However, the motivation for the category TV/VP[inf] (as opposed to the category (VP/VP[inf]/NP), and therefore the motivation for (some effect of) wrapping in this construction, does not really seem to me to be on firm ground; see Dowty (1982a) and Dowty (1982b). English almost surely requires wrapping (or the equivalent) in other cases, however, such as *too hot to eat* and *easy man to please.*

11. A related idea was proposed by Ross (1967, sec. 3.1), though not in an LP-framework but as an output filter on a transformational grammar. Another perhaps relevant fact (if not one observed already) is that constituents containing a verb are placed at the end of the clause; this could have a disambiguating effect, as NPs or PPs placed after such a verb-containing constituent could sometimes be ambiguously parsed as belonging to the constituent in question or to the main clause.
12. Zwicky also deals with another class of sentences where an unstressed subject pronoun is prohibited, namely inversions:

    Across the plane came the 20th Century Limited. *Across the plane came it.

    "Gee whillikers!" exclaimed Ona, with great feeling. *"Gee whillikers!" exclaimed she, with great feeling.

    and argues that their ill-formedness is due to their having a somewhat different structure from that in (37)-(41), though one that his condition applies to nonetheless. These sentences, unlike the ones discussed above, permit adverbial material, or, for that matter, further auxiliary and main verbs to separate the subject from the main verb, as in (Zwicky's examples):

    "Gee whillikers!" suddenly exclaimed Ona with great feeling. Across the plains would come the train every few days.

    However, I think there is reason to wonder whether the pronoun unacceptability here is due to the fact that these are presentational sentences (at least the second), whose function is to introduce a new discourse referent. Personal pronouns by their meaning, on the other hand, cannot introduce a new referent. And in fact, I find even a stressed pronoun rather strange here, though Zwicky's analysis assume that stressed pronouns should always be acceptable:

    (*) Around the corner came SHE, of all people!
    (*) And now "Gee whillikers!" exclaimed SHE, as well.
13. I find the judgments in the following example a bit clearer than in Zwicky's, for reasons I am not sure of:

    John obviously has never lied.
    John has obviously never lied.
    Never has John obviously lied.
    *Never has obviously John lied.
14. We will deal with Heavy-NP Shift below, which is an exception to this principle.
15. That is, direct object is redefined as the "first NP argument" that a verb combines with, while subject is the "last NP argument". Rules like Passive, which apply to direct objects (or to direct objects only) can be given a schematized definition that permits "first NP argument" to be affected, over a variety of verbal types. This schematic form for relation-changing rules is motivated by the need to

give parameterized definitions of relation-changing rules, as explained in Dowty (1982a).

16. The other method would require us to suppose that the first NP to combine with a ditransitive verb is attached to it: {give} and {a, book} combine to give {give+{a, book}}. Then when the second NP is added, the syntactic operation again being attachment, and requiring us to attach the new NP to the head of the TV, the result is that this new NP "displaces" the old one: {give+{a, book}} plus {Harold} gives {give+{Harold}+{a,book}}. A question for this approach is what happens to the original attachment that is broken: is {a, book} reattached to {Harold}? Some requirement of a link is needed to explain the badness of *I gave Harold it.
17. Since S is a bounding category, this raises the question what exactly happens to its bound when an S/S combines with it. Clearly, we want to make an exception, so that the "outer" S created by this combination is bounded, but the "inner" S is not, to get the right adverb positions. Cf. the similar discussion about modifiers of NP below, so maybe there is a cross-categorial principle about modifiers of bounded categories. Other than just stipulating this exception, another option would be to postulate something like an S-bar node and make it, not S, the bounded category. However, S-bar has no natural definition (and possibly no need) in categorial grammar, at least in the positions where we would need it. Another possibility is general type-raising for adverbs, i.e. S/S ⇒ VP/VP (⇒ TV/TV, etc.), which has a number of independent motivations. This would bring S-adverbs inside the S-bound. Possibly Obviously, *John hasn't left yet* has an S/S adverb (outside the bound) and *John obviously hasn't left yet* has its adverb in VP/VP.
18. Coordinated adjectives within NPs are an exception to these general principles, as one can sometimes felicitously insert parenthetical material after the and:

    A handsome and, if I'm not mistaken, expensive overcoat was lying on the sofa.

    But if coordinated conjuncts are each bounded expressions (as we would need to say in this approach for several reasons, such as producing the right word order within coordinated VP's and in non-constituent coordinations), then there is no contradiction in saying that a coordinated attributive adjective expression is attached to its CN (and the determiner subsequently attached to it), even though there are unattached expressions within the coordinated adjective expression; that is, the coordination construction itself can be assumed not to involve attachment but only ordering.
19. Though I will not discuss them in detail, it can be noted briefly that this treatment produces a "wrapping" effect in several other CN and Adj modifier constructions, e.g.
    (i) taller than Susan ⇒ taller woman than Susan
    (ii) easy to please ⇒ easy man to please
    (iii) too to enter ⇒ too tall to enter

I assume the attachment operation that attaches attributive modifiers to nouns (adjectives) is really head-attachment. Thus if the adjective (or Adj/Adj) is a phrasal one, the head is attached to the left of the CN (or Adj) by syntactic head attachment, and the rest of the adjective phrase is unattached and appears whereever the LP principles order it. In the above examples, the phrases are PPs or infinitive VPs, so they follow it. This treatment also predicts the possibility of extraposing these phrases. (Why the complements of easy-adjectives do not extrapose, I cannot explain presently.)

20. The present account makes no provision for NPs in which one modifier has been extraposed and another left behind (remaining with the NP). If such sentences exist, and they apparently do, a more sophisticated definition of "optionally bounded" must be worked out.
21. As already mentioned, I do not attempt to deal with leftward extraction in this paper, though some other theories of leftward extraction are not incompatible with what I am proposing here: cf. footnote 2.
22. Note the difference between the hypothetical "nesting" explanation rejected for (89)-(91) above and those discussed here (and in the following section): in (89)-(91) we were talking about two predicative modifiers of the same NP. Even if it made sense to talk about the "original" vs. "final" order of the modifiers (which I am claiming it doesn't, since no movement is involved), "nesting" could not make any difference, since the semantic interpretation would be the same no matter in which order the two modifiers were combined. In this example, we are dealing with modifiers of two different NPs (or later, of an NP vs. of a complement of a verb), so getting the right element with the right head is crucial for the right semantic interpretation.
23. Note, therefore, that analyses which treat multiple so-sentences simply as having multiple, independent so-operators in semantic interpretation or in their logical form, without summing the extents somehow to get the relevant causal force, would not get the meanings of the sentences right. This would apprear to be a problem with Gueron and May's (1984) analysis, for example.
24. The only reason I can think of that we would want this is to capture sentences, known to me only in (King James) biblical English, such as *She brought us bread,* that we might eat, which looks suspiciously like a result clause (in the subjunctive) without the preceding so phrase. But I have not had a chance to check the history of the construction.
25. The only reason I have given the syntax in this form is because of the anaphora data in (98); otherwise, the syntactic rule could, more simply, take two sentences d and y to form { d that+y }. For all I know, alternative accounts of the anaphora data could be given which are compatible with this structure. See Gueron and May (1984), who also use a structure somewhat like that in (103), for some discussion.

26. Stucky suggests (p. 388) that this sentence is also accepted by May and Gueron, but they exhibit it only as a D-structure (p. 3, 8b); there seem to be no non-extraposed (S-structure) examples in their paper.

References

Andrews, Avery
1975 *Studies in the Syntax of Relative and Comparative Clauses.* Cambridge, MIT Linguistics Dissertation.

Bach, Emmon
1980 In Defense of Passive. *Linguistics and Philosophy,* 3: 297–342.

Bach, Emmon
1983 On the Relationship between Word Grammar and Phrase Grammar. *Natural Language and Linguistic Theory,* 1.1: 65–90.

Bach, Emmon and Robin Cooper
1978 The NP-S Analysis of Relative Clauses and Compositional Semantics. *Linguistics and Philosophy,* 2:145–150.

Bach, Emmon and Barbara H. Partee
1980 Anaphora and Semantic Structure. *Papers from the Parasession on Pronouns and Anaphora,* Chicago, Chicago Linguistic Society, 1–28.

Baltin, Mark
1981 Strict Bounding. In: Carl L. Baker and John McCarthy (eds.), *The Logical Problem of Language Acquisition,* MIT Press.

Baltin, Mark
1982 A Landing Site Theory of Movement Rules. *Linguistic Inquiry,* 14: 1–38.

Curry, Haskell B.
1963 Some Logical Aspects of Grammatical Structure. In: R. Jakobson (ed.), *Structure of Language and its Mathematical Aspects: Proceedings of the Twelfth Symposium in Applied Mathematics.* American Mathematical Society, 56–68.

Dowty, David
1982a Grammatical Relations and Montague Grammar. In: Pauline Jacobson and Geoffrey Pullum (eds.), *The Nature of Syntactic Representation.* Dordrecht, Reidel, 79–130.

Dowty, David
1982b More on the Categorial Theory of Grammatical Relations. In: Annie Zaenen (ed.), *Subjects and Other Subjects: Proceedings of the Harvard Conference on the Representation of Grammatical Relations.* Bloomington, Indiana University Linguistics Club, 115–153.

Dowty, David
1989 On the Semantic Content of the Notion "Thematic Role". In: Barbara Partee, Gennaro Chierchia and Ray Turner (eds.), *Properties, Types and Meanings: vol. II.* Dordrecht, Kluwer, 69–130.

Dowty, David R.
1979 *Word Meaning and Montague Grammar.* Dordrecht, Reidel.

Gazdar, Gerald and Geoffrey K. Pullum
1981 Subcategorization, Constituent Order, and the Notion "Head". In: M. Moortgat, H. van der Hulst, and T. Hoekstra (eds.), *The Scope of Lexical Rules.* Dordrecht, Foris.

Gazdar, Gerald, Ewan Klein, Geoffrey Pullum, and Ivan Sag
1985 *Generalized Phrase Structure Grammar.* Harvard University Press/Blackwell's.

Gueron, Jacqueline – Robert May
1984 Extraposition and Logical Form. *Linguistic Inquiry*, 15: 1–32.

Hankamer, Jorge and Ivan Sag
1975 Result Clauses in English: So-Flip or So What? Paper presented at NWAVE 4, Georgetown University, Washington, DC.

Kaplan, Ronald M. and Annie Zaenen
1989 Long-Distance Dependencies, Constituent Structure, and Functional Uncertainty. In: Mark Baltin and Anthony Kroch (eds.), *Alternative Conceptions of Phrase Structure.* Chicago, The University of Chicago Press, 12–42.

Karttunen, Lauri
1989 Radical Lexicalism. In: Mark Baltin and Anthony Kroch (eds.), *Alternative Conceptions of Phrase Structure.* Chicago, The University of Chicago Press, 43–65.

Keenan, Edward
1974 'The Functional Principle: Generalizing the Notion of "Subject of"'. *Proceedings of the Tenth Annual Meeting of the Chicago Linguistics Society.* Chicago, University of Chicago, 298–303.

Liberman, Mark
1974 Conditioning the Rule of Subject-Aux Inversion. In: Ellen Kaisse and Jorge Hankamer (eds.), *Proceedings of the Fifth Regional Meeting of the Chicago Linguistic Society.* Department of Linguistics, University of Chicago.

Pollard, Carl
1984 *Generalized Phrase Structure Grammars, Head Grammars, and Natural Languages.* (Stanford University Linguistics Dissertation), Stanford, Stanford University.

Pollard, Carl and Ivan A. Sag
1987 Information-Based Syntax and Semantics, vol. I. *CSLI Lecture Notes No. 13.* Stanford, Center for the Study of Language and Information.

Pollard, Carl and Ivan A. Sag
1994 *Head-Driven Phrase Structure Grammar*. Stanford, Center for the Study of Language and Information.

Postal, Paul
1974 *On Raising*. Cambridge, MIT Press.

Powers, Joyce
1988 Exceptions to ECPO. New Orleans, *Paper Presented to the 63rd Annual Meeting of the Linguistic Society of America*.

Pullum, Geoffrey
1982 Free Word Order and Phrase Structure Rules. In: James Pustejovsky and Peter Sells (eds.), *Proceedings of the 12th Annual Meeting of the North Eastern Linguistic Society*. Amherst, Department of Linguistics, University of Massachusetts, 209–220.

Reinhart, Tanya
1979 Syntactic Domains for Semantic Rules. In: F. Guenthner and S. J. Schmidt (eds.), *Formal Semantics and Pragmatics for Natural Languages*. Dordrecht, Reidel.

Ross, John R.
1967 *Constraints on Variables in Syntax*. MIT Linguistics Dissertation [Available from Indiana University Linguistics Club].

Steedman, Mark J.
1985a Dependency and Coordination in the Grammar of Dutch and English. *Language*, 61: 523–568.

Steedman, Mark J.
1985b Combinators and Grammars. In: Richard T. Oehrle et al. (eds.), *Categorial Grammars and Natural Language Structures*. Dordrecht, Kluwer.

Stucky, Susan
1981 Free word order languages, free constituent order languages, and the grey area in between. *NELS 11*, 364–376.

Stucky, Susan
1987 Configurational Variation in English: A Study of Extraposition and Relation Matters. In: Geoffrey Huck and Almerindo Ojeda (ed.), *Discontinuous Constituency, Syntax and Semantics* 20. Orlando, etc., Academic Press, 337–405.

Williams, Edwin
1974 *Rule Ordering in Syntax*. Cambridge, Massachusetts, MIT Linguistics Dissertation.

Zeevat, Henk, Ewan Klein, – Jo Calder
1987 Unification Categorial Grammar. In: Nicholas Haddock, Ewan Klein, and Glyn Morrill (eds.), *Edinburgh Working Papers in Cognitive Science I*. Edinburgh, Centre for Cognitive Science, University of Edinburgh, 195–222.

Zwicky, Arnold
1986 Concatenation and Liberation. In: Anne M. Farley et al. (eds.), *Proceedings of the Twenty-Second Regional Meeting (General Session) of the Chicago Linguistics Society*. Chicago, Chicago Linguistics Society, 65–74.

Zwicky, Arnold
1986a The Unstressed Pronoun Constraint in English. In: Arnold Zwicky (ed.), *Ohio State University Working Papers in Linguistics*, 32: 114–124, Ohio State Department of Linguistics.

Zwicky, Arnold M.
1982 Stranded 'to' and Phonological Phrasing in English. *Linguistics*, 20: 3–57.

Formal tools for describing and processing discontinuous constituency structure

Harry Bunt

Abstract. This contribution is concerned with the development of formal tools for the description and processing of discontinuous constituency structures. It is argued first that the traditional tree representations of constituent structure are too limited, and that these representations in general should be allowed to have crossing branches. A precise mathematical definition of *discontinuous trees* is provided, plus a linear precedence relation for expressing a kind of concatenation operation on these structures.

The formal concepts introduced here are theory-neutral and can be applied in a wide variety of grammatical frameworks and their computer implementations. Their use in phrase-structure grammars is explained in some detail, developing a grammatical formalism called *Discontinuous Phrase Structure Grammar* (DPSG); their possible use in Categorial Grammar is considered very briefly.

The paper concludes with a section on computational issues, in particular in relation to the computer implementation of DPSG for parsing and generation.

1. Introduction

This paper takes the view that discontinuity in constituent structure is nothing to be afraid of, and gives substance to this view by developing formal tools that can be used both in the description of discontinuous constituency in a wide range of grammatical formalisms, and in the formulation of efficient algorithms for parsing and generating sentences with discontinuities.

One way of expressing the basic idea underlying this paper is that constituents can fruitfully be regarded not as *sequences* of words, but as partially ordered *sets* of words[1] with certain precedence relations amongst themselves and with surrounding words. Central in the elaboration of this idea is the notion of a *discontinuous tree*, which is a tree-like structure with crossing branches describing discontinuous constituency.

The idea of allowing discontinuous constituent structures is not new; for example, McCawley (1982) has suggested to analyse the sentence *John talked of course about politics* as having the constituent structure displayed in (1). We will return to his proposal below.

(1)

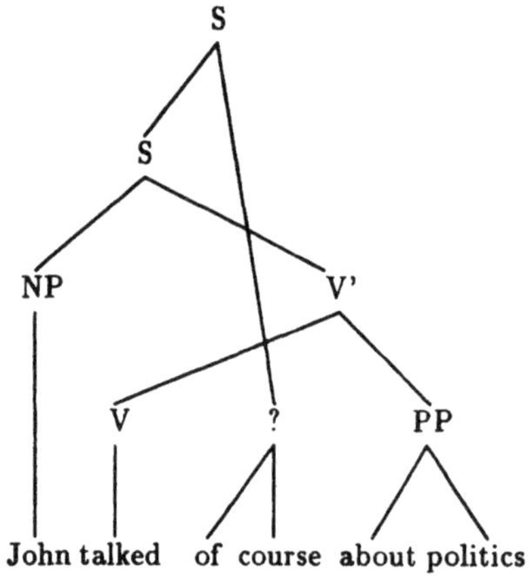

When it is not possible to analyse a given sentence into continuous NPs, VPs, APs, etc., we can choose between either analysing the sentence differently, or allowing NPs, VPs, etc. to be discontinuous. There are two very good reasons for opting for the latter possibility.

Firstly, the syntactician in the generative tradition has the task to describe in her grammar ultimately all patterns of words that form correct sentences; the syntactician tries to achieve this not just in any odd way, but in a way which reveals syntactic generalizations. From this point of view it is attractive to be able to express a generalization like 'An S consists of an NP and a VP' without implying that the NP and VP must be continuous. Allowing phrases to be discontinuous thus makes it possible to express stronger generalizations about constituency at higher levels.

Secondly, components like NP, PP and AP have a clear semantic status, and are therefore attractive building blocks in a compositional semantics. The semantic argument is partly one of good taste, since, according to the compositional view, the words making up a phrase have an independent meaning of their own that can in principle be used instead of the phrase meaning. The semantic argument reinforces the syntactic generalization argument, though: when discontinuous constituents are allowed, a semantic rule gets coupled to a syntactic rule that describes a larger class of structures, which is the more satisfactory since discontinuous phrases, like those caused by parentheticals, are often semantically equivalent to their continuous form.

Independent motivation for discontinuous structures in linguistic representations have also been given by Bach (1979; 1980) in his analysis of transitive verb phrases. Bach (1979) offers an analysis of control verbs in Montague Grammar in which various kinds of control verbs combine with complements to form transitive verb phrases. In the transformational account, verbs like *persuade* and *consider* share the common designation as 'control verbs' since their NP objects control the subject of their sentential complements. Bach classifies control verbs lexically (cf. (2)) as verbs which combine with controlled complements to form transitive verb phrases (TVPs) that lack only the controlling complement to form intransitive verb phrases (IVPs).

(2)	persuade to go	–	Vt/ViP + ViP
	consider competent	–	Vt/AdjP + AdjP

Since the controlled complement is combined first with the control verb, the combination of the resulting TVP with its NP complement cannot happen as the product of simple concatenation. Rather, a discontinuous operator called 'Right-Wrap' (RWRAP) is used to form an IVP by sticking the NP into the TVP right after the head. This operator is formalized in (3).

(3)	RWRAP(a,b)	=	a + b	if a is simple
			X + b + W	if a has the form $[_{XP}$ X W]

RWRAP (with + defined as concatenation) gives structures like the one depicted in (4), which have a clear interpretation in terms of trees with crossing branches.[2]

(4)

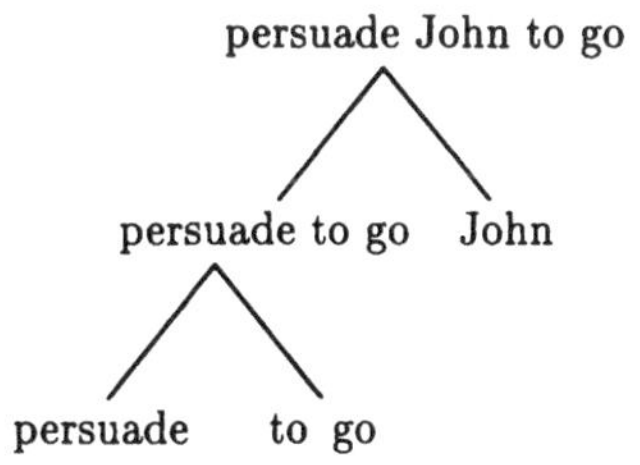

Bach takes advantage of the argument structure allowed by representing the combination of discontinuous TVPs with their objects to characterize passivization as a rule which applies solely to TVPs. This accounts for the constraints on passivization of control verbs relative to raising verbs in accord with the fact that, among lexical classes of transitive and intransitive verbs (belonging to the phrasal classes by default), only the transitive verbs passivize. The overall simplicity of this account provides a strong argument in favour of representing discontinuous constituents.

Jacobson (1987) accepts Bach's analysis with RWRAP and uses it to also characterize verb-particle constructions as TVPs, as they occur in sentences like (5).

(5) *Mary will wake me up at seven-thirty.*

In cases like this, *wake* combines with its particle to form a TVP and the NP object is wrapped into the TVP to form an IVP. Jacobson recasts the RWRAP operation in the GPSG framework as context-free promotion of the SLASH feature.

(6) $\text{VP} \Rightarrow \text{V}_1\ \text{NP}\ \text{TVP[SL:V}_1]$

Promotion of the SLASH feature is used to account for the discontinuity created by relative clause extraposition as well as that represented by crossing branches in tree representations.

The work of all three, McCawley, Bach, and Jacobson, suggests that there is sufficient linguistic motivation to maintain the constituent structure implied by discontinuous tree representations, in spite of the tendency to avoid drawing trees with crossing branches.

This paper does not so much present a *theory* about discontinuous constituency, but it develops certain *tools* which are simple yet quite powerful for the description of discontinuous structures, and which can be used in a wide variety of grammar formalisms and their computer implementations. Central is the notion of a *discontinuous tree*, which is a tree-like structure describing discontinuous constituency. A second important notion is that of *adjacency sequence*, which generalizes the notion of adjacency pair (or left-right neighbourship) in a way that applies to structures with discontinuities. This latter notion makes it possible to formulate rewrite rules which describe discontinuous structures. We outline the incorporation of such rules in a (generalized) phrase-structure grammar; the resulting formalism we call *Discontinuous Phrase-Structure Grammar*, or *DPSG*. We briefly consider an ID/LP format for DPSG which allows us to express strong generalizations in terms of ID rules.

We also briefly consider the possible use of discontinuous trees in Categorial Grammar and Head-driven Phrase Structure Grammar. We conclude with a few words on algorithmic complexity and on the computer implementation of DPSG for purposes of parsing and generation.

2. Trees with discontinuities

When we want to represent that a phrase P has constituents A and C, while there is an intervening element B, we must allow the node corresponding to P to dominate the A and C nodes without dominating the B node, even though this node is located between A and C (7). This will have the consequence that the structure gets crossing branches, if we still want every node to be dominated by a higher node. In what respects exactly do these structures differ from ordinary trees? McCawley (1982) has tried to answer this question, suggesting a formal definition for trees with discontinuities by amending the definition of an ordinary tree.

(7)

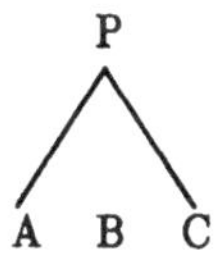

An ordinary tree is often defined as a set of elements, called NODES, on which two relations are defined, immediate dominance (D) and linear precedence ($<$). These relations are required to have certain properties, to the effect that a tree has exactly one root (or 'top') node, which dominates every other node; that every node in a tree has exactly one 'mother' node, etc. (see e.g. Wall, 1972). Two of the required properties that are worth considering here, are the following.

First, the precedence relation has the property that a nonterminal node x precedes a node y if and only if every node dominated by x precedes every node dominated by y:

(8) For any two nodes x and y in a tree, $x < y$ iff for all nodes u and v, if x dominates u and y dominates v, then $u < v$.

Second, any two nodes are required to either dominate or precede one another, but not both:

(9) For any two nodes x and y in a tree, then either x D' y, or y D' x, or x $<$ y, or y $<$ x. (D' designates the relation of dominance: the reflexive and transitive closure of D.)

Together, (8) and (9) have the effect of excluding discontinuities in a tree. For suppose a node x would dominate nodes y and z without having a dominance relation with node w, where y $<$ w $<$ z. Since neither x dominates w nor w dominates x, by (9) either x $<$ w or w $<$ x. But x dominates a node to the right of w, so by (8) x does not precede w; and w is to the right of a node dominated by x, so w does not precede x either. A structure like (7) is thus excluded, since P neither dominates nor precedes B.

McCawley's definition of trees with discontinuities consists of a list of seven axioms like (8) and (9) which include, instead of (9), the requirement that a node has no precedence relation to any node it dominates:

(10) For any two nodes x and y in a tree, if x D' y then neither x $<$ y nor y $<$ x.

McCawley's definition is inaccurate in some respects; it is redundant, and it unintentionally allows structures to be cyclic or not wholly connected. An attractive alternative to an 'axiomatic' definition of tree-like structures is a recursive one, which is especially attractive in connection with top-down generation. Ordinary trees are very easy to define recursively since their building blocks are again trees, if we consider terminal nodes as atomic trees. Such a definition may run as follows:

(11) Let N be a non-empty set whose elements are called NODES.
- (i) If t $\in$ N, then <t,[ ]> is a tree, where [ ] represents the empty list;
- (ii) If $X_1, X_2, \ldots, X_k$ are disjoint trees and a $\in$ N, then <a, [X_1,X_2, …,X_k]> is a tree. Instead of '<a,[X_1,X_2,…,X_k]>', we shall also write more simply: 'a(X_1,X_2,…,X_k)'.
- (iii) No other structures than those defined by (i) and (ii) are trees.

According to this definition, a tree is an ordered pair consisting of a node and a list. The node is said to be the top of the tree and to dominate the members of the list. The top node is also said to be the 'mother' of the members of that list, which are called the 'daughters'. A node in a tree <t,[ ]> dominates zero subtrees, and is called a *terminal node*.

A recursive definition of a tree with discontinuities, or 'DISCOTREE', is not so easily given, since such a structure is built up of substructures which themselves are not necessarily (disco-)trees. Example (12) illustrates this.

(12)

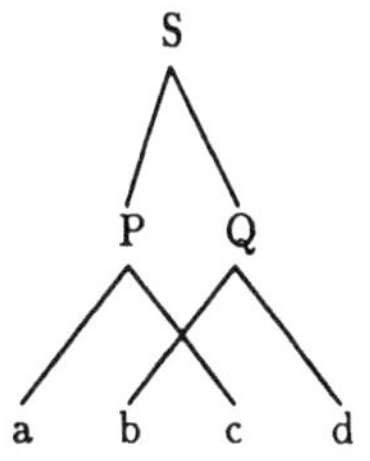

'Crossing discontinuities', which would give rise to structures like (12), do occur quite easily; examples are provided in (13). (In these examples, one of the crossing discontinuous constituents is underlined; the other italicized. Example a is from Williams (1974); b is from Stucky (1987); c is from Dowty (1992).)

(13) a. *Everybody* is so strange *whom I like* that I can't go out in public with them.
b. An impeccably dressed man struck up *a conversation* with me on the plane last month *about 'Situations and Attitudes'* who was going to Missoula, Montana.
c. *Some guy* was hired *that Sue knew* to fix the plumbing.
d. *He invited* the vice-chairman, *I think it was*, of the committee.

The discotree S in (12) is made up of the substructures with top nodes P and Q:

(14a)

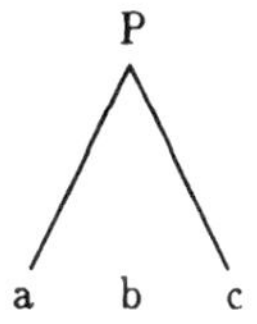

(14b)

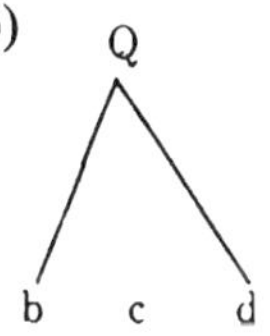

These structures are not well-formed discotrees since they contain 'loose' nodes (b and c), not connected to the rest of the structure. Therefore, we first define these substructures ('SUBDISCOTREES') separately; this can be done recursively.

(15) Let N be a non-empty set whose elements are called NODES.
- (i) If $t \in N$, then the pair $<t,[\ ]>$ is a subdiscotree; such a subdiscotree is called ATOMIC;
- (ii) If $x \in N$ and $X_1, \ldots, X_k$ are subdiscotrees that do not share any subdiscotrees[3] then the pair $<x, [X_1, Y_2, \ldots, Y_j, X_k]>$ is a subdiscotree, where $Y_i = X_i$ or Y_i a sub-list of $X_2, \ldots, X_{k-1}$.
- (iii) No other structures than those defined by (i) and (ii) are subdiscotrees.

Instead of '$<x, [X_1, \ldots, [\ldots], \ldots, X_k]>$', we also write, more simply: '$x(X_1, X_2, \ldots, [\ldots], \ldots, X_k)$'. The idea is that a subdiscotree consists of a top node x and a sequence of nodes dominated by x (daughter nodes), possibly interrupted by lists $[X_i, X_j, \ldots]$ of nodes *not* dominated by x; these are called INTERNAL CONTEXT of x, or CONTEXT DAUGHTERS of x.

For example, the structure in (14a) can be viewed as a graphical representation of the subdiscotree written in full and in simplified form in (16):

(16) $X = <P, [a, [b], c]> = P(a, [b], c)$

Similarly, the graph (12) is a visualization of (17):

(17) $X = <S, [<P, [a, [b], c]>, <Q, [b, [c], d]>]> = S(\ P(a, [b], c), Q(b, [c], d)\ )$

We define the notions of dominance and direct dominance for subdiscotrees as follows:

(18) Direct dominance (*D*):
- (i) in an atomic subdiscotree $<x, [\ ]>$, there is no node that is dominated by node x;
- (ii) in a subdiscotree $<x, [X_1, Y_1, \ldots, Y_j, X_k]>$ the node x directly dominates the top nodes of X_1, of X_k, and of every Y_i that is a subdiscotree (but not of those Y_i that are a list of subdiscotrees; a node does not dominate its context daughters).

Dominance (D^*) is defined as usual, as the reflexive and transitive closure of direct dominance.

A discontinuous tree is now simply a subdiscotree without any 'loose' nodes (nodes that are not connected to the rest of the structure through the dominance relation). In other words, every node in a discotree has a mother node.

(19) Discontinuous tree (DISCOTREE):
A discontinuous tree is a subdiscotree X where every node is dominated by some other node in X.

Since the top node of a (sub)discotree dominates all the nodes which have a mother node, it follows that the top node of a discotree dominates every node in the structure.

We now have a reliable definition of discontinuous tree structures. The next point to consider is how these structures can be generated by a grammar. We know that ordinary tree structures are generated by phrase-structure grammars; can discontinuous trees also can be produced by some sort of phrase-structure rules? This question (which to our knowledge has not been addressed before) turns out to be far from trivial; to answer it, we will have to look closely at linear precedence and adjacency in discotrees.

2.1 Linear precedence and adjacency in discontinuous trees

A phrase-structure rule rewrites a constituent into a sequence of pairwise adjacent constituents. The formulation of phrase-structure rules for discontinuous trees thus requires a notion of adjacency in such structures. Since adjacency is a special case of linear precedence, we first have to define the precedence relation for discotrees. We may try to do this in the same way as usual for ordinary trees.

In the axiomatic definition of trees, the set of terminal nodes is assumed to be ordered and the precedence relation is defined in a 'bottom-up' way on the basis of this ordering (see (8)).

In the recursive approach, where trees are defined in a 'top-down' fashion, no ordering of the terminal nodes is assumed (see (15)). Instead, linear precedence (<) is defined recursively in a top-down way by (20):

(20) (i) In a tree $A(X_1, \ldots, X_n)$, $X_i < X_j$ iff $i < j$.
(ii) If P, Q, x and y are nodes in a tree such that $P < Q$, $P\ D\ x$, and $Q\ D\ y$, then $x < y$.

The first clause in this definition defines a partial ordering between 'sister' nodes. The second clause makes this ordering total, and rules out weird structures like (21).

(21a)

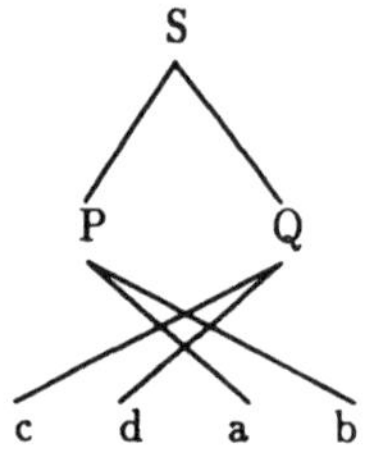

(21b)

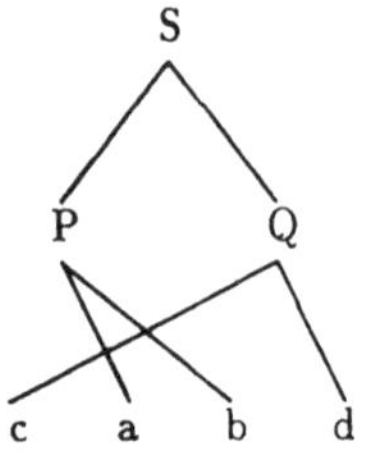

It is easily verified that the precedence relation defined in this way is transitive, as an ordering should be. The obvious disco-counterpart of this definition is:

(22) (i) In a subdiscotree $A(X_1, \ldots, [\ldots, X_i, \ldots], \ldots, X_n)$, $X_i < X_j$ iff $i < j$.
(ii) If P, Q, x and y are nodes in a subdiscotree such that P < Q, P *D* x, and Q *D* y, then x < y.

Adjacency is now simply precedence without intervening nodes:

(23) two nodes x and y in a discotree are adjacent iff x < y and there is no z such that x < z < y.

We shall write 'x + y' to indicate that x and y are adjacent.

Unfortunately, this notion of adjacency is inadequate for formulating grammar rules that operate with discontinuous constituents. We turn to the issue of grammar rules for generating discontinuous trees in the next section.

3. Discotrees in grammar rules

3.1 Adjacency and concatenation

The following example shows that the notion of adjacency, introduced above, is not adequate for use in rewrite rules. Suppose we want to generate the discontinuous tree structure (24):

(24)

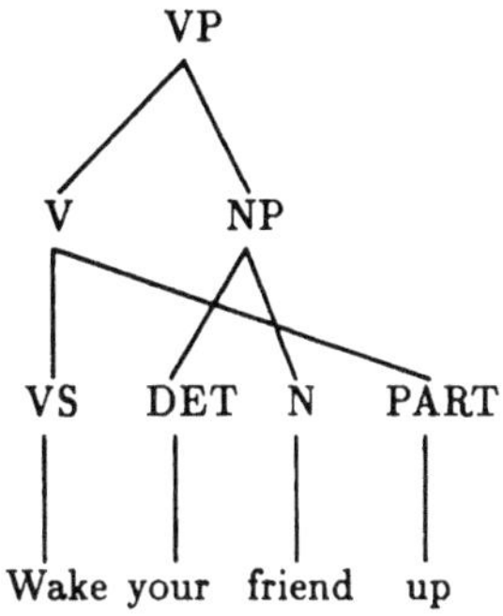

To generate this structure, we need rules like the following, where square brackets indicate internal context elements:

(25)

VP	→	V + NP
V	→	VS + [DET] + [N] + PART
NP	→	DET + N
VS	→	wake
DET	→	your
N	→	friend
PART	→	up

According to the second clause in (22), however, the particle *up* precedes the determiner and the noun, so these rules generate the incorrect structure (26). This problem occurs generally when a discontinuous constituent is to be concatenated with some other constituent. We thus need a different precedence relation for discontinuous trees.

(26)

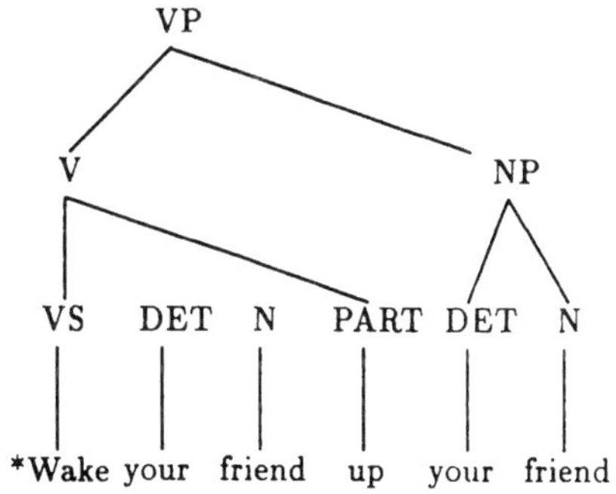

The source of the problem is that, by the second clause in (22), a node x which is an internal context daughter of node P and a 'real' daughter of another node Q, either precedes or is preceded by all the daughter nodes of P, depending on whether P precedes Q or Q precedes P. But characteristic of an internal context node is precisely that it is located *in between* the 'real' daughters of a node (of node P, in this case). We therefore relax the second clause in (22) to (27):

(27) if X and Y are nodes in a subdiscotree such that $X < Y$, then X's leftmost daughter precedes Y's leftmost daughter.

The notion 'leftmost daughter' *Lm* (X) of X is defined by (28):

(28) (i) if X is an atomic subdiscotree <x, [ ]>, then *Lm*(X) = x;
(ii) else X is a subdiscotree of the form <x, [X_1,..., [...], ..., X_n]> and *Lm*(X) = X_1.

With this notion of precedence, and the notion of adjacency that follows from it, the rules (25) give besides the incorrect structure (26) also the correct possibility (24). To prevent the generation of incorrect structures like (26), we define adjacency slightly differently:

(29) Two nodes x and y are adjacent iff:
(i) $Lm(x) < Lm(y)$;
(ii) for every node z such that $Lm(x) < z < Lm(y)$: x *D* z.

In other words, x and y are adjacent if x precedes y and y's leftmost daughter is the first node to the right of x's leftmost daughter which does not belong to x. With this definition of adjacency the rules (25) do not generate the structure (26), since the V and NP in that case are not adjacent.

3.2 Discotrees in Phrase-Structure Grammar

Upon closer inspection, the adjacency relation as now defined is still not quite satisfactory from the point of view of formulating rewrite rules. The following example illustrates this.

(30)

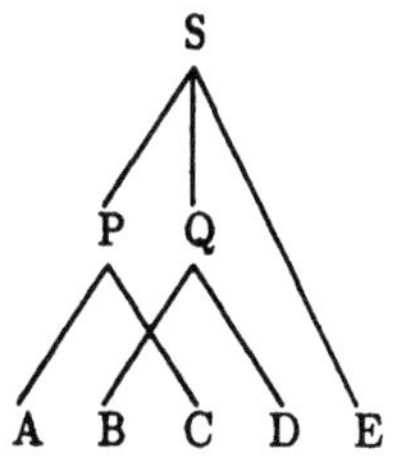

Suppose we want to generate the structure (30). To generate the S node, we would like to write a phrase-structure rule that rewrites S into its constituents, like (31):

(31) $S \rightarrow P + Q + E$

But this rule would not apply here, since Q and E are not adjacent; according to (29), Q has C as its right neighbour, not E. Therefore, the correct rule for generating (30) would be (32):

(32) $S \rightarrow P + Q + [C] + [D] + E$

This is ugly, and even uglier rules are required in more complex cases with discontinuities at different levels. Moreover, there seems to be something fundamentally wrong, since the C and D nodes are on the one hand internal context for the S node, according to rule (32), while on the other hand they are also dominated by S. That is, these nodes are both 'real' constituents of S and internal context of S.

To remedy this we introduce a new concept called ADJACENCY SEQUENCE, which generalizes the traditional notion of sequence of adjacency pairs. The definition goes as follows:

(33) A sequence <a, b,. . . , n> is an adjacency sequence iff:
(i) every pair <i,j> in the sequence is either an adjacency pair or is connected by a sequence of adjacency pairs of which all members are a constituent of some element in the subsequence <a, b,. . . , i>;
(ii) the elements in the sequence do not share any constituents.

For example, in the structure (30) the triple <P, Q, E> is an adjacency sequence since <P, Q> is an adjacency pair and Q and E are connected by the sequence of adjacency pairs Q-C-D-E, with C and D constituents of P and Q, respectively. Moreover, P, Q, and E do not share any substructures. The triple <P, B, C>, on the other hand, is not an adjacency sequence since P and C share the constituent C.

This notion of adjacency sequence can now be used to define phrase-structure rules for discontinuous trees as prescriptions to rewrite a nonterminal into a sequence of constituents which forms an adjacency sequence, like (31), where some of the elements (but not the first and not the last) may be marked as internal context elements. A phrase-structure grammar consisting of rules of this kind we call a *Discontinuous Phrase-Structure Grammar (DPSG)*.

A DPSG rule A → B + C generates exactly those structures where the immediate daughters of B and C are interwoven, or 'sequence-unioned' (Reape, 1990), with the additional constraint that B's leftmost daughter precedes C's leftmost daughter.

It is worth emphasizing that this notion of phrase-structure rule is a generalization of the standard notion, since an adjacency sequence as defined by (33) subsumes the traditional notion of sequence of adjacency pairs. We have also seen that trees with discontinuities are a generalization of the traditional tree concept. Therefore, phrase-structure rules of the familiar sort coincide with DPSG rules without discontinuous constituents, and they produce the familiar sort of trees without discontinuities. In other words, DPSG rules can simply be added to an ordinary PSG (including a generalized or augmented PSG), with the result that the grammar generates trees with discontinuities for sentences with discontinuous constituents, while doing everything else as before.

3.3 Discotrees in Categorial Grammar

Categorial Grammars do not aim at the explicit generation of constituent structures, but they are based on string concatenation; therefore, it can hardly come as a surprise that discotrees can be introduced in Categorial Grammar just as easily as in PSGs.

The following example illustrates this possibility. Consider first the simple sentence

(34) *John kissed Mary.*

To analyse this in a CG-fashion, the following categories may be assigned to the individual lexical items:

(35) John : NP
kissed : (NP\S)/NP
Mary : NP

Right concatenation of the verb with the object-NP gives a verb phrase of category NP\S, which concatenates to the left with the subject-NP to form an S.

Now consider the similar sentence with a discontinuity in the verb phrase:

(36) *John woke Mary up.*

To generate this sentence, we keep the NPs as before but assign the following categories to the verb and the particle:

(37) woke : (NP\S)[/NP]/PART
up : PART

The notation [...] has been used here, as in the case of discontinuous PSG rules, to indicate that the material inside the brackets is internal context. To make this work, all we have to do is amend the right concatenation rule of CG to one that allows internal context:

(38) $A[/C]/B + [C] + B \Rightarrow A/C$

This says that an element of category A[/C]/B combines with an element of category B occurring to its right while there is an intervening element of category C. The resulting element combines with a C on its right to form an A. (This could, of course, be generalized for sequences of more than one intervening elements.) Application of the scheme (38) to (36) and (37) gives the reduction of *woke ... up* to a discotree, with category (NP\S)/NP, and the rest goes the same as before.

For a really satisfactory treatment of cases like sentence (36) we should, of course, take into account that the particle which 'concatenates' with the verb is the one that the verb is expecting, and not just any particle. In this respect, the situation is the same as in PSG rules, and the solution is again to add features and unification to the grammar; see for instance Van der Linden (1989).

3.4 An ID/LP format for discontinuous rules

Sofar, we have considered the use of discotrees in rewrite rules only for their classical form, in which they state something about immediate dominance as well as about linear precedence. One of the important innovations of GPSG has been the decoupling of these aspects, which makes it possible to formulate rules that express much greater generalizations.

A rule that generates a discontinuous tree must by its very nature say something about immediate dominance as well as about linear precedence, so it seems, and an ID/LP format for such rules therefore might appear strange.

This is a wrong impression, however. A rule like (39) is equivalent to the ID/LP rules (40), where CD stands for (immediate) context daughters:

(39) $R \rightarrow A + [B] + [C] + D$

(40) ID: $R \rightarrow A, D$
CD: B, C
LP: $A < D$; $B < C$.

In this example, the ID/LP-like formulation clearly has no advantages whatsoever over the traditional formulation; such advantages can only be expected if the same dominance rule allows various linear orders. This is precisely what is often the case with discontinuities; for example, in Dutch an intervening adverb (phrase) can be placed on a variety of positions. If, in the case of example (39), the B and C constituents may appear in arbitrary order, the ID/LP-like format becomes more attractive:

(41) ID: $R \rightarrow A, D$
CD: B, C
LP: $A < D$.

The LP rule has now become very simple, since internal context elements by definition can only stand in between the 'real' daughters of the top node.

The exact ID/LP-like format of DPSG rules is rather complex, when more 'real' or context daughters are involved, features are taken into account and semantics is added; the reader is referred to Bunt (1990) for more details.

The strict separation of dominance and precedence is also one of the features of Head-driven Phrase Structure Grammar (HPSG; see Pollard – Sag, 1987; 1991). For bounded discontinuities, which is what the DPSG concepts are useful for, HPSG like GPSG faces the problem of having to specify the bounded internal contexts which may separate the parts of a discontinuous constituent. In HPSG we can do this by 'simulating' the use of discotrees as follows.

HPSG does not build phrase structure representations of the usual kind, but builds attribute-value matrices where some of the attributes represent dominance relations. More precisely, the attributes HEAD-DAUGHTER, COMPLEMENT-DAUGHTERS, ADJUNCT-DAUGHTER, FILLER-DAUGHTER are used to represent mother-daughter relations with certain functional characteristics. We can add to this an attribute corresponding to the 'context daughter' relation of DPSG: CONTEXT-DAUGHTER, and thus build feature structures corresponding to (sub)discotrees, useful in parsing or generation of sentences with bounded discontinuities. Expectations (or requirements) concerning the presence of certain types of daughters in certain types of phrases are expressed in HPSG by means of attributes whose values propagate according to certain general principles, like the Subcat Principle. Expectations concerning complement daughters are expressed in the values of the SUBCAT attribute, those concerning filler daughters in the SLASH attribute, and those concerning head-adjunct daughter combinations either in the ADJUNCTS feature (Pollard – Sag, 1987) of the head daughter or in the MOD feature of the adjunct daughter (Pollard – Sag, 1991). Similarly, for internal context daughters we introduce a feature whose values propagate in a way more or less similar to the SUBCAT feature. The details of how this might work are beyond the scope of the present paper.

4. Complexity and computer implementation of DPSG

DPSG obviously has greater than context-free generative capacity; on the other hand, it has restrictions that make it less powerful than context-sensitive grammar. Exactly where DPSG sits in between these two has not yet been established precisely. Vogel – Bunt (1992) and Vogel – Erjavec (1994) argue that, especially when DPSG is restricted slightly in the kinds of crossing branching it allows,[4] it has properly less power than the Mildly Context-Sensitive Grammars (Joshi, Vijay-Shanker – Weir, 1989).

A first computer implementation of DPSG has been made within the context of the TENDUM dialogue project (see Bunt *et al.*, 1985). A parser-interpreter has been built, based on the chart parsing technique,[5] where the syntactic side of DPSG that has been outlined here, is combined with a somewhat Montague-like semantic theory, called *two-level model-theoretic semantics* (Bunt, 1985), and with a pragmatic theory which construes the communicative functions of utterances in dialogues in terms of the kind of information transfer they accomplish upon correct understanding (Bunt, 1989).[6] The output of the parser consists of one or more triples, depending on ambiguity in the input, each formed by

1. a syntactic analysis in the form of a discotree;
2. a semantic representation in the form of an expression of the logical language EL/F, a type-logical language based on Ensemble Theory, an extension of standard set theory; see Bunt (1985);
3. a pragmatic analysis in the form of a bundle of features, relevant for the determination of the input's communicative functions.

The parsing algorithm is based on the active chart parsing concept; it uses a special matrix-driven strategy for the application of rules, and it incorporates additional bookkeeping devices for the correct handling of context daughters and the n-ary adjacency-sequence relation of DPSG. Above, we have already emphasized that trees with discontinuities are a generalization of the traditional tree concept, and that the DPSG notion of phrase-structure rule is a generalization of the standard notion. As a result, phrase-structure rules of the traditional sort coincide with DPSG rules without discontinuous constituents, and they produce the familiar sort of trees without discontinuities. A PSG parser equipped with the additional bookkeeping devices mentioned above can thus process a grammar consisting partly of ordinary PSG rules and partly of DPSG rules, producing syntactic (disco-)trees with discontinuities for sentences with discontinuous constituents, while operating in the usual way for sentences without discontinuities. The reader is referred to Bunt (1991) for a description of this chart parser.

The use of DPSG in the generation of sentences, starting from formal representations of semantic content and communicative function, has been explored both theoretically and in an experimental computer implementation discussed in Bunt (1987).

An interesting recent development is the expression of feature structures and DSPG rules in an extended version version of the semantic representation language EL/F, mentioned above. This allows the expression of syntactic and semantic information in a single representation formalism, and gives a formal, model-theoretic interpretation of the syntactic part of a DPSG grammar. The extended representation language is called 'GEL', for Generalized Ensemble Language. In contrast with the traditional view of phrase-structure rules as recipes for building phrase structures, and with the declarative view in the parsing-as-deduction paradigm as a proposition which is true if the conditions for building the phrase structure are satisfied, a rule in GEL is best viewed as a proposition in Dynamic Semantics: it can be evaluated recursively and evaluates not to true or false, but to the minimal change in the model[7] needed to make the proposition true. This idea and its implementation in a chart parser for DPSG are described in Bunt & Van der Sloot (1993).

Notes

1. Or rather, *multisets* of words, i.e. unordered collections, possibly with duplicates.
2. See Vogel & Bunt (1992) for a discussion of the relation between Right-Wrap and a restricted form of the Discontinuous Phrase Structure Grammar formalism, described below, called $DPSG^R$.
3. Two subdiscotrees X and Y share a subdiscotree T if both X and Y contain a node dominating T.
4. The restriction considered in these studies is that any node *c*, which occurs as a context daughter of a node *t*, must also be directly dominated by some node *s*, distinct from *t*, that bears a 'generalized dominance' relation to *t*. The 'generalized dominance' relation combines the ordinary dominance relation with that of the relation between a node and its context daughters.
5. See Bunt – Thesingh – Van der Sloot (1987).
6. For developments in this pragmatic theory since the TENDUM project see Bunt (1990; 1994).
7. That is, in this case, in the chart.

References

Bach, E.
1979 Control in Montague Grammar. *Linguistic Inquiry 10*, 515–531.

Bach, E.
1980 In Defense of Passive. *Linguistics and Philosophy 3*, 297–341.

Bunt, H.C.
1985 *Mass terms and model-theoretic semantics*. Cambridge University Press, Cambridge, England.

Bunt, H.C.
1987 Utterance generation from semantic representation augmented with pragmatic information. In: G. Kempen (ed.), *Natural language generation.* Kluwer/Nijhoff, The Hague.

Bunt, H.C.
1989 Information dialogues as communicative action in relation to partner modelling and information processing. In: M.M. Taylor, F. Neel, and D.G. Bouwhuis (eds.), *The Structure of Multimodal Dialogue.* North-Holland Elsevier, Amsterdam, 48–73.

Bunt, H.C.
1990 DIT – Dynamic Interpretation in Text and Dialogue. In: L. Kalman and L. Polos (eds.), *Papers from the Second Symposium on Logic and Language.* Akademiai Kiado, Budapest.

Bunt, H.C.
1991 DSPG and its use in parsing. In: M. Tomita (ed.), *Parsing Technologies.* CMU, Pittsburgh.

Bunt, H.C.
1994 Context and Dialogue Control. *THINK Quarterly 3(1)*, 17–29.

Bunt, H.C., Beun, R.J., Dols, F.J.H., Linden, J.A. van der, and Schwartzenberg, G.O. thoe
1985 The TENDUM dialogue system and its theoretical basis. IPO Annual Progress Report 19, 105–113.

Bunt, H.C., Thesingh, J.C. and Sloot, K. van der
1987 Discontinuities in trees, rules and parsing. In: *Proceedings of the Third Conference of the European Chapter of the ACL*, Copenhagen, 203–211.

Bunt, H.C. and Sloot, K. van der
1993 Parsing as Dynamic Evaluation. In: *Proceedings of the Third International Workshop on Parsing Technologies IPWT'93*, ITK, Tilburg, 27–37.

Dowty, D.R.
1996 Toward a minimalist theory of syntactic structure. *This volume*, 11–63.

Emonds, J.E.
1979 Appositive relatives have no properties, *Linguistic Inquiry*, vol. 10, 211–243.

Gazdar, G., Klein. E., Pullum, G.K. and Sag, I.A.
1985 *Generalized Phrase Structure Grammar.* Harvard University Press, Cambridge, Massachusetts.

Linden, E.-J. van der
1989 Lambek Theorem Proving and Feature Unification. In: *Proceedings of the 4th EACL Conference*, Manchester.

Jacobson, P.
1987 Phrase Structure, grammatical relations, and discontinuous constituents. In: G.J. Huck and A.E. Ojeda (eds.), *Discontinuous Constituency*, Academic Press, New York etc.

McCawley, J.D.
1982 Parentheticals and Discontinuous Constituent Structure. *Linguistic Inquiry*, vol. 13, 91–106.

Pollard, C.J. and Sag, I.A.
1987 *Information-based Syntax and Semantics*, vol. 1, CLSI, Stanford.

Pollard, C.J. and Sag, I.A.
1991 *Topics in Constraint-Based Syntactic Theory*. Universität des Saarlandes, Saarbrücken.

Reape, M.
1996 Getting things in order. *This volume*, 209–253.

Stucky, S.
1987 Configurational Variation in English: A Study of Extraposition and Relation Matters. In: G. Huck and A. Ojeda (eds.), *Discontinuous Constituency. Syntax and Semantics 20*. Academic Press, New York etc.

Vogel, C.M. and Bunt, H.C.
1992 Representing Discontinuous Constituency: Motivations and Complexity. In: *Proceedings of Pacific Rim International Conference on Artificial Intelligence*, Seoul.

Vogel, C.M. and Erjavec, T.
1994 Restricted Discontinuous Phrase Structure Grammar and Its Ramifications. In: C. Martin-Vide (ed.), *Current Issues in Mathematical Linguistics*. Elsevier, Amsterdam.

Wall, R.E.
1972 *Introduction to Mathematical Linguistics*. Prentice-Hall, Englewood Cliffs.

Williams, E.
1974 *Rule Ordering in Syntax*. MIT Linguistics Dissertation, Cambridge, Massachusetts.

Expressing discontinuous constituency in Dislog

Patrick Saint-Dizier

Abstract. In this short document, we present several applications of Dislog to language processing. Dislog uses the power of logic and the high conceptualization level of Prolog as an operational vehicle to express the notion of constraint or relation between discontinuous elements in a structure. A Dislog clause is a set of definite clauses, possibly sharing common variables, which must co-occur in a proof (or parse) tree. The notion of non-continuity is expressed by the fact that there are no a priori restrictions on the location of these definite clauses in the proof tree.

1. Introduction

Dislog mainly emerged from the specification of a computational model for Government and Binding theory (noted hereafter as GB) (Chomsky 1982; 1986), in particular to model movement theory and Quantifier raising and their related constraints and filters. Our goal is not to model GB theory, but we feel that the transfer of some of its principles to natural language processing is worth investigating and very promising (Saint-Dizier 1989). The GB description of linguistic phenomena turns out to be concise, modular and parametrized; more interestingly, it is a constraint-based linguistic description of language. All these reasons make GB attractive to logic programmers. Finally, our preliminary experiences show that some GB principles, paired with other natural language processing devices dealing with lexical issues (e.g. lexical semantics), with feature representation and logical form construction, can form an efficient and well-designed system.

Dislog is not only a tool appropriate for GB modelling: more generally, it permits us to express relations or constraints between non-contiguous elements in a structure in a simple, modular and declarative way. The examples developed in section 3 show several application domains: expressing free-phrase order, computing the semantic representation of temporal expressions and its use for other computational approaches, like unification grammars. Dislog has also been used in other areas than natural language processing, such as compiler design and planning, where long-distance relations need to be expressed. Finally, we present in this document the main lines of the compiler we have designed.

2. Introducing DISLOG

2.1 Dislog clauses

A Dislog clause is a finite, unordered set of Horn clauses or of literals f_i of the form:

$$\{ f_1 , f_2 , \ldots , f_n \}.$$

The informal meaning of a Dislog clause is: if a clause or a literal f_i in a Dislog clause is used to construct a given proof tree, then all the other f_j of that Dislog clause must be used to construct that proof tree, with the same substitutions applied to identical variables. Moreover, there are no hypotheses made on the location of these clauses or these literals in the proof (or parse) tree.

For example, the following Dislog clause composed of two Prolog facts:

{ arc(a,b), arc(e,f) }.

means that, in a graph, the use of arc(a,b) to construct a proof is conditional on the use of arc(e,f). If one is looking for paths in a graph, this means that all paths going through the arc (a,b) will have to go through the arc (e,f) or conversely. A Dislog clause thus permits us to express co-occurence of constraints of clauses or of literals in a proof tree. The constraint stating that all identical variables in an instance of a Dislog clause must be substituted for the same term permits the transfer of feature values between non-contiguous elements in a very convenient way.

2.2 Constraining Dislog clauses

A Dislog clause can be subject to various types of restrictions. A first type of restriction is the imposition of constraints on the order in which clauses or literals are used in a Dislog clause. We say that an instance of a clause or a literal r_i precedes an instance of a clause or of a literal r_j in a proof tree if either r_i appears in that proof tree to the left of r_j or if r_i dominates r_j. Notice that this notion of precedence is independent of the strategy used to build the proof tree. To model this notion of precedence, we add to Dislog clauses the traditional linear precedence restriction notation: a < b means that the definite clause with head a (or the literal a) precedes the clause with head b (or the literal b). This can be illustrated by the following Dislog clause:

{ arc(a,b), arc(c,d), arc(e,f) } arc(a,b) < arc(e,f).

which imposes that the literal (or fact) arc(a,b) precedes arc(e,f) in a proof tree using an instance of that Dislog clause.

When the clause order in a Dislog clause is complete, we use the more convenient notation:

f_1 / f_2 / ... / f_n.

which means that f_1 precedes f_2 which precedes f_3 etc ... The relation '/' can be viewed as an accessibility relation.

Another improvement to Dislog clauses is the adjunction of *modalities*. We want, for example, to allow definite clauses or literals in a Dislog clause to be used several times. This permits us, for example, to deal with parasitic gaps and with pronominal references. We introduce the modality *m*, applied to a clause or to a literal, to express that it can be used any number of times in that Dislog clause. For example, in:

{ f_1 , f_2 , m(f_3) }.

the clause f_3 can be used any number of times, provided that f_1 and f_2 are used. Substitutions for identical variables remain the same as before.

Finally, we introduce in Dislog the notion of bounding domain. In linguistics, roughly speaking, Bounding theory states constraints on the way in which constituents can be moved, or, in non-transformational terms on the way to establish relations between non-contiguous elements in a sentence. The main type of constraint is expressed in terms of domains over the boundaries of which relations cannot be established. For example, if A is a bounding node (or a subtree which is a sequence of bounding nodes), then the domain of A is the domain it is the root of and no constituent X inside that domain can have relations with a constituent outside it (at least not directly).

This phenomenon can be transposed to Dislog: if an instance of a Dislog clause is activated within a bounding domain, then the whole Dislog clause has to be used within that domain. For a given application, bounding nodes are specified as a small database of facts and are interpreted by the Dislog system.

2.3 General form of Dislog clauses

The general form of a Dislog clause is the following:

$$\{ m_1(r_1), m_2(r_2), \ldots, m_n(r_n) \} \text{ constraints}(r_1, r_2, \ldots, r_n).$$

where:
- r_i are Horn clauses (or Definite Clause grammar rules which are grammar rules encoded in Prolog). They can also be extensions to Horn clauses like modal Horn clauses, clauses of the Constrained Logic Programming framework or logical types construction rules.
- m_i are modalities: m, m+, the empty modality, etc.
- constraints($r_1, r_2, \ldots, r_n$) is a conjunction of constraints.

These constraints are global to the Dislog clause and thus cannot be encoded in a particular r_i; they can be of very different types, for example linear precedence restrictions and bounding constraints.

In Saint-Dizier (1988), we give the theoretical foundations of Dislog and show that it is sound and complete.

3. Dislog for natural language processing

3.1 Parsing and generating sentences with Dislog

A Dislog clause can be a set of Definite Clause grammar rules. Compared to other approaches dealing with discontinuous constituency, Dislog has the following specific features:

- Dislog clauses are declarative, no procedural commitment (e.g. computation rule or parsing strategy) is made, moreover each clause is independent from the others.

- Discontinuous constituency is expressed in a modular way, apart from other grammatical aspects. These other aspects are dealt with by other rules of the grammar.
- Discontinuous constituency is expressed in a concise and simple way, with no complex apparatus or meta-level of abstraction.
- No additional argument is used to carry gap introduction and gap satisfaction information as is the case for GPSGs (with slash categories or, more recently, with slash features) and for LFGs (with meta-variables indexed by category values). Discontinuous consistuency in Dislog is only expressed by grammar symbols and a co-occurence constraint.
- No strong hypothesis is made on the nature of the elements in a Dislog clause (cf. section 3.2). Dislog can thus be used in a number of different linguistic and computational linguistics approaches like Logic Grammars, Unification Grammars and Tree-Adjoining Grammars. It is thus not committed to any particular linguistic theory.

3.2 Modeling movement theory in GB

Dislog was first designed to model (Saint-Dizier 1987; 1989) move-α, quantifier raising and bounding theory in GB theory (Chomsky 1982; 1986). Move-α needs to be somewhat instantiated to be computationally tractable; this instantiation, however, does not affect the generality of the rule. Let us consider the case of the relative clause. In a relative clause, an N is pronominalized and moved to the left and adjoined to a COMP node. A trace of N is left behind and co-indexed with the pronominalized N. Here is the general frame of this construction:

[COMP N(+Pro)$_i$ ... [N2 trace $_i$] ...]
as in:
[COMP that$_i$ John met [N2 trace $_i$] yesterday]

This construction is expressed in a straightforward way in Dislog. The first clause deals with the left adjunction of the N(+Pro) to the COMP and the second clause deals with the derivation of the N2 into a trace. Both rules must be present in the proof (or parse) tree to make the proof (or parse tree) correct. A shared variable '*i*' permits us to non-ambiguously establish a co-indexation link. Notice that what is in between the pronoun and the trace is of no current interest and will be processed by other rules. The Dislog clause is the following, in which we adopt the X-bar syntax terminology:

xp(comp,0,_,_) → xp(n,0,pro(Case),I) , xp(comp,0,_,_). /
xp(n,2,Case,I,) → trace(I).

An xp is a predicate which represents any category. The category is specified in the first argument, the bar level in the second, syntactic features in the third one (oversimplified here), the fourth argument is the co-indexation link. Notice that using identical variables (here *I* and *Case*) in two different clauses in a Dislog clause permits us to transfer feature values in a very simple and transparent way. The Dislog rule given above operates like a rewriting rule, constructing a well-formed annotated surface form of a sentence. We have the following diagram for the above relativization rule:

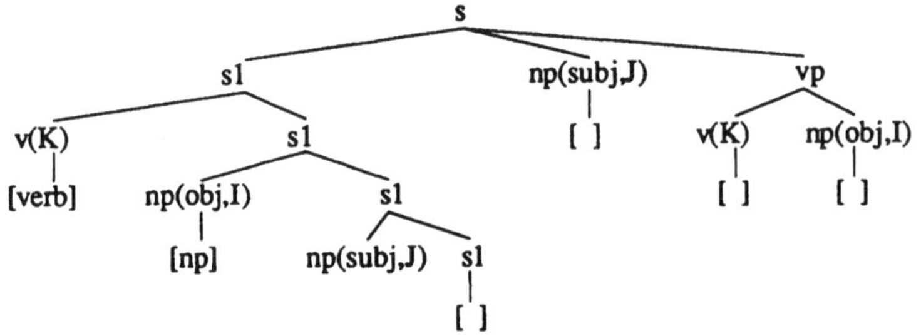

Figure 1.

Other examples of rules are given in Saint-Dizier (1989) such as: NP-movement, subject-to-subject raising and wh-construal at Logical Form. The use of modality m permits us to deal with constructions like parasitic gaps.

3.3 Unification Grammars and Dislog

The same type of phenomenon can be expressed within the Unification Grammar's representational system using for example a type-based representation. To represent grammatical and lexical elements objects we use Login, which is introduced below.

3.3.1 An overview of Login

Login (Aït-Kaçi – Nasr 1986), is an extension to Prolog in which first-order terms are replaced by a more general notion: Ψ-terms. These terms allow the integration of taxonomies directly into the unification mechanism. This enhances the expressiveness of the language as well as the efficiency of the resolution-based inference mechanism of Prolog. The syntactic representation of a structured term is called a Ψ-term. It consists of:

(1) a root symbol, which is a type constructor and denotes a class of entities,
(2) attribute labels, which are record field symbols. Each attribute denotes a function in extenso, from the root to the attribute value.
(3) coreference constraints among paths of labels, which indicate that the corresponding attributes denote the same function. They are indicated by variables.

Here is an example:

```
person( id ⇒ name (first ⇒ string, last ⇒ X: string),
        born ⇒ date(day ⇒ integer, month ⇒ monthname,
        year ⇒ integer),
        father ⇒ person(id ⇒ name(last ⇒ X ))).
```

The root symbol is person; id, born and father are three sub-Ψ-terms. X indicates a coreference. All different type structures are tagged by different symbols. Notice also that in the latter field only relevant information about person is mentioned. Infinite structures can also be specified by coreference links.

3.3.2 Using Login for parsing

The X-bar rules used in GB theory can be translated into a typed-based form. Here is, as an illustration, the rule:

X2 → spec, X1.

where X is a category like N, A, V, P, INFL or COMP.

Let us consider the operator:

A with B unify C.

which means that A and B unify to give C. A, B and C are (partial) type specifications. This permits us to have unification rules directly for X-bar syntax; this instead of deduction or rewrite rules. We then have the rule above expressed as follows, where mod refers to a specifier database:

```
xp(syn ⇒ category(cat ⇒ C1, bar ⇒ B )) with % X2 → spec, X1.
    xp(syn ⇒ category(cat ⇒ C, bar ⇒ 1 ))   unify
```

```
  xp(syn ⇒ category(cat ⇒ C, bar ⇒ 2 )) :-
mod(spec,C,C1,B).
mod(spec,n,det,0).   % specifier database
mod(spec,aux,v,0).   % aux with bar level 0 is the spec of v.
```

3.3.3 Dealing with discontinuous constituency

Movement rules are expressed in the same way as in section 3.2. Instead of having grammar rules in Dislog clauses, we have unification rules. Here is the example of the relativisation rule:

```
{ ( xp(syn ⇒ category(cat ⇒ n, bar ⇒ 2, pronoun ⇒ rel))
      % first rule with
      xp(syn ⇒ category(cat ⇒ comp, bar ⇒ 2))  unify
      xp(syn ⇒ category(cat ⇒ comp, bar ⇒ 2), trace ⇒ I) ),
      xp(empty ⇒ yes)  unify                      % second rule
      xp(syn⇒category(cat⇒n,bar⇒2),trace ⇒ I, empty ⇒ yes ) }.
```

The informal meaning of this Dislog rule is that if one of the unification rules is used during the parse, then the other one must also be used with identical variable substitutions applied to identical variable identifiers.

3.4 Free word order in Dislog

Dislog is well-adapted to deal with languages exhibiting a certain degree of free word order. Consider, as an example, the following grammar:

```
s → np(subj), vp.
vp → v, np(obj).
```

If we want to have a free np order in the language recognized by this grammar, then the grammar will have to be composed of 6 context-free rules. Instead, we can write the following Dislog rule, keeping the generality of the free np order. To avoid repetition of the axiom s, we introduce a 'working' node s1:

```
s → s1.  s1 → [ ].
{ (s1 → np(subj), s1), (s1 → v, s1), (s1 → np(obj), s1) }.
```

If we want, at the same time, to reconstruct a 'normalized' parse tree corresponding to the above grammar, we can write the following grammar:

s → s1, np(subj, I), vp. s1 → [ ].
vp → v(J), np(obj, I).
s1 → np(Case, I), s1 / np(Case, I) → [ ].
s1 → v(J), s1 / v(J) → [ ].

Symbols beginning with a capital letter represent variables. The variables I and J are co-indexes, they permit us to relate overt elements with their traces, as in GB theory. The grammar above permits us to obtain a tree like the following:

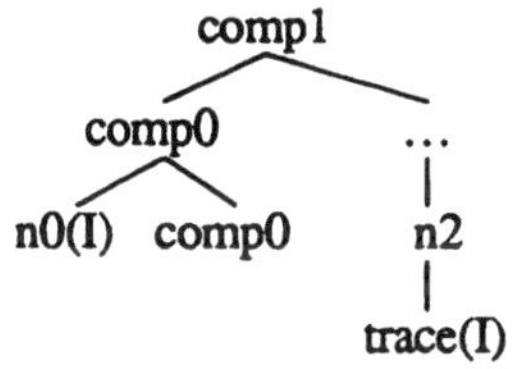

Figure 2.

where the normalized form of the parse tree is reconstructed by means of co-indexation variables in the right-hand part of the tree.

Notice that, at this level, Dislog rules are not a re-interpretation of the ID/LP system since rules in a Dislog rule need not appear at the same level in the parse tree (i.e. to be sisters), which is the case for symbols in ID/LP rules. If the structures are not completely free to occupy any position of their category, constraints can be formulated (see section 2.2).

3.5 Relations between syntax and semantics, compositionality

Syntactic phenomena described by Dislog rules can be associated with semantic representations specifically expressing the semantics of movements or long-distance relations. Dislog also permits us to specify in a simple and declarative way the semantics of constructions involving discontinuous constituents, like temporal expressions. We will give here two examples.

Topicalizing an NP means that it becomes, for example, the focus of the sentence. If we assume that the topicalized NP is adjoined to a phrasal node like COMP, then we have the following rule, where the semantic representation of the NP is R and its representation is focus(R). S is the representation of the remainder of the sentence, elaborated on under the COMP symbol in the right-hand side of the first rule in the Dislog rule below:

comp(and(focus(R), S)) → np(R), comp(S) / np(_) → trace.

The expression of the semantics of temporal expressions involving, for example, temporal connectors like *when* need to take into account non-contiguous constituents in the sentence (Bras 1989; Bras – Saint-Dizier 1989). For example, in French, in 'P_1 quand P_2' (P_1 when P_2), where propositions P_1 and P_2 denote events e_1 and e_2, then, depending on tenses t_1 and t_2 of the verbs in P_1 and P_2, and on their semantic types cat_1 and cat_2 (for example: achievement, state, accomplishment, etc.), e_1 can either precede, follow, partly or completely overlap e_2. For example, in the following sentence:

Jean entra quand Marie parlait.
'John came in when Mary was talking'

the event e_1 (denoted by *Jean entra*) is included in the event e_2 (denoted by *Marie parlait*) because the two events are in, respectively, the 'Passé simple' and the 'Imparfait' and the first verb expresses achievement and the second one a state. In the following sentence:

Jean entra quand Marie sortit.
'John came in when Mary left'

the event e_1 follows the event e_2. We can model this latter example by the following Dislog rule, involving here literals and not rules:

v(passé_simple,achievement,E1) / quand(events(precede,E1,E2))
→ [quand] / v(passé_simple,achievement,E2).

More generally, the semantics of *quand* can be expressed in a more parametrized way by a rule of the form:

v(T1, Cat1, E1) / quand(event(P,E1,E2)) →
[quand] / v(T2, Cat2, E2) :-
semantics_of_quand(T1, T2, Cat1, Cat2, P).

where semantics_of_quand( ) refers to a semantic database with elements of the form:

> semantics_of_quand(passé_simple, passé_simple, accomp, accomp, follows).

if we consider the example above.

Notice that these Dislog rules make use of literals instead of rules or clauses. This is a way to express long-distance context-sensitivity.

Features could be used instead of having the first and the third rule in the above Dislog rule; however, percolation of these features in the tree up to the connector is not trivial and, furthermore, this is not linguistically motivated since these features are not proper features of temporal connectors. As we can see from these two examples, the Dislog rule format appears to be well-adapted to deal with the semantics of constructions involving discontinuous constituents. Dislog rules do not strictly follow compositionality principles but the level at which they operate (mainly at the phrasal and the propositional levels) still preserves the basic assumptions of compositionality: assembling the semantics of (non-contiguous) constituents to construct the semantics of the whole construction.

4. An implemenation of Dislog in Prolog

We now present the main features of an implementation of Dislog in Prolog. We have built a complete compiler translating Dislog clauses into Prolog. For the sake of clarity, we will present here a simple translation method and then a more elaborated meta-interpreter having the same functionality as our compiler.

Dislog clauses are translated into Prolog using additional arguments. Two arguments are used to store the list of instances of rules in Dislog rules which have to be executed in the future for the proof or parse tree to be correct. We call these two arguments the input and the output list of pending rules. When a new instance of a Dislog clause is activated, the pending rules are added to the current list of pending rules. When a pending rule is being used to construct a proof, it is withdrawn from the list of pending rules. If it is marked with modality m, it is simply consulted (without instantiating its free variables in the list of pending rules) and it remains in the list. Let us consider here a simple example. A Dislog clause of the form:

as → a, as / bs → b, bs.

is translated as follows into Prolog:

```
as(X,Y,LE,LS) :- append(LE,[d(bs,b,bs,I)],LE1),
a(X,Z,LE1,LE2),   as(Z,Y,LE2,LS).
bs(X,Y,LE,LS) :- check_withdraw(LE,d(bs,b,bs,I),LS1),
b(X,Z,LS1,LS2),   bs(Z,Y,LS2,LS).
```

The call check_withdraw(X,Y,Z) checks whether Y is in X and Z is X without Y. The structure d(_,_,_,I) permits the system to store pending rules in a convenient way, the variable I is used to carry the index of co-indexation. All variables shared by clauses or literals in Dislog clauses receive appropriate unifications because they are appended to the list of pending rules. Let us now consider a more general schema. We will present it by means of a meta-interpreter. For that purpose, we have extended the Prolog meta-interpreter presented in Sterling – Shapiro (1986):

```
solve(L,L,true).
solve(L,L1,(A,B)) :-
solve(L,L2,A),
solve(L2,L1,B).
solve(L,L1,A) :-
clause(A,B),
solve(L,L1,B).
solve(L,L1,A) :-
dislog_clause(C),          %call to a Dislog rule,
find(A,C,L,L2,[J], Body),       % strategy encoding,
solve(L2,L1,Body).
```

The built-in predicate clause(A,B) is true if it finds a clause with head A and body B. A Prolog fact with an empty body has a body B equal to 'true'. The Dislog meta-interpreter itself manages the list of pending rules L.

Dislog clauses are stored in dislog_clause facts, together with precedence restrictions (not shown here, see Carn (1989)). The call to *find* permits us to encode a Dislog clause traversal strategy and the way a clause with head A and body Body is extracted from a list (in the second argument), the variable H is used to memorize the rules in the pending list which have been examined as possible candidates but have been rejected:

```
find(A,[(A:-Body)  Tail ], L, L2, H, Body) :-
    append(L, H, L3),
    append(L3, Tail, L2).
find(A, [H  Tail], L, L2, H1, Body) :-
    append(H1, [H], H2),
    find(A, Tail, L, L2, H2, Body).
```

Dislog is used to build a parser and a generator for a natural language computational model we have designed from GB theory (Saint-Dizier et al. 1989b; Saint-Dizier 1989c).

Acknowledgements. I am very grateful to Myriam Bras, Nathalie Carn, Guy Lapalme and Franz Günthner for their discussions which helped improving this work.

References

Aït-Kaçi, H. and Nasr, R.
1986 Login: A Logic Programming Language with Built-in Inheritance. *Journal of Logic Programming*, vol. 3.

Bras, M.
1989 Representing Discursive Temporal Knowledge: A Computational Application of DRT. *Proceedings of KBCS'89*, Bombay, India, in: S. Ramani Edt. (ed), Springer-Verlag.

Bras, M., and Saint-Dizier, P.
1989 Representing Temporal expressions by Contextual Discontinuous Grammars,. *Proceedings of 1st Computational Linguistics Conference*, Lisbon University.

Carn, N.
1989 *Un compilateur de Dislog en Prolog*, rapport de DEA, Université Paul Sabatier, Toulouse, France.

Chomsky, N.
1981 *Lectures on Government and Binding*, Foris Pub., Dordrecht.

Chomsky, N.
1986 *Barriers*. Linguistic Inquiry monograph no.13, MIT Pres.

May, R.
1986 *Logical Form*. Linguistic Inquiry monograph no. 12, MIT Press.

Saint-Dizier, P.
1987 Contextual Discontinuous Grammars, In: V. Dahl and P. Saint-Dizier (ed.), *Natural Language Understanding and Logic Programming II*. North Holland.

Saint-Dizier, P.
1988 Foundations of Dislog, programming in Logic with Discontinuities. *FGCS'88*, Tokyo.

Saint-Dizier, P.
1989 Programming in Logic with Constraints for Language Processing. *ACL '89*, Manchester.

Saint-Dizier, P., Toussaint, Y., Delaunay, C., Sebillot, P.
1989 A Natural Language Processing System Based on Government and Binding Theory. In: P. Saint-Dizier and S. Szpakowicz (eds.), *Logic, Logic Grammars and Logic Programming*. Ellis Horwood.

Saint-Dizier, P.
1989 A Generation Method Based on Government and Binding Principles, *The 2nd European workshop on Natural Language Generation*, Edinburgh.

Sterling, L. and Shapiro, E.
1986 *The Art of Prolog*. MIT Press.

Discontinuous Rewrite Grammar, a description of discontinuities by separating recognition and structure assignment

Erik Aarts

Abstract. The grammar formalism Discontinous Rewrite Grammar (DRG) is described. In DRG structure assignment is not seen as a subprocess of recognition. Recognition and structure assignment are viewed as two separate processes which proceed in parallel. DRG can handle discontinuous constituents, including unbounded dependencies. A parsing algorithm for DRG is outlined, and the implementation of a small fragment is sketched.

1. Introduction

In natural language, constituents that form a syntactic and semantic unit are often separated by other constituents. This phenomenon is generally referred to as discontinuous constituency. Context-free grammars are simple and powerful tools to describe languages, but they are not powerful enough to handle discontinuous constituency in natural language. In a context-free rule, the daughters must be adjacent and no intermediate constituents are allowed. I propose here a formalism, called Discontinuous Rewrite Grammar, in which a mother does not (really) dominate all its daughters. This is also the basic idea in Discontinuous Phrase Structure Grammar (DPSG, see Bunt 1988 and in this volume), on which DRG is based. The (formal) elaboration of this idea (not-real daughters and crossing branches) is different, however.

2. Discontinuous Rewrite Grammar

In a context-free system, a rule is specified as a pair consisting of a symbol (the lefthand side) and a list of symbols (the righthand side). In DRG the rules are a bit more complicated. The righthand side of a DRG rule is a list of lists with three elements: a symbol, a boolean variable and a variable which can have three values. The boolean variable (with possible values `real` and `notreal`) indicates whether the mother and daughter must be related in the parse tree or not. A related daughter is called a real daughter. The other variable (with possible values `notlhs`, `left` and `right`) indicates whether the daughter is copied to the lefthand side of the rule and, if so, whether it appears to the left of the mother or to the right of the mother.

Examples of rules are:

(1) S ⇒ [NP,VP] , (context-free)

(2) S ⇒ [[NP,real,notlhs],[VP,real,notlhs]] , (DRG)

(3) VP ⇒ [[V,real,notlhs],[ADV,notreal,right],[NP,real, notlhs]], (DRG)

Below I give a formal description of DRG in Prolog.

Suppose we have a 4-place Prolog-predicate `append3` which appends three lists into a new list or splits a list in three sublists (see Appendix A). In a context-free model we can define a predicate that can decide for every string whether it is grammatical as follows:

```
recognize([S]) :- startsymbol(S).
 recognize(Inlist) :-
     append3(Begin,Rhs,End,Inlist),
     rule(Lhs,Rhs),
     append3(Begin,[Lhs],End,Outlist),
     recognize(Outlist).
 rule(s,[np,vp]).        % example rule
 ?- recognize([np,vp]). % example query
```

We can define a mapping `changerule` from DRG rules onto ordinary rewrite rules:

```
changerule(Lhs,Rhs,Newlhs,Newrhs) :-
     extract(Rhs,[_,dontcare],[_,dontcare],Newrhs),
     extract(Rhs,[_,dontcare],[left,select],Left),
     extract(Rhs,[_,dontcare],[right,select],Right),
     append3(Left,[Lhs],Right,Newlhs).
```

The predicate extract is defined in Appendix A. It extracts from the righthand side all daughters whose variables have a certain value. Once the function changerule is defined, we can build a recognizer which is a small extension of the recognizer for context-free systems.

```
recognize([S]) :- startsymbol(S).
 recognize(Inlist) :-
     append3(Begin,Middle,End,Inlist),
     rule(Lhs,Rhs),
     changerule(Lhs,Rhs,Newlhs,Middle),
     append3(Begin,Newlhs,End,Outlist),
     recognize(Outlist).
 rule(s,[[np,real,notlhs],[vp,real,notlhs]]).   % example rule
 ?- recognize([np,vp]).    % example query
```

We shall assume that grammar rules in DRG always have at least one daughter with the value notlhs as its third argument. Under this assumption, the recognition problem is decidable.[1]

A generator, which generates all sentences, is defined by changing the first clause of recognize and swapping the third and fourth argument of changerule. With some slight alterations we can define a parser. The reader is referred to Appendix A for a detailed description of the parser. In the parser, the symbol *, which matches any string of symbols, is introduced. It is like the wildcard often used in terminal input. It will become clear later why this has been done.

The parser performs two separate tasks:

- recognition: the parser tries to reduce the input string by repeatedly replacing a substring which matches a right-hand side of a rule with the corresponding left-hand side.
- structure assignment: the dominance relations between nodes are defined.

The decision whether a rule is applicable is taken solely by the recognition part. Application of a rule defines new mother-daughters relations. The assignment of structure follows the recognition process. Therefore, the parser can be called a recognition driven structure assigner. These two processes are guided by the second and third variable in the daughter list. The recognition process is guided by the values left, right and notlhs. These values define the left-hand side which replaces the right-hand side. Structure assignment is done by the two values real and notreal. The value real defines a dominance relation between the daughter and the mother and notreal does not.

The daughters in the right-hand side of a rule can be divided in six groups, numbered from 1 to 6, as follows:

Table 1. Types of daughters

	left	right	notlhs
real	◁1	2▷	3
notreal	◁[4]	[5]▷	[6]

Table 1 gives some notational conventions which can be used to indicate the type of a daughter. If we were to allow only daughters of type 3, DRG behaves as a context-free model. Admitting daughters of type ◁[4] and [5]▷ results in a formalism in which every node has exactly one mother node.

When we also admit types ◁1, 2▷, and [6] we get a formalism whose performance on recognition is the same. The difference is that, in theory, 'strange' structures can be assigned: nodes can have zero, one, two, three ... mothers. In practice we exclude nodes with zero mothers by using features. For a description of natural language, we extend the grammar with monadic symbols to a phrase structure grammar with feature bundles. In this paper, I shall use a simple feature system as described by Shieber (1986).

In the remainder of this paper I shall argue that this model, in combination with a feature system, can describe unbounded dependencies properly. But first I want to show that this strong formalism has not lost much efficiency in parsing in comparison with context-free models.

3. Efficient parsing

The parser from Appendix A is not very fast. We can implement an efficient algorithm by making use of a well-formed substring table. It is widely investigated how to use a well-formed substring table (or a chart) in parsing in context-free models. Winograd (1983: 72–132) gives an introduction. The vertices in such a chart form a linear ordering. In parsing DRG, we use a chart in which the vertices form a partial ordering. We get a partial ordering by adding vertices after completion of an edge which contains daughters of type ◁1, 2▷, ◁[4] or [5]▷.

By adding vertices, we create a new path through the chart. Along this path we place the mother of the complete edge and her daughters of type ◁1, 2▷, ◁[4] or [5]▷.

This is illustrated by an example. Suppose we have a grammar and a chart as in table 2 and figure 1.

Table 2. Example grammar

S ⇒ NP VP	PP ⇒ P NP	P ⇒ met 'with'
VP ⇒ PART NP	NP ⇒ ik 'I'	N ⇒ man 'man'
NP ⇒ DET N	AUX ⇒ heb 'have'	N ⇒ hoed 'hat'
NP ⇒ NP ◁[PART] PP	PART ⇒ gezien 'seen'	DET ⇒ een 'a'
VP ⇒ AUX VP		

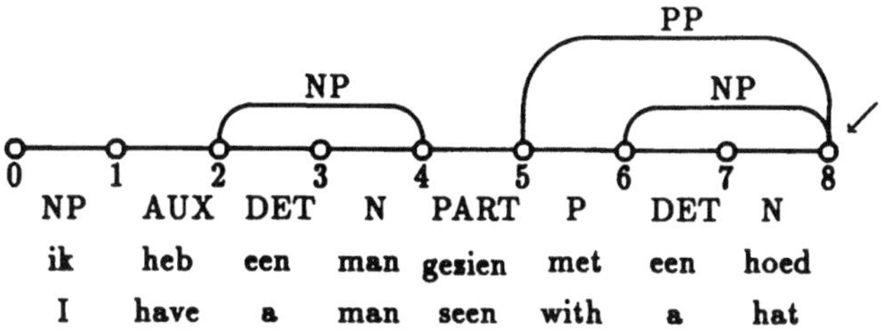

Figure 1. Chart during parsing

Rule "NP ⇒ NP ◁[PART] PP" is applicable now. We add a (black) vertex (number 9), which creates a new path. From 2 to 9 an edge is built for the daughter PART and from 9 to 8 for the mother NP. After this operation the chart looks like figure 2.

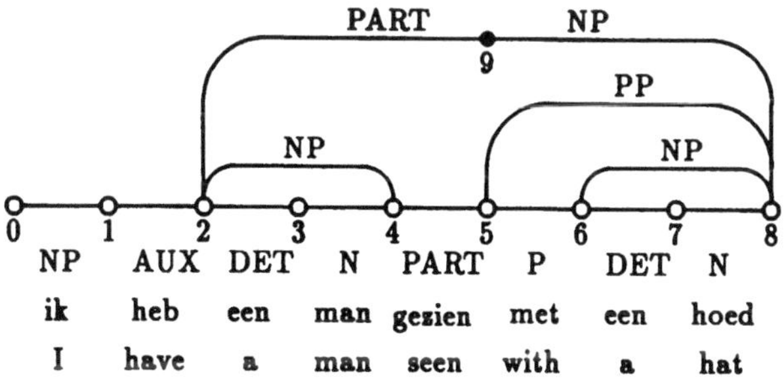

Figure 2. Chart with added vertex

The algorithm now computes new (pending) edges as a result of finding the PART and the NP. The final chart is in figure 3.

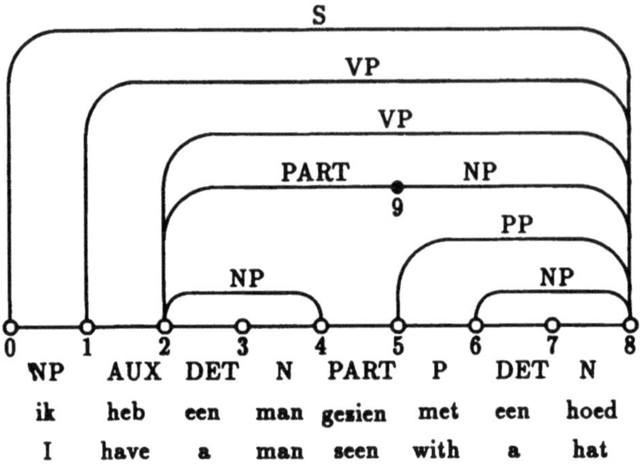

Figure 3. Result chart

This chart parser has been implemented. It is not clear what the complexity of the parsing problem for DRG is. DRG-rules are transformed into ordinary context-sensitive rules by the predicate `changerule`. The general recognition problem for DRG seems therefore PSPACE-complete (Garey – Johnson 1979). We can restrict ourselves to acyclic rules[2] when we use DRG for linguistic purposes, however.

The recognition problem for acyclic DRG seems to be equivalent[3] to the recognition problem for acyclic context-sensitive grammars as they have been defined in Aarts (1991a; see also Aarts 1992). Recognition for acyclic context-sensitive grammars is NP-complete (Aarts 1991a). For any fixed grammar the problem seems polynomial, however (Aarts 1991b). This would mean that when the parser is fast for small inputs, it will be fast for long inputs too. For a more extended discussion of the formal properties of acyclic context-sensitive grammars see Aarts (1995).

4. Unbounded dependencies

We have already seen that we can define a subsystem in which only daughters of type 3, ⊲[4] and [5]⊳ are allowed. We have seen that in this system parsing can be done efficiently. So why do we not restrict ourselves to this subsystem?

The answer is that we get in trouble when we consider unbounded dependencies. Unbounded dependencies occur when two elements that are separated by an infinitely large string are related to each other. In the subsystem these elements cannot be related because we should sum up infinitely many daughters of type ◁[4] or [5]▷.

A possible solution for unbounded dependencies is the introduction of the `slash` feature of GPSG (Gazdar 1981). Introduction of the `slash` feature has two major disadvantages, however:

- Too many slash categories can be built. All sorts of constituents which are not present in the sentence can be regarded as missing elements. This is a consequence of the fact that the solution with the `slash` feature is a local solution. This problem can be solved by using predictive (bottom-up) parsing, but grammar formalisms and parsers should be as independent from each other as possible. Furthermore, the predictor does not reduce the number of slash categories in case of rightward dependencies.
- Constituents which form a (semantic) unit are not taken together.

To solve these problems I admit daughters of type $\triangleleft 1, 2 \triangleright$, and [6] and the wildcard *. With these tools it is possible to apply rules to daughters which are separated by strings of unbounded length. These strings match the wildcard.

We further need a feature `fromfar`, which indicates that a constituent dominates another constituent at a long distance (separated by *). In the examples in the next section we will see how this feature is used. It is similar to the `slash` feature, appearing in those cases where in GPSG `slash` would appear. An essential difference, however, is that the `fromfar` feature cannot possibly have a constituent as value which is absent from the sentence.

5. Some examples

Gazdar (1981) gives examples of unbounded dependencies and coordination. I shall demonstrate here how DRG would handle the examples cited there:

(4) The kennel which Mary made and Fido sleeps in has been stolen.

(5) The kennel in which Mary keeps drugs and Fido sleeps has been stolen.

(6) * The kennel (in) which Mary made and Fido sleeps has been stolen.

These sentences can be described by the grammar (in short form) in table 3.

Table 3. Example grammar for unbounded dependencies

1. S ⇒ NP VP	8. PP ⇒ ◁NP ◁[*] P
2. NP ⇒ NP R	9. VP ⇒ HAS BEEN STOLEN
3. NP ⇒ DET NOUN	10. VP ⇒ ◁PP ◁[*] VP
4. R ⇒ [NP] S	11. R ⇒ [PP] S
5. S ⇒ S CONJ S	12. PP ⇒ P NP
6. VP ⇒ VP PP	13. VP ⇒ V NP
7. VP ⇒ ◁NP ◁[*] V	

The full grammar can be found in Appendix B. The tree structure which is assigned to sentence (4) is figure 4. This structure is equivalent to Gazdar's structure. The only difference is that "which" is not related to any gaps in the sentence but is taken directly instead.

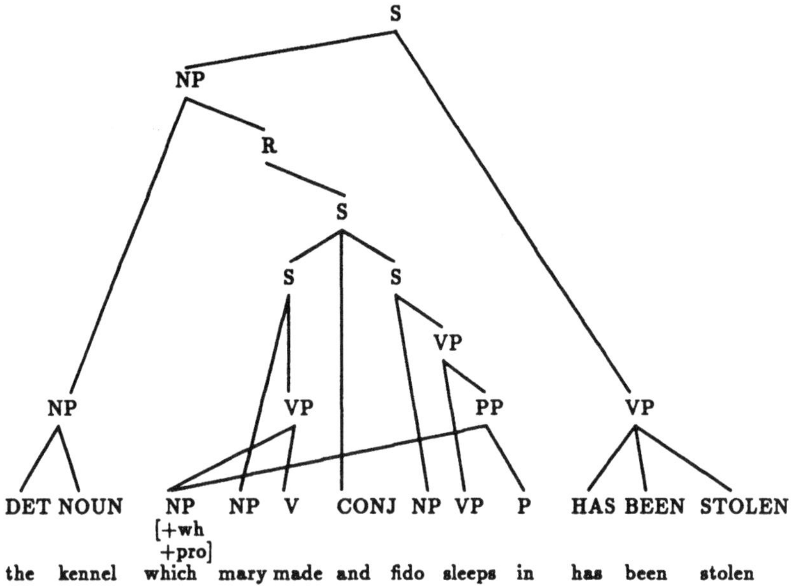

Figure 4. Tree assigned to sentence (4)

In sentence (5) rule 10 is applied twice. In sentence (6), *The kennel in which ...* , rules 7 and 10 are applied. Application of rule 5 is not possible, however, because the two S's differ in their feature `fromfar` (also when 10 is not applied). Sentence (6), *The kennel which* ... , is ungrammatical too: rule 7 is applied and rule 5 is again not applicable.

Elliptic constructions like (7) can also be treated by DRG:

(7) Mary kissed John and Michael Raisa.

This example is described by four rules: 1, 5, 13 and 14:

14. VP ⇒ ◁V ◁[*] NP

These rules also admit:

(8) Mary kissed John and Michael Raisa and Pamela Bobby.

and so on.

The complexity result from section 2 does not hold anymore. It is not clear as yet what the complexity of parsing is when daughters of all types and the * are used. We can make the chart parser more efficient by admitting only terminal daughters and the ('terminal') daughters along new paths to match *. Otherwise a rule "A ⇒ B ◁[*] C" would introduce many new paths instead of one.

6. Conclusion

Discontinuous Rewrite Grammar is a formalism which is near to ordinary (context-sensitive) rewrite systems. Therefore it is fairly elegant. A parser can be defined by six Prolog predicates only. The formalism can assign crossing branches for both bounded and unbounded dependencies and makes gaps superfluous. Sentences are efficiently parsable. It seems ellipsis can be treated in a simple way. It is not clear whether solutions for ellipsis overgenerate or not.

Notes

1. Under this assumption `length(Outlist)` $\leq$ `length(Inlist)`. If `Outlist` is shorter there is no problem. To avoid 'loops' in case of equal length we can add the predicates `\+ wellformed(Outlist) , assert(wellformed(Outlist))` in the definition of the predicate `recognize`.
2. We remove all `left` and `right` daughters from the righthand sides. When the remaining (context-free) grammar is acyclic (contains no rules like A $\Rightarrow$ B, B $\Rightarrow$ C, C $\Rightarrow$ A) the original DRG was acyclic.
3. This has not been proven as yet.

References

Aarts, E.
1991a *Recognition for Acyclic Context-sensitive Grammars is NP-complete. ITK Research Report 29*. Tilburg University, Tilburg.

Aarts, E.
1991b *Recognition for Acyclic Context-sensitive Grammars is probably Polynomial for Fixed Grammars. ITK Research Memo 8*. Tilburg University, Tilburg.

Aarts, E.
1992 Uniform Recognition for Acyclic Context-Sensitive Grammars is NP-complete. *Proceedings of COLING'92*, Nantes, 1157–1161.

Aarts, E.
1995 *Investigations in Logic, Language and Computation*. Ph.D. Thesis, Utrecht University.

Bunt, H.
1988 DPSG and its use in sentence generation from meaning representations. In: Zock M. and G. Sabah (eds.), *Advances in Natural Language Generation*. Pinter Publishers, London.

Bunt, H.
1996 Formal tools for describing and processing discontinuous constituency structure. *This volume*, 63–85.

Gazdar, G.
1981 *Unbounded dependencies and coordinate structure. Linguistic Inquiry 12*, 155-184.

Garey, M. and D. Johnson
1979 *Computers and Intractability: A Guide to the Theory of NP-Completeness.* W.H. Freeman and Company, San Francisco, CA.
Shieber, S.
1986 *An introduction to unification-based approaches to grammar. CSLI Note 4.* Center for the Study of Language and Information, Stanford.
Winograd, T.
1983 *Language as a cognitive process – Volume 1: Syntax.* Addison Wesley, Reading, Massachusetts.

Appendix A. A parser for DRG

```
parse([[S|Tree]]):- startsymbol(S),write([S|Tree]),nl.
 parse(Inlist) :-
     append3(Begin,Middle,End,Inlist),
     rule(Lhs,Rhs),
     fit(Rhs,Middle,Newrhs),
     makenewlhs(Lhs,Newrhs,Newlhs),
     append3(Begin,Newlhs,End,Outlist),
     parse(Outlist).

fit([],[],[]).
 fit([[*,B,C]|R1],[[A|Struc]|R2],[[[A|Struc],B,C]|R3]) :-
     fit(R1,R2,R3). % for * at least one element necessary
 fit([[*,B,C]|R1],[[A|Struc]|R2],[[[A|Struc],B,C]|R3]) :-
     fit([[*,B,C]|R1],R2,R3).
 fit([[A,B,C]|R1],[[A|Struc]|R2],[[[A|Struc],B,C]|R3]) :-
     fit(R1,R2,R3).

makenewlhs(Lhs,Newrhs,Newlhs) :-
     extract(Newrhs,[_,dontcare],[left,select],Left),
     extract(Newrhs,[_,dontcare],[right,select],Right),
     extract(Newrhs,[real,select],[_,dontcare],Daughters),
     append3(Left,[[Lhs|Daughters]],Right,Newlhs).

extract([],_,_,[]).
 extract([[A,X,Y]|L0],[C,D],[E,F],[A|L1]) :-
     equalifselect(X,C,D),equalifselect(Y,E,F),
     extract(L0,[C,D],[E,F],L1).
```

```
extract([[A,X,Y]|L0],[C,D],[E,F],L1) :-
    (\+ equalifselect(X,C,D) ; \+ equalifselect(Y,E,F) ),
    extract(L0,[C,D],[E,F],L1).

equalifselect(A,A,select).
equalifselect(_,_,dontcare).

append3([A|B],C,D,[A|E]) :- append3(B,C,D,E).
append3([],[A|C],D,[A|E]) :- append3([],C,D,E).
append3([],[],D,D).

rule(s,[[np,real,notlhs],[vp,real,notlhs]]). % example rule
?- parse([[np,_],[vp,_]]).            % example query
```

Appendix B. Grammar rules

```
startsymbol([cat:s,fromfar:none]).
1. rule([cat:s,fromfar:P],
       [[[cat:np,r:min,wh:min,pro:min],real,notlhs],
        [[cat:vp,fromfar:P],real,notlhs]]).
2. rule([cat:np,r:min,wh:min,pro:min],
       [[[cat:np,r:min,wh:min,pro:min],real,notlhs],
        [[cat:r],real,notlhs]]).
3. rule([cat:np,r:min,wh:min,pro:min],
       [[[cat:det],real,notlhs],
        [[cat:noun],real,notlhs]]).
4. rule([cat:r],
       [[[cat:np,r:plus,wh:PM,pro:plus],notreal,notlhs],
        [[cat:s,fromfar:[cat:np,r:plus,wh:PM,pro:plus]],real,
          notlhs]]).
% The first daughter must unify with the value of fromfar.
  In order
% to force identity we need an indexing mechanism or
  reentrancies.
5. rule([cat:s,fromfar:Ind],
       [[[cat:s,fromfar:Ind],real,notlhs],
        [[cat:conj],real,notlhs],
        [[cat:s,fromfar:Ind],real,notlhs]]).
```

```
6. rule([cat:vp,fromfar:P],
       [[[cat:vp,fromfar:none],real,notlhs],
        [[cat:pp,fromfar:P],real,notlhs]]).
7. rule([cat:vp,fromfar:[cat:np,r:PM,wh:plus,pro:plus]],
       [[[cat:np,r:PM,wh:plus,pro:plus],real,left],
        [*,notreal,left],
        [[cat:v],real,notlhs]]).
8. rule([cat:pp,fromfar:[cat:np,r:plus,wh:plus,pro:plus]],
       [[[cat:np,r:plus,wh:plus,pro:plus],real,left],
        [*,notreal,left],
        [[cat:p],real,notlhs]]).
9. rule([cat:vp,fromfar:none],[[[cat:has],real,notlhs],
       [[cat:been],real,notlhs],[[cat:stolen],real,notlhs]]).
10. rule([cat:vp,fromfar:[cat:pp,fromfar:none]],
       [[[cat:pp,fromfar:none],real,left],
       [*,notreal,left],
       [[cat:vp,fromfar:none],real,notlhs]]).
11. rule([cat:r],
       [[[cat:pp,fromfar:none],notreal,notlhs],
        [[cat:s,fromfar:[cat:pp,fromfar:none]],real,notlhs]]).
12. rule([cat:pp,fromfar:none],
       [[[cat:p],real,notlhs],
        [[cat:np,r:_,wh:_,pro:_],real,notlhs]]).
13. rule([cat:vp,fromfar:none],
       [[[cat:v],real,notlhs],
        [[cat:np,r:min,wh:min,pro:min],real,notlhs]]).
14. rule([cat:vp,fromfar:none],
       [[[cat:v],real,left],
        [*,notreal,left],
        [[cat:np,r:min,wh:min,pro:min],real,notlhs]]).
```

Non-compositional discontinuous constituents in Tree Adjoining Grammar

Anne Abeillé and Yves Schabes

Abstract. Lexicalized TAGs, which associate sets of elementary trees with lexical items, define linguistic units of extended domain of locality that have both syntactic and semantic relevance. This formalism offers a very natural representation for constituents that follow regular syntactic composition rules, and may exhibit internal discontinuities, but lack semantic compositionality. This representation considers non-compositional constituents as one semantic unit without having to stipulate any element to be semantically empty, and is thus kept strictly increasing. In this paper, we rely on Synchronous TAGs as an underlying formalism for building up our semantic representation. We also sketch the advantages of our treatment for natural language processing applications. Most of our examples are taken from idioms and light-verb constructions in French and English.

1. Introduction to Lexicalized TAGs

Lexicalized Tree Adjoining Grammars, as defined in Joshi (1985; 1988) and Schabes – Abeillé – Joshi (1988), consist of a set of elementary trees associated with lexical items anchoring them in the lexicon. Elementary trees can be of two types: initial or auxiliary (Figure 1) and are combined together by substitution or adjunction (Figure 2).

Because of the operation of adjunction, Tree Adjoining Grammars are more powerful than context-free grammars but only mildly so. An elementary tree defines an extended domain of locality over which phrase structures are encoded. They also correspond to complete predicate argument structures. Subjects and complements both belong to sentential elementary trees, as well as both fillers and gaps. Elementary trees define syntactic and semantic units at the same time. They are gathered in Tree families which encode the different lexical and syntactic rules which may apply to them.

Sentences of the language generated by a TAG are associated with two kinds of objects: one or more derived tree which is the resulting tree structure

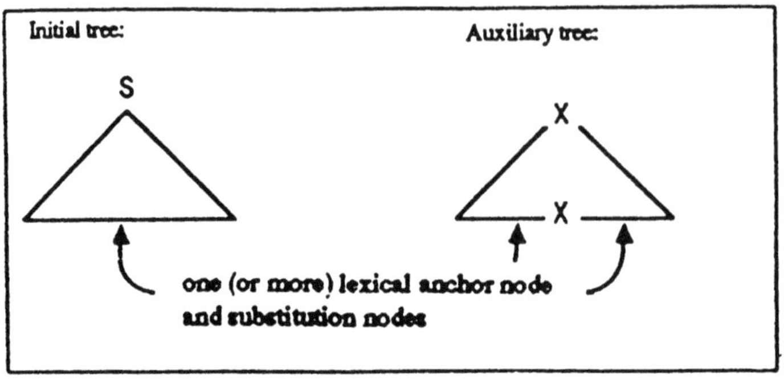

Figure 1. Schematic initial and auxiliary trees

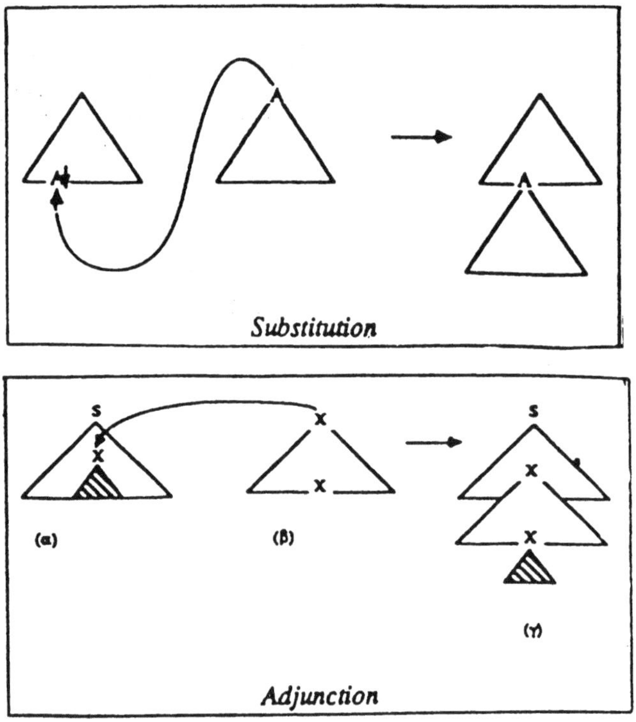

Figure 2. Combining operations

after all combinations have been performed, and one (or more) corresponding derivation tree that tells which elementary trees have been combined together and at which nodes. Derived trees are thus different from derivation trees, as opposed to context free grammars. The basis for semantic interpretation in a TAG is the derivation tree, not the derived tree (which corresponds to syntactic properties).[1]

Feature structures can be associated at each node in an elementary tree and constraints on combining trees can be expressed in terms of success or failure of unification. We refer the reader to Vijay-Shanker – Joshi (1988) for a precise definition of feature-based TAGs and to Abeillé (1991b) for an application to French. A sentence is well-formed with respect to a TAG iff:

- it can be derived from an initial tree rooted in S,
- all features unify at each node in the corresponding derived tree.

Lexicalized feature-based Tree Adjoining Grammar has been used for describing a number of syntactic phenomena across several languages (Kroch – Joshi 1985; Abeillé 1991a). The main linguistic advantages of such a formalism are that:

- it provides a larger domain of locality than a CFG or other augmented CFG-based formalisms such as HPSG or LFG,
- it allows factoring of recursion from the domain of dependencies.

As far as discontinuous constituency is concerned, wh-movement and topicalization have been treated by Kroch – Joshi (1985) in a particularly "natural" way. Factoring recursion out of local dependencies allows one to handle filler-gap relations locally, i.e. at the level of the one elementary tree to which they both belong. Unbounded dependencies such as: *Who do you think John loves?* are thus derived from the adjunction of the auxiliary tree corresponding to the matrix clause *do you think S?* into the tree of *Who John loves*, and the filler-gap relation is thus kept strictly local (see Figures 3 and 4).

Such cases of compositional discontinuous constituents can thus be treated as continuous ones, in the sense that their corresponding nodes belong in both cases to one and the same elementary tree.

Other cases of syntactic discontinuities have been treated in the TAG formalism, such as extraposition out of an NP (Kroch – Joshi 1986) or long-distance scrambling, which involve more powerful variants of TAGs

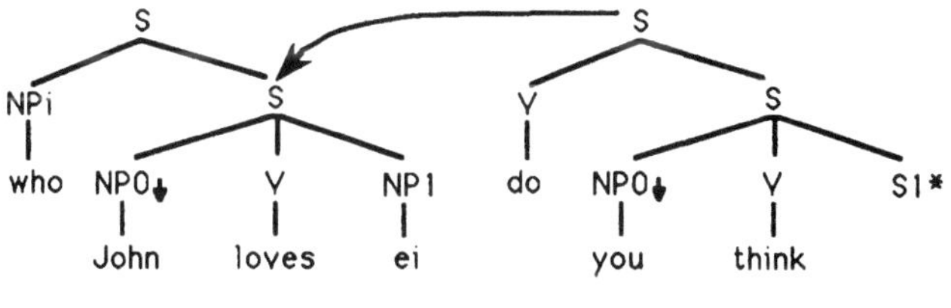

Figure 3. Unbounded dependency in the course of derivation

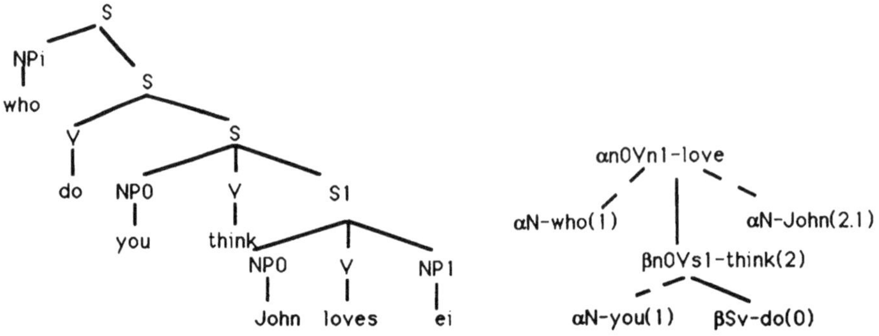

Figure 4. Final derived and derivation trees for *Who do you think John loves?*

(Becker – Joshi – Rambow 1991). We focus here on more lexical cases of discontinuities, those involving idiomatic and non-compositional constructions.

Because of their two-fold perspective on syntactic description, TAGs are a fruitful formalism to explore discrepancies between syntactic properties (as exhibited by the derived trees) and semantic ones (as exhibited by the derivation trees). The idiomatic (or semi-idiomatic) expressions studied here are clearly of this kind: their syntax is regularly compositional, while their semantics is not. Their derived trees are thus the same as those of non-idiomatic constructions, but their derivation trees are different.

2. Non-compositionality and discontinuities

Complex predicates can be of different kinds. They can either be totally unanalysable semantically such as the English idiom *kick the bucket*, or exhibit unpredictable distributional restrictions as can be observed between English verbs and particles, or between light verbs and predicative nouns: *to take a walk, to have a drink, to give a cough.*[2] These complex predicates exhibit syntactic properties ranging from total fixity to total flexiblity. Light verb constructions are usually considered flexible ones. With idioms, a distinction is usually made between fixed ones (such as *kick the bucket*, or *saw logs*) and flexible ones (*take advantage of NP, pull strings*), although most of them are clearly intermediate cases, allowing for certain rules and refusing others. It has been proposed that more flexible idioms be assigned a more compositional semantics (Wasow – Sag – Nunberg 1983). However, extensive listings of idioms for French has shown no clear link between their undergoing certain syntactic rules or not and semantic differences between them (Gross 1982; 1988).[3] Important to note here is the fact that even idioms usually considered as fixed syntactically may exhibit disturbing discontinuities. We also show that assigning a compositional syntactic representation to flexible idioms, that would account for their possible discontinuities, would be conflicting with some specific syntactic properties presented by these constructions such as double passsives or Complex NP Constraint violations. However, a representation based on trees of extended domain of locality gives a motivated account of all desired discontinuities and is also consistent with the idea of a continuum between "fixed" and "frozen" idiomatic phrases.

Discontinuities can be of several kinds, depending on whether they come from the insertion of modifiers, the application of syntactic rules (possibly adding some word order variation), or from the definition of the complex predicate itself. The existence of idioms intrinsically discontinuous has long been noted. Examples are: *take NP into account, send NP to the showers, have NP over a barrel* (Emonds 1972). Gross' (1982 – 1989) extensive listings of French idioms, and Freckelton's (1984) listings of English idioms show that about 15% of idioms in each language are of this kind. But what has less often been noted is that discontinuities may arise dynamically in almost any idiom even those which seem the most frozen ones, as a result of the application of regular syntactic or lexical rules or of adjunct insertion (Laporte 1988).

2.1 Discontinuities with "fixed" idioms

We will start with the most "fixed" idioms[4] and show that they may present two kinds of discontinuities: those of bounded length but also truly unbounded ones. Discontinuities are of bounded length in the case of intrinsically discontinuous predicates, since heavy-NP shift applies regularly, in English or in French:[5]

(1) a. *He took Mary's words into account.*
b. *He took into account all the nasty things Mary has been telling him when they were living together.*

They are also bounded when a free possessive (binded externally to the sentence) occurs inside a frozen complement of an English idiom, because the alternation, NP's → of NP, applies regularly when the NP is too long:

(2) a. *John is raining on his brother's parade.*
b. *John is raining on the parade of everyone he met since then.*

In French, another case of bounded discontinuity arises when a clitic (coming either from an adverb or a free argument of the idiom) is inserted between the frozen subject and the verb in idioms such as:

(3) a. *La moutarde monte au nez de Jean = La moutarde lui monte au nez.*
'Jean becomes angry'
b. *Des ailes poussent à Jean = Des ailes lui poussent.*
'Jean becomes ambitious'

But there are cases where two frozen elements of a non-compositional predicate can be infinitely far apart. In French "fixed" idioms, adverbials are inserted quite regularly between verb and object, just as auxiliaries or raising verbs between subject and verb:

(4) a. *Jean cassera certainement sa pipe bientôt*
'John will certainly soon kick the bucket'
b. *La moutarde risque probablement de monter au nez de Jean.*
c. *Le marchand de sable va bientôt passer.*
'It will be soon time to go to bed'

Similarly, in English, unbounded discontinuities (for idioms refusing most syntactic transformations) may arise from the insertion of auxiliaries or adverbials between the frozen subject and the verb:

(5) a. *The roof will soon cave in on John.*
b. *All hell seemed to be likely to break loose.*

All insertions are regularly predictable from the syntactic category of the idiomatic element that is modified; for example, the adjective *proverbial* in: *John kicked the proverbial bucket.*

These discontinuities show that even so-called "fixed" idioms (not undergoing passive or wh-movement on their frozen parts) cannot be dealt with by syntactic reanalysis nor any kind of morphological incorporation. The regular insertion of modifiers also shows that these idioms always need be assigned a syntactic internal structure.

2.2 Discontinuities with "flexible" idioms

"Flexible" idioms exhibit the same discontinuities as free sentences, and are usually assigned the same syntactic structures. Adjectives may be inserted in their frozen parts (more easily than with "fixed" idioms), for example the French adjective *réel* in: *Jean prend une réelle veste* ('Jean really comes a cropper') or the English *legal* in *We should leave no legal stone unturned* (Wasow et al. 1983). Unbounded discontinuities may arise from the application of the passive to an idiom with a frozen complement, which gives rise to an idiom with a frozen subject where adverbials and auxiliaries insert regularly:

(6) a. *Pat spilled the beans.*
b. *The beans were spilled by Pat.*
c. *The beans continue to appear to be certain to be spilled.* (Wasow et al. 1983)

They may also come from the application of wh-question, relativation, topicalization or cleft extraction, giving rise to unbounded dependencies:

(7) a. *Which strings did they pull?*
b. *Which strings do you think that everybody knows that they pulled?*

(8) a. *Jean a cassé du sucre sur le dos de Luc.*
'Jean ran Luc down'
b. *Sur le dos de qui Jean a-t-il cassé du sucre?*
'who did Jean run down'
c. *C'est sur le dos de Luc que tout le monde s'accorde à dire que Jean a cassé du sucre.*
'It is Luc that everybody agrees to say that Jean ran down'

However, flexible idioms do not undergo syntactic rules in exactly the same way as "free" sentences. As has often been noted, light verb constructions regularly exhibit Complex NP Constraint violations, allowing for example both: *The trip to Spain that John took*, and *Spain, where John took a trip to*, or, in French, *Quelle attaque contre Marie Jean a-t-il lancée?* (Which attack against Marie did Jean launch) as well as *Contre qui Jean a-t-il lancé une attaque?* (Against whom did Jean launch an attack). The complex predicate cannot be reanalysed as a verb, but it exhibits more syntactic cohesion than 'free' verb-object combinations. Similarly, a standard compositional analysis of English idioms such as *make use of* or *take advantage of* will predict the regular passive: *No advantage was taken of her talents*, but not: *Her talents weren't taken advantage of*. Such phenomena lead Bresnan (1982) to posit a double analysis: a regular one, and one incorporating the idiomatic object and the following preposition into the verb. This hypothesis is contradicted by these sentences not being ambiguous. TAG's representation using extended locality domains allows for a very natural account of such phenomena.

3. Representation in a Lexicalized Tree Adjoining Grammar

An elementary tree defines an extended domain of locality over which all structures are encoded. They also correspond to complete predicate argument structures, with both subject and complements, as well as both fillers and gaps. They are thus syntactic and semantic units at the same time.

Trees of extended domain of locality enable one to define semantically non-compositional (but possibly discontinuous) constituents (Abeillé – Schabes 1989). To each elementary tree is associated a semantic representation. When trees are combined by adjunction or substitution, the corresponding semantic representations are combined.

Non-compositional predicates are represented by extended trees, capturing all the frozen pieces of the expression which behave as one multiple "anchor".[6] (See Figure 5)

Such a representation naturally extends to light-verb constructions and English verb-particle combinations which are also considered as extended elementary trees with multicomponent anchors (Abeillé et al. 1990).[7]

Discontinuities coming from the insertion of modifiers are captured by the very topology of the tree (adjunction of such modifiers being allowed at any interior node), in exactly the same way as for compositional sentences, and all idioms are predicted to exhibit such discontinuities. Bounded discontinuities are taken care of by the regular application of heavy-NP shift, or constraints specific to clitic insertion.

We will now consider how these extended elementary trees enable one to account for the specific syntactic and semantic properties of the idioms. We will rely on the general principles governing the composition of Tree

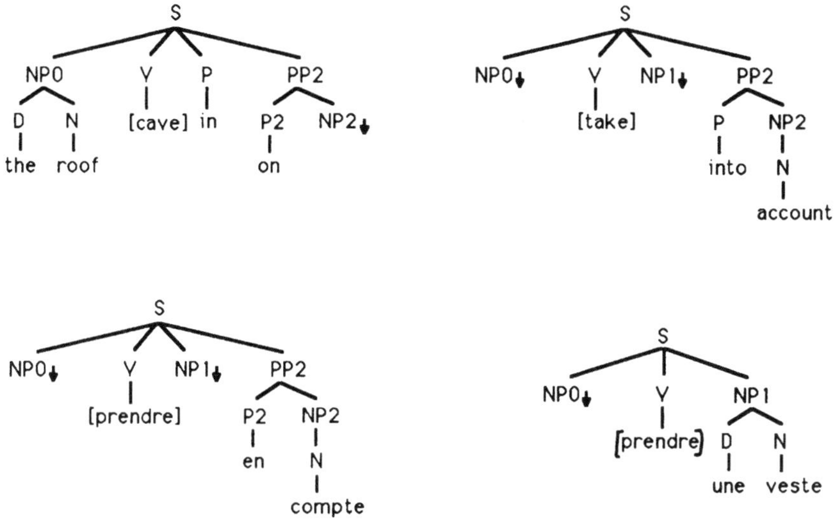

Figure 5. Elementary trees for idiomatic expressions

families for the former and on the semantic interpretation associated with TAG's derivation trees for the latter.

3.1 Extended elementary trees and syntactic properties

Such extended trees make idioms fall naturally into the same grammar as "free" sentences, since they are elementary trees corresponding exactly to regular derived trees.

This predicts, for example, that idioms present the same range of syntactic structures as non-idiomatic sentences, with either frozen subjects, frozen objects or frozen PPs: *Il pleut* ('It rains'); *Jean perd les pédales* ('Jean is getting mixed-up'), *Jean monte sur ses grands chevaux* ('Jean is very touchy').

They also present the same range of syntactic rules: there is no rule which would not apply to any idiom (Newmeyer 1974; Wasow et al. 1983). As in the general case of sentential predicates in Lexicalized TAGs, idioms select sets of elementary trees (Tree Families), which gather all their possible syntactic realizations such as wh-question, relative clauses, passive ... The Tree family for the French idiom *NP0 prendre une veste* comprises, among others, the elementary trees[8] in Figure 6.

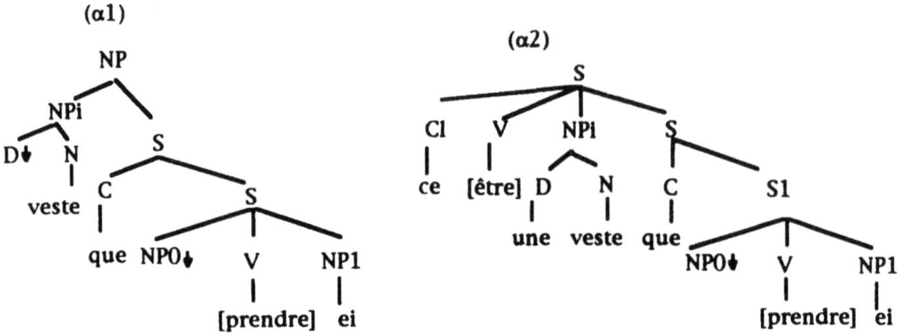

Figure 6. Elementary trees associated with *NP0 prendre une veste*

Notice that the free NP subject will produce a discontinuity in the idiom in $\alpha1$, e.g.: *J'ai été surprise par la veste que Jean a prise hier* ('I was surprised by Jean coming a cropper'). Unbounded discontinuities coming from the adjunction of a matrix clause to the S1 node in $\alpha2$ such as: *C'est une sacrée veste qu'on a dit que Jean avait prise hier* ('They said that Jean really came a cropper yesterday'), are localized in the same way as unbounded dependencies for free sentences, and no special device is needed.

Specific syntactic properties of idioms such as CNPC violations, or double passives, noted above (section 2.2), can also be naturally accounted for (Abeillé 1988). Since all phrasal nodes (except the root node) of an elementary sentential tree can be considered as possible arguments for syntactic (or lexical) rules, *take* in $\alpha1$ (Figure 7) will be considered syntactically as having three complements: the NP headed by *advantage*, the PP headed by *of* and the NP *Mary*. The family thus includes two different passive trees $\alpha2$: *No advantage of Mary was taken* and $\alpha3$: *Mary was taken advantage of by John*, and (at least) three for relative clauses: *Mary, of which John took advantage, is a witch; Mary, which John took advantage of, didn't realize that;* and *This advantage of Mary that John took was unfair.* There is no need for noun or preposition incorporation, and the PP behaves at the same time as a verbal complement (independent from the frozen NP) and as a complement being included in a higher NP, without reanalysis being necessary.

One may notice that our representation actually allows more syntactic flexibility for idiomatic constructions than for "free" sentences, since their elementary trees are more expanded (and may comprise more phrasal constituents). This might seem counterintuitive but is necessary if one wants to account for the "extreme" cases just mentioned. Note that these are only po-

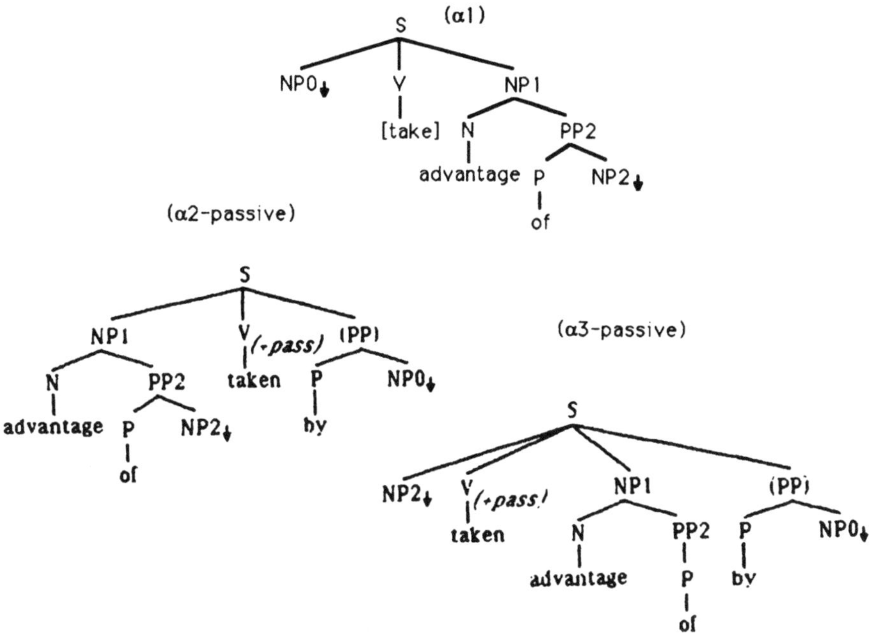

Figure 7. Passive trees in the family of *NP take advantage of NP*

tential structures for a given idiom. Many idioms will rule out some or most of them; and this is done by specific features on their tree families marked in their lexical entries.[9]

3.2 Derivation trees and non-compositionality

An idiomatic sentence will be generally analysed as being ambiguous between idiomatic and literal readings as long as all its words also appear as autonomous entries in the lexicon with a similar construction. Literal and idiomatic interpretations of such ambiguous sentences correspond to two identical derived trees, but to two different derivation trees, as shown by the example in Figure 8 of the French sentence *Jean prend une veste* ('Jean takes a jacket'-literal meaning or 'Jean comes a cropper'-idiomatic reading).[10]

Such ambiguous interpretations will not arise for an idiom as *to play hooky*; as *hooky* does not occur elsewhere, there will not be any means of deriving the phrase from the free verb *play*. This will neither be the case for idioms such as *aller son train* (='to go one's way') or *mettre le paquet* (='to spare nothing'), since free verbs *aller* and *mettre* require, respectively,

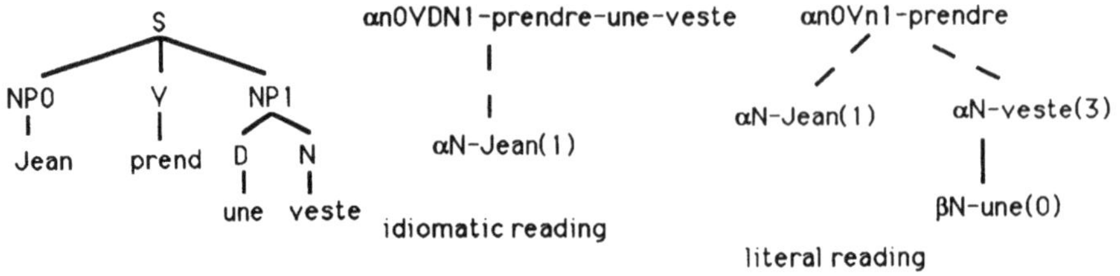

Figure 8. Derived and derivation trees for the ambiguous sentence *Jean prend une veste*

a prepositional complement (not a direct one) and a second locative complement.

The restricted derivation tree corresponding to the idiomatic reading has interesting consequences for semantic theory. It mimicks semantic reanalysis (*to kick the bucket* = *to die*) without imposing syntactic reanalysis. Notice that the derivation tree does not encode word order, contrary to the derived one. All discontinuities are thus eliminated at this level: *to take NP into account* = *to consider NP*.

Our representation with multiple anchors allows one to deal with semantic non compositionality in a unified way for fixed and flexible idioms. This is different from LFG representation of flexible idioms which assigns all semantic content to one part of the idiom and considers the others as semantically empty (Bresnan 1982). This is also different from Chomsky's (1981) "quasi" arguments bearing a dummy theta-role in flexible idioms or light verb constructions, and from Wasow et al. (1983) who have to assign arbitrary parts of idiomatic meaning to the different elements of flexible idioms in order to keep a structural parallelism between syntactic and semantic analysis. Our semantic analysis both accounts in a natural way for non-compositional phenomena and is kept strictly increasing in its representation.

This advantage is independent of the particular semantic representation chosen for interpreting the TAG syntactic structures as long as the interpretation is based on the derivation trees. We are going to develop here some examples of idiomatic interpretation for discontinuous constructions based on the formalism of Synchronous TAGs.

4. Synchronous TAGs and semantic interpretation

Synchronous TAGs are a variant of TAGs introduced by Shieber – Schabes (1990) to characterize correspondences between Tree Adjoining languages. In Synchronous TAGs, TAG syntactic units are matched with semantic units expressed in a logical form language which is also a lexicalized TAG. As both the syntactic and the semantic representations use tree structures, the correspondences are stated as tree pairings with some of the nodes of the paired trees possibly linked. The following are examples of such pairings for some of the idioms displayed in Figure 5.

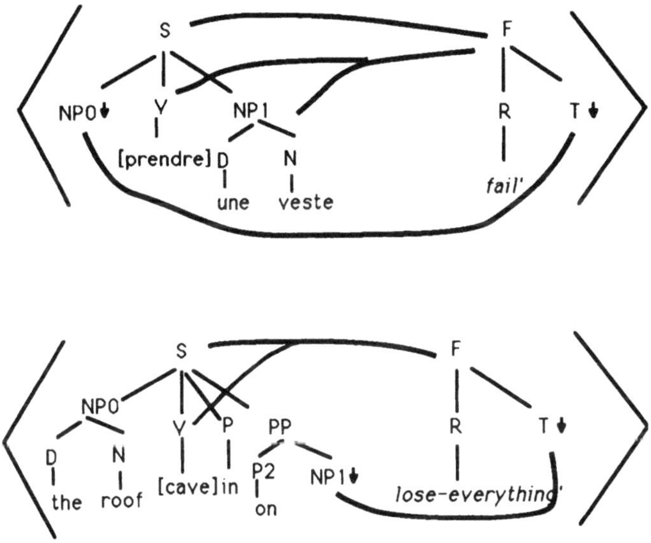

Figure 9. Pairing with semantic trees for *NP0 prendre une veste* and *The roof cave in on NP1*

The links (drawn with thick lines) between syntactic and semantic nodes mean that an operation at one node in the syntactic tree has an equivalent combination at the linked node in the semantic tree (and vice versa)[11]. More precisely, the semantic interpretation of a sentence is built "synchronously" with its syntactic derivation, as follows (Shieber – Schabes 1990):

- choose a link between two nodes n1 and n2 in a pair (syntactic tree, LF tree),
- choose another pair of elementary trees (T2 and L2), the root nodes of which match the respective categories of the two nodes chosen above,
- form a new pair by combining T2 at node n1 and L2 at node n2 and remove the link[12],
- repeat for every combination until the sentence has been completely parsed.

The sentence *Jean prend une veste* will thus have the corresponding logical form for its idiomatic reading: *fail′(jean′)*, provided the NP *Jean* is paired with a semantic Term tree *jean′*[13].

Notice that all elementary trees in an idiomatic tree family are paired with the same LF semantic tree. The elementary tree $\alpha 1$ (Figure 6) corresponding to the relative clause *La veste que NP prend* is thus paired with an F-rooted semantic tree (and not with a semantic Term as usual NPs are). *La veste que Jean a prise surprend Marie* thus has the interpretation *surprise′(fail′(jean′,marie′))* which is the same as that of: *Que Jean ait pris une veste surprend Marie* ('(the fact) that Jean was put down surprises Marie').

We can now move on to the semantic interpretation of adjuncts inserted between the frozen parts of an idiomatic expression. It is easy to see how adverbs, auxiliaries or raising verbs can only modify the idiom as a whole (they are paired with semantic auxiliary trees rooted if F). A more subtle question arises with adjectives adjoining to frozen parts of the idiom. We will show that our representation guarantees that these adjectives are always interpreted with respect to the idiom as a whole, but that they may have either an adverbial or an argumental interpretation depending on the semantic structure of the idiom and on that of the adjective. We thus distinguish between what we call semantically intransitive and semantically transitive idioms (this distinction being different from Wasow et al's (1983) between non-compositional and (more) compositional ones). Let us begin with the first case.

4.1 Syntactic adjuncts with adverbial interpretation

Semantic equivalence between certain adjectives and adverbs has often been noted for idiomatic and light verb constructions. Some examples for English are:

(9) a. *John took unfair advantage of the proposition.*
= *John unfairly took advantage of the proposition.*

b. *The conservative majority could thumb its collective nose at Speaker O'Neil.* (*New York Review of Books*, July 1989)
= *The conservative majority could collectively thumb its nose at Speaker O'Neil.*

Such expressions behave semantically as one unit towards all possible modifiers and the adjectives have an adverbial interpretation.

We show that our representation enables us to correctly handle the equivalence between the following French sentences:

(10) a. *Jean prend une réelle veste.*
= b. *Jean prend réellement une veste.*
'Jean is really coming a cropper'

This equivalence relies on the potential synonymy between the adjective and the adverb but also on the semantic equivalence between their attachment points (N in sentence 10a and V in sentence 10b). Notice that the synonymy between *réel* and *réellement* is not realized with a non-idiomatic predicate such as *NP0 aimer NP1:*

(11) a. *Jean aime les réels amis.*
'Jean likes real friends'
*= b. *Jean aime réellement les amis.*
'Jean really likes friends'

In our representation of the idiom *NP0 prendre une veste* (Figure 9), the F semantic node is linked to three different syntactic nodes: S, V and N. The different frozen pieces of the idiom (here the verb *prendre* and the noun *veste*) which are lexically and syntactically distinct are thus made semantically equivalent since syntactic combination on any of them triggers a synchronous combination on the same semantic node.

We also rely on the fact that the adjective *réel*, which can take either NP or S subjects, is semantically ambiguous between a Term and a Formula semantic scope (as opposed to adjectives like *bleu* which only have NP subjects and Term semantics and are thus prevented to adjoin to our idiomatic tree[14]. The semantic trees for the adjective *réel* and the adverb *réellement* are as follows:

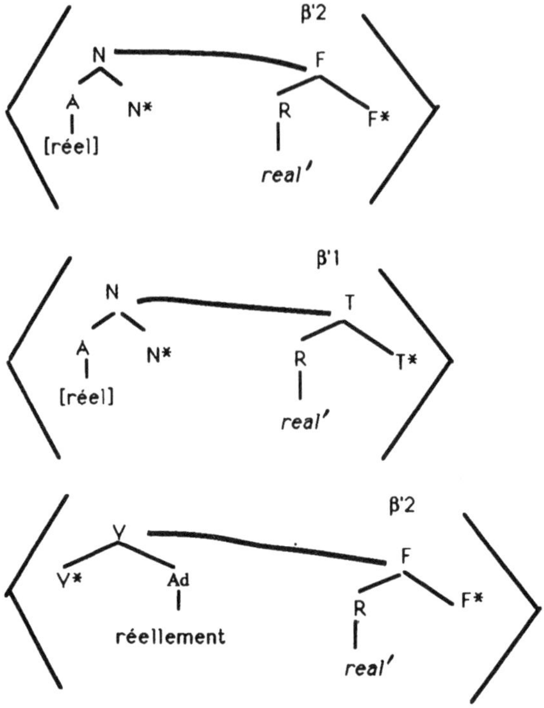

Figure 10. Semantic trees for the adjective *réel* and the adverb *réellement.*

In sentence (10a), the adjective *réel* has regularly been adjoined at the N internal node of the idiomatic tree *prendre une veste*. Since this N node is linked to a semantic F node, only the semantic tree $\beta'2$ can be used for the adjective, for the sentence to be synchronously interpreted. The resulting interpretation is exactly the same as the one for sentence (10b) where an equivalent adverb (*réellement*) adjoins to the V node, since there is a link between the syntactic V node and the semantic F node of the idiom[14] (Figure 11).

The two sentences are thus analysed as synonymous. Informally speaking, one might say that the idiom has its frozen parts reanalysed semantically as an unanalysable predicate and that, as a consequence, the syntactic category and the attachment point of its modifiers do not matter (of course, for modifiers with a possible sentential scope).[16]

If one now considers the literal reading of the same sentence: *Jean prend une réelle veste* ('Jean takes a real jacket'), the selected semantic tree for the adjective will have to be $\beta'1$ since the literal verb *prendre* is paired with

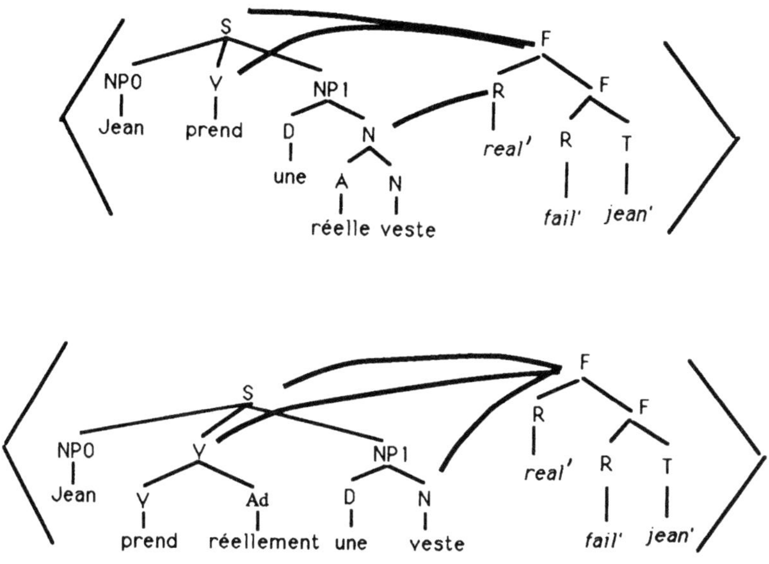

Figure 11. Synchronous interpretations of *Jean prend une réelle veste* and *Jean prend réellement une veste*

a semantic tree with two Term nodes, respectively linked to its NP0 and NP1 syntactic arguments. In this case, there is no F node where $\beta'2$ could adjoin (assuming a synchronous interpretation of the sentence). This is the same for the non-idiomatic sentences (11a) and (11b) that we repeat here for convenience:

(11) a. *Jean aime les réels amis.*
'Jean likes real friends'
*= b. *Jean aime réellement les amis.*
'Jean really likes friends'

The elementary tree for the simple verb *aimer* is paired with a semantic tree with two terms, and its complement is only linked to a T node. Only the pairing of *réel* with a T-rooted semantic auxiliary tree can thus be used. The two sentences thus have two different semantic trees and the possible synonymy between *réel* and *réellement* is not realized:

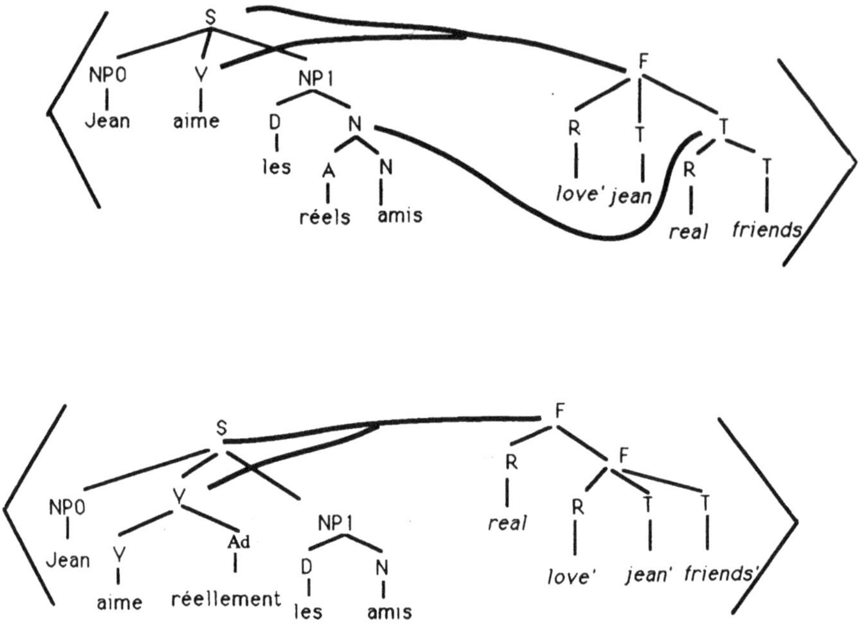

Figure 12. Different interpretations for *Jean aime les réels amis* and *Jean aime réellement les amis*

We have focused here on adjectives but the same treatment would hold for relative clauses. The adjunction of a relative clause to the frozen *veste* is semantically equivalent to a relative clause attaching to the whole S in the idiomatic context:

(12) a. *Il a pris une veste qu'il avait bien méritée.* (NP-relative clause)
= b. *Il a pris une veste, ce qu'il avait bien mérité.* (S-relative clause)
'He came a cropper, which he deserved'

It is thus both unnecessary and misleading to think (as Wasow et al. (1983) do) that adjunction of relative clauses to frozen parts of an idiom forces one to give them a compositional semantics. Only a non-compositional analysis can predict such semantic equivalences.

4.2 Syntactic adjuncts with argumental interpretation

There are cases in which an adjective adjoining to a frozen part of an idiom does not have an adverbial interpretation. The sentence: *This is grist for the linguistic mill* does not mean *?? This is grist for the mill linguistically*. Such cases involve different idioms than those seen in section 4.1 and usually different adjectives.

In these cases, the modifying adjective actually plays the role of a semantic (optional) argument of the idiom, as with the English idiom *be grist for the mill:*[17]

(13) a. *This is grist for the mill* = this helps
b. *This is grist for the linguistic mill* = this helps linguistics (or linguists)

This is the other way in which an idiom behaves as one semantic unit towards an adjective adjoining at one of its frozen parts. Semantically the adjective modifying *mill* plays the role of an argument and the whole idiom behaves as a transitive predicate. We consider such idioms as having a more complex logical form than the ones considered in section 4.1. and one (or more) optional T node(s) linked to its frozen part(s)[18] (see Figure 13).

Notice that the adjectives involved here are different from the ones in section 4.1. In French, a test for such adjectives is their being equivalent to PPs (or NPs) and not to adverbs: *apporter de l'eau au moulin palestinien* = *apporter de l'eau au moulin des palestiniens* ('to be grist for the palestinian mill'). They are usually derived from nouns, especially political and national ones: *linguistic/linguistics; French/ France ...*)[19]. We assign them a Term semantics and pair them with T initial trees (as for NPs) and not only with semantic auxiliary trees[20]. The idiomatic sentence *Idioms are grist for the linguistic mill* thus receives the interpretation *help'(idioms',linguistics')* provided the adjective *linguistic* is paired with the term *linguistics'*. Notice that in this "synchronous" interpretation, the combining operation on the syntactic side (an adjunction) is not formally the same as the one performed on the semantic side (a substitution), which is what our formalism allows for.

The same treatment holds for idioms with more than one frozen NP and more than one optional adjectival argument as in the following example:

(14) a. *"Cet examen prétend séparer le bon grain individualiste de l'ivraie collectiviste"* (*Le Monde*, October 1989)

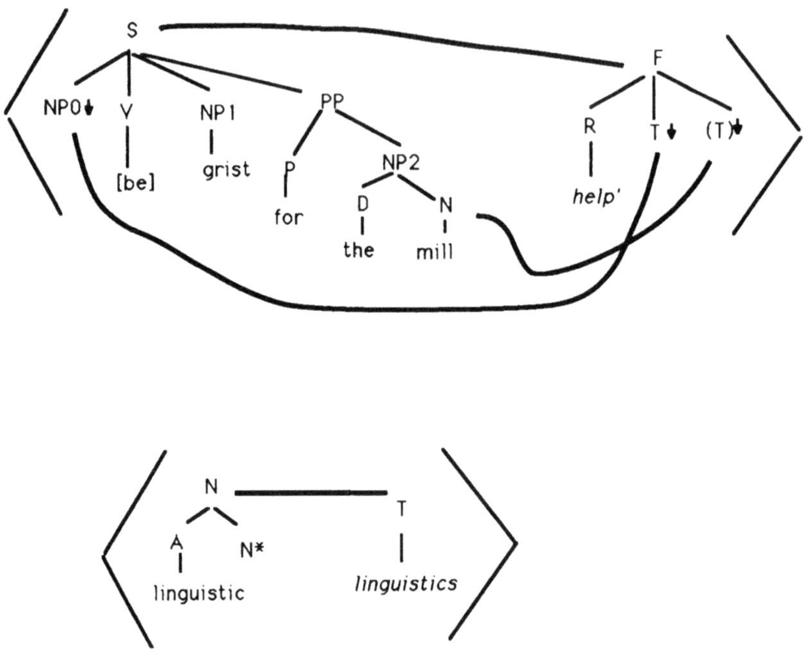

Figure 13. Semantic trees associated with *be grist for the mill* and the adjective *linguistic.*

= b. *Cet examen prétend* <u>*séparer le bon grain*</u> *de l'individualisme* <u>*de l'ivraie*</u> *du collectivisme.*
'this inquiry claims to distinguish individualism from collectivism'

The French idiom *séparer le bon grain de l'ivraie* ('to separate the wheat from the chaff') is thus paired with a F semantic tree with three Term nodes: one for its free subject, and one for each frozen complement.

To give an informal summary of our discussion, we have proposed in this section a semantic distinction between two kinds of idioms:

- idioms semantically "intransitive": e.g. *kick the bucket, saw logs, casser sa pipe, prendre une veste*; they may have various syntactic complements; some permit adjectives (which only have an adverbial interpretation) on their frozen pieces, others permit only adverbs (this being a purely syntactic constraint), but these adjectives only have an adverbial interpretation.
- idioms semantically "transitive": their free arguments are either predicted in their syntax (as specific leaf nodes in the syntactic tree): e.g. *take NP*

into account, casser du sucre sur le dos de NP, or only in the semantics (as leaf nodes in the semantic tree, linked with internal syntactic nodes): e.g. *be grist for the mill, separate the wheat from the chaff.*

This is the aspect in which we follow Wasow et al.'s (1983) claim that not all idioms should be assigned the same kind of semantics. But for us, the semantics of idioms is always non-compositional (it is not built up from an individual piece of meaning assigned to any frozen parts) even if not all their frozen syntactic nodes are linked to the same semantic nodes, in order to account for different possible interpretations of their modifiers. Secondly, and contrary to them, we do not correlate such semantic differences with differences in syntactic properties, since the same syntactic flexibility may arise with semantically "intransitive" idioms and semantically "transitive" ones, as the following examples of cleft extractions show:

(15) a. *C'est au moulin palestinien qu'il apporte de l'eau.* (idiom semantically transitive)
b. *C'est une sacrée veste qu'il a prise.* (idiom semantically intransitive)

5. Relevance of this representation for natural language processing

The NLP community has recently paid increasing attention to discontinuities, proposing extensions of existing formalisms (e.g. DPSG, see Bunt 1991) or specific parsing algorithms (Johnson 1985; Van Noord 1991). But the question of non-compositional discontinuous constituents has seldom been adressed.

Non-compositional constituents are usually considered to be a problem for automatic processing, and have received only partial solutions so far (e.g. Stock 1987). Preprocessing is unavailable for discontinuous idioms, and, more generally, has to be rejected as soon as one considers that the non compositional elements obey regular syntactic rules, which makes their recognition dependent on the whole syntactic analysis (Schenk 1986; Abeillé – Schabes 1989). In TAGs non-compositional constituents fall into the same grammar as "regular" sentences and their processing does not require any special mechanism. Since TAGs factor recursion from local dependencies, their possible discontinuities are captured straighforwardly without any special devices.

Furthermore, the Synchronous TAGs formalism guarantees that their semantic interpretation (although non-compositional) be kept strictly monotonic, a property crucial for generation as explained in Shieber – Schabes (1991).

Parsing non-compositional constituents is thus reduced to the general parsing of Lexicalized TAGs, which follows the two-step offline parsing strategy described in Schabes – Abeillé – Joshi (1988): first scan the input string to select all the trees anchored by the diferent lexical items; then try to combine these elementary structures to obtain a well-formed structure.[21]

The selection of an idiomatic (elementary) tree by the parser obeys the following conditions (Abeillé – Schabes 1989; Schabes 1990):

- all the lexical heads of the idiomatic tree must be present in the input string,
- the syntactic features in the lexical entry of the idiom must indeed allow for the rule corresponding to this idiomatic tree,
- the order imposed for the preterminals in the tree must match the order in which the pieces appear in the input string. The different idiomatic pieces thus need not be contiguous in the input string and may appear in several possible orders (depending on the composition of the Tree family of the corresponding idiom).

Our representation of non-compositional constituents also has advantages for another NLP application, namely machine translation, which can also be based on Synchronous TAGs. The strategy adopted for machine translation using Lexicalized TAGs (Abeillé – Schabes – Joshi 1990) consists of matching the source TAG derivation of the sentence to a target TAG derivation. Both derivations have to be built "synchronously". In this application, the English elementary trees are not paired with semantic trees but with French elementary trees (and vice versa), with some of their nodes possibly linked, in a bilingual transfer lexicon. The mapping of derivation trees from source to target languages, using the formalism of synchronous TAGs, makes possible to state direct correspondences between structures quite different syntactically without the need for a mediating interlingual representation (Abeillé – Schabes – Joshi 1990).

Discrepancies in the elementary structures being paired in the lexicon are not a problem, discrepancies in the derived structures are also expected and no special mechanism is required for them. English idioms, for example, can easily be paired with French idioms of quite different syntactic structure, or with simple verbs: *NP's dander is up= la moutarde monte au nez de NP; to take NP to task= passer un savon à NP; to sweap NP under the rug = escamoter NP*. Elementary trees with internal discontinuous constituents are paired in the same way and their transfer does not require any special mechanism.

Furthermore, the equivalence between adjectives and adverbs in non-compositional constructions noted in section 4.1. can be carried over cross-linguistically using the same double-link device: *faire confiance à NP = to trust NP ⇒ faire une totale confiance à NP = to totally trust NP*. And similarly for the equivalence between adjectives and NPs (or PPs) explained in section 4.2.: *prendre le train en marche = to jump on the band-wagon ⇒ prendre le train communautaire en marche = to jump on the Common market band-wagon.*

Conclusion

We have shown how English and French idioms may exhibit various discontinuities. We have described how to deal in a TAG with semantic non compositionality in idioms and light verb constructions, without losing the internal syntactic composition of these structures. TAG's extended domain of locality allows one to handle, within a single level of syntactic description, phenomena that in other frameworks require either dual analyses or reanalysis. The treatment of such discontinuous constituents is reduced to the general representation of constituency in TAGs. The extension of Synchronous TAGs makes particularly explicit how they can be syntactically and semantically localized and enables one to handle their non-compositional semantics in a strictly monotonic way.

Acknowledgments. The authors have benefited from their discussions with L. Danlos, M. Gross, A. Joshi and S. Shieber. The second author has received partial support from ARO grant DAAL03-89-C0031PRI, DARPA grant N00014-90-J-1863 and NSF grant IRI90-16592 at the University of Pennsylvania.

Notes

1. As for the semantic representation itself, we follow here Shieber – Schabes (1990a) who assume a correspondence between the syntactic elementary trees and elementary logical forms which are themselves lexicalized trees (see section 4 below for more on this).
2. To be contrasted with the impossible: **to take a run, *to have an eat, *to give a laugh.*
3. For light verb constructions, a semi-compositional semantic might sometimes be necessary. Although this paper focuses here on non-compositional phenomena, semi-compositionality can also be dealt with in Lexicalized Tree Adjoining Grammar.
4. By fixed, we mean that no syntactic or lexical rule (such as wh-question, relativization, passive, pronominalisation) ... apply to the frozen arguments of the idiom. In most of the cases, though, idioms are in between fixed and flexible, since only certain rules apply to them, not others, with puzzling idiosyncrasies (Gross 1989).
5. In what follows, the frozen parts of the idiom are underscored.
6. We use standard TAG notation: '↓' stands for nodes to be substituted, * annotates the foot node of an auxiliary tree and the indices correspond to grammatical functions. The term "head" denotes the lexical item(s) projecting to the given construction. Heads are also required to be neither lexically, nor semantically empty.
7. The only difference between idioms and light verb constructions is that in the latter's Tree families, there are complex NP trees corresponding to the predicative noun occurring without the light verb. For more details about the composition of these Tree Families that force several elementary trees to be associated together with a given lexical item see Abeillé (1991a).
8. Empty nodes are used here for commodity of reading only. They are superfluous both for our syntax and our semantics.
9. Gross (1989) and Abeillé (1990) suggest some means of predicting the applicability of syntactic rules to idioms (which mainly rely on the value of the determiner of the frozen complement).
10. We use standard TAG notation for the derivations trees: unbroken lines for adjoined trees and dashed lines for substituted ones, Gorn adresses for the parent node at which combination takes place.
11. The non-terminal names in the logical form grammar are mnemonic for Formula, Term and Relation (or function).
12. The definition allows for the operation performed at each node to differ, one being an adjunction and the other a substitution for example. It also allows for a node to be linked to several other nodes: in this case, only the "consumed"

link is removed. See Shieber – Schabes (1990a) for more formal details about Synchronous TAGs.

13. In what follows we leave aside the representation of tense, aspect, determination or quantification in our semantic interpretations.
14. It will be the case for all adjectives entering only *NP0 être Adj* constructions. They are prevented to adjoin to the node *veste* in the idiomatic tree because it is linked to an F node in the semantic tree. There is thus no place where the T-rooted tree of such adjectives could adjoin in the semantic tree of the idiom. This is what we may call semantic ill-formedness (when no synchronous LF is possible for a given syntactic derivation) and enables us to rule out the idiomatic reading for *Jean prend une veste bleue/trop petite* ('Jean takes a blue/too small jacket') without the need of ad hoc features.
16. We leave aside the possible distinction between adverbs with S or VP scoping and consider here all adverbs as having the widest scope.
17. Interpretation of adjectives modifying frozen parts of such idioms may be more complex than the simple case above, but we are guaranteed that they will have an adverbial interpretation: *to kick the proverbial bucket = to kick the bucket, as the proverb says* (or *in the proverbial sense of the word*).
18. We leave aside the possibility of a possessive determiner, as in *This is grist for John's mill*, which is to be analysed as an (obligatory) syntactic adjunct with a Term semantics.
19. With a more refined semantics, the semantic T node(s) linked with the frozen part(s) of the idiom need not be optional. When one says: *This is grist for the mill*, one usually means: *This helps what we are talking about.* We should thus remember that when no adjunction takes place on their linked syntactic nodes, these T nodes are filled with an anaphor.
20. Some adjectives are analysed as semantically ambiguous (although they yield the same syntactic structure). For example the adjective *politique* is paired with a semantic tree adjoining to T (as any adjective), with one adjoining to F (*il a pris une veste politique = politiquement*), and with a simple Term initial tree (*il apporte de l'eau au moulin politique = au moulin de la (vie) politique*).
21. Notice that other adjectives such as color ones are prevented to adjoin on the N node of the idomatic tree, since they are only paired with auxiliary (T-rooted) semantic trees: *Il apporte de l'eau au moulin bleu* ('He brings water to the blue mill') will thus not receive an idiomatic interpretation.
22. We are using the Earley parser for TAGs described in Schabes – Joshi (1988), Schabes (1990;1991). The semantic component of the parser (based on Synchronous TAGs) has not been implemented yet.

References

Abeillé, A.
1988 Light verb constructions and extraction out of NP in Tree Adjoining Grammar. *Papers from the 24th Regional Meeting of the Chicago Linguistic Society*, Chicago.

Abeillé, A. and Y. Schabes
1989 Parsing Idioms with a Lexicalized Tree Adjoining Grammar. *Proceedings of the 4th European Conference of ACL*, Manchester.

Abeillé, A.
1990 Lexical and syntactic rules in a Tree Adjoining grammar. *Proceedings of 28th ACL meeting*, Vancouver.

Abeillé, A., K. Bishop, S. Cote and Y. Schabes
1990 *A lexicalized Tree Adjoining grammar for English*. Technical Report, CIS Department, University of Pennsylvania, Philadelphia.

Abeillé, A., Y. Schabes and A. Joshi
1990 Using Lexicalized TAGs for Machine Translation, *Proceedings of 13th COLING*, Helsinki.

Abeillé, A.
1991(a) *Une grammaire lexicalisée d'arbres adjoints pour le français*. Thèse de Doctorat, Université Paris 7, Paris.

Abeillé, A.
1991(b) L'unification dans une grammaire d'arbres adjoints: quelques exemples en syntaxe française. *TA Informations*, 30: 1-2, Paris.

Becker, T., A. Joshi and O. Rambow
1991 Long-distance scrambling and Tree Adjoining Grammars. *Proceedings of the 5th European Conference of ACL*, Berlin.

Bunt, H.
1991 DSPG and its use in parsing. In: M. Tomita (ed.), *Current Issues in Parsing Technology*. Kluwer, Boston.

Bresnan, J.
1982 The passive in lexical theory. In: J. Bresnan (ed.), *The mental representation of grammatical relations*. MIT Press, Cambridge, MA.

Chomsky, N.
1981 *Lectures on Government and Binding*. Foris, Dordrecht.

Emonds, J.
1972 Evidence that indirect object movement is a structure preserving rule. *Foundations of Language, 8.*

Freckelton, P.
1984 *Une taxonomie des expressions idiomatiques anglaises*. Thèse de 3ème cycle, Université Paris 7, Paris.

Gross, M.
1982 Classification des phrases figées en français. *Revue québécoise de linguistique,* 11:2, Montréal.

Gross, M.
1988 Les limites de la phrase figée. *Langages* 90, Paris: Larousse.

Gross, M.
1989 *Les expressions figées du français*, Rapport technique, ADL, Université Paris 7, Paris.

Johnson, M.
1985 Parsing with discontinuous elements. In: *Proceedings of 23th ACL meeting*, Chicago.

Joshi, A.
1985 How much context-sensitivity is necessary for characterizing structural descriptions: Tree Adjoining grammars. In: D. Dowty, L. Karttunen and A. Zwicky (eds.), *Natural Language Processing: Psycholinguistic, Computational and Theoretical Perspectives.* Cambridge University Press, Cambridge.

Joshi, A.
1988 An Introduction to Tree Adjoining Grammars. In: A. Manaster-Ramer (ed.), *Mathematics of Language.* J. Benjamins, Amsterdam.

Kroch, A. and A. Joshi
1985 Some Aspects of the linguistic relevance of Tree Adjoining Grammar. Technical Report MS-CIS 85-18, CIS Department, University of Pennsylvania, Philadelphia.

Laporte, E.
1988 La reconnaissance des expressions figées lors de l'analyse automatique, *Langages,* 90, Paris: Larousse.

Newmeyer, F.
1974 The regularity of idiom behaviour. *Lingua, 34.*

Schabes, Y. and A. Joshi
1988 An Earley-type parsing algorithm for Tree Adjoining grammars. *Proceedings of 26th ACL meeting*, Buffalo.

Schabes, Y., A. Abeillé and A. Joshi
1988 Parsing strategies with lexicalized grammars: Tree adjoining grammars, *Proceedings of 12th COLING*, Budapest.

Schabes, Y.
1990 *Mathematical and computational properties of lexicalized grammars.* PhD Thesis, University of Pennsylvania, Philadelphia.

Schabes, Y.
1991 The valid Prefix Property and Left to Right parsing of Tree-Adjoining Grammar. *Proceedings of the 2nd International Workshop on Parsing Technologies*, Cancun.

Schenk, A.
1986 Idioms in the Rosetta machine translation system. *Proceedings of 11th COLING*, Bonn.
Shieber, S. and Y. Schabes
1990 Synchronous Tree adjoining grammars. *Proceedings of 13th COLING*, Helsinki (vol. 3, pp. 253-260).
Shieber, S. and Y. Schabes
1991 Generation and Synchronous Tree Adjoining Grammars. *Computational Intelligence*, 4:7, pp. 220-228. Pittsburg.
Stock, O.
1987 Getting idioms in a lexicon-based parser's head. *Proceedings of 25th ACL meeting*, Stanford.
Noord, G. van
1991 Head corner parsing for discontinuous constituency. *Proceedings of 29th ACL meeting*, Berkeley.
Vijay-Shanker, K. and A. Joshi.
1988 Feature based Tree Adjoining Grammar. *Proceedings of 12th COLING'88*, Budapest (vol. 2, pp. 714-719).
Wasow, T., I. Sag and G. Nunberg.
1983 Idioms: an interim report. *Proceedings of the XIIIth International Congress of Linguists*, Tokyo.

Discontinuous constituency in Segment Grammar

Koenraad De Smedt and Gerard Kempen

Abstract. Segment Grammar (SG) is a grammar formalism which is especially suited to model the incremental generation of sentences. SG is characterized by a dual level of syntactic description: f-structures, which are unordered functional structures composed out of syntactic segments, and c-structures, which represent left-to-right order of constituents. True discontinuities in SG are viewed as differences between immediate dominance (ID) relations in c-structures and those in corresponding f-structures. Constructions which are treated in this way include clause union, right dislocation, and fronting. Separable parts of words such as verbs and compound prepositions are not viewed as true discontinuities but as lexical entries consisting of separate syntactic segments.

1. Word order in Segment Grammar

1.1 Introduction

Segment Grammar (SG) was originally proposed by Kempen (1987) undcr the name of Incremental Grammar. It is a unification-based formalism which is especially suited to model the incremental generation of sentences. In order to account for the fact that human speakers normally produce utterances to some extent in a piecemeal fashion, certain requirements are imposed on a grammar formalism. Specifically, the grammar must define the left-to-right order of partial sentences as well as of complete ones. Moreover, the grammar must allow a partial utterance to be extended, if possible, in vertical as well as horizontal orientation (De Smedt – Kempen 1987: 369–370).

A stronger requirement for incremental generation is that the grammar must fit into a detailed predictive model of language behaviour which explains how utterances are actually produced by speakers. In this chapter, we will, for instance, not be content to merely describe that certain continuous constituents have discontinuous counterparts, but we will also try to explain what are the conditions in the sentence generation process favouring discontinuities and what are the conditions obstructing them. Various timing factors within the incremental generation process will play a crucial role in this account.[1]

We have developed an SG for Dutch and we have implemented a computer simulation program on a Symbolics Lisp Machine which uses this grammar to construct Dutch sentences in an incremental mode. A number of simulations have been run so far which have produced some of the discontinuous constructions described in this chapter. In the remainder of this section, we will briefly describe the way in which left-to-right order of constituents is determined in SG. After that, we will turn our attention to the treatment of discontinuities in SG.

1.2 F-structures and c-structures in Segment Grammar

Somewhat like a lexical-functional grammar (LFG) as proposed by Kaplan – Bresnan (1982: 175–231), an SG assigns two distinct descriptions to every sentence of the language which it generates. The *constituent structure* (or "c-structure") of a sentence is a conventional phrase structure (PS), which is represented as an ordered tree-shaped graph. It indicates the surface grouping and ordering of words and phrases in a sentence. The *functional structure* (or "f-structure") provides a more detailed representation of grammatical relations between words and phrases, as traditionally expressed by subject, direct object, etc. The representation in f-structures also accounts for agreement, and it does so by using features like number, gender, etc.

When an SG is used for generation, semantic and discourse information is mapped into f-structures, which in turn are mapped into c-structures. C-structures are then subjected to morpho-phonological processing, producing phonetic strings which are eventually uttered as speech sounds. This overall process is depicted in Figure 1.

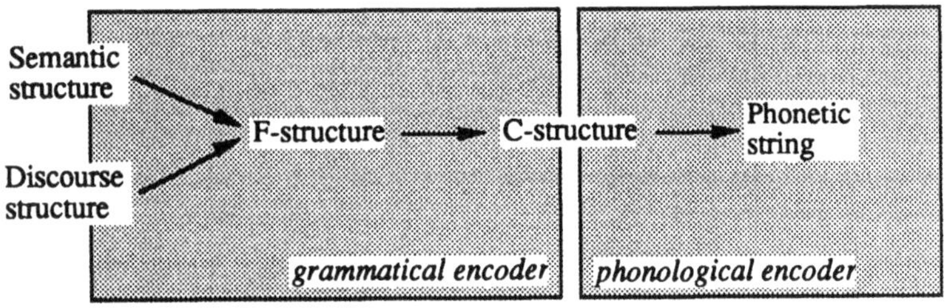

Figure 1. The generation of successive linguistic descriptions during sentence formulation.

1.3 Syntactic segments and ID/LP format

In order to encapsulate grammatical knowledge into units small enough for incremental sentence generation, Kempen (1987) proposes that a grammar consist solely of a set of *syntactic segments*, each representing a single immediate dominance (ID) relation. A segment consists of two nodes representing grammatical categories linked by an arc labeled with a grammatical function. They are graphically represented in vertical orientation, where the top node is called the *root* and the bottom node the *foot*. Syntactic segments join to form a syntactic structure (f-structure) by means of a general unification operation. The f-structure (1d) for the Dutch examples (1a) as well as (1b) consists of six segments (1c).

(1) a. *Ik belde Marie op.*
'I called Marie up'
b. *Marie belde ik op.*
Marie called I up
'Marie I called up'

c.
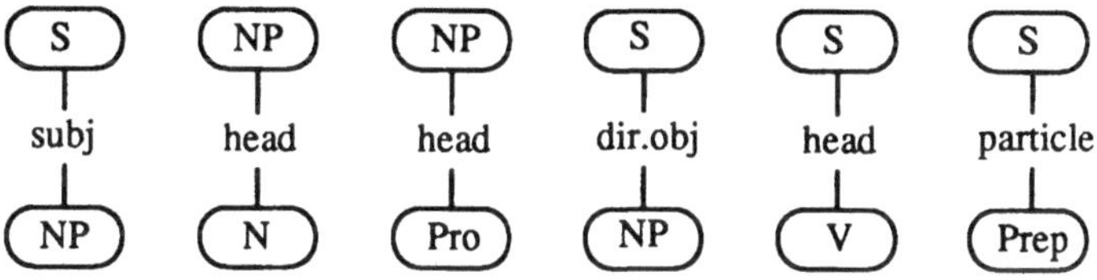

d.
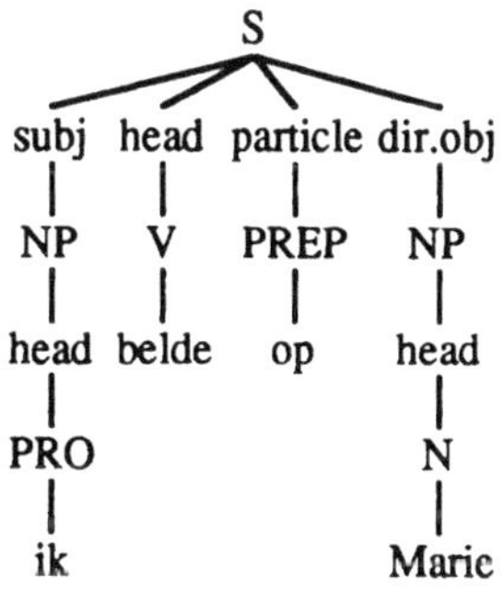

e.
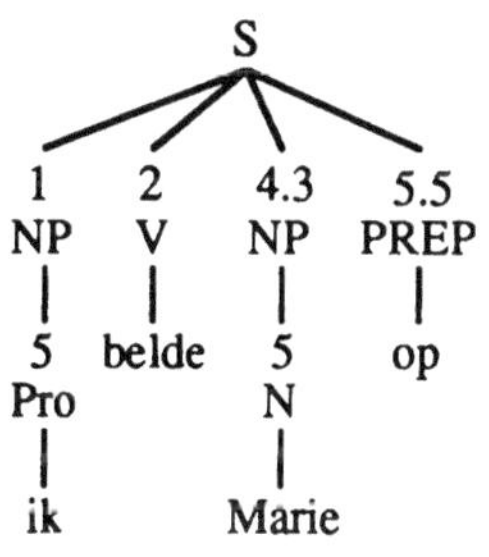

The assignment of left-to-right positions to constituents is modeled as the piecemeal derivation of a different kind of structure – a c-structure. By way of example, c-structure (1e) is assigned to (1a).

Somewhat like the ID/LP format for PS rules, SG handles ID relations and linear precedence (LP) relations separately. This enables the grammar to account for systematic variations of word order in a more general way. For example, both (1a) and (1b) could be assigned the same f-structure (1d). However, there are two crucial differences. First, whereas a PS-based system specifies a relative ordering of sister nodes, SG assigns a position to a constituent independently of its sisters; therefore, a system of absolute positions is used, as shown by the numbered slots in (1e). Second, the assignment of LP in SG may be attended with a revision of ID relations. Consequently, the ID relations in the f-structure and the c-structure for a sentence may not be isomorphic. We will therefore explain in some more detail how left-to-right positions are assigned in SG.

1.4 Destinations

The procedure which assigns left-to-right positions works in a bottom-up fashion: the foot node of a segment is attached in the c-structure directly under its *destination.* The destination of a constituent is determined by its matrix in the f-structure, that is, the node which is root of the segment where the constituent is the foot. Normally, the address which the matrix constituent assigns as destination of its dependents is the matrix constituent itself, that is, ID relations in the c-structure are by default the same as those in the corresponding f-structure. Figure 2 is a schematic representation of this process.

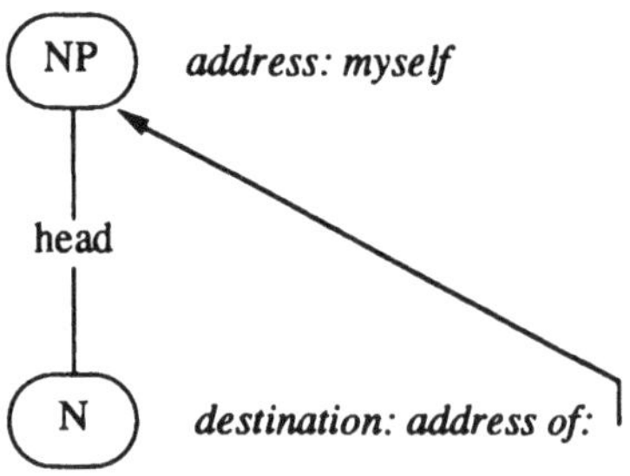

Figure 2. Finding the destination of a node via the address of its mother.

Such indirect determination of the destination may seem complicated, but it guarantees that the root node of a segment in f-structure exerts control over the ID relation of the foot node. This will prove useful in the treatment of constructions where nodes go to higher-level destinations, as discussed below.

1.5 Holders and word order variation

Since f-structures are constructed in a piecemeal fashion, it is natural to assign word order incrementally as well. As soon as a node has been attached to its mother in the f-structure, SG attempts to assign it a left-to-right position in the corresponding c-structure. Because not all constituents are available at the same time, it is difficult to encode word order relative to other constituents. Therefore, SG prefers an absolute order of constituents. For this purpose, a *holder* is associated with each phrase. A holder is a vector of numbered slots that can be filled by constituents. Figure 3 schematically shows some holders associated with c-structure (1e).

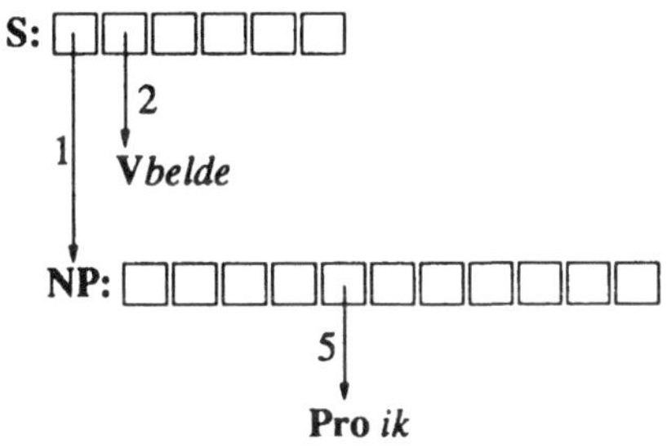

Figure 3. Diagram showing some holders for (1e); the first and second positions of the S and the fifth position of the NP have just been occupied.

The foot node of each segment in the grammar has a feature called *positions* which lists all possible slot positions that the node can occupy in its destination. Word order variation is accounted for by listing more than one possibility where appropriate. For instance, in the grammar of Dutch it is specified that the foot of a S-subject-NP segment may go to holder slots 1 or 3. Constituents will try to occupy the first available slot in this list. For instance, when the foot of a S-subject-NP segment is assigned a position in the holder of its destination, it will first attempt to occupy position 1. Suppose, for instance, that the first slot in the holder has already been occupied (indicated by the crossed out slot in Figure 4); the NP will consequently attempt to insert a pointer to itself into the third slot (indicated by the arrow

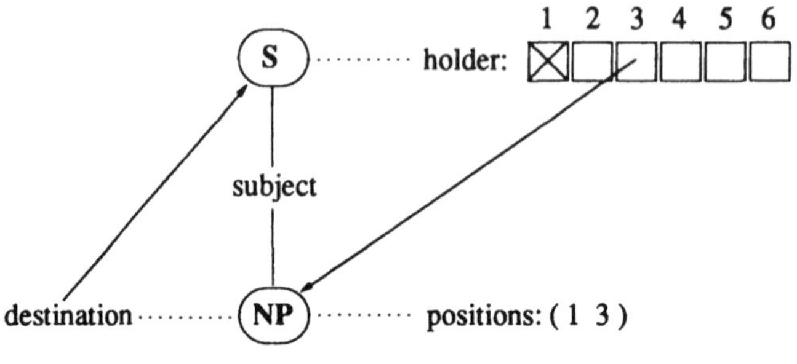

Figure 4. Destination ånd linearization processes: assign NP to the third slot in the holder of its destination when the first slot is already occupied.

in Figure 4). This situation may give rise to the word order in (1b), where the subject *ik* 'I' takes third position rather than first.

Several constituents can make attempts to fill the same slot; SG presupposes a "first come, first serve" principle in dealing with these situations. This principle, in combination with the previously mentioned mechanisms, may give rise to different word order choices in different circumstances. If the utterance has proceeded beyond the point where a constituent can be added, a syntactic dead-end occurs and a self-correction or restart may be necessary. Alternatively, the constituent may end up somewhere else. For instance, the final slot in the S holder is a "dump" for late material (as occurs in right dislocation). The relative clause in (2a) is an instance of such a construction. In spontaneous speech, right dislocation sometimes occurs even if the result is not quite grammatical (2b).

(2) a. *Marie belde ik op, die ziek was.*
Marie called I up, who ill was
'I called up Marie, who was ill'
b. * *Dat was prettig, redelijk.*
That was nice, quite
'That was quite nice'

Although human speakers do not always make perfect sentences, and sometimes produce clear ordering errors, it seems generally possible, at least in languages like English and Dutch, to determine the order of single fragments one after the other incrementally during sentence generation. In fact, it seems that incremental production is only possible if for the assignment of left-to-right position to a constituent, the simultaneous presence of all other constituents in the phrase is not required. If this empirical claim is true, the necessary knowledge to determine word order can be encoded locally on the level of single segments, as is done in SG.

The number of holder slots in a Dutch clause is substantial. In order to keep an overview, positions within positions are sometimes used. The Dutch sentence can be divided into six main parts, each having its own internal ordering. Decimal notation is used to represent such slots; for instance, the number 3.2 denotes the second slot in the third main slot. Some holder slots can be occupied by a single constituent only; others may be occupied by an unspecified number of constituents, for instance, an indefinitely long list of adjectival phrases in front of a noun. We will not further elaborate on general aspects of word order in an SG for Dutch. For further discussion of SG and its role in generation we refer to De Smedt (1990b) and De Smedt – Kempen (1991). We will now turn to those aspects dealing with discontinuous constituency.

2. Discontinuous constituency in Segment Grammar

As indicated above, the assignment of left-to-right positions to constituents in a sentence may be accompanied by changes in the ID relations. Thus, a c-structure need not be isomorphic to the corresponding f-structure. SG accounts for various kinds of discontinuous constituents – including right dislocation, S-O raising, and Wh-fronting – by assigning different ID relations in the c-structure.

2.1 Overview of discontinuities

Even languages with a relatively fixed word order allow constituents of a phrase to be non-adjacent. In (3–7), five important kinds of discontinuities in Dutch are summed up (see also Bunt 1988).

The examples in (3) contain broken-up constituents (indicated by means of underlining) which in part have been dislocated to the right, across another constituent.

(3) a. *Ik heb een auto gekocht met zes deuren.*
I have a car bought with six doors
'I have bought a car with six doors'

b. *Een van zijn vrienden kwam, die in Brussel woont.*
One of his friends came, who in Brussels lives
'One of his friends came, who lives in Brussels'

c. *Een betere film dan ik verwachtte draaide gisteren*
A better film than I expected was shown yesterday
in Calypso.
in Calypso
'A better film than I expected was shown at Calypso yesterday'

d. *Een betere film draaide gisteren in Calypso*
A better film was shown yesterday in Calypso
dan ik verwachtte.
than I expected
'A better film than I expected was shown at Calypso yesterday'

Example (3a) shows a discontinuous NP with an extraposed PP. Extraposition is optional here and tends to occur more often in spontaneous speech. Example (3b) shows a similar construction with a right dislocated relative clause rather than a PP. Again, extraposition is optional, but tends to be more acceptable as the relative clause is longer and the rest of the sentence (*kwam*) is shorter. In (3c), it is an adjectival phrase (ADJP) which is discontinuous; this right dislocation is obligatory and can extend not only to the NP level (3c) but also to the S level (3d).

A second kind of discontinuity consists of compound words which are split up, for instance the verb *opbellen* in (4a) and (1a,b) and the preposition *doorheen* (through) in (4b).

(4) a. *Bel me morgen op om dit te bevestigen.*
Call me tomorrow up in-order-to this to confirm
'Call me up tomorrow in order to confirm this

b. *Het vliegtuig gaat nu door de geluidsbarrière heen.*
The airplane goes now through-1 the sound barrier through-2
'The airplane now breaks the sound barrier'

In SG, these cases are not really considered discontinuities, but the "split" elements are listed in the lexicon as already consisting of several segments. Consequently, they are realized as separate constituents on all levels of representation. They may be assigned left-to-right positions in such a way that other constituents may intervene. The French negative *ne* ... *pas* is also an instance of this kind of lexical entry.

Examples of *clause union* are given in (5). In (5a), the constituents of the infinitival clause (underlined) are not kept together as a whole but are assigned positions in the main clause. Thus, objects are grouped irrespective of the clause where they functionally belong, and likewise for non-finite verbs. Clause union may result in crossed dependencies in Dutch, as shown schematically in (5b).

(5) a. *Ik heb Otto een appel zien eten.*
I have Otto an apple seen eat
'I have seen Otto eat an apple'

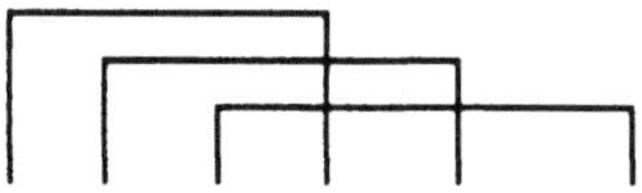

b. *Ik dacht dat Jan Piet Marie zag helpen zwemmen.*
I thought that Jan Piet Marie saw help swim
'I thought that Jan saw Piet help Marie swim'

A fourth kind of discontinuities involves unbounded dependencies, for instance, wh-fronting in (6a) and fronting of a focused element from subordinate clauses in (6b).

(6) a. *Wie dacht je dat ik opbelde?*
Who thought you that I up-called
'Who did you think I called up?'
b. *Dat blonde meisje dacht ik dat je opbelde.*
That blond girl thought I that you up-called
'That blond girl I thought you called up'

A fifth kind of discontinuity contains the pronoun *er* 'there' and similar "R-words". When the object in a PP does not have a person as its antecedent, it is pronominalized by means of the special pronoun *er* (often also called a pronominal adverb), which is placed before the preposition. This combination of *er* and a preposition may be interrupted by some other constituents, as in (7).

(7) *De vloeistof gaat er nu in.*
The liquid goes there now in
'The liquid now goes in it'

Since the various kinds of discontinuous constructions which are summed up above are more or less problematic for PS-based grammars, it has been proposed to amend the definition of an ordinary PS tree to accommodate discontinuities. For sentence (1a), this could result in the modified tree structure (8).

(8)

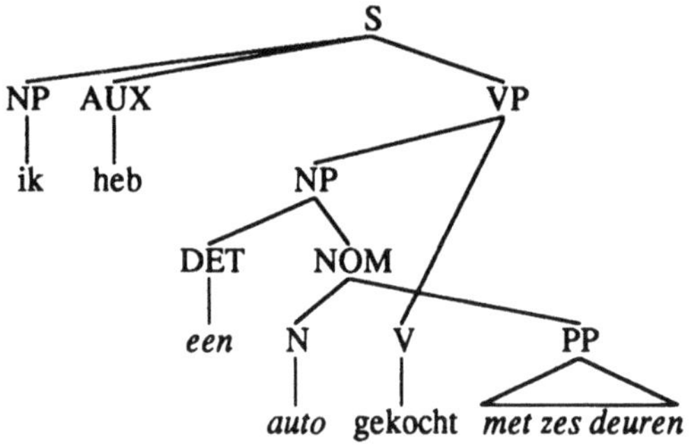

In order to generate such structures within a context-free framework, Bunt (1988) proposes Discontinuous Phrase Structure Grammar (DPSG) which introduces and formalizes the notion of adjacency into PS grammars. DPSG is motivated by the claim that other generation algorithms for a language with discontinuities would first have to generate a continuous ordered tree representation and then identify and apply the transformations which produce the correct word order for discontinuities. However, this need not be the case for a grammar which distinguishes between an unordered functional structure (f-structure) and an ordered surface structure (c-structure). In SG, the correct word order is produced directly.

In the remainder of this section, it is shown how various discontinuities are handled by changes in ID relations at the time when left-to-right order is determined.

2.2 Right dislocation

At the level of f-structure, SG assigns the right dislocated PP in (3a) a functional relation to the NP *een auto* as shown in f-structure (9a). However, the PP is not part of the NP in the c-structure. Rather, it has an ID relation to the S, as shown in c-structure (9b). Since the f-structure is unordered, the computation of a c-structure is not a transformation in the TGG sense, but an assignment of left-to-right order accompanied by a simple reassignment of an ID relation.

(9) a.

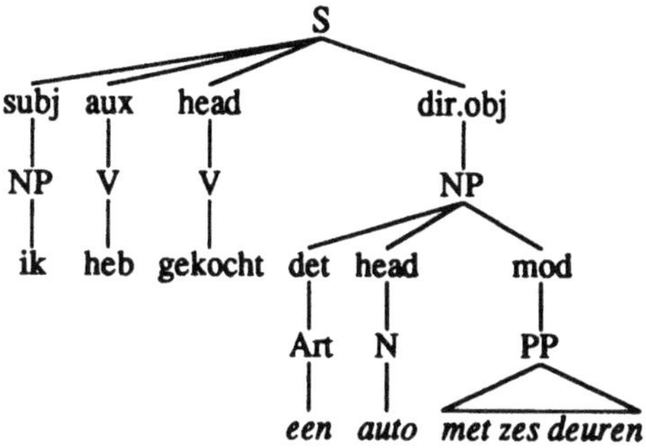

b.

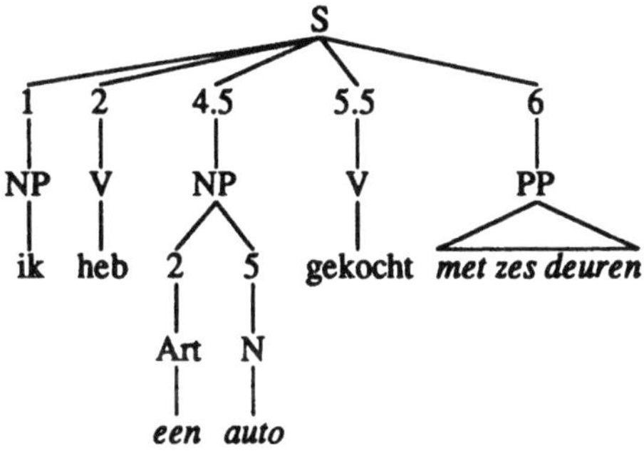

The right dislocation of a PP fits naturally into the incremental generation process. It is triggered by the fact that the extraposed PP cannot be added incrementally to the holder of the NP, because the utterance has already proceeded beyond that point. Therefore the PP is exceptionally allowed to move to the S level, which has a holder slot where some kinds of "late" constituents can be placed. Preferably, this slot (numbered 6) contains at most one constituent; more than one constituent is not impossible though, as in (10a,b). The character of such constituents as "afterthoughts" becomes clearer if more constituents are added.

(10) a. *Ik heb een auto gekocht vorige week met zes deuren.*
I have a car bought last week with six doors
'I have bought a car last week with six doors'

b. *Ik heb een auto gekocht met zes deuren vorige week.*
I have a car bought with six doors last week
'I have bought a car with six doors last week'

Right dislocation is sometimes obligatory, for instance (3c,d). Such obligatory right dislocation must be specified in the lexicon. In SG this is achieved by a specification of possible destinations on the foot of the AP-mod-S segment which is associated with the lexical entries for *beter ... dan* 'better than' and other comparatives. F-structure (11) contains a schematic indication of these possibilities.

(11)

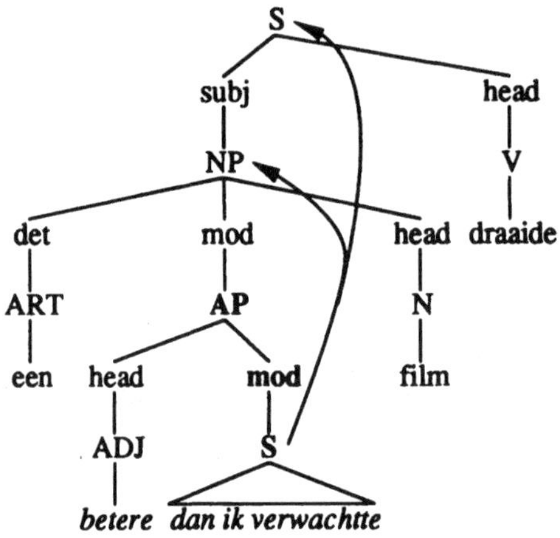

2.3 Clause union and "raising"

This section deals with subject-to-object raising. This construction (henceforth *S-O raising*) is characterized by a direct object, for instance, *Otto* in (3), which simultaneously serves as the logical subject of an infinitival complement clause. According to SG, as well as certain other contemporary accounts, this construction does not actually involve raising in the transformational sense. The direct object *Otto* in (5a) is always the object of the matrix clause and never subject of the embedded clause at any point during the generation process. This is compatible with the LFG analysis of such constructions, which has also been argued for independently on the basis of cross-language investigation by Horn (1985).

The "raised" object must be semantically related to the matrix S as well as to the complement (comp) S. For instance, in sentence (5a), which is assigned f-structure (12), the "raised" direct object realizes the thematic role *theme* of the proposition expressed by the matrix S. It also holds the *agent* role to the action expressed by the complement S. This would normally result in the addition of a subject. It is indeed a precondition that the direct object in the matrix S is coreferential with the subject in the complement S. However, the subject in the complement S is not realized because non-finite clauses never have subjects.

(12)

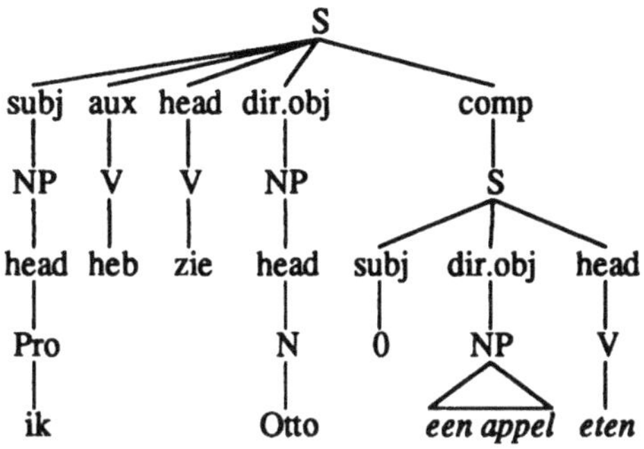

The discontinuity of the infinitival clause, as shown by means of underlining in (5), is accounted for by means of *clause union*: the complement S forms one surface unit with the matrix S. That is, the constituents of the embedded S are assigned positions in the holder of the matrix S. Although both infinitives collocate in one positional slot, the infinitives from deeper clauses– which are positioned later – are added at the end. The resulting c-structure is shown in (13).

(13)

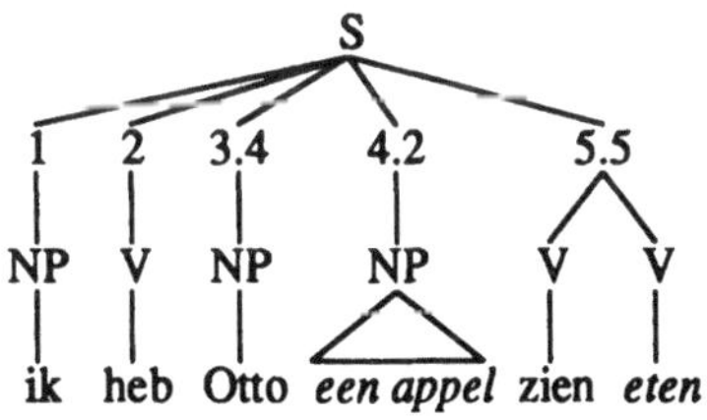

Clause union is brought about by the same destination mechanism which constructs "normal" c-structures. As mentioned in Section 4.4, the destination of a constituent is determined by its mother node in the f-structure. Normally, the mother assigns a dependent constituent a position in its own holder. However, clauses whose constituents are "raised" do not function as destinations. Rather, they use their mother nodes as the destination addresses for their constituents,[2] as shown in Figure 5.

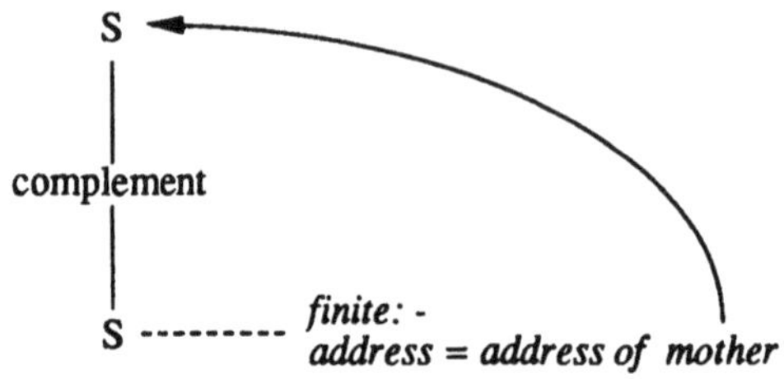

Figure 5. Segment for object complement clause.

Raised constituents may themselves contain raised constituents: pointers are followed step by step upward in the tree until a node is found which will function as the destination address. The infinitival complement S node itself occurs nowhere in the c-structure; since all its dependent constituents are put elsewhere, there is no need to assign it a position.

S-O raising requires substantial planning ahead: if only the subject and head are planned ahead and realized early, the sentence will come out as (14), where the first part cannot be complemented by an S-O raising construction, but can – in this case – be complemented with a finite subclause (a that-clause). In order for S-O raising to be successful in an incremental mode of generation, it is therefore necessary that the thematic roles involved in this construction are established well in advance.

(14) *Ik heb gezien dat hij een cake bakt.*
I have seen that he a cake bakes
'I have seen that he bakes a cake'

The requirement of semantic coreferentiality of the direct object of the matrix clause with the subject of the embedded clause may force a passivization, as shown in (15). Suppose that in an incremental mode of generation, the direct object of the matrix clause is generated first. If this constituent is coreferential with the direct object of the (active) embedded clause, then that clause cannot be realized as an active one, because coreferentiality with its subject is required. The lexicalization process may then apply lexical rules to the lemma of the embedded clause. Passivization will produce a lemma where the subject is coreferential with the direct object of the matrix clause.

(15) *Jan ziet Piet door Marie gekust worden.*
Jan sees Piet by Marie kissed be
'Jan sees Piet being kissed by Marie'

2.4 Cross-serial dependencies

When multiple instances of clause union are embedded in a finite subclause in Dutch, the c-structure may exhibit so-called cross-serial dependencies. Example (16a) is taken from Bresnan et al. (1982). The horizontal brackets indicate dependency relations between NPs and main verbs. In (16b), the vertical brackets indicate the grouping of constituents in surface positions. The German translation equivalent (16c) shows that the ordering of the infinitives is language-specific.

(16) a. *dat Jan Piet Marie zag helpen zwemmen.*
that Jan Piet Marie saw help swim
'that Jan saw Piet help Marie swim'
b. *dat Jan [Piet Marie] [zag helpen zwemmen]*
c. *daß Jan [Piet Marie] [schwimmen helfen sah]*

As shown in f-structure (17a), example (16a) is a doubly embedded S-O raising construction. The collocation of the raised objects in one surface position, as well as the collocation of the infinitives in one surface position, cf. (17b), is accomplished by clause union, as explained in Section 5.3.

(17a)

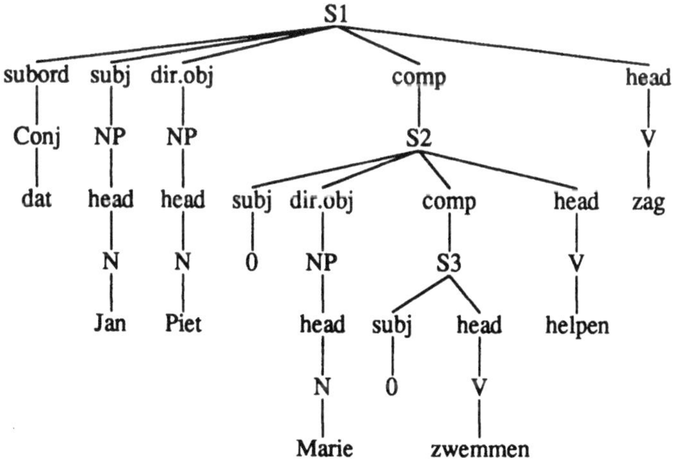

(17b)

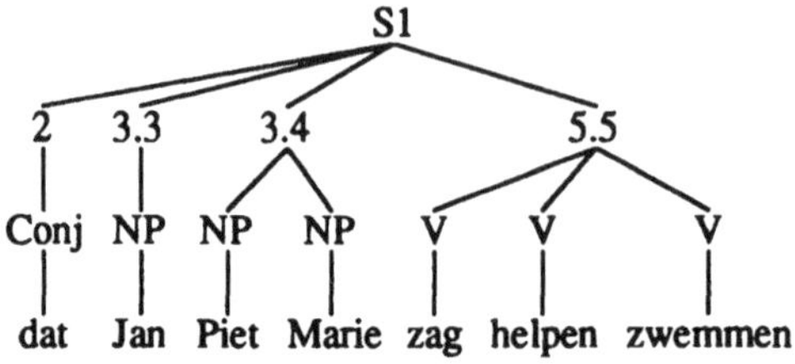

The relative ordering of objects and verbs remains to be explained. Recall that a single position in a holder can be occupied by a list of several constituents. For instance, the position of the clause-final verb cluster contains an ordered list of verbs. The relative ordering of the verbs follows from a rule which specifies that, in Dutch, constituents are by default added to the end of the list. Thus, the cross-serial pattern emerges quite automatically, since deeper embedded constituents are added later than shallower ones. For a language like German, which is quite similar but accumulates the verbs in the reverse order, the opposite rule which adds verbs to the front of the list is postulated (as suggested by Kempen – Hoenkamp 1987: 230). Finally, the English equivalent is simply accounted for by the absence of clause union, so that the embedded clauses are retained in the c-structure. It can be concluded that the same f-structure can easily account for the different surface phenomena in the three languages mentioned.

2.5 Unbounded dependencies

Interrogatives in Dutch are characterized by a marked word-order. Yes-no questions, for instance (18a), show subject-verb inversion. In wh-questions, the interrogative pronoun is normally fronted (18b) although this is not necessary (18c). Wh-fronting in itself is not seen as a discontinuity in SG. However, certain verbs allow a wh-constituent to escape from an embedded clause in order to be fronted in the matrix clause; this results in a discontinuity which will be called *wh-extraction* (18d). Optional fronting and possible resulting discontinuities are also observable with focused elements (18e), which suggests that wh-extraction and focus extraction can be treated in a similar fashion.

(18) a. *Eet Otto een appel?*
Eats Otto an apple
'Is Otto eating an apple?'

b. *Wat eet Otto?*
Wat eats Otto
'What is Otto eating?'

c. *Otto eet wat?*
Otto eats what
'Otto is eating what?'

d. *Wat denk je dat Otto eet?*
What think you that Otto eats
'What do you think Otto is eating?'

e. *Een appel denk ik dat Otto eet.*
An apple think I that Otto eats
'An apple I think Otto is eating.'

The treatment proposed below roughly follows the lines suggested by Kempen – Hoenkamp (1987: 231–238) but works more incrementally and is extended to cover focus fronting as well; actually, wh-constituents will be considered focused. The discontinuities are accounted for in terms of a non-isomorphism between corresponding f-structures and c-structures. A treatment similar to that of clause union may cause an embedded constituent to be "raised" to a higher level in the c-structure, where it occupies the clause-initial position, which is reserved for focused constituents. Let us now have a closer look at this process.

As with other word order variations, the temporal properties of the generation process are considered primarily responsible for the marked word order of focused constituents. It is assumed that those parts of the semantic input which are to be realized as focused constituents, are passed to the grammatical encoder at a very early stage in the sentence generation process. This causes them to occupy a sentence-initial position. However, if for some reason the focused semantic elements are not accessible in time, the grammatical encoder may already have assigned another constituent a position in the first holder slot. This may result in a question with unmarked (declarative) word order as in (18c).[3]

For sentences involving wh-extraction (18d) and focus extraction (18e), the moment when focused elements are accessible is important as well, but some additional machinery is necessary to allow the extraction of a constituent from an embedded clause to a higher level clause. This possibility must be indicated at the level of the lexical entry. Unlike clause union, where the destination of all constituents of a clause is transferred to a higher level, we must be more selective now. A special feature called *focus – destination*[4] is proposed, which handles the destination of focused elements. A focused element will first attempt to occupy a specified spot (position 1) in the holder of its focus-destination, otherwise it will go to its normal (default) destination. An analysis of (18d) is presented as f-structure (19a) and c-structure (19b).

(19) a.

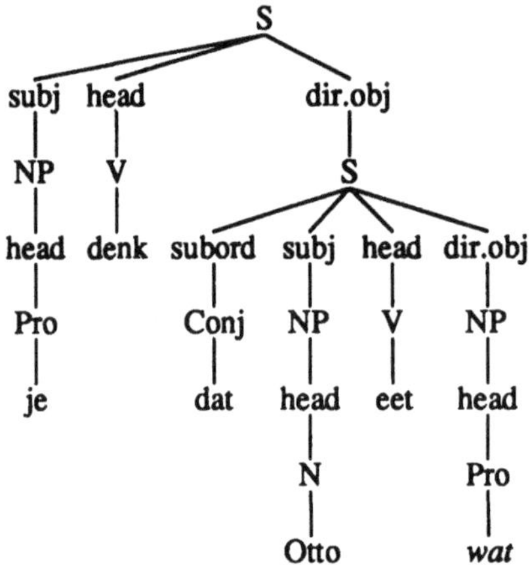

b.

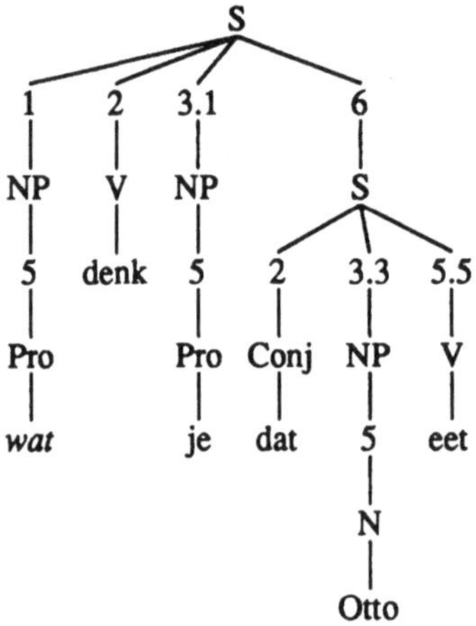

In lexical entries which allow focus extraction (and wh-extraction), this feature is specified on the segment for the object complement clause which is associated with the entry. If the lexical entry allows focus extraction, for instance Dutch *zeggen* 'to say' or *zien* 'to see', then the feature in the foot node of the segment S-direct-object-S will refer to the feature in the root node. This is schematically shown in Figure 6. If the lexical entry does not allow focus extraction, for instance Dutch *weten* 'to know', then the feature will be absent.

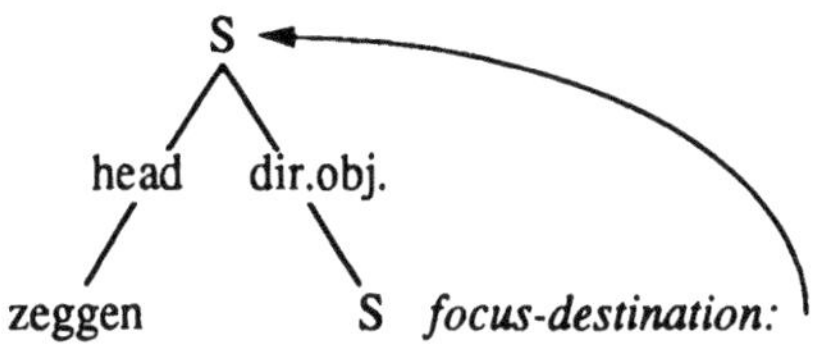

Figure 6. Dutch *zeggen* (to say) is a lexical entry allowing focus extraction.

In a fashion similar to the treatment of clause union, the value of the feature focus-destination may recursively refer upward in multiple embedded clauses. A remaining question is then, when and how to stop referring upward. In declarative clauses and direct questions, the final destination for focused elements is clearly the main clause. However, the mechanism should also work for indirect questions, for instance (20a,b), where the final destination of the focused element is a subordinate clause.

(20) a. *Ik weet wat je ziet dat Otto eet.*
I know what you see that Otto eats
'I know what you see Otto is eating'
b. *Ik weet dat je ziet wat Otto eet.*
I know that you see what Otto eats
'I know that you see what Otto is eating'

It seems to be necessary for grammatical encoding to know exactly which clause is being questioned. This can be indicated by means of a feature *interrogative* on the S in question. It is assumed that this feature has been set as a consequence of processing the semantic input structure. When such a feature is present, the focus-destination of an S refers to that S itself rather than upward.

2.6 Pronominal adverbs

The Dutch adverbs *er, daar* 'there' and *hier* 'here' sometimes serve as variants on the pronouns *het* 'it', *dat* 'that' and *dit* 'this' respectively, because the latter pronouns are not tolerated by many prepositions, for instance (21a).

This use of pronominal adverbs may result in a discontinuity of the prepositional phrase (cf. 21b).

(21) a. * *De vloeistof gaat nu <u>in</u> <u>het</u>.*
The liquid goes now in it
'The liquid now goes into it'
b. *De vloeistof gaat <u>er</u> nu <u>in</u>.*
The liquid goes there now in
'The liquid now goes into it'

Apparently *er* and the other "R-words" are part of the S at the level of c-structure and thus must be allowed to escape from the PPs where they belong in f-structure. The destination of *er* is in this case not the default, that is, its mother node in the f-structure, but the next higher node. This is a property of the lexical entries for the pronominal adverbs; so this exception does not interfere with the general mechanism. F-structure (22) shows the destination of the pronominal adverb in example (21b). The S holder uses slot 3.5 for this constituent.

(22)

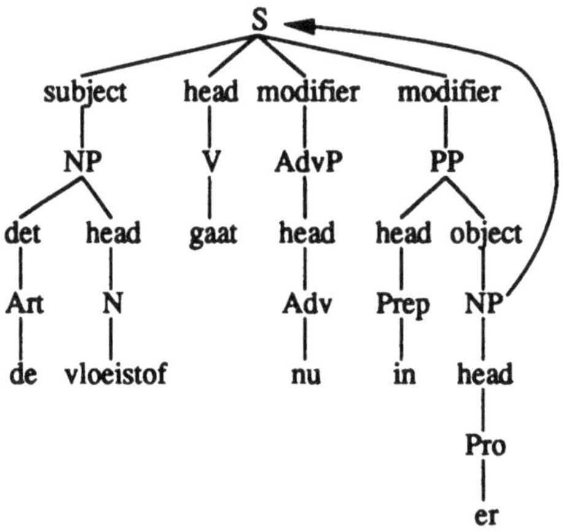

There are constraints on the number of occurrences of *er* in the same c-structure clause. For instance, suppose that the sentence gets an indefinite subject and is initiated by means of the "situating" *er*, as in (23a,b), then if a pronominal adverb *er* is present, one of the occurrences of *er* must be omitted (23b). We have not studied this phenomenon.

(23) a. *Er gaat een vloeistof in de fles.*
There goes a liquid into the bottle
'A liquid is poured into the bottle'
b. *Er gaat een vloeistof in.*
There goes a liquid in
'A liquid is poured into it'

2.7 Concluding remarks

We have presented discontinuities not only from a structural viewpoint but also from a processing viewpoint. Several kinds of discontinuities seem to offer advantages for an incremental strategy in sentence generation. This holds especially for the optional dislocations. Right dislocation allows the generator to utter constituents which are ready, and to postpone uttering more complex (or "heavy") ones, which are still being processed, to a later stage. In addition, right dislocation allows the incorporation of new semantic input as afterthoughts. Fronting of focused constituents is also natural in an incremental mode of generation if we assume that prominent concepts are passed on to the grammatical encoder earlier than other parts of the semantic input. In contrast, S-O raising benefits less from an incremental mode because it seems to require some planning ahead.

True discontinuities in SG are viewed as differences between ID relations in c-structures and those in corresponding f-structures. Constructions which are treated in this way include clause union, right dislocation, and fronting. Separable parts of words such as verbs and compound prepositions are not viewed as true discontinuities but have their origin in lexical entries consisting of multiple segments.

The use of c-structures in SG is somewhat similar to LFG, but contrasts with other approaches such as DPSG which are based on PS grammar. Whereas DPSG attempts to fit both functional relations and surface constituency into one structure, SG distinguishes between an unordered functional structure and an ordered constituent (surface) structure.

We make the following tentative generalizations about SG mechanisms for discontinuities. The destination of a constituent must always be a node which dominates it – but not necessarily immediately. There seem to be two major variants of the destination mechanism allowing constituents to go to nonimmediately dominating destinations. The first is root initiated. In these cases, for instance clause union, a node refers its constituents to another dominating node. This operation may be recursive. The second mechanism is foot initiated. In these cases, for instance, PPs with pronominal adverbs, a node directly presents itself to a higher-level destination.

Notes

1. A similar enterprise was undertaken by De Smedt (1993) for some aspects of word order variation.
2. The implementation of this rule is shown in De Smedt (1990a: 137–138).
3. Kempen – Hoenkamp (1987: 233) account for "declarative" word order in questions by assuming that wh-fronting occurs only in the presence of a special ?X tag. The treatment proposed in the current work does not rely on this special tag but exploits the incremental assignment of word order to choose between alternatives.
4. This feature takes the role of the variable wh-dest in IPG (Kempen – Hoenkamp 1987: 232).

References

Bresnan, J., R. Kaplan, S. Peters and A. Zaenen
1982 Cross-serial dependencies in Dutch. *Linguistic Inquiry* 13, 613-635.

Bunt, H.
1988 DPSG and its use in sentence generation from meaning representations. In: M. Zock and G. Sabah (ed.), *Advances in natural language generation,* Vol 2. London, Pinter Publishers, 1-26.

De Smedt, K.
1990a *Incremental sentence generation: a computer model of grammatical encoding*. Ph. D. dissertation. *NICI technical report 90-01*, NICI, University of Nijmegen, Nijmegen.

De Smedt, K.
1990b IPF: An incremental parallel formulator. In: R. Dale, C. Mellish and M. Zock (eds.), *Current research in natural language generation*. London, Academic Press, 167-192.

De Smedt, K.
1991 Parallelism in incremental sentence generation. In: G. Adriaens and U. Hahn (eds.), *Parallel models of natural language computation*. Norwood, NJ, Ablex.

De Smedt, K. and G. Kempen
1987 Incremental sentence production, self-correction and coordination. In: G. Kempen (ed.), *Natural language generation: new results in Artificial Intelligence, psychology and linguistics*. Dordrecht/Boston/Lancaster, Kluwer Academic Publishers, 365-376.
De Smedt, K. and G. Kempen
1991 Segment Grammar: a formalism for incremental sentence generation. In: C. Paris, W. Swartout and W. Mann (eds.), *Natural language generation in Artificial Intelligence and Computational Linguistics*. Boston/Dordrecht/London, Kluwer Academic Publishers, 329-349.
Horn, G.
1985 Raising and complementation. *Linguistics* 23, 813-850.
Kaplan, R. and J. Bresnan
1982 Lexical-functional grammar: A formal system for grammatical representation. In: J. Bresnan (ed.), *The mental representation of grammatical relations*. Cambridge, MA, MIT Press, 173-281.
Kempen, G.
1987 A framework for incremental syntactic tree formation. *Proceedings of the 10th IJCAI, Milan*, Los Altos, Morgan Kaufmann, 655-660.
Kempen, G. and E. Hoenkamp
1987 An incremental procedural grammar for sentence formulation. *Cognitive Science* 11, 201-258.

Discontinuity and the *wat voor*-construction

Norbert Corver

Abstract. This paper examines the internal syntax and the movement behavior of the interrogative *wat voor (een) N*-phrase in Dutch. It is argued that this noun phrase consists of an interrogative nonargument *wat*, which functions as the head of the noun phrase, and a predicative PP headed by *voor*, which is adjoined to *wat*. On the basis of this structure, an analysis of the discontinuous *wat voor (een) N*-phrase will be presented within the Barriers-framework as proposed in Chomsky (1986).

1. Introduction

This paper investigates the internal syntax and the movement behavior of a particular type of interrogative noun phrase in Dutch, namely the *wat voor (een) N*-noun phrase (literally: what for (a) N; meaning: 'what kind of N').[1] This phrase asks for the nature, quality or sort of person, thing or object. It further has the property of allowing subextraction of the left branch question element *wat*, yielding a discontinuous pattern. So, besides removal of the entire noun phrase to [Spec,CP] as in (1a), extraction only of *wat* is permitted as well (as in (1b)).[2]

(1) a. *[Wat voor honden]$_i$ heb je t_i gezien?*
What for dogs have you seen
'What kind of dogs did you see?'
b. *Wat$_i$ heb je [t_i voor honden] gezien?*
What have you for dogs seen
'What kind of dogs did you see?'

The paper is organized as follows. First, I will examine the external and internal structure of the *wat voor (een) N*-phrase. A number of syntactic phenomena will be discussed which have led to the proposal in the literature that the N is the head of the entire noun phrase, and *wat voor (een)* some sort of complex specifier of the noun. Next, I will present an alternative analysis of the internal structure, arguing that *wat* is the head of the noun phrase and *voor een N* a predicative PP, which is adjoined to *wat*. Finally, an account will be given of the (im)possibility of various discontinuous *wat voor*-patterns.

2. Some notes on the internal and external structure

Externally the *wat voor (een) N*-phrase is a noun phrase.[3] It occurs as complement of verbs that are subcategorized for noun phrases (see (2a)); it can undergo noun phrase-movement, as in the raising construction (2b);

(2) a. Wat voor een hond$_i$ heb jij t$_i$ geslagen?
What for a dog have you hit
b. Wat voor een man$_i$ schijnt t$_i$ deze talen te spreken?
What for a man seems these languages to speak

With respect to the internal structure of this noun phrase, the question arises how the phrase breaks down into smaller constituents. According to previous analyses of the *wat voor*-construction (Bennis 1983; Den Besten 1985) a phrase like *wat voor een hond* should be analyzed as follows: The noun *hond* is the head of the phrase and the string *wat voor (een)* is a complex specifier of the noun. A first argument for considering the noun which follows the preposition *voor* to be the head of the *wat voor*-phrase comes from the subject-finite verb agreement phenomenon. If the interrogative phrase *wat voor (een) N* is subject of a finite clause, then the finite verb agrees in number with the headnoun. If *wat* is the headnoun, we would expect that the finite verb is always singular, since this question word has the lexical property of being [+singular], as opposed to the question word *wie* 'who', for example, that can be both [+ singular] and [+plural]. This is exemplified in (3) below.

(3) a. *Ik weet niet wat hem heeft/ *hebben gebeten.*
I know not what him has/ have bitten
b. *Ik weet niet wie hem heeft/ hebben gebeten.*
I know not who him has/ have bitten

Consider now (4):

(4) *Ik weet niet [wat voor honden] mij *heeft / hebben gebeten.*
I know not what for dogs me *has / have bitten
'I don't know what kind of dogs have bitten me.'

This sentence suggest that the noun *honden* is the head of the noun phrase *wat voor honden,* since that noun agrees with the finite verb.

A second argument in favor of an analysis in which the noun following *voor* is the head of the *wat voor*-phrase comes from the binding requirement that the reciprocal *elkaar* 'each other' requires a [+plural] antecedent (Bennis 1983). If the [-plural] *wat* were the head of the noun phrase, we would expect that the noun phrase headed by *wat* cannot bind the [+ plural] reciprocal *elkaar.* If, on the other hand, the noun following *voor* is the head of the interrogative phrase, then it is predicted that the noun phrase can bind *elkaar* in case this noun is [+ plural]. Now, the following fact shows that the *wat voor*-noun phrase can bind a reciprocal, and therefore suggests that the noun following *voor* is the head of the interrogative phrase.

(5) *Wat voor honden$_i$ hebben elkaar$_i$ gebeten?*
What for dogs have each other bitten
'What kind of dogs have bitten each other?'

Another important fact about the *wat voor*-construction is that the preposition *voor* does not have any case assigning function within the noun phrase (Den Besten 1985). Although this is not visible in Dutch (since Dutch lacks overt case realizations), the German *was für*-construction clearly shows that the material following the preposition *für,* which usually assigns accusative case, does not receive case from this preposition. Consider, for example, the following sentence:

(6) *[Mit [was für einem Mann/ *einen Mann]] haben Sie*
With what for a-DAT man/ *a-ACC man have you
gesprochen?
spoken

Einem Mann bears dative case. It cannot receive this case from *für.* Instead, it receives its case from the preposition *mit,* a dative case assigner. One could argue that this absence of case assignment by the P *voor/für* is due to the fact that being part of the specifier it does not govern the noun (N) and therefore cannot assign accusative case to it.

In order to account for the discontinuous *wat voor*-phrases such as (1b), the above-mentioned previous analyses of the *wat voor*-construction make use of restructuring processes which make the left branch element *wat*, which is part of the complex specifier, accessible to wh-movement without violating such principles as the Subjacency Condition or the Empty Category Principle (ECP).[4] In the next section I will investigate the *wat voor*-phrase more closely and propose a different internal structure, on the basis of which I will present an analysis of the split *wat voor*-phrases.

3. An alternative analysis

I assume that the proper analysis for the *wat voor*-phrase is the one given in (7):

(7)

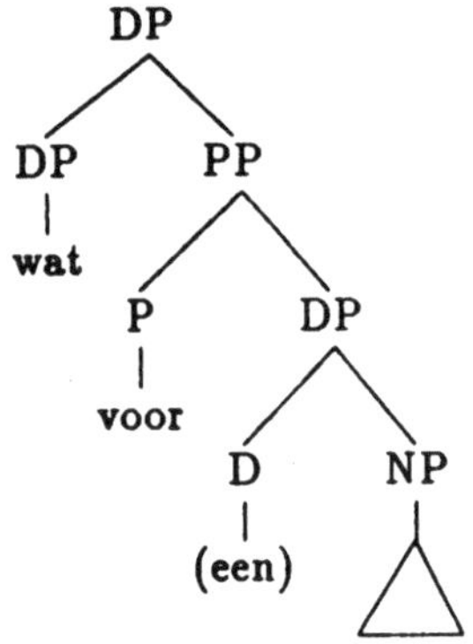

The interrogative element *wat* is the head of this phrase and the string *voor (een) hond* 'for (a) dog' forms a PP which is base-adjoined to DP. The optional indefinite article *een* occupies the lower D-position and takes an NP-complement (i.c. *hond*).

Let us turn to some arguments in favor of this structure. For the sake of simplicity of argumentation, I will begin with the issue of the constituenthood of the string *voor (een) N*. A first piece of evidence for the constituenthood of this string is the fact that it is possible to extrapose it (i.e. it can be moved to a postverbal position):[5]

(8) *Wat heb je gezien [voor honden]?*
What have you seen for dogs

As is well-known, only constituents can be moved. Notice also that the extraposability suggests that *voor een N* is a PP and not, for example, a noun phrase, since generally noun phrases cannot undergo extraposition in Dutch.

Another argument in favor of the constituenthood of *voor (een) N* comes from coordination. Under the assumption that only constituents can be coordinated, consider the various coordination patterns that are possible with the *wat voor*-phrase.

(9) a. *[[Wat voor honden] en [wat voor katten]] heb jij gezien?*
What for dogs and what for cats have you seen
b. *[Wat [[voor honden] en [voor katten]]] heb jij gezien?*
What for dogs and for cats have you seen
c. *[Wat voor [[honden] en [katten]] heb jij gezien?*
What for dogs and cats have you seen
'What kind of dogs and what kind of cats did you see?'

(9a) is a coordination of two *wat voor*-phrases (i.e. DP's). (9b) exemplifies a coordination of the PP *voor DP*. Note that this supports the assumption that *voor DP* forms a constituent. (9c), finally, could be analyzed as a coordination of two NPs. Note that the coordination pattern (9b) is unexpected under an analysis in which *wat voor (een)* is a complex specifier forming a constituent, since under such an analysis *voor honden* and *voor katten* are not constituents.

So far I have motivated the fact that the string *voor DP* is a PP. I have further made the assumption that *wat* is a DP, and that PP is base-adjoined to it. The question arises whether there is any evidence for this adjunction structure. Why not assume, for example, that the PP voor DP is a sister of D, as in (10)?

(10)

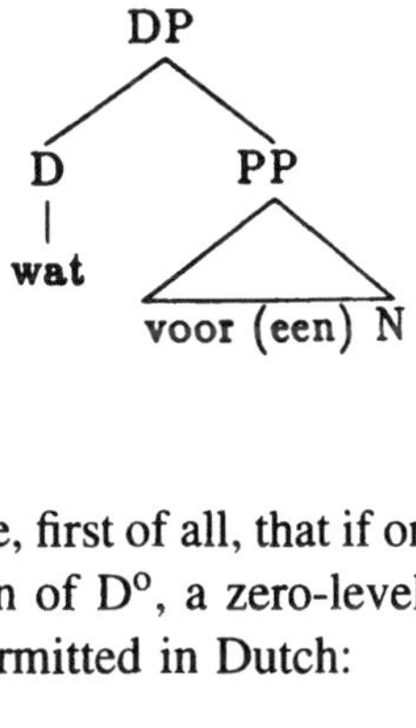

Notice, first of all, that if one adopts structure (10), removal of *wat* involves extraction of D°, a zero-level category. Extraction of determiners, however, is not permitted in Dutch:

(11) **De/deze$_i$ heb jij [$_{DP}$ t_i honden] gezien.*
The/these have you dogs seen

Within a Barriers system (Chomsky 1986), the nonextractability of determiners can be accounted for as follows. Since the D, being a head, cannot adjoin to VP, movement out of the DP will always yield an ECP-violation, because there is no local antecedent governor for the trace in D°-position. The Subjacency Condition will be violated as well, since the fronted D° can neither adjoin to VP nor to IP and therefore will cross two L-barriers (IP by inheritance). Furthermore, if the structure preservingness hypothesis applies to substitution, the D° cannot be moved into [Spec,CP] because that position only allows maximal projections.

So, if one adopts a structure like (10), a subextraction analysis of the split *wat voor*-pattern is no longer possible. Notice that an analysis in which the PP is extraposed to a position external to the *wat voor*-phrase (either before or after moving the *wat voor*-phrase to [Spec,CP]) is not adequate, since extraposition would always move the extraposed PP to a postverbal position and consequently would always generate structures such as (8) but not such as (1b).

A piece of evidence which seems to support the adjunction structure given in (7) is based on the behavior of certain lexical items in Dutch which typically "hang around" (i.e. are adjoined to) maximal projections: *ongeveer* 'about/approximately', *zoal* 'among others', *precies* 'exactly', etc. As the following example shows, these so-called free adjuncts can appear in different positions within the *wat voor*-phrase, one of the positions being in between *wat* and the PP.

(12) a. *[Ongeveer wat voor een bedrag] heb jij uitgegeven?*
Approximately what for an amount have you spent
'How much money approximately did you spend?'
b. *[Wat ongeveer voor een bedrag] heb jij uitgegeven?*
c. *[Wat voor een bedrag ongeveer] heb jij uitgegeven?*

Notice that in these sentences the *wat voor*-phrases containing the free adjunct-like element occupy [Spec,CP], which shows that they are really constituents.[6] The question now arises whether in the b-sentence the free adjunct *ongeveer* is attached to the DP *wat* or to the PP *voor (een) N*. The fact that it can reasonably well move along with the fronted interrogative element *wat*, but not with the extraposed PP *voor een bedrag* suggests that it is adjoined to the former.

(13) a. *?Wat ongeveer heb jij voor een bedrag uitgegeven?*
b. **Wat heb jij uitgegeven ongeveer voor een bedrag?*

Now that we know that the free adjunct *ongeveer* in the *wat voor*-phrase *wat ongeveer voor een bedrag* is base-adjoined to the maximal projection *wat* (i.e. DP), the conclusion must be that the PP headed by *voor*, which follows the DP *wat ongeveer*, is also adjoined to the maximal projection DP.[7]

Having established the internal syntax of the *wat voor*-phrase, let us discuss the semantic and syntactic properties of the question word *wat* in the *wat voor*-construction, starting with its categorial status. On the basis of its identity to the question word *wat* and in the absence of evidence to the contrary, I propose that *wat* is a nominal element (i.e. DP). A piece of evidence in favor of its nominal status comes from the categorial matching condition on free relative constructions in Dutch (Bennis 1983). If the free relative is in a position where noun phrases may occur, then there can only be a nominal element (e.g. relative pronoun) in the COMP of the free relative (Groos — Van Riemsdijk 1981). The following sentence shows that *wat* can occur in the COMP-position (or better [Spec,CP]) of a free relative clause which appears in a typical noun phrase position. This suggests that *wat* is a nominal element.

(14) *Piet droeg [wat Karel voor kleren droeg]*
Pete wore what Charles for clothes wore
'Pete wore the sorts of clothes that Charles wore.'

Another question with respect to *wat* concerns the semantic status of this element, i.e. is it an argument expression (i.e. an element bearing an internal or external theta-role) or not? Notice first of all, that *wat* in the *wat voor*-construction differs from the "normal" question word *wat* in that it does not have a non-interrogative counterpart.

(15) a. *Wat$_i$ heeft Jan t_i gekocht?*
What has John bought
b. *Jan heeft dat gekocht.*
John has that bought

(16) a. *Wat$_i$ heeft Jan [t_i voor boeken] gekocht?*
What has John for books bought
b. **Jan heeft dat voor boeken gekocht.*
John has that for books bought

The nonargument status of *wat* in the *wat voor*-phrase is suggested by some other properties of this question word. First, as is well-known, extraction of argument noun phrases out of wh-islands is much better than extractions of nonarguments out of these island configurations. Argument extractions only yield Subjacency violations, but nonargument extractions violate both the Subjacency Condition and the ECP. Notice now the following sentences:

(17) a. ??*[Wat]$_i$ vraag jij je af [wanneer Jo t_i gekocht heeft]?*
What wonder you REFL PRT when Joe bought has
'What do you wonder when John bought?'
b. **[Wat]$_i$ vraag jij je af [wanneer Jo [t_i voor boeken] gekocht heeft?*
What wonder you REFL PRT when Joe for books bought has

In (17a), the argument noun phrase *wat* has been moved out of a wh-island, yielding a Subjacency violation. The b-sentence, in which *wat* has been removed from a *wat voor*-phrase is much worse, since it violates both the ECP and the Subjacency Condition.

A second argument comes from parasitic gap constructions. As is well-known, a fronted argument noun phrase can be the antecedent for a parasitic gap, as is shown in (18a). Notice now that the fronted *wat* in (18b), which is extracted from a *wat voor*-phrase, cannot license a parasitic gap. This asymmetry suggests that the question phrase *wat* in the *wat voor*-phrase is not an argument expression.

(18) a. *Wat$_i$ heeft Jan [zonder [pg te lezen]] t_i weggegooid?*
What has John without to read thrown-away
b. **Wat$_i$ heeft Jan [zonder [pg voor tijdschriften] te lezen]* [t_i *voor boeken] weggegooid?*
What has John without for magazines to read for books thrown-away

Given these facts, I will assume that the DP *wat* is not an argument expression but a kind of interrogative nonargument expression. The entire *wat voor*-phrase, however, is an argument noun phrase receiving an internal or external theta-role from some theta-assigner. The fact that movement of it across a wh-island only yields a weak subjacency violation and the fact that it can license a parasitic gap are in accordance with its argument status:

(19) a. ??*[Wat voor boeken]$_i$ vraag jij e af [wanneer*
What for books wonder you REFL PRT when
Jo t_i gekocht heeft]?
Joe bought has
b. *Wat voor boeken$_i$ heeft Jan [zonder [t_i te lezen]] t_i*
What for books has John without to read
weggegooid?
thrown-away

Given this interpretation of *wat*, how do we analyze the PP headed by *voor*? I assume that it behaves as a secondary predicate with regard to *wat*. It specifies some type or property of the interrogative word *wat*.

The interpretation of *voor een N* as a predicative phrase is justified by the fact that the preposition *voor* can head a predicate PP in other contexts as well.[8] This is exemplified in (20):

(20) a. *Ik schold hem uit voor slappeling.*
'I called him a weakling'
b. *Ik maakte hem uit voor (een) bedrieger.*
'I called him an impostor'

Notice also that it is possible for other noun phrases that are not true arguments to be linked to secondary predicates:

(21) a. *Het ruikt er als een beerput.*
It smells there like a cesspool
b. *Het regent [als een gek].*
It rains like a fool
'It rains very heavily'

In terms of my analysis of the *wat voor*-phrase, the various syntactic phenomena discussed in the previous section (i.e. subject-verb agreement, binding of the reciprocal *elkaar*, absence of case assignment by the P *voor*) can be accounted for in a straightforward way. Let us first consider the absence of case assignment by *voor*. Recall that there are two nominal elements inside the *wat voor*-phrase, *wat* and the noun phrase (i.e. DP) following *voor*. Both need case in order not to violate the Case Filter. That noun phrases which are arguments need case is shown by the following facts:

(22) a. *It$_i$ seems [t_i to rain].*

b. **It was believed it to rain.*

Sentence (22a) is well-formed because the quasi-argument *it* receives nominative case after it has been raised into the subject position of the matrix clause. (22b), however, is ruled out by the Case Filter, since the quasi-argument *it* in the embedded clause cannot receive case from a governor.

I assume that *wat* receives its case as follows: Case is assigned to the entire *wat voor*-phrase and it percolates down to the head of this phrase, which is the DP *wat*. How does the nominal following *voor* receive its case? I assume that it receives its case from *wat* under predication. In fact, this case assignment procedure can be found in other syntactic environments as well. Consider, for example, the following sentences from German (van Riemsdijk 1983).

(23) a. *Ich behandelte [den Mann] [wie [einen Bruder]].*
I treated the man-ACC as a brother-ACC
b. *Er schreit [wie [ein Rasender]].*
He-NOM cries like a madman-NOM

These sentences show that the predicate nominal after *wie* must agree in morphological case with the noun it modifies. So, in fact, the non-case assigning property of the preposition *voor/für* in the *wat voor*-construction is not exceptional at all. The noun phrase-complement of the preposition receives its case via a normal case assignment procedure, viz. predication.

The agreement facts also follow from the predication structure. Recall that the argument question word *wat* is [+ singular]. The same holds for its non-interrogative counterpart *het*. The inherent [+ singular] feature of the argument *het* makes it impossible to combine it with a plural verb, as in (24).

(24) *Het staat/ *staan in de kast.*
It stands/ *stand in the cupboard

In predicative structures, however, the subject pronouns *het/wat* can cooccur with plural finite verbs. This is illustrated below:[9]

(25) a. *Het zijn/ *is grote honden.*
It are/ *is big dogs
b. *Wat worden/ *wordt grote honden?*
What become/ *becomes big dogs

It is typical of these predicative constructions that the predicate nominal determines the agreement relation with the finite verb. This can be formalized by having a coindexing relation between the predicate nominal and the subject. So, in a way, the subject noun phrase inherits the agreement features ([+ plural] in (25)) from the predicate nominal under predication. So, the property of *wat* in the *wat voor*-phrase of receiving number features from its predicate is a much more general syntactic phenomenon. The subject-verb agreement phenomenon is not an argument in favor of considering the non-interrogative noun in the string *wat voor een N* as the head of the entire phrase. The DP *wat* gets its person/number features from the nominal contained within the PP under predication. These features percolate upwards to the dominating (subject) DP (i.e. the highest DP in (7)) which enters into an agreement relation with the finite verb.

The binding phenomena can also be explained under my analysis. Recall that the fact that a subject *wat voor*-phrase could bind the plural anaphor *elkaar* was considered an argument in favor of interpreting the non-interrogative noun within the interrogative phrase as the head of the entire phrase. This binding fact, however, also follows from an analysis in which *wat* is the head of the entire phrase. As I have argued, *wat* receives the [+plural]-feature under predication from its predicate attribute. This plural-feature percolates to the dominating DP, and hence the [+ plural] DP can bind *elkaar*.

4. Discontinuity in the *wat voor*-construction

Having established the internal structure of the *wat voor*-phrase, I will proceed with an analysis of the discontinuous *wat voor*-construction. The following examples show that the split pattern can occur in certain syntactic environments, but not in others (Den Besten 1985):

(26) a. *Wat heb jij [- voor boeken] gelezen?*
What have you for books read
'What sort of books have you read?'

b. *Wat ben jij [[- voor talen] machtig]?*
What are you for languages competent
'What sort of languages do you master?'

c. **Wat hebben [- voor mensen] hun huis verkocht?*
What have for persons their house sold
'What kind of people have sold their house?'

d. **Wat heb jij [op [- voor iemand]] gerekend?*
What have you on for someone counted
'What kind of person have you counted on?'

In (26a), *wat* has been reordered out of a direct object *wat voor*-phrase. Neither the Subjacency Condition nor the ECP is violated, since the fronted *wat* can reach the [Spec,CP] without crossing any L-barrier (i.e. a maximal projection which is not L-marked). The direct object-DP itself is L-marked (i.e. assigned a theta-role by a lexical category) and therefore not an L-barrier. The potential barrierhood of VP can be voided via adjunction to it, and IP is not an L-barrier (although a BC) by stipulation.

In (26b), *wat* has been removed from within the DP-complement of the adjective *machtig*. It can be fronted to [Spec,CP] without violating ECP or subjacency in the following way: It can leave the object-DP, which is L-marked by the adjective, and subsequently move to [Spec,CP] via intermediate adjunctions to AP and VP, which are both non-argument type categories and therefore can function as hosts for adjunction operations.

Sentence (26c) involves extraction of *wat* from within the subject-DP. Note that the subject-DP is not L-marked and therefore is an L-barrier. Movement of *wat* to [Spec,CP] does not violate subjacency, however, since it crosses only one L-barrier, viz. IP, which inherits barrierhood from the subject-DP. Notice that the subject-DP is not an L-barrier for *wat*, since *wat* is not dominated by this category because only one segment of DP contains *wat*. Although subextraction does not violate the Subjacency Condition, it does violate ECP. The moved question word *wat* occupying [Spec,CP] does not antecedent govern the trace within the DP, because IP is an intervening L-barrier.

In (26d), *wat* has been removed from within the DP-complement of a preposition. DP is L-marked by the P, and the PP is L-marked by the verb. So, *wat* can move to [Spec,CP] via adjunction to VP, without violating subjacency. Notice, however, that this extraction violates ECP. Of course, not because of the intervening L-barriers, as we have just seen. But Minimality is violated.[10] Note that the moved *wat* cannot adjoin to PP, since the latter is an argument type category. Hence, the first adjunction site is VP. The intermediary trace adjoined to VP does not antecedent govern the trace in DP, because PP is a M-barrier. It is a M-barrier, because it contains (i) the trace itself, (ii) a maximal projection including the trace (namely PP), and (iii) a head c-commanding the trace (i.e. P).

Consider also the ill-formedness of the sentences b and c in the paradigm below:

(27) a. *Wat voor een boek heb jij gekocht?*
What for a book have you bought
'What kind of book did you buy?'
b. **Wat voor een heb jij boek gekocht?*
c. *Wat voor heb jij een boek gekocht?*
d. **Wat heb jij voor een boek gekocht?*

In (27a) the entire *wat voor*-phrase is fronted, and in (27d) only the interrogative phrase *wat*. (27b and c) are ruled out by the principle which states that Move alpha can only apply to constituents. The strings *wat voor een* and *wat voor* do not form constituents and therefore cannot be extracted.

In conclusion, the presence or absence of discontinuous *wat voor*-phrases in various syntactic environments can be accounted for in terms of the Subjacency Condition and the ECP on the basis of the internal structure of the *wat voor*-phrase which has been defended in this paper.

Acknowledgements. I am grateful to Henk van Riemsdijk for his comments on an earlier version of this paper. I would also like to thank for discussion the participants in the Grammaticamodellen seminar at Tilburg University and the audience at the symposium on discontinuous constituency. All errors are mine.

Notes

1. This type of interrogative phrase also appears in other Germanic languages such as German (Den Besten 1985) and Norwegian (Lie 1982).
2. The extractability of the left branch question element *wat* from within a noun phrase is exceptional, since generally subextraction of a left branch specifier or modifier from within a noun phrase is impossible in Dutch.
3. I will assume the so-called Determiner Phrase-hypothesis for nominals in this paper. According to this analysis, (cf. Brame 1981; Abney 1987), the determiner heads the maximal projection DP and takes an NP-complement. For the sake of

clarity, I will still use the term 'noun phrase' to refer to DPs in the text. When I use 'NP', I refer to the complement of D.

4. Reasons of space prevent me from discussing and criticizing these previous analyses. See Corver (1990) for discussion.
5. For some speakers of Dutch these sentences sound odd. They agree, however, that they are much better than sentences in which a noun phrase is extraposed (as in (i)):
   (i) **Ik geloof dat Jan* t_i *las [dit boek]*$_i$.
   I believe that John read this book
6. I should say that speakers of Dutch sometimes differ in their acceptability judgments of these sentences. This is related to the fact that for some of these speakers these free adjuncts have a greater freedom of position than others. All speakers I have consulted, however, agree that a sentence like (12b) is much better than for example, the b-sentence in the following paradigm:
   (a) *[Ongeveer welk bedrag] vind je aanvaardbaar?*
   Approximately which amount consider you acceptable
   (b) ***[Welk ongeveer bedrag] vind je aanvaardbaar?*
   (c) *[Welk bedrag ongeveer] vind je aanvaardbaar?*
   In (a) and (c), the free adjunct is respectively left-adjoined and right-adjoined to the DP which is headed by the determiner *welk*. The illformedness of (b) is caused by the fact that the NP-complement *bedrag*, which is selected by the determiner *welk*, is not a sister of this functional category because of the intervening free adjunct which is adjoined to DP.
7. Note that the following orders are also possible:
   (a) *Wat heb jij ongeveer voor een bedrag uitgegeven?*
   (b) *Wat heb jij ongeveer uitgegeven voor een bedrag?*
   (c) *Wat ongeveer heb jij uitgegeven voor een bedrag?*
   In (a), the interrogative element *wat* is fronted to [Spec,CP], leaving behind the free adjunct. In (b), the PP headed by *voor* has been extraposed and *wat* has been fronted. In (c), the PP is extraposed and *wat* is moved to [Spec,CP] together with the free adjunct.
8. In English, The preposition *for* can also be used as a predicative adjunct, as is shown by the following examples:
   (a) *John mistook her [for a foreigner].*
   (b) *They had duck [for dinner] yesterday.*
9. Notice that *het* can also appear as subject of a [+plural] predicate (*dogs*) in the following small clause structures, which are also predication configurations:
   (a) *Ik vind het mooie honden.*
   I consider it beautiful dogs
   (b) *Wat vind jij mooie honden?*
   What consider you beautiful dogs

10. I assume the following definition of Minimality: A is a Minimality-barrier for B iff A includes B, D (an X^0 c-commander of B), and G (a maximal projection not necessarily distinct from A) (Chomsky 1986: class lectures Fall).

References

Abney, S.
1987 The English noun phrase in its sentential aspect. Unpublished Ph.D. Dissertation, MIT.

Bennis, H.
1983 A case of restructuring. In: Bennis, H. and W. van Lessen Kloeke (eds.), *Linguistics in the Netherlands*. Dordrecht, Foris.

Besten, H. den
1985 The ergative hypothesis and free word order in Dutch and German. In: Toman I. (ed.), *Studies in German grammar*. Dordrecht, Foris.

Brame, M.
1981 The general theory of binding and fusion. *Linguistic Analysis* 7.3.

Chomsky, N.
1986 *Barriers*, MIT Press, Cambridge (MA).

Corver, N.
1990 The syntax of left branch extractions. Unpublished Doctoral dissertation, Tilburg, Tilburg University.

Groos, A. and H. van Riemsdijk
1981 Matching effects in free relatives, a parameter of core grammar. In: A. Belletti et al. (eds.), *Theory of Markedness in generative grammar: proceedings of the 1979 GLOW conference*, Pisa, Scuola Normale Superiore.

Lie, S.
1982 Discontinuous questions and subjacency in Norwegian, In: E. Engdahl and E. Ejerhed (eds.), *Readings on unbounded dependencies in Scandinavian languages*. Umea.

Riemsdijk, H. van
1983 The case of German adjectives. In: F. Heny et al. (eds.), *Linguistic categories: auxiliaries and related puzzles*. Dordrecht, Reidel.

Generalized quantifiers and discontinuous type constructors*

Michael Moortgat

1. A sign-based categorial framework

This paper investigates discontinuous type constructors within the framework of a sign-based generalization of categorial type calculi. The paper takes its inspiration from Oehrle's (1988) work on generalized compositionality for multidimensional linguistic objects, and, we hope, may establish a bridge between work in Unification Categorial Grammar or HPSG, and the research that views categorial grammar from the perspective of substructural type logics. Categorial sequents are represented as composed of multidimensional *signs*, modelled as tuples of the form

$$\langle Type; Semantics; Syntax \rangle$$

They simultaneously characterize the semantic and structural properties of linguistic objects in terms of a type-assignment labelled with semantic information (a lambda term) and structural, syntactic information. As argued elsewhere (Moortgat 1988), the structural information refers to *phonological* structuring of linguistic material, rather than to syntactic structure in the conventional sense. For the purposes of this paper, structural information is simplified to a string description.

The move to a sign-based perspective requires adjustment in the logical machinery of sequent calculus. The inference rules that decompose complex types into their subtypes simultaneously specify the corresponding operations in the semantic and string algebras. Linearization of the terminal string is expressed in terms of *string equations*, and resolution proof search is extended with string unification, along the lines of Calder's (1989) work on morphology. Within this framework, we present a complete logic for extraction '$\uparrow$' and infixation '$\downarrow$' type constructors, improving on our earlier proposals. Finally, we introduce a generalized quantifier type constructor $q(A; B; C)$, definable in terms of '$\uparrow$' and '$\downarrow$', and indicate how this can lead to a uniform approach to binding phenomena in categorial terms.

1.1 Types and terms

Categorial type deductions can be associated with a lambda recipe coding their meaning along the lines of the so-called Curry-Howard correspondence. We take this correspondence between proofs and semantic recipes as our starting point and show in the next section that the approach can be generalized to other dimensions, such as the dimension of linguistic structure.

Consider first the Curry-Howard correspondence between categorial proofs and lambda terms. In order to associate a lambda term with the proof of a sequent $\Gamma \vdash B$, we associate each antecedent type $A \in \Gamma$ with a fresh parameter of the appropriate type, and compute the lambda term for the succedent type B in terms of these parameters, as indicated in Figure 1. Some notational conventions: Greek uppercase letters are used as variables over sequences of tuples $\langle Type, Term \rangle$, C as a variable over a tuple $\langle Type, Term \rangle$. The antecedent must be non-empty. For the directional Lambek system **L**, the antecedent has to be interpreted as a *sequence*, i.e. the comma in Δ, Γ represents the concatenation of the sequences Δ and Γ. In order to obtain the non-directional system **LP**, one can add a structural rule of Permutation to the set of inference rules, or alternatively interpret the comma in the antecedent as multiset union rather than concatenation.

$$[\mathrm{Ax}]\frac{}{\langle A,t\rangle \vdash \langle A,u\rangle}\quad \{u=t\}$$

$$[\mathrm{R}/]\frac{\mathrm{T},\langle B,v\rangle \vdash \langle A,u\rangle}{\mathrm{T}\vdash \langle A/B,\lambda v.u\rangle} \qquad [\mathrm{L}/]\frac{\mathrm{T}\vdash \langle B,u\rangle \quad \Gamma,\langle A,tu\rangle,\Lambda \vdash C}{\Gamma,\langle A/B,t\rangle,\mathrm{T},\Lambda \vdash C}$$

$$[\mathrm{R}\backslash]\frac{\langle B,v\rangle,\mathrm{T} \vdash \langle A,u\rangle}{\mathrm{T}\vdash \langle B\backslash A,\lambda v.u\rangle} \qquad [\mathrm{L}\backslash]\frac{\mathrm{T}\vdash \langle B,u\rangle \quad \Gamma,\langle A,tu\rangle,\Lambda \vdash C}{\Gamma,\mathrm{T},\langle B\backslash A,t\rangle,\Lambda \vdash C}$$

$$[\mathrm{L}\bullet]\frac{\Gamma,\langle A,\pi_0(t)\rangle,\langle B,\pi_1(t)\rangle,\Lambda \vdash C}{\Gamma,\langle A\bullet B,t\rangle,\Lambda \vdash C} \qquad [\mathrm{R}\bullet]\frac{\Delta\vdash \langle A,u\rangle \quad \mathrm{T}\vdash\langle B,v\rangle}{\Delta,\mathrm{T}\vdash \langle A\bullet B,\langle u,v\rangle\rangle}$$

$$[\mathrm{Cut}]\frac{\mathrm{T}\vdash \langle A,u\rangle \quad \Gamma,\langle A,t\rangle,\Gamma' \vdash C}{\Gamma,\mathrm{T},\Gamma' \vdash C}\quad \{t=u\}$$

Figure 1. Lambda semantics for Lambek calculus

From the general algebraic perspective of Montague's Universal Grammar, the inference rules above can be seen as realisations of the mapping from an algebra of proofs to the algebra of lambda terms interpreting these proofs. The syntactic objects (types) are associated with semantic objects (terms) and the operations in the algebra of proofs (inferences) are associated with operations in the term algebra – functional application and functional abstraction in the case of [L/],[L\] and [R/],[R\], pairing and projection in the case of [R•] and [L•], substitution in the case of [Cut]. Cut is an admissible rule in this formulation of the calculus: it does not yield any theorems that could not be obtained without the use of Cut. And from the semantic point of view, it does not yield any readings (lambda recipes) that would not be logically equivalent to readings associated with cut-free derivations. So for the remainder of this paper we can safely ignore the Cut inference.

As an illustration, we present the syntactic derivation of an instance of functional composition in (1), and the construction of the corresponding lambda recipe in (2).

$$\cfrac{\cfrac{\cfrac{n \vdash n \quad np \vdash np}{(np/n), n \vdash np} \quad pp \vdash pp}{(pp/np), (np/n), n \vdash pp}}{(pp/np), (np/n) \vdash (pp/n)} \tag{1}$$

$$\cfrac{\cfrac{\cfrac{\cfrac{\{t'' = v\}}{v_n \vdash t''_n} \quad \cfrac{\{t' = \mathbf{g}(v)_{np}\}}{\mathbf{g}(v)_{np} \vdash t'_{np}}}{\mathbf{g}_{(np/n)}, v_n \vdash t'_{np}} \quad \cfrac{\{t = \mathbf{f}(\mathbf{g}(v))_{pp}\}}{\mathbf{f}(\mathbf{g}(v))_{pp} \vdash t_{pp}}}{\mathbf{f}_{(pp/np)}, \mathbf{g}_{(np/n)}, v_n \vdash t_{pp}}}{\mathbf{f}_{(pp/np)}, \mathbf{g}_{(np/n)} \vdash (\lambda v.t)_{pp/n}} \tag{2}$$

Some comments on the procedural aspects of proof search may be useful here. We start the search with the goal sequent

$$\langle pp/np, \mathbf{f}\rangle, \langle np/n, \mathbf{g}\rangle \vdash \langle pp/n, \mathit{Term}\rangle$$

The antecedent types are associated with known parameters **f**, **g** – black boxes for the semantics of the antecedent assumptions, or thc lexical semantics of the input expressions in a concrete application. The succedent is associated with the unknown *Term*. The proof unfolds by backward-chaining: we try to match the goal sequent against the conclusion of one of the [L],[R] inferences, and continue search on the premises. The matching takes place under unifying substitutions, which gradually instantiate the unknown recipe *Term* as the proof unfolds. The first step of the proof, for example, matches the goal sequent against the conclusion of the [R/] inference, instantiating *Term* as $\lambda v.t$, where t is the new unknown associated with the new succedent goal type pp. Notice that, from this resolution point of view, the [Axiom] scheme forces *unification* of the term *structure* built up in the antecedent with the term *variable* associated with the succedent.

1.2 Types and strings

The representation of sequent elements as pairs ⟨*Type*, *Term*⟩ leaves one component of the derivation implicit: the *terminal symbols* associated with the assumptions $A_1, \ldots, A_n$ in a sequent $A_1, \ldots, A_n \vdash B$. Suppose we add this information, and extend the representation of sequent elements to three-dimensional objects

$$\langle \mathit{Type}, \mathit{Term}, \mathit{String} \rangle$$

i.e. *signs* in the sense of UCG or HPSG. Each inference rule in the algebra of proofs will now also be associated with an operation in the *string algebra*, realising the mapping from type combinations to the combinations of the strings associated with these types. As soon as we make this move, antecedent ordering becomes redundant: the linearization of the terminal string underlying a sequent is expressed on the *String* component of our linguistic objects, just as the construction of the lambda recipe is expressed on the *Term* component. The antecedent, in other words, can be interpreted as a multiset of signs, for **L** as well as for **LP**.

In the remainder of this paper, we will give a declarative formulation of the operations in the string algebra in terms of *string equations*. See Calder (1989) for the use of string equations in morphology, and Siekmann (1985) for the logical background. Strings are sequences of syntactic atoms combined by an operator '+', which in the case of **L** is interpreted as associative and non-commutative. In the semantic algebra, we build up partial descriptions of lambda terms that get further instantiated in the course of unfolding a proof by means of term-unification. Likewise, in the string algebra, inference rules will be associated with partial descriptions of strings. The solution of string equations requires the extension of resolution proof search with *string unification* to determine whether two partial descriptions match the same string.

In order to introduce the shifted perspective, consider the sequent rules for the concatenative connectives '/','\' in their new guise. The antecedent can be read now as a multiset of signs. (Interpret [as multiset union). The variable conventions are as before, with lowercase greek letters as metavariables for the *String* component. In the Axiom case, we have unification of the lambda term labels and the string labels of the antecedent and succedent signs.

$$[\mathbf{Ax}]\frac{}{\langle A,1,t,\sigma\rangle \vdash \langle A,0,u,\tau\rangle}\{u=t,\tau=\sigma\} \tag{3}$$

$$[\mathrm{L}/]\frac{\mathrm{T} \vdash \langle B, u, \tau\rangle \quad \langle A, tu, \phi\rangle \cup \Delta \vdash C}{\langle A/B, t, \sigma\rangle \cup \mathrm{T} \cup \Delta \vdash C} \quad \phi = \sigma + \tau$$
$$[\mathrm{R}/]\frac{\langle B, v, \tau\rangle \cup \mathrm{T} \vdash \langle A, u, \phi\rangle}{\mathrm{T} \vdash \langle A/B, \lambda v.u, \sigma\rangle} \quad \phi = \sigma + \tau \tag{4}$$

$$[\mathrm{L}\backslash]\frac{\mathrm{T} \vdash \langle B, u, \tau\rangle \quad \langle A, tu, \phi\rangle \cup \Delta \vdash C}{\langle B\backslash A, t, \sigma\rangle \cup \mathrm{T} \cup \Delta \vdash C} \quad \phi = \tau + \sigma$$
$$[\mathrm{R}\backslash]\frac{\langle B, v, \tau\rangle \cup \mathrm{T} \vdash \langle A, u, \phi\rangle}{\mathrm{T} \vdash \langle B\backslash A, \lambda v.u, \sigma\rangle} \quad \phi = \tau + \sigma \tag{5}$$

Consider first the rules of *use* [L/] and [L\]. In order to use a functor A/B associated with a string σ, we have to prove B computing the associated string τ and use A which is then associated with the concatenation of the functor string σ with the argument string τ. Likewise for the use of $B\backslash A$, where the string associated with A consists of the argument string τ concatenated with the suffix functor string σ. Whereas in the case of the rules of use, functional application goes hand in hand with string concatenation, in the case of the rules of *proof* [R/] and [R\], functional abstraction is mirrored in the string algebra by string subtraction. In order to prove an A/B, we prove an A using a hypothetical assumption B. The strings associated with the active types have to satisfy the equation $\phi = \sigma + \tau$, i.e. the string computed for A/B is what remains after dropping the right-peripheral string τ associated with the hypothetical B from the string computed for A. Likewise for the proof of $B\backslash A$.

The reader is invited to work through our earlier example in this threedimensional setting. The goal sequent would now become:

$$\langle pp/np, \mathbf{f}, \text{“f”}\rangle \cup \langle np/n, \mathbf{g}, \text{“g”}\rangle \vdash \langle pp/n, \mathit{Term}, \mathit{String}\rangle$$

which could be paraphrased as the question: what semantic recipe *Term* and structure *String* in type pp/n can we compute from the multiset of antecedent lexical assumptions? Or we could further instantiate the goal sequent to:

$$\langle pp/np, \mathbf{f}, \text{“f”}\rangle \cup \langle np/n, \mathbf{g}, \text{“g”}\rangle \vdash \langle pp/n, \mathit{Term}, \text{“fg”}\rangle$$

where the question becomes: can we compute the structure “fg” in type pp/n from the multiset of antecedent lexical assumptions, and if so, what lambda recipe *Term* goes with the computation?

From the general algebraic perspective adopted here, it becomes possible to uniformly characterize the well-known calculi of the categorial hierarchy in terms of the inference patterns given above, by simply varying the properties attributed to the string combinator '+'. **L** and **LP** are obtained under an associative interpretation of '+'. For the non-associative variants we switch to a domain of *bracketed strings*, and the derivability relation is sensitive to this bracketing. This yields the system **NL** of Lambek (1961) in case of a non-commutative '+' and a commutative 'mobile' variant **NLP**, with a non-directional but structure preserving derivability relation (i.e. a characterization of immediate dominance but no linear precedence).

CALCULUS	ASSOCIATIVE	COMMUTATIVE
LP	yes	yes
L	yes	no
NLP	no	yes
NL	no	no

These options will be adequate for the discussion of this paper. Interesting additional calculi can be obtained by enriching the *String* component of our linguistic objects to, say, *labeled* bracketed strings (i.e. trees, either at the morphosyntactic level, with categorial labeling, or at the prosodic level, with (sw) prominence labeling). In Moortgat – Morrill (1991), such dimensions and their interplay are investigated in depth. Alternatively, one can explore *non-concatenative* interpretations of the string combinator '+', for example, interleaving (sequence union). See Reape (this volume) for linguistic applications of interleaving.

1.3 Intermezzo: proof net unfolding

The presentation above characterizes the properties of the type constructors in terms of the familiar sequent format. Sequent calculus has some drawbacks, when one considers computational efficiency or notational economy. As to the latter: sequent proofs are exceedingly verbose in copying the inert assumptions from conclusion to premises, whereas the real action of the proof is to be found in the *active* types – the types that are decomposed in their immediate subtypes by the logical inference rules. From a computational point of view, sequent proof search is redundant in another way: there is no one-to-one correspondence between sequent proofs and lambda terms, a redundancy caused by irrelevant orderings of rule applications. Both forms of inefficiency of sequent proof search can be overcome by switching to a more succinct representation of derivations in terms of a categorial version of the *proof nets* of Linear Logic. See Roorda (1991), and Moortgat (1990b) for the connection between proof net unfolding and partial deduction. In this paper, we are not concerned with the computational aspects of proof search. But our heavily annotated categorial signs make a compact notation for type deductions highly desirable. Hence this intermezzo on proof net type decomposition.

The translation from sequent inferences to proof net links is straightforward. A sequent $\Gamma \vdash \mathbf{B}$ is represented as a multiset of *signed* labeled types, i.e. structures of the form

$$\langle \textit{Type}, \textit{Polarity}, \textit{Term}, \textit{String} \rangle$$

The new element here is the polarity label. It keeps track of the positive/negative nature of types, which in the sequent format is encoded in their occurrence to the left or to the right of the $\vdash$ sign. Antecedent types $A \in \Gamma$ are assigned polarity 1, the succedent type B is signed with polarity 0. The association of types with a lambda term and a string term is exactly as before. Proof net unfolding of types then assumes the following form.

$$[\mathbf{Ax}]\frac{}{\langle A,1,t,\sigma\rangle \quad \langle A,0,u,\tau\rangle}\{u=t,\tau=\sigma\} \tag{6}$$

Axiom links cancel an antecedent atom against a matching succedent atom under the unifying substitution for the lambda term and string term. The logical links recursively decompose types of arbitrary complexity into their atomic subtypes.

$$\begin{array}{ll} [\mathbf{L}/]\dfrac{\langle A,1,tu,\phi\rangle \quad \langle B,0,u,\tau\rangle}{\langle A/B,1,t,\sigma\rangle} & \phi=\sigma+\tau \\ [\mathbf{R}/]\dfrac{\langle D,1,v,\tau\rangle \quad \langle A,0,u,\phi\rangle}{\langle A/B,0,\lambda v.u,\sigma\rangle} & \phi=\sigma+\tau \end{array} \tag{7}$$

$$\begin{array}{ll} [\mathbf{L}\backslash]\dfrac{\langle A,1,tu,\phi\rangle \quad \langle B,0,u,\tau\rangle}{\langle B\backslash A,1,t,\sigma\rangle} & \phi=\tau+\sigma \\ [\mathbf{R}\backslash]\dfrac{\langle B,1,v,\tau\rangle \quad \langle A,0,u,\phi\rangle}{\langle B\backslash A,0,\lambda v.u,\sigma\rangle} & \phi=\tau+\sigma \end{array} \tag{8}$$

$$\begin{array}{ll} [\mathbf{L}\bullet]\dfrac{\langle A,1,\pi_0(t),\sigma\rangle \quad \langle B,1,\pi_1(t),\tau\rangle}{\langle A\bullet B,1,t,\phi\rangle} & \phi=\sigma+\tau \\ [\mathbf{R}\bullet]\dfrac{\langle B,0,t_0,\sigma\rangle \quad \langle A,0,t_1,\tau\rangle}{\langle A\bullet B,0,\langle t_0,t_1\rangle,\phi\rangle} & \phi=\sigma+\tau \end{array} \tag{9}$$

In order to determine whether a sequent is derivable, we have to be able to match, by means of the axiom links, the atoms with opposite signature in the structure obtained by decomposing the complex types into their atomic subtypes. In Moortgat (1990b) we have shown that this problem can be tackled with familiar resolution techniques. (Resolution extended with string unification in the present case.) Let $\mathcal{L}$ be the multiset of atomic leaves of an unfolded proof frame. From $\mathcal{L}$ we reconstruct a definite clause representation of the underlying sequent by collecting the definite clauses

$$C = \{\langle A, 1, t, \sigma\rangle\} \cup \{\langle B, 0, u, \tau\rangle \mid u \in FV(t)\}$$

$$[\mathrm{L}/]\frac{\langle A,1\rangle \quad \langle B,0\rangle}{\langle A/B,1\rangle} \qquad \frac{\langle B,1\rangle \quad \langle A,0\rangle}{\langle A/B,0\rangle}[\mathrm{R}/] \tag{10}$$

for all A, 1, t, σ, $\in$, $\mathcal{L}$. SLD resolution then provides the proof search algorithm. Alternatively, the SLD resolution search for the clausal representation can be reinterpreted as the following 'goal driven' set of proof net travel instructions, starting from the (unique) negative succedent type. However, the point of the clausal transformation is that all information needed for the construction of a proof is already recorded in the atomic leaves of the unfolded proof frame. In the examples that follow, we can therefore ignore the underlying proof frame structure, and just present the labeled leaves, as input for the resolution algorithm.

$$\begin{array}{lcl@{\qquad}lcl}
\downarrow\langle A,1\rangle & \rightsquigarrow & \uparrow\langle B,0\rangle & \uparrow\langle A/B,0\rangle & \rightsquigarrow & \uparrow\langle A,0\rangle\\
\downarrow\langle B,0\rangle & \rightsquigarrow & \downarrow\langle A/B,1\rangle & \downarrow\langle A,0\rangle & \rightsquigarrow & \downarrow\langle A/B,0\rangle\\
\uparrow\langle A/B,1\rangle & \rightsquigarrow & \uparrow\langle A,1\rangle & \downarrow\langle B,1\rangle & \rightsquigarrow & \uparrow\langle B,1\rangle
\end{array}$$

$$[\mathrm{Ax}]\frac{}{\langle A,1\rangle \quad \langle A,0\rangle}$$

$$\begin{array}{lcl}
\uparrow\langle A,0\rangle & \rightsquigarrow & \downarrow\langle A,1\rangle\\
\uparrow\langle A,1\rangle & \rightsquigarrow & \downarrow\langle A,0\rangle
\end{array}$$

As an illustration of the definite clause transformation, consider the lexical representation for the verb *need*, i.e. the structure

$$\langle (np\backslash s)/(s/(np\backslash s)), 1, \text{need}, \mathbf{need}\rangle.$$

Unfolding of the complex type yields a multiset of five signed atoms, with the associated semantic recipes and partial string descriptions shown in (11). (In order to distinguish variables from parameters, we use (subscripted) uppercase V (lambda terms), T (strings) for the former, and lowercase x, s for the latter.)

$$\begin{array}{l} \langle s, 1, \text{need}(\lambda x_5.V_0)(V_1), T_{23} + \textbf{need} + T_{45}\rangle \\ \langle np, 0, V_1, T_{23}\rangle \\ \langle s, 0, V_0, T_{45} + s_5\rangle \\ \langle s, 1, x_5(V_6), T_{78} + s_5\rangle \\ \langle np, 0, V_6, T_{78}\rangle \end{array} \tag{11}$$

This multiset of literals is not in definite clause form: it contains two heads (the s atoms with positive signature). Grouping the heads with the dependent body literals (i.e. the atoms with negative polarity which show their dependency on the head through variable sharing as indicated in (10)), yields the two definite clauses below.

$$\{\langle s, 1, \text{need}(\lambda x_5.V_0)(V_1), T_{23} + \textbf{need} + T_{45}\rangle, \langle np, 0, V_1, T_{23}\rangle, \langle s, 0, V_0, T_{45} + s_5\rangle\}$$

$$\{\langle s, 1, x_5(V_6), T_{78} + s_5\rangle, \langle np, 0, V_6, T_{78}\rangle\}$$

In a more familiar Logic Programming notation, these clauses would assume the following form.

$$\text{s}(\text{need}(\lambda x_5.V_0)(V_1), T_{23} + \textbf{need} + T_{45}) \leftarrow \text{np}(V_1, T_{23}), \text{s}(V_0, T_{45} + s_5). \tag{12}$$

$$\text{s}(x_5(V_6), T_{78} + s_5) \leftarrow \text{np}(V_6, T_{78}). \tag{13}$$

2. Discontinuous type constructors

After these preparatory sections, we are ready now to address the real subject matter of the paper, and investigate how Lambek calculus can be extended with type-constructors that have a non-concatenative interpretation.

From a logical perspective, the directional calculus **L** can be characterized as a logic without structural rules (cf. Lambek 1990). The system can be extended to full intuitionistic propositional logic by gradually adding structural rules, as shown in Van Benthem (1991), Wansing (1990).

From a linguistic point of view, it is attractive to have *controlled* access to the power of structural rules. Linear Logic (cf. Girard 1987) reintroduces the expressivity of structural rules in a type-controlled manner as extra connectives – the 'modalities'. Linguistic applications of this strategy can be found in Morrill (1990), Morrill et al. (1990), Hepple (1990), Moortgat – Morrill (1991).

From the modal perspective, one could try to reduce non-concatenative phenomena to a permutation modality 'β_p': a type βA then represents a datum of type A which does not have a fixed position, but is free to move in the course of a deduction until it finds a place where it can be used as an A. The present section follows a different line. We discuss a number of functional type constructors directly capturing extraction and infixation operations at a suitable level of linguistic generalization. Whether or not these type constructors are ultimately reducible to more elementary ones is a matter of further research.

In the figure below, one finds a graphical illustration of the type constructors under discussion, in terms of the triangles of parsing theory. A triangle

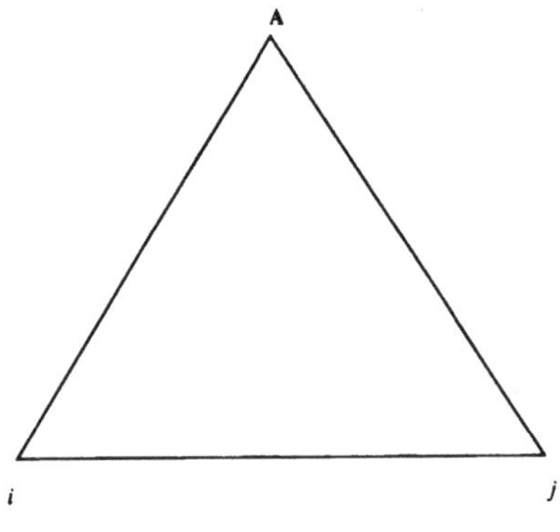

expresses the fact that a string running from positions i to j reduces to type A. How can we cut up the triangle in a functor component and an argument component? The concatenative type-constructors cut it up into the continuous portions (i, j) and (j, k), with either a prefix functor A/B covering (i, j) or a suffix functor $B\backslash A$ covering (j, k). See the top row in the illustration, where the argument component is shaded. In the non-concatenative mode we want to explore below, the triangle is cut up into the discontinuous component $(i, j) + (k, l)$ and its completion (j, k). As in the concatenative case, we have a choice as to which region we want to shade as the argument. In the case of the extraction functor $A \uparrow B$ we have a discontinuous functor covering $(i, j) + (k, l)$, which wraps itself around its argument. In the case of the infix functor $A \downarrow B$, it is the B type argument which covers the discontinuous string $(i, j) + (k, l)$, and the infix functor fills up the missing (j, k) part.

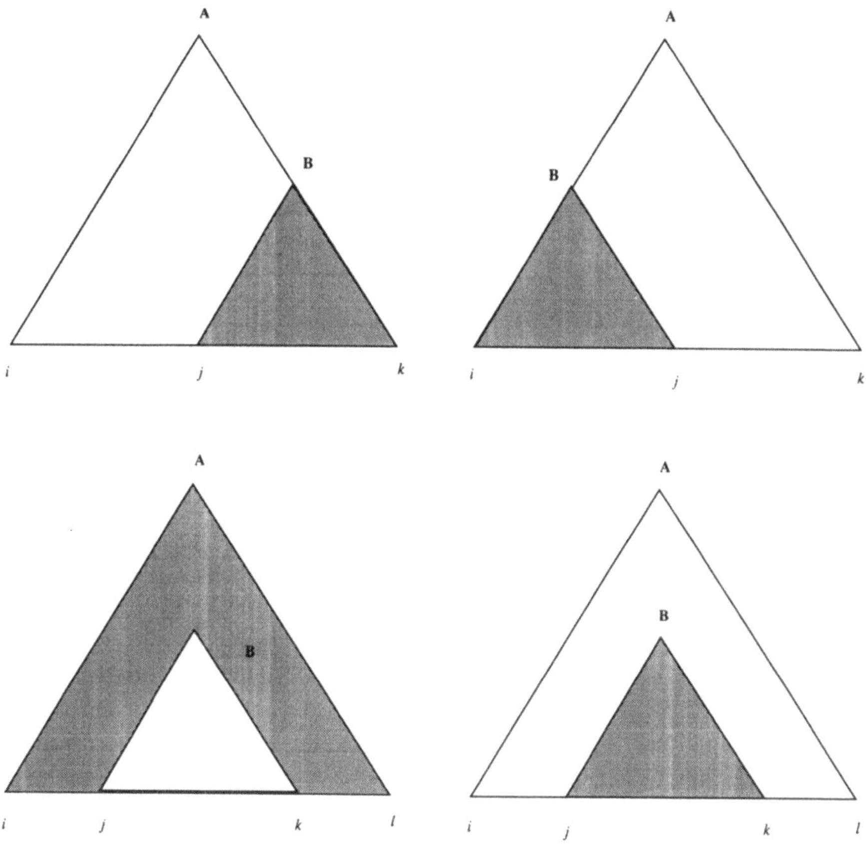

2.1 Partial logics for extraction and infixation

Extraction and infixation type constructors are discussed in Moortgat (1988) in an attempt to accomodate Emmon Bach's work on discontinuity (e.g. his 1981 or 1984 papers) within the categorial type logic approach. It is shown there that within the expressive limits of the sequent language (without labeling annotation!) a *partial* logic for the discontinuous type constructors '↑' (extraction) and '↓' (infixation) can be given, but that this partial logic cannot be extended into a *complete* one, with matching left and right rules for these connectives, if the ordering of antecedent types is the only means of expressing the structural combination of types. A calculus with an incomplete characterization of its type constructors does not enjoy the pleasant logical properties of the original system **L**. The purpose of this section is to improve on our earlier proposal by presenting a complete logic for extraction and infixation type constructors, in terms of the sign-based approach to categorial deduction.

Consider first the sequent rules [L↓] and [R↑] as originally presented in Moortgat (1988).

$$[\mathrm{L}\downarrow]\frac{\mathrm{T}',\mathrm{T}''\vdash\langle B,u\rangle \quad \Gamma,\langle A,tu\rangle,\Lambda\vdash C}{\Gamma,\mathrm{T}',\langle A\downarrow B,t\rangle,\mathrm{T}'',\Lambda\vdash C} \tag{14}$$

$$[\mathrm{R}\uparrow]\frac{\mathrm{T}',\langle B,v\rangle,\mathrm{T}''\vdash\langle A,u\rangle}{\mathrm{T}',\mathrm{T}''\vdash\langle A\uparrow B,\lambda v.u\rangle} \tag{15}$$

What we have here is a rule of use ([L↑]) for infixation, and a rule of proof ([R↑]) for extraction. Why is it impossible to complete these inferences with [R↓] and [L↑]? In the standard sequent format, the linearization of an expression has to be characterized completely in terms of the ordering of types in the *antecedent*. There is no problem, then, with the rule of use for an infix type $A \downarrow B$, which represents the infix functor in the context of the material that has to make up the argument subtype B: T′, $A \downarrow B, t$, T″. Likewise, the succedent inference for an extraction type $A \uparrow B$ can represent the extraction site of the argument subtype B in terms of the antecedent factorization T′, T″ $\vdash A \uparrow B, \lambda v.u$. Conceptually, the matching left rule [L↑] would have to represent the fact that a functor $A \uparrow B$ wraps itself around its argument, rather than simply preceding or following it. But this structural manipulation is not expressible in terms of ordering of types in the antecedent. Similarly, for the succedent inference [R↓] it is impossible to express in terms of antecedent ordering the fact that the argument subtype B envelops the infix functor $A \downarrow B$.

2.2 String equations for extraction and infixation

With the enriched sign-based representation ⟨*Type*, *Semantics*, *String*⟩ extraction and infixation type constructors can be characterized in terms of the string equations relating the *String* information associated with functor, argument and result types. Consider first the extraction type constructor. Below in (16) and (17) are the matching rule of use and rule of proof, first in sequent format.

$$[\mathrm{L}\uparrow]\frac{\mathrm{T}\vdash\langle B,u,\tau\rangle \quad \langle A,tu,\sigma\rangle\cup\Delta\vdash C}{\langle A\uparrow B,t,\phi\rangle\cup\mathrm{T}\cup\Delta\vdash C} \quad \begin{cases}\phi=\phi_1+\phi_2\\ \sigma=\phi_1+\tau+\phi_2\end{cases} \tag{16}$$

$$[\mathrm{R}\uparrow]\frac{\langle B,v,\tau\rangle\cup\mathrm{T}\vdash\langle A,u,\sigma\rangle}{\mathrm{T}\vdash\langle A\uparrow B,\lambda v.u,\phi\rangle} \quad \begin{cases}\phi=\phi_1+\phi_2\\ \sigma=\phi_1+\tau+\phi_2\end{cases} \tag{17}$$

To obtain the corresponding proof net links, we add the polarity information, as indicated before.

$$[\uparrow L]\frac{\langle A,1,tu,\sigma\rangle \quad \langle B,0,u,\tau\rangle}{\langle A\uparrow B,1,t,\phi\rangle} \quad \begin{cases} \phi = \phi_1 + \phi_2 \\ \sigma = \phi_1 + \tau + \phi_2 \end{cases} \tag{18}$$

$$[\uparrow R]\frac{\langle A,0,u,\sigma\rangle \quad \langle B,1,v,\tau\rangle}{\langle A\uparrow B,0,\lambda v.u,\phi\rangle} \quad \begin{cases} \phi = \phi_1 + \phi_2 \\ \sigma = \phi_1 + \tau + \phi_2 \end{cases} \tag{19}$$

Some comments are in order here. Consider first the rule of proof [R$\uparrow$]. Suppose one can prove an A consuming a B in the process; the string label τ associated with B showns up somewhere within the full string label σ computed for A: $\sigma = \phi_1 + \tau + \phi_2$. Now one can withdraw the B assumption, at the same time erasing its trace from σ, and one obtains a proof of $A \uparrow B$ associated with the remainder of σ after removal of τ. From the linguistic point of view, then, the rule of *proof* for $\uparrow$ captures extraction phenomena, and does the work of the SLASH feature in GPSG, as discussed in Moortgat (1988). But our logical framework invites us to consider a matching rule of *use* for the type constructor. How could we use an assumption $A \uparrow B$ given that such an assumption is associated with a discontinuous string label $\phi_1 + \phi_2$? An expression of type $A \uparrow B$ is used as a *discontinuous* functor which forms an expression of type A by wrapping itself around the argument expression of type B. The inherent [R],[L] duality of the logical framework thus unifies linguistic phenomena of extraction and wrapping, representing the [R] and [L] action of one type constructor $\uparrow$.

As an illustration of a lexical wrapping functor, consider discontinuous determiner expressions of the type *more ... than ...* (cf. Keenan – Stavi 1986 for many examples). The functor combines with two common noun arguments to give a generalized quantifier noun phrase, wrapping itself around its first argument. The type assignment then can be $(gq/n) \uparrow n$. But now, since this is a lexical wrapper, we do not have a proof telling us at what position the first n argument has to be enveloped. We assume therefore that the factorization $\phi_1 + \phi_2$ of the discontinuous functor is given as part of the lexical representation. The unfolded lexical representation of the discontinuous determiner *more ... than ...* is presented below in (20).

$$\frac{\dfrac{\langle gq,1,\mathbf{more\text{–}than}(u)(v),\mathbf{more}+\tau+\mathbf{than}+\phi\rangle \quad \langle n,0,v,\phi\rangle}{\langle gq/n,1,\mathbf{more\text{–}than}(u),\mathbf{more}+\tau+\mathbf{than}\rangle} \qquad \langle n,0,u,\tau\rangle}{\langle (gq/n)\uparrow n,1,\mathbf{more\text{–}than},\mathbf{more}+\mathbf{than}\rangle} \tag{20}$$

Consider next the case of infixation. The rule of use [L$\downarrow$] and rule of proof [R$\downarrow$] for the infixation type constructor are obtained by switching around the ϕ and τ labels: in the case of infixation, it is the *argument* B which is associated with the discontinuous string $\phi = \phi_1 + \phi_2$ which wraps itself around the infix functor $A \downarrow B$. Here are the rules in sequent format.

$$[\mathrm{L}\downarrow]\frac{\mathrm{T} \vdash \langle B,u,\phi\rangle \quad \langle A,tu,\sigma\rangle \cup \Delta \vdash C}{\langle A\downarrow B,t,\tau\rangle \cup \mathrm{T} \cup \Delta \vdash C} \quad \begin{cases} \phi = \phi_1 + \phi_2 \\ \sigma = \phi_1 + \tau + \phi_2 \end{cases} \tag{21}$$

$$[\mathrm{R}\downarrow]\frac{\langle B,v,\phi\rangle \cup \mathrm{T} \vdash \langle A,u,\sigma\rangle}{\mathrm{T} \vdash \langle A\downarrow B,\lambda v.u,\tau\rangle} \quad \begin{cases} \phi = \phi_1 + \phi_2 \\ \sigma = \phi_1 + \tau + \phi_2 \end{cases} \tag{22}$$

The proof net links for the infixation type constructor $\downarrow$ are given below.

$$[\downarrow\mathrm{L}]\frac{\langle A,1,tu,\sigma\rangle \quad \langle B,0,u,\phi\rangle}{\langle A\downarrow B,1,t,\tau\rangle} \quad \begin{cases} \phi = \phi_1 + \phi_2 \\ \sigma = \phi_1 + \tau + \phi_2 \end{cases} \tag{23}$$

$$[\downarrow\mathrm{R}]\frac{\langle A,0,u,\sigma\rangle \quad \langle B,1,v,\phi\rangle}{\langle A\downarrow B,0,\lambda v.u,\tau\rangle} \quad \begin{cases} \phi = \phi_1 + \phi_2 \\ \sigma = \phi_1 + \tau + \phi_2 \end{cases} \tag{24}$$

In the concatenative system **L** the operators '/' and '\' behave as right and left-residuals of the '•' operator. Analogously, we could match the extraction/infixation operators with an explicit substring product '$\odot$'.

$$[\odot\mathrm{L}]\frac{\langle A,1,\pi_0(t),\phi\rangle \quad \langle B,1,\pi_1(t),\tau\rangle}{\langle A\odot B,1,t,\sigma\rangle} \quad \begin{cases} \phi = \phi_1 + \phi_2 \\ \sigma = \phi_1 + \tau + \phi_2 \end{cases}$$

$$[\odot\mathrm{R}]\frac{\langle A,0,t_0,\phi\rangle \quad \langle B,0,t_1,\tau\rangle}{\langle A\odot B,0,\langle t_0,t_1\rangle,\sigma\rangle} \quad \begin{cases} \phi = \phi_1 + \phi_2 \\ \sigma = \phi_1 + \tau + \phi_2 \end{cases}$$

2.3 Illustration: wh-extraction

We close this section with a worked out example of the derivation of the Dutch embedded clause *wie het meisje kust* 'who the girl kisses'. The example allows for two readings, depending on whether the extraction site for *wie* is the subject or the object of the transitive verb. The lexical type assignments are given below.

$$\begin{array}{l} \langle s/(s\uparrow np),1,\mathrm{wie},\mathbf{wie}\rangle \\ \langle np/n,1,\mathrm{het},\mathbf{het}\rangle \\ \langle n,1,\mathrm{meisje},\mathbf{meisje}\rangle \\ \langle np\backslash(np\backslash s),1,\mathrm{kust},\mathbf{kust}\rangle \end{array} \tag{25}$$

Unfolding of the lexical type assignments yields the set of literals 1–9 below. The negative atom 10 represents the goal type.

$$\begin{array}{ll}
1. & \langle s, 1, \mathrm{wie}(\lambda x_2.V_0), \mathbf{wie} + T_1 + T_2\rangle \\
2. & \langle s, 0, V_0, T_1 + s_2 + T_2\rangle \\
3. & \langle np, 1, x_2, s_2\rangle \\
4. & \langle np, 1, \mathrm{het}(V_3), \mathbf{het} + T_4\rangle \\
5. & \langle n, 0, V_3, T_4\rangle \\
6. & \langle n, 1, \mathrm{meisje}, \mathbf{meisje}\rangle \\
7. & \langle s, 1, \mathbf{kust}(V_6)(V_7), T_8 + T_{10} + \mathbf{kust}\rangle \\
8. & \langle np, 0, V_7, T_8\rangle \\
9. & \langle np, 0, V_6, T_{10}\rangle \\
10. & \langle s, 0, \mathrm{Term}, \mathbf{wie} + \mathbf{het} + \mathbf{meisje} + \mathbf{kust}\rangle
\end{array} \tag{26}$$

The resolution problem has two solutions, depending on whether one resolves 8 against 3 and 9 against 4, or 9 against 3 and 8 against 4. The first solution represents the subject extraction case, the second direct object extraction.

Subject extraction: wie $(\lambda x_2.\mathrm{kust}(\mathrm{het}(\mathrm{meisje}))(x_2))$.

Resolution	Lambda terms	String terms
$10+1$	$\mathrm{Term} = \mathrm{wie}(\lambda x_2.V_0)$	$\mathbf{wie} + \mathbf{het} + \mathbf{meisje} + \mathbf{kust} = \mathbf{wie} + T_1 + T_2$
$2+7$	$V_0 = \mathrm{kust}(V_6)(V_7)$	$T_1 + s_2 + T_2 = T_8 + T_{10} + \mathbf{kust}$
$8+3$	$V_7 = x_2$	$T_8 = s_2$
$9+4$	$V_6 = \mathrm{het}(V_3)$	$T_{10} = \mathbf{het} + T_4$
$5+6$	$V_3 = \mathrm{meisje}$	$T_4 = \mathbf{meisje}$

Object extraction: $\mathrm{wie}(\lambda x_2.\mathrm{kust}(x_2)(\mathrm{het}(\mathrm{meisje})))$.

Resolution	Lambda terms	String terms
$10+1$	$\mathrm{Term} = \mathrm{wie}(\lambda x_2.V_0)$	$\mathbf{wie} + \mathbf{het} + \mathbf{meisje} + \mathbf{kust} = \mathbf{wie} + T_1 + T_2$
$2+7$	$V_0 = \mathrm{kust}(V_6)(V_7)$	$T_1 + s_2 + T_2 = T_8 + T_{10} + \mathbf{kust}$
$9+3$	$V_6 = x_2$	$T_{10} = s_2$
$8+4$	$V_7 = \mathrm{het}(V_3)$	$T_8 = \mathbf{het} + T_4$
$5+6$	$V_3 = \mathrm{meisje}$	$T_4 = \mathbf{meisje}$

3. Quantifiers

3.1 Earlier attempts

Let us turn finally to the analysis of generalized quantifier expressions and reformulate the proposal of Moortgat (1990) in terms of the type constructors '↑' and '↓'. It is shown in Hendriks (1990), Emms (1990), that within the order-preserving calculus **L** no directional type assignment to generalized quantifier noun phrases (e.g. $s/(np\backslash s)$ or $(s/np)\backslash s$) generates the proper set of possible quantifier scopings. The quantifier scope problem leads these authors to substantial modifications of the categorial architecture – a relaxation of the functional mapping from syntactic categories to semantic types in the case of Hendriks, and the introduction of irreducible lexical (as opposed to derivational) polymorphism in the case of Emms. Commenting on these proposals, Moortgat (1990) investigates the relation between quantifier scoping and the structural rule of Permutation. It is shown that **L** can be extended with a restricted form of Permutation which allows one to derive non-local quantifier scopings underivable within pure **L** while retaining the preservation of thematic structure of the original calculus. Following the strategy of the modalities of Linear Logic, the extension of **L** is implemented in the form of a new type constructor, lifting exponentiation A^B. The *logical* rules for the new type constructor encapsule the restricted use of the *structural* rule of Permutation which is needed to handle quantifier scope phenomena. The objective of this move is to reduce quantifier polymorphism to *derivational* polymorphism of the new type constructor, and to retain the functional category-to-type mapping. The proposed inference rules for types A^B are given below, in the original sequent format, i.e. with the sequence interpretation of the antecedent.

$$[\mathrm{QL}]\frac{\mathrm{T}', \langle A, v\rangle, \mathrm{T}'' \vdash \langle B, u\rangle \quad \Gamma, \langle B, t(\lambda v.u)\rangle, \Lambda \vdash C}{\Gamma, \mathrm{T}', \langle A^B, t\rangle, \mathrm{T}'', \Lambda \vdash C} \tag{27}$$

$$[\mathrm{QR}]\frac{\mathrm{T} \vdash \langle A, u\rangle}{\mathrm{T} \vdash \langle A^B, \lambda v.vu\rangle} \tag{28}$$

The idea behind [QR] and [QL] is that syntactic types A^B are mapped to semantic types $\langle\langle\langle t(A), t(B)\rangle\rangle, t(B)\rangle$. The inference rules for types A^B can then be interpreted as the compilations by partial execution of the **LP** derivations for $\langle\langle\langle t(A), t(B)\rangle\rangle, t(B)\rangle$.

Intuitively, an expression A^B is to be interpreted as an *infix* functor binding a variable of type $t(A)$ within a domain of type $t(B)$. Syntactically, the binder A^B and the bound element A occupy the same position in the terminal string, thus guaranteeing preservation of thematic structure. For example: a generalized quantifier expression of type np^s occuring in direct object position binds a direct object variable in the thematic structure.

Given this characterization of A^B as an infix functor, it is not surprising that the inference rules above suffer from the same defect as the partial characterizations of '↑' and '↓' discussed in the previous section. The [QL] rule faithfully captures the intended interpretation of exponentiation. The [QR] rule, however, cannot properly represent the context which *surrounds* the infix expression (rather than simply preceding or following it). As Hendriks (p.c.) has pointed out, [QR] as stated above is incomplete with respect to the intended interpretation. It is impossible, for example, to derive the valid type transition of (29) below, which would turn a sentence level quantifier into a verb phrase level one. That such type transitions should indeed be validated by the type calculus, appears from the fact that verb phrase quantifiers (e.g. reflexives) are conjoinable with sentential quantifiers (e.g. *he saw himself and two girls*).

$$np^s \vdash np^{np\backslash s} \tag{29}$$

Another problem with the exponentiation type constructor A^B is its limited generality. The fact that the associated semantic type is $\langle\langle\langle t(A), t(B)\rangle\rangle, t(B)\rangle$ suggests an extra degree of flexibility: the type of the binding domain could in principle be distinct from the type of the resulting expression. This suggests a more general three-place type constructor $q(A, B, C)$ with the case $B = C$ as an instance. As we will see below, linguistic motivation for the more general type constructor can be found in quite diverse binding phenomena.

3.2 Quantifiers as infix functors

In (30) and (32) we reformulate the quantifier type constructor in terms of '↑' and '↓'. It turns out that the type constructor $q(A, B, C)$ can be characterized as the special case of $C \downarrow (B \uparrow A)$ where the unfolding steps for '↑' and '↓' impose *the same* factorization $\phi = \phi_1 + \phi_2$ on the string associated with the subtype $B \uparrow A$. In the normal case of a type $C \downarrow (B \uparrow A)$, the '↓' unfolding would be associated with a string equation $\phi = \phi_1 + \phi_2$, and the '↑' unfolding with an equation $\phi = \phi_3 + \phi_4$, without enforcing $\phi_1 = \phi_3$ and $\phi_2 = \phi_4$. The identity of the constraints on the unfolding steps for '↑' and '↓' justifies the introduction of $q(A, B, C)$ as a separate type constructor: expressions of type $q(A, B, C)$ are not completely characterizable in terms of $C \downarrow (B \uparrow A)$. In (30) below we present the antecedent unfolding in terms of $C \downarrow (B \uparrow A)$. (31) is the compiled antecedent unfolding for the type constructor $q(A, B, C)$.

$$\frac{\langle C, 1, t(\lambda v.u), \chi\rangle \quad \dfrac{\langle B, 0, u, \sigma\rangle \quad \langle A, 1, v, \tau\rangle}{\langle B \uparrow A, 0, \lambda v.u, \phi\rangle}}{\langle C \downarrow (B \uparrow A), 1, t, \psi\rangle} \qquad \begin{cases} \phi = \phi_1 + \phi_2 \\ \sigma = \phi_1 + \tau + \phi_2 \\ \chi = \phi_1 + \psi + \phi_2 \end{cases} \tag{30}$$

$$[QL]\frac{\langle C, 1, t(\lambda v.u), \chi\rangle \quad \langle B, 0, u, \sigma\rangle \quad \langle A, 1, v, \tau\rangle}{\langle q(A, B, C), 1, t, \psi\rangle} \qquad \begin{cases} \sigma = \phi_1 + \tau + \phi_2 \\ \chi = \phi_1 + \psi + \phi_2 \end{cases} \tag{31}$$

The corresponding succedent unfolding rules are obtained by reversing the polarities, and switching from functional application to functional abstraction. Again, we first present the unfolding in terms of $C \downarrow (B \uparrow A)$ in (32), then in (33) the compiled succedent unfolding for the type constructor $q(A, B, C)$.

$$\frac{\langle C, 0, u, \chi\rangle \quad \dfrac{\langle B, 1, vz, \sigma\rangle \quad \langle A, 0, z, \tau\rangle}{\langle B \uparrow A, 1, v, \phi\rangle}}{\langle C \downarrow (B \uparrow A), 0, \lambda v.u, \psi\rangle} \qquad \begin{cases} \phi = \phi_1 + \phi_2 \\ \sigma = \phi_1 + \tau + \phi_2 \\ \chi = \phi_1 + \psi + \phi_2 \end{cases} \tag{32}$$

$$[QR]\frac{\langle C, 0, u, \chi\rangle \quad \langle B, 1, vz, \sigma\rangle \quad \langle A, 0, z, \tau\rangle}{\langle q(A, B, C), 0, \lambda v.u, \psi\rangle} \qquad \begin{cases} \sigma = \phi_1 + \tau + \phi_2 \\ \chi = \phi_1 + \psi + \phi_2 \end{cases} \tag{33}$$

As an example, we derive the type transition from a sentence level to a verb phrase level quantifier. Recall that with the [QL], [QR] rules of Moortgat (1990) this type transition was underivable.

$$\langle q(np, s, s), \text{someone}, \mathbf{someone}\rangle \vdash \langle q(np, np\backslash s, np\backslash s), \text{Term}, \mathbf{someone}\rangle \tag{34}$$

Proof net unfolding yields the set of signed literals (35), of the form

<Type, Polarity, Semantics, Strings>

The structures are numbered for further reference. Literals 1–3 represent the atoms of the input type $q(np, s, s)$. Literals 4–8 represent the atoms of the goal type $q(np, np\backslash s, np\backslash s)$. To distinguish variables from parameters, I use (subscripted) uppercase V, T for the former, and lowercase x, s for the latter.

$$\begin{array}{ll}
1. & \langle \mathbf{np}, 1, \boldsymbol{x}_{15}, \boldsymbol{s}_{15} \rangle \\
2. & \langle \boldsymbol{s}, 0, V_8, T_9 + \boldsymbol{s}_{15} + T_{11} \rangle \\
3. & \langle \boldsymbol{s}, 1, \text{someone}(\lambda \boldsymbol{x}_{15}.V_8), T_9 + \textbf{someone} + T_{11} \rangle \\
4. & \langle \mathbf{np}, 0, V_3, T_4 \rangle \\
5. & \langle \boldsymbol{s}, 1, \boldsymbol{x}_{13}(V_3)(V_5), T_6 + \boldsymbol{s}_{131} + T_4 + \boldsymbol{s}_{132} \rangle \\
6. & \langle \mathbf{np}, 0, V_5, T_6 \rangle \\
7. & \langle \boldsymbol{s}, 0, V_0, \boldsymbol{s}_{14} + \boldsymbol{s}_{131} + T_1 + \boldsymbol{s}_{132} \rangle \\
8. & \langle \mathbf{np}, 1, \boldsymbol{x}_{14}, \boldsymbol{s}_{14} \rangle
\end{array} \tag{35}$$

Resolution requires solutions for the set of string equations below.

Resolution	Lambda terms	String terms
$1+4$	$V_3 = \boldsymbol{x}_{15}$	$T_4 = \boldsymbol{s}_{15}$
$2+5$	$V_8 = \boldsymbol{x}_{13}(V_3)(V_5)$	$T_9 + \boldsymbol{s}_{15} + T_{11} = T_6 + \boldsymbol{s}_{131} + T_4 + \boldsymbol{s}_{132}$
$3+7$	$V_0 = \text{someone}(\lambda \boldsymbol{x}_{15}.V_8)$	$\boldsymbol{s}_{14} + \boldsymbol{s}_{131} + T_1 + \boldsymbol{s}_{132} = T_9 + \textbf{someone} + T_{11}$
$6+8$	$V_5 = \boldsymbol{x}_{14}$	$T_6 = \boldsymbol{s}_{14}$

The problem can be solved under the additional unifying substitutions of (36), which produces the desired reading (37) for the type transition. The lambda term for the derived type $np\backslash^{np\backslash s}$ is a function from transitive predicates to intransitive ones, with x_{13} a variable of type $t(np\backslash(np\backslash s))$ and x_{14} a variable of type $t(np)$. The original semantics of the input quantifier binds the direct object variable in the thematic structure, as required.

$$\{T_9 = \boldsymbol{s}_{14} + \boldsymbol{s}_{131}, T_{11} = \boldsymbol{s}_{132}, T_1 = \textbf{someone}\} \tag{36}$$

$$\text{Term} = \lambda \boldsymbol{x}_{13} \lambda \boldsymbol{x}_{14}.\text{someone}(\lambda \boldsymbol{x}_{15}.\boldsymbol{x}_{13}(\boldsymbol{x}_{15})(\boldsymbol{x}_{14})) \tag{37}$$

4. Binding

The discontinuous type constructors discussed above and their sign-based categorial type logic have been applied since the original presentation of this material to a wide range of phenomena in work of a.o. Morrill (1990), Oehrle (1991), Van der Linden (1991), Raaijmakers (1991) and Hendriks (1991). These applications suggest a uniform approach to *binding* phenomena in terms of a family of type constructors fitting the general patterns given below.

$$op(A, B, C)$$

$$t(op(A, B, C)) = (t(A) \rightarrow t(B)) \rightarrow t(C)$$

A: bound expression
B: binding domain
C: resultant expression

In this final section, we briefly review some of the instantiations of the pattern. The semantic action of $op(A, B, C)$ in these various cases is uniform; they differ in the syntactic realization of the binding type constructor. Among the syntactically available operations one would like to distinguish *substitution* binders, where the binder occupies the position of the bound element in the binding domain, from *prefixation* binders, where the binder precedes the binding domain. Generalized quantifiers exemplify the former, *wh*-extraction binders the latter. There is another dimension for variation, as suggested by the work of Oehrle (1991), Van der Linden (1991) and Raaijmakers (1991). The generalized quantification and extraction binders are *lexically* realized expressions. They have analogues in the *intonational* dimension in the form of focus and topicalisation binders. These cannot take the form of type assignments to specific lexical items: the type shift from A to the higher order $op(A, B, C)$ in these cases is triggered by the focus/topicalisation intonation contour. The table below summarizes the options.

	SUBSTITUTION	PREFIXATION
LEXICAL	$q(A, B, C)$ Generalized quantification	$wh(A, B, C)$ Extraction
INTONATIONAL	$f(A, B, C)$ Focus	$t(A, B, C)$ Topicalisation

4.1 Generalized quantification

The ordinary generalized quantifier instantiating the pattern $q(A, B, C)$ is of type $q(np, ss)$: a binder of an np type variable within a sentential domain, returning a sentence. We have already seen other instantiations, such as the verb-phrase level reflexive quantifier of type $q(np, np\backslash s, np\backslash s)$. As an illustration of the generality of the quantificational pattern $q(A, B, C)$, in particular of the case $B \neq C$, consider Comparative Subdeletion cases, as in the example below.

$$\text{John bought } \textbf{more} \text{ books } \textbf{than} \text{ Mary sold records} \tag{38}$$

Comparative Subdeletion is discussed by Hendriks (1991) in a categorial setting. Hendriks assimilates the construction to coordination, and accounts for the missing determiner in the *than* clause in terms of the extraction type constructor $\uparrow$. Here we present an alternative analysis, where *more ... than* is treated as a three-place determiner relation, in the sense of Keenan – Moss (1985). Intuitively, where the ordinary two-place determiner expresses a relation between two properties, we want the *more ... than* determiner to operate on three properties: the one obtained from its common noun argument, the property obtained by binding a np variable at the position occupied by *more N* in the main clause, and, finally, a property obtained from the *than* clause. The *more ... than* relation holds in case the cardinality of the intersection of the common noun property and the noun-phrase abstraction property for the main clause is greater than or equal to the cardinality of the *than* clause property. The latter is obtained by taking the boolean meet of the property corresponding to the common noun argument of the hypothetical determiner in the *than* clause and the noun-phrase abstraction property of the *than* clause. So our example would be paraphraseable as: 'the number of books bought by John is greater than the number of records sold by Mary'.

$$\|\textbf{more-than}\|(CN) = \{\langle X, Y\rangle \in E^2 \mid |X \cap \|CN\|| \geq |Y|\} \tag{39}$$

Now let us see how we can capture the syntactic fine-tuning in terms of a type assignment to the head of the construction – the determiner *more* in the main clause – so that it can reach out discontinuously to the *than* clause. The essential point is that the result of np binding in the main clause s domain is not a complete sentence, but a sentence still looking for a *than* complement. (Compare the type assignment to an ordinary s level determiner: $q(np, s, s)/n$.) The *than* clause is headed by the complementizer *than* which combines with a clause missing a determiner: $s \uparrow (q(np, s, s)/n)$.

$$\begin{array}{lcl} \textbf{more} & \in & q(np, s, s/s_{\text{than}})/n \\ \textbf{than} & \in & s_{\text{than}}/(s\uparrow(q(np, s, s)/n)) \end{array}$$

To make the semantics explicit, we can assign the complementizer *than* a lexical lambda term which takes the boolean meet of the property corresponding to the common noun argument of the hypothetical determiner and the noun-phrase abstraction property of the *than* clause.

$$\textbf{than} = \lambda Q_{((et)(et)t)t} \lambda x_e . Q(\lambda P_{et} \lambda Q_{et} . P(x) \wedge Q(x)) \tag{40}$$

Below, the reader can find the semantic recipes computed for the main clause and for the *than* clause.

$$\textbf{John bought more books} \mapsto \lambda Q_{et}.\text{more}(\textbf{books})(\lambda x_e.\text{bought}(x)(\text{john}))(Q) \tag{41}$$

$$\textbf{than Mary sold records} \mapsto \text{than}(\lambda D_{(et)(et)t}.D(\text{records})(\lambda y_e.\text{sold}(y)(\text{mary}))) \tag{42}$$

Working out the lexical recipe for *than*, they combine to the term given below.

$$\text{more}(\textbf{books})(\lambda x_e.\text{bought}(x)(\text{john}))(\lambda y.(\textit{records}(y) \wedge \textit{sold}(y)(\textit{mary}))) \tag{43}$$

4.2 Focus, gapping

Work by Oehrle (1991) and Van der Linden (1991) on the semantic impact of prosodic organisation shows that one can analyse focus assignment in terms of a focus binder

$$f(A, B, C)$$

analogous to the generalized quantifier substitution binder $q(A, B, C)$. Such an approach can be implemented in a way that it is compatible with Rooth's (1985) and Krifka's (1991) analysis of the semantics of focus phenomena. In order to obtain a focus binder, we need a type transition associated with the focus intonation pattern. Below, we use the $\stackrel{focus}{\longrightarrow}$ arrow to indicate such a transition. Explicit focus particles (such as *only*) in this perspective would be lexical functors of type $f(A, B, C)/A$.

$$t : A \stackrel{focus}{\longrightarrow} t' : f(A, B, C) \tag{44}$$

$$t' = \lambda x_{(t(A),t(B))}[x(t) \sqcap \text{FOREGROUND}(t)(x)]_{t(C)} \tag{45}$$

Semantically, the type transition is associated with a recipe which to the truth-functional content adds an element of information structuring in terms of a foreground/background opposition.

Let us illustrate the analysis of focus-as-binding with the following examples, where the transitive verb is focussed.

$$\textbf{John KISSED Mary} \tag{46}$$

The $\stackrel{focus}{\longrightarrow}$ type transition turns a first-order transitive verb into a higher order focus binder, abstracting over a transitive verb variable in a clausal domain s and yielding a sentence with focus information structuring s_f.

$$\text{kissed} : (np\backslash s)/np \stackrel{focus}{\longrightarrow} \text{KISSED} : f(((np\backslash s)/np), s, s_f) \tag{47}$$

The semantic recipes going with this type transition, and with the derivation of the complete sentence, are given below.

$$\text{KISSED} = \lambda x_{(eet)t}[x(\text{kissed}) \sqcap \text{FOREGROUND}(\text{kissed})(x)]_t \tag{48}$$

$$\text{KISSED}(\lambda y_{(eet)}.y(\text{mary})(\text{john})) \tag{49}$$

Raaijmakers (1991) shows that gapping can be analysed along parallel lines: the material that is foregrounded in the focus construction is backgrounded in the left conjunct of a gapping conjunction; the material missing from the right conjunct is of the type of the bound variable of the gapping binder.

These examples must be enough to illustrate the generality of the binding pattern $op(A, B, C)$. Many questions are left unanswered here. The reader will have realized that the arrow $\stackrel{focus}{\longrightarrow}$ for prosodically triggered type transitions is only a promisory note: what we would really like to develop here is a type calculus where the derivability relation $\vdash$ is sensitive to prosodic structuring. See Bird (1991), Oehrle (1991) or Moortgat – Morrill (1991) for explorations of this line of research. Also, we have not discussed the interaction of quantification and binding with locality domains. Morrill (1990) and Hepple (1990) develop categorial accounts of locality constraints in terms of domain modalities. These accounts are compatible with the basic semantic action of the type constructors discussed in this paper.

Notes

* Earlier versions of this paper were presented at the Tilburg Symposium on Discontinuous Dependencies (January 1990), the Second European Summer School in Language, Logic and Information (Leuven, August 1990), and the Finse Workshop on Computational Semantics (Finse, Norway, August 1990). I thank these audiences for comments. The sign-based approach to categorial deduction introduced here is further developed in Moortgat (1991) in terms of Gabbay's (1991a;b) Labelled Deductive Systems. Rather than completely rewrite the paper, I have kept it more or less in its 1990 form, adding references to more recent work where appropriate in the text. The final section gives pointers to some work where the type-constructors discussed in this paper have found wider applications.

References

Bach, E.
1981 Discontinuous constituents in generalized categorial grammars. *NELS XI*. Amherst, MA, 1–12.

Bach, E.
1984 Some generalizations of Categorial Grammars. In: Landman and Veltman (eds.), *Varieties of Formal Semantics*. Foris, Dordrecht, 1–23.

Benthem, J. van
1988 The Lambek Calculus. In: Oehrle – Bach – Wheeler (eds.), *Categorial Grammars and Natural Language Structures*, 35–68. Reidel, Dordrecht.

Benthem, J. van
1991 Language in Action. Categories, Lambdas, and Dynamic Logic. *Studies in Logic*. North-Holland, Amsterdam.

Bird, S.
1991 A declarative model of semantics-phonology interactions. In: Bird (ed.), *Declarative Perspectives on Phonology*. Edinburgh Working Papers in Cognitive Science, CCS, Edinburgh.

Calder, J.
1989 Paradigmatic morphology, *Proceedings of the 4th EACL Conference*, Manchester, 58–65.

Emms, M.
1990 Polymorphic quantifiers, *Proceedings 7th Amsterdam Colloquium*. ITLI, Amsterdam.

Gabbay, D.
1991a Labelled Deductive Systems. Draft, to appear. Oxford University Press, Oxford.

Gabbay, D.
1991b A general theory of structured consequence relations. Draft, to appear, Theoretical Foundations for Non-Monotonic Reasoning-Part 3.

Girard, J.Y.
1987 Linear Logic. *Theoretical Computer Science* 50, 1–102.

Girard, J.Y., Y. Lafont and P. Taylor
1989 Proofs and types. *Cambridge Tracts in Theoretical Computer Science* 7. Cambridge.

Hendriks, H. – M. Moortgat
1990 Theory of Flexible Interpretation. *Esprit DYANA Report R1.2.A.*

Hendriks, P.
1991 Subdeletion and the incompleteness of Noun Phrases, Adjective Phrases and Adverb Phrases. Ms. Talk presented at the 8th Amsterdam Colloquium, December 17–20 1991. To appear in the Proceedings.

Hepple, M.
1990 The Grammar and Processing of Order and Dependency: A Categorial Approach. Ph.D. Dissertation, Edinburgh.

Keenan, E. and L. Moss
1985 Generalized quantifiers and the expressive power of natural language. In: Van Benthem – ter Meulen (eds.), *Generalized Quantifiers in Natural Language*. Foris, Dordrecht, 73–126..

Keenan, E. – J. Stavi
1986 A semantic characterization of natural language determiners. *Linguistics & Philosophy* 9, 253–326.

Krifka, M.
1991 Focus, semantic partition and dynamic interpretation. Talk presented at the 8th Amsterdam Colloquium, December 17–20, 1991. To appear in the Proceedings.

Lambek, J.
1990 Logic without structural rules. (Another look at Cut Elimination). ms., McGill University, Montreal.

Linden, E.J. van
1991 Accent placement and focus in categorial logic. In: Bird (ed.), *Declarative Perspectives on Phonology. Edinburgh Working Papers in Cognitive Science*. CCS, Edinburgh.

Moortgat, M.
1988 *Categorial Investigations. Logical and Linguistic Aspects of the Lambek Calculus*. Foris, Dordrecht.

Moortgat, M.
1990a The quantification calculus: questions of axiomatisation. In: Hendriks & Moortgat (eds.).

Moortgat, M.
1990b Unambiguous proof representations for the Lambek Calculus. *Proceedings 7th Amsterdam Colloquium.*

Moortgat, M.
1996 Generalized quantifiers and discontinuous type constructors. *This volume*, 181–207.

Moortgat, M.
1991 Labelled Deductive Systems for categorial theorem proving. Talk presented at the 8th Amsterdam Colloquium, December 17-20. To appear in the Proceedings.

Moortgat, M. – G. Morrill
1991 Heads and phrases. Type calculus for dependency and constituent structure. *OTS Working Papers.* RUU, Utrecht.

Morrill, G.
1990 Grammar and logical types, In: Barry – Morrill (eds.), *Studies in Categorial Grammar.* Edinburgh Working Papers in Cognitive Science, Volume 5.

Morrill, G.
1990 Rules and derivation: binding phenomena and coordination in categorial logic. *dyana Deliverable R1.2.D.*

Morrill, G., N. Leslie, M. Hepple and G. Barry
1990 Categorial deductions and structural operations, In: Barry – Morrill (eds.), *Studies in Categorial Grammar.* Edinburgh Working Papers in Cognitive Science, Volume 5.

Oehrle, R.T.
1988 Multidimensional compositional functions as a basis for grammatical analysis. In: Oehrle – Bach – Wheeler (eds.), *Categorial Grammars and Natural Language Structures.* Reidel, Dordrecht, 349–390.

Oehrle, R.T.
1991 Prosodic constraints on dynamic grammatical analysis. In: Bird (ed.), *Declarative Perspectives on Phonology.* Edinburgh Working Papers in Cognitive Science, CCS, Edinburgh.

Raaijmakers, S.
1991 *Lexicalism and gapping.* Ms. Tilburg University, Tilburg.

Roorda, D.
1991 Resource Logics: Proof-theoretical Investigations. Ph.D. Dissertation, Amsterdam.

Rooth, M.
1985 Association with Focus. Ph.D. dissertation, University of Massachusetts, Amherst.

Siekmann, J.H.
1984 Universal unification. In: Shostak (ed.), *Proceedings of the 7th International Conference on Automated Deduction*. Lecture Notes in Computer Science. Springer, Berlin.

Wansing, H.
1990 Formulas-as-types for a hierarchy of sublogics of intuitionistic propositional logic. *Berichte der Gruppe Logik, Wissenstheorie und Information* 9/90. Freie Universität, Berlin.

Getting things in order

Mike Reape

1. Introduction

Nearly all modern grammatical theories derive word order from the terminal yield of phrase structure trees. This includes theories as disparate as GB, LFG (Bresnan 1982), and GPSG (Gazdar et al. 1985). Another way to put this is to say that the word order domain of a constituent is the sequence of the leaves of its constituent structure tree. Therefore, any attempt to explain apparent cases of discontinuous constituency requires that "continuous" surface phrase structure trees be assigned whose terminal yield exhibits the apparent discontinuity. In GB this is done via movement rules which "reorder" *D*-structure trees into *S*-structure trees. In LFG and GPSG this is done by assigning phrase structure trees to strings which do not necessarily correspond to intuitively-motivated subcategorisation requirements, e.g., Dutch and German control constructions may not include any controlled, infinitival VPs at the level of syntax. This can make the task of giving an interpretive, compositional semantics very difficult. The problem of discontinuous constituency has prompted numerous proposed solutions within and without the GB community. In nearly all cases, these proposals either employ operations on trees (e.g., clause union or movement) or a redefinition of the notion of tree (e.g., "tangled" or "discontinuous" trees; see Bunt 1996). That is, the strategy is to somehow produce a tree whose terminal string exhibits the apparent discontinuity. This strategy makes sense as long as one is committed to *surface syntax* as the basis of word order, as has of course been the case in most linguistic theory since the publication of *Syntactic Structures* (Chomsky 1957).

There is another approach however which is represented to some degree by the dependency grammar tradition and HPSG (Pollard and Sag 1987; 1994) and, to a lesser extent, by categorial grammar. This approach denies the existence of, or at least reduces the importance of, an independent level of surface syntactic structure and its role in determining word order. However, most versions of dependency grammar and categorial grammar require a *strict adjacency condition* on strings which is consistent with the phrase structure tradition. That is, the string derived by a phrasal constituent is still the left-to-right concatenation of the strings of its ordered daughters. To my knowledge, there are only two other approaches which allow word order to be derived from syntactic structure without necessarily requiring the adjacency condition. In theory, this is possible in HPSG since daughters are not ordered and the *Constituent Ordering Principle* allows an arbitrary mapping from syntactic structure to phonological theory in principle. So far, this does not seem to have been taken seriously by the HPSG community yet. The second approach is that taken by David Dowty (1991) which is reported in this volume. It is similar in many ways to the approach adopted here.[1]

I will present an approach which rejects surface syntax and its role in determining word order. In its simplest, most general form, the approach claims that

1. phrasal word order is determined within locally definable *word order domains* which are ordered sequences of constituents,[2]
2. phrasal word order domains are composed compositionally from their daughter word order domains,
3. lexical entries do not have word order domains,
4. the *functor* of a phrasal constituent is an element of its mother's domain and
5. either
   (a) a nonfunctor daughter is an element of its mother's domain or
   (b) the elements of a nonfunctor daughter's domain are elements of its mother's domain and furthermore they may appear discontinuously or nonadjacently in the mother's domain provided the relative order of the elements of the daughter domain are preserved in the mother's domain.

When the last option is chosen, we say that the daughter domain has been *domain unioned* into its mother's domain. We can also speak of two or more domains being domain unioned together.

Domain union can be formalised as a ternary relation $\bigcirc$ over sequences called *sequence union*, which is related to the *shuffle* operator of formal language theory.[3] (Cf. Hopcroft and Ullman 1979). Let ϵ be the *empty sequence*, σ_1, σ_2 and σ_3 be sequences and $\circ$ the string concatenation operator. Then

(1)
$$\bigcirc(\epsilon, \epsilon, \epsilon)$$
$$\bigcirc(x \circ \sigma_1, \sigma_2, x \circ \sigma_3) \leftrightarrow \bigcirc(\sigma_1, \sigma_2, \sigma_3)$$
$$\bigcirc(\sigma_1, x \circ \sigma_2, x \circ \sigma_3) \leftrightarrow \bigcirc(\sigma_1, \sigma_2, \sigma_3)$$

Clearly, $\bigcirc$ is very similar to $\circ$. Let σ also be a sequence. Then

(2) $\circ(\epsilon, \sigma, \sigma)$
$\circ(x \circ \sigma_1, \sigma_2, x \circ \sigma_3) \leftrightarrow \circ(\sigma_1, \sigma_2, \sigma_3)$

Note, however, that while $\circ$ is an operator (i.e., a *function*), $\bigcirc$ is not. (The definition of $\circ$ should be very familiar to Prolog programmers. It is just the definition of append/3.)

E.g., Let $A = \langle a, b\rangle$ and $B = \langle c, d\rangle$. Then $\bigcirc(A, B, C)$ iff C is one of the sequences in (3).

(3) $\langle a, b, c, d\rangle$
$\langle a, c, b, d\rangle$
$\langle a, c, d, b\rangle$
$\langle c, d, a, b\rangle$
$\langle c, a, d, b\rangle$
$\langle c, a, b, d\rangle$

Informally, C contains all and only the elements of A and B and the order of the elements of A and B are preserved in C. That is, for each value of C in (3), $a < b$ as in A and $c < d$ as in B.

In what follows, we assume a level of *syntactic-semantic functor-argument structure*. This functor-argument structure encodes (nonsurface) syntactic structure. However, since word order domains determine word order, this level of syntactic representation is unordered. Therefore, if we say that the phrase VP_1 is of the form $[_{VP_1}\ NP_1\ VP_2\ V_1]$ for example, the order of the daughter elements NP_1, VP_2 and V_1 is undefined. When we refer to syntactic constituents in the sequel, it is to this level of representation that wc refer.

A convenient way to think about domain union informally is in terms of bracket erasure of labelled bracketed strings.[4] If VP_1 is a phrase of the form $[_{VP_1}\ NP_1\ VP_2\ V_1]$ and we assume for the sake of argument that NP_1 precedes V_1 in the domain of VP_1 (written $D(VP_1)$) then $D(VP_1)$ can be any of the domains in (4) by virtue of the fact that a daughter can be an element of its mothers domain.

(4) $[_{VP_1}\ VP_2\ NP_1\ V_1\ ]$
$[_{VP_1}\ NP_1\ VP_2\ V_1\ ]$
$[_{VP_1}\ NP_1\ V_1\ VP_2\ ]$

Now assume that $D(VP_2)$ is $[_{VP_2}\ NP_2\ V_2]$. This means that NP_2 precedes V_2 in any domain which $D(VP_2)$ is domain unioned into. Informally, we can think of domain unioning $D(VP_2)$ into $D(VP_1)$ by placing $D(VP_2)$ anywhere in $D(VP_1)$, erasing the brackets $[_{VP_2}]$ and then allowing NP_2 and V_2 to "float" arbitrarily far to the left or right within $D(VP_1)$ so long as NP_2 precedes V_2. This means that any of the labelled bracketed strings in (5) can be derived (which are all possible domains of VP_1 in addition to those shown in (4)).

(5)
(a) $[_{VP_1}\ NP_1\ V_1\ NP_2\ V_2\ ]$
(b) $[_{VP_1}\ NP_1\ NP_2\ V_1\ V_2\ ]$
(c) $[_{VP_1}\ NP_1\ NP_2\ V_2\ V_1\ ]$
(d) $[_{VP_1}\ NP_2\ V_2\ NP_1\ V_1\ ]$
(e) $[_{VP_1}\ NP_2\ NP_1\ V_2\ V_1\ ]$
(f) $[_{VP_1}\ NP_2\ NP_1\ V_1\ V_2\ ]$

Now substitute $[_{VP_2}\ NP_2\ V_2]$ for $D(VP_2)$ in (4).

(6)
(a) $[_{VP_1}\ [_{VP_2}\ NP_2\ V_2]\ NP_1\ V_1\ ]$
(b) $[_{VP_1}\ NP_1\ [_{VP_2}\ NP_2\ V_2]\ V_1\ ]$
(c) $[_{VP_1}\ NP_1\ V_1\ [_{VP_2}\ NP_2\ V_2]\ ]$

Then (5a) will produce the same word order as in (6c), (5c) will produce the same word order as in (6b) and (5d) will produce the same word order as in (6a), although in the (5) domains, the $[_{VP_2}]$ brackets have been eliminated while in the (6) domains they are preserved. This means that if a (6) domain is unioned into another domain, then $D(VP_2)$ will necessarily be continuous in that domain whereas if a (5) domain is unioned into another domain, $D(VP_2)$ might appear discontinuously in it.

The order of elements in a domain which has been domain unioned is partially determined by the domain union relation but we have said nothing so far which determines the order of elements within a non-unioned domain. Domain order is also partially determined by *linear precedence* (LP) constraints of a form similar to those in GPSG. However, LP constraints are defined here as well-formedness conditions on word order domains (sequences) as opposed to GPSG where they are defined as well-formedness conditions on local trees. There are two types of LP constraints. A sequence σ satisfies an LP constraint of the form $\phi_1 \in \phi_2$ iff every element of σ which satisfies ϕ_1 in σ precedes every element of σ which satisfies ϕ_2. A sequence σ satisfies an LP constraint of the form $\phi_1 < \phi_2$ iff every element of σ which satisfies ϕ_1 in σ precedes (or is equal to) every element of σ which satisfies ϕ_2. The $\preceq$ form will become important in section 4.

For example, let $A = \langle$NP[DAT]$v_1\rangle$ and $B = \langle$NP[ACC]$v_2\rangle$ and assume the LP constraints NP[DAT] $<$ NP[ACC] and NP $<$ V. Then $\bigcirc(A, B, C)$ where C is one of the sequences in (7).

(7) ⟨NP[DAT] NP[ACC] V_1 V_2⟩
⟨NP[DAT] NP[ACC] V_2 V_1⟩

LP constraints apply to *every* domain. So, although NP[DAT] < NP[ACC] has no affect on *A* or *B*, it requires that the NP[DAT] from *A* precedes the NP[ACC] from *B*.

We will now turn to a simple example.

2. An example from German

Before we proceed with a detailed analysis of German verb projections, we will present a simple example of a German "cross-serial" subordinate clause. In (8), the subscripts indicate the head-complement dependencies. Each NP is separated from its head by other constituents. *es* 'it' is the direct object of the verb *zu lesen* 'to read', *ihm* 'him' is the dative object of the past participle *versprochen* 'promised' and *jemand* 'someone' is the subject of the finite auxiliary *hat*. *zu lesen* subcategorises for a nominative subject and an accusative object, *versprochen* subcategorises for a nominative subject, a dative object and a *zu*-infinitival VP and *hat* subcategorises for a nominative subject and and a past participle VP.

(8) daß es_3 ihm_2 $jemand_1$ zu $lesen_3$ $versprochen_2$ hat_1
that it(ACC) him(DAT) someone(NOM) to read promised has
'that someone promised him to read it'

To analyze this clause, we only need to make four assumptions beyond those made in section 1. First, the configuration [$_S$ NP[NOM] VP] is ungrammatical in German. Instead, verbs take all their complements as sisters in clauses. This does not mean that there are no VPs, just that they never form a clause with a subject. Second, we assume the LP constraint NP<V. Third, a verb follows any verb that it *governs*.[5] A verb V_i governs a verb V_j iff V_j is the head verb of a VP complement of V_i or V_i governs V_k and V_k governs V_j. (This is expressed using $\preceq$ but we will delay this until section 4.) Fourth, all of the verbs in (8) domain union their VP complements. (This is artificially trivial but is all we need to analyze this example.)

The verb *zu lesen* 'to read' subcategorises for a direct object so we can form the VP *es zu lesen* 'to read it' with domain (9).

(9) **[$_{VP}$ [$_{NP}$ es] [$_{V}$ zu lesen]]**

The NP *es* ‘it’ precedes the verb as required by the LP statement NP<V. The past participle *versprochen* ‘promised’ subcategorises for an indirect object and a *zu*-infinitival VP. *es zu lesen* is such a VP and *ihm* ‘him’ is the masculine, third person dative pronoun. If we union the domain of *es zu lesen* into the VP domain of which *versprochen* is the head we can form the VP *es ihm zu lesen versprochen* ‘promised him to read it’ with domain (10).

(10) **[$_{VP}$ [$_{NP}$ es] [$_{NP}$ ihm] [$_{V}$ zu lesen] [$_{V}$ versprochen]]**

Since the order of the two NPs with respect to each other is unconstrained they may appear in this order.[6] Both NPs precede both verbs as required and the governed verb *zu lesen* precedes its governing verb *versprochen* as required. *hat* ‘has’ subcategorises for a past participial VP. *es ihm zu lesen versprochen* is such a VP and *jemand* ‘someone’ is a nominative pronoun. If we union the domain of *es ihm zu lesen versprochen* into the finite clause domain we can form the clause *es ihm jemand zu lesen versprochen hat* ‘someone has promised him to read it’ with domain (11).

(11) **[$_{VP}$ [$_{NP}$ es] [$_{NP}$ ihm] [$_{NP}$ jemand] [$_{V}$ zu lesen] [$_{V}$ versprochen] [$_{V}$ hat]]**

Again, all NPs precede all verbs and *zu lesen* and *versprochen* precede the governing auxiliary *hat* so the domain is well-formed. The assumptions made above account for the possible permutations of NPs in the Mittelfeld and the canonical order of verbs in the verb sequence. Figure 1 is the syntax tree of (8) and Figure 2 is the domain tree of (8). Domain trees have domains as the nodes of trees instead of categories. In a local domain tree, the mother domain node is constructed from the daughter domain nodes according to the domain construction rules introduced in section 1.

Both syntax trees and domain trees are unordered. Furthermore, the structure of the trees in Figure 1 and Figure 2 is the same (modulo the order of the daughters, which is irrelevant). This isomorphism between syntax trees and domain trees always holds given the rules for domain construction. This means that domain construction is strictly compositional in the Montagovian sense. However, unlike composition of meaning translation in Montague semantics where the composition rules are all functional, domain construction is relational (because of the relational character of domain union and the non-determinism in applying domain union or not). So, for (8) we could derive a

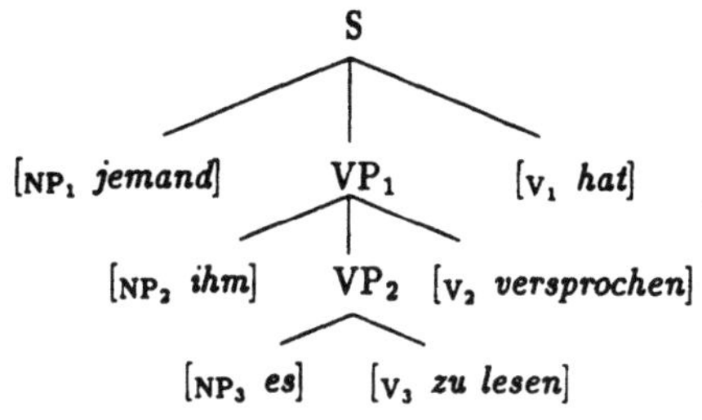

Figure 1. Syntax tree for (8)

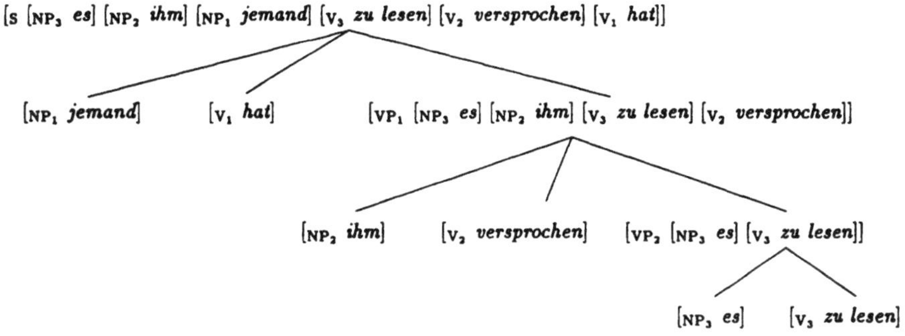

Figure 2. Domain tree for (8)

total of six domain trees corresponding to the clauses in (12) since the order of NPs is unconstrained.

(12)

es ihm jemand zu lesen versprochen hat
es jemand ihm zu lesen versprochen hat
ihm es jemand zu lesen versprochen hat
ihm jemand es zu lesen versprochen hat
jemand es ihm zu lesen versprochen hat
jemand ihm es zu lesen versprochen hat

3. An Analysis of German

We will now give an informal and somewhat idealised presentation of how this approach accounts for word order in German V2 (verb-second) and subordinate clauses. We will assume the 'TVX' analysis for V2 clauses, i.e., a topic followed by the finite verb followed by 'everything else'. The order of constituents in the 'X' domain is the same as the order of the post-complementiser field in subordinate clauses so we will primarily consider subordinate clauses. We assume, following Uszkoreit (1987), that the structure of a V2 clause is $[_{CP//}$ XP $[_{S/XP//}$ V[FIN] ...]], i.e., that the topic is filled by unbounded movement of a phrasal constituent from the post-verbal field. Furthermore, we assume that the finite verb is initial in the domain of the S in contrast to assumptions about the verb moving to COMP. In this structure there is no COMP position. The category of the V2 clause is labelled CP even though there is no COMP position present. CP is used because the topic does seem to be in a specifier-like position.

As in the discussion of (8), the characteristic Mittelfeld order of a sequence of NPs followed by a sequence of verbs is produced by unioning the domains of VPs and Ss together. We maintain the two previous LP constraints that NPs precede verbs and for canonical verb order, a governing verb is preceded by all the verbs it governs.

(13) a **daß der Mann versuchte, das Buch zu lesen**
that the man tried the book to read
'that the man tried to read the book'

b **daß der Mann versucht hat, das Buch zu lesen**
that the man tried has, the book to read
'that the man has tried to read the book'

(14) **daß der Mann versucht hat, zu behaupten, das Buch gelesen zu haben**
that the man tried has, to claim, the book read to have
'that the man has tried to claim to have read the book'

(13) and (14) contain *extraposed* VPs. An extraposed VP is one which occurs to the right of the verb cluster which contains the verb that governs it. In (13a), the VP *das Buch zu lesen* is not unioned but is extraposed and appears in clause-final position after the finite verb. To analyse this, we prohibit extraposed clauses from being unioned and add the LP constraint [EXTRA -] < [EXTRA +]. EXTRA (EXTRAPOSED) is a binary-valued feature which indicates whether a constituent is extraposed or not. This LP constraint

forces all nonextraposed elements to proceed all extraposed elements within a domain. (In this fragment, only VPs are allowed to be extraposed.) Since the VP is extraposed it will not be unioned and will be marked [EXTRA +]. (Cf. Figures 3 and 4.)

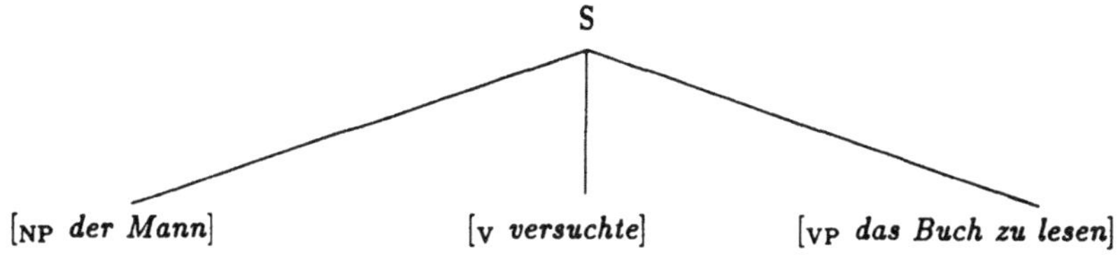

Figure 3. Syntax tree for (13a)

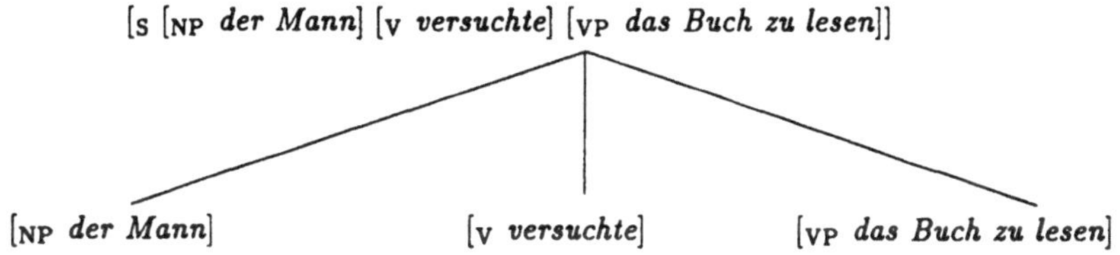

Figure 4. Domain tree for (13a)

(13b) is slightly more interesting. Here, *das Buch zu lesen* is subcategorised by the participle *versucht* from which it is separated and is not subcategorised by the finite auxiliary *hat*. The domain of the VP *das Buch zu lesen* is not unioned and so the VP is in domain-final position in the domain of the VP *versucht, das Buch zu lesen* due to the LP constraint. Its domain is (15).

(15) [$_{\text{VP}}$ [$_{\text{V}}$ **versucht**] [$_{\text{VP}}$ **das Buch zu lesen**]]

(15) is then unioned into the finite clause domain resulting in domain (16).

(16) [$_{\text{VP}}$ [$_{\text{NP}}$ **der Mann**] [$_{\text{V}}$ **versucht**] [$_{\text{V}}$ **hat**] [$_{\text{VP}}$ **das Buch zu lesen**]]

Since [$_{\text{VP}}$ das Buch zu lesen] is [EXTRA +] and an element of the finite clause's domain it must be domain final which it is. *versucht* appears to the left of *hat* since *hat* governs it. Finally, the NP *der Mann* appears to the left of all the verbs as required by the LP constraint. (Cf. Figures 5 and 6.)

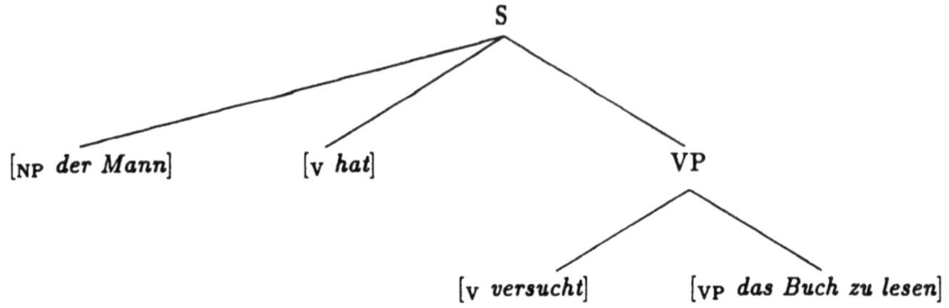

Figure 5. Syntax tree for (13b)

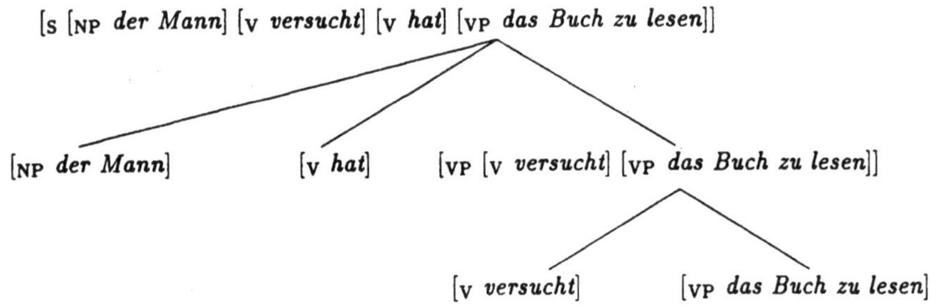

Figure 6. Domain tree for (13b)

(14) is a bit more complicated. The VP *das Buch gelesen* and the verb *zu haben* form the VP *das Buch gelesen zu haben.* It may not look like it but this actually involves unioning the domain of *das Buch gelesen* into the VP domain of which *zu haben* is the head. In general, we require that nonextraposed VPs are unioned. The extraposed VP *das Buch gelesen zu haben* forms a VP with the verb *zu behaupten.* Its domain is (17).

(17) [VP [V **zu behaupten**] [VP **das Buch gelesen zu haben**]]

Then this VP is extraposed in the VP *versucht, zu behaupten, das Buch gelesen zu haben.* Its domain is (18).

(18) [VP [V **versucht**] [VP [V **zu behaupten**] [VP **das Buch gelesen zu haben**]]]

Finally, this VP domain is unioned into the domain of the finite clause as in (13b). Cf. Figures 7 and 8.

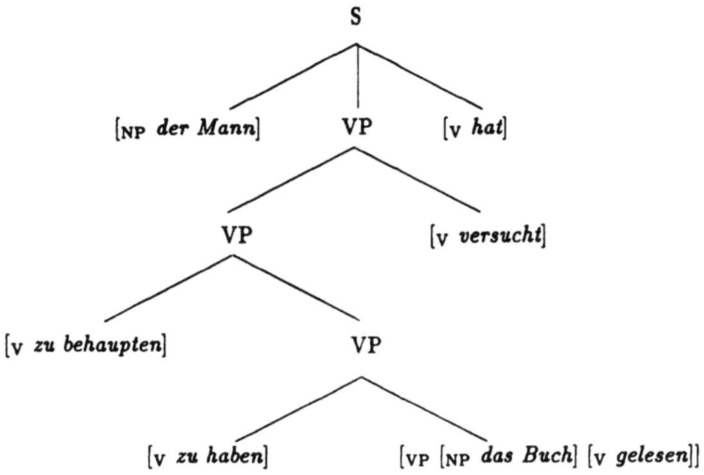

Figure 7. Syntax tree for (14)

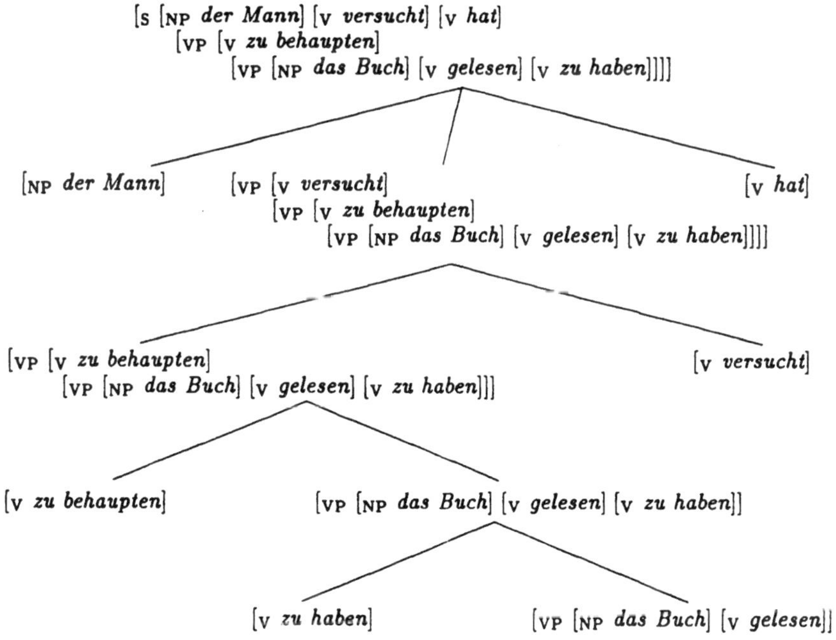

Figure 8. Domain tree for (14)

Notice that VP extraposition is not taken to be clause-bounded rightward movement as in English relative clause extraposition. Rather VP extraposition is analyzed as a VP occuring in domain final position in a VP or S domain. In cases of "recursive" extraposition like (14), the VP *das Buch gelesen zu haben* is "trapped" inside of the domain of the VP *zu behaupten, das Buch gelesen zu haben*. Therefore when this VP is extraposed within the finite clause, we will get the characteristic recursive extraposition order of [... VC VP_1 VP_2 VP_3 ...] where VC is the verb cluster.

This treatment of VP extraposition has interesting implications for topicalisation of VPs in V2 clauses. Assume that constituents are not unioned in topic position. In other words, the topic must be in clause-initial position. Then it should be possible to topicalise entire VPs and also recursively extraposed VPs. This is precisely what we find.

(19) **dem Jungen das Buch schenken wollte Peter**
the boy the book give wanted Peter
'Peter wanted to give the boy the book'

(20) a **Hans hat sich geweigert, dem Richter zu gestehen, die Tat begangen zu haben**
Hans has himself refused the judge to confess, the act committed to have
'Hans has refused to confess to having committed the act to the judge'

b **Dem Richter zu gestehen, die Tat begangen zu haben, hat Hans sich geweigert**

In (19), the VP complement *dem Jungen das Buch schenken* of the finite verb *wollte* has been topicalised. (20a) is a V2 clause where the VP *die Tat begangen zu haben* is recursively extraposed in the VP *dem Richter zu gestehen, die Tat begangen zu haben* which is extraposed in the finite clause itself. (20b) shows that the VP *dem Richter zu gestehen, die Tat begangen zu haben* can be topicalised instead of extraposed and that the VP *die Tat begangen zu haben* is in fact a daughter of the VP headed by *zu gestehen* and not the finite clause. (Cf. Figure 9.)

Examples like (21) would appear to cause problems, however.

(21) **?versucht zu behaupten hat er, das Buch gelesen zu haben**

At first sight, (21) looks very problematic.[7] The VP *das Buch gelesen zu haben* is dependent on *zu behaupten* (which in turn is extraposed in the topicalised VP *versucht zu behaupten*) but it is in clause-final position rather than in topic-final position as we would expect from the account of VP extraposition above. This is rather disturbing since it would appear to require

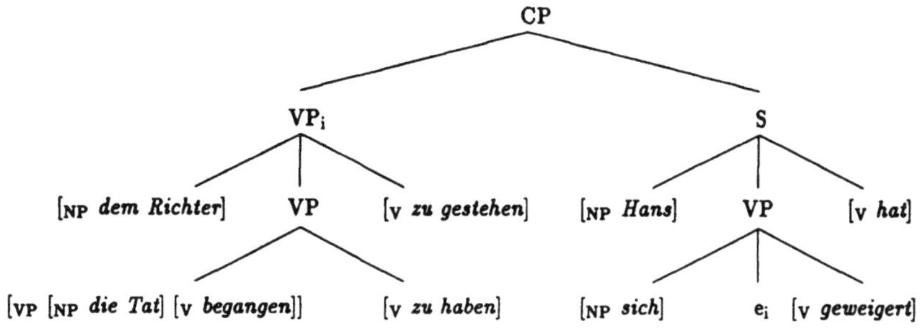

Figure 9. Syntax tree for (20b)

a special rule or device to allow clause-final extraposition in just this one case when we have derived the other cases from general properties of the analysis. However, there is other data which is relevant to this problem. As is well-known, it is possible to front a verb with some or none of its complements.

(22)
a **dem Jungen das Buch schenken wollte Peter**
b **dem Jungen schenken wollte Peter das Buch**
c **das Buch schenken wollte Peter dem Jungen**
d **schenken wollte Peter dem Jungen das Buch**

One explanation that has been proposed by den Besten and Webelhuth (1988) is that the complements which are "left behind" have been "moved out" of the VP to the finite clause prior to its topicalisation. I.e., *dem Jungen schenken*, *das Buch schenken* and *schenken* in (22b)–(22d) respectively, are really VPs and not nonmaximal verb projections. Given this analysis, the null hypothesis predicts that constituents can be "moved up" from extraposed VPs as well. Uszkoreit (1987) provides examples of just this type (cf. (23)).

(23) **Letztes Jahr hatte Peter [das große Haus]$_i$ der Stadt versprochen e$_i$ zu reparieren**
last year had Peter the big house the city promised to repair
'Peter promised the city to repair the big house last year'

(23) shows that this movement can cooccur with topicalisation. Uszkoreit also provides examples that show that it can cooccur with *wh*-movement and that more than one constituent can be moved. All of these examples, however, involve movement to the post-finite verb field. The null hypothesis should

be that these constituents can move up to VPs which intervene between the extraction site and the finite clause. However, the only way to see this theory-neutrally is to see if constituents move from an extraposed VP governed by a VP which is itself extraposed (i.e., a case of recursive extraposition) to the extraposed governing VP itself. Hans den Besten (p.c.) has shown that there are examples in both German and Dutch where this is in fact possible.

How then can these facts be integrated into the account outlined above? At a purely descriptive level, we want to say that such "raised" constituents are moved to the domain of the VP or S that they appear in. Then the LP constraints and other grammatical factors come into play to treat them just like any other element of that domain. All the evidence seems to support that this "equal treatment" does in fact hold. We are now in a position to explain (21). Assume that raised constituents can also be marked [EXTRA +], i.e., can be extraposed. Then (21) can be explained by assuming that *das Buch gelesen zu haben* is marked [EXTRA +] and raised out of the VP *versucht zu behaupten, das Buch gelesen zu haben* into the domain of the finite clause. Since *das Buch gelesen zu haben* is marked [EXTRA +] it will appear in clause-final position.

A few words are in order concerning the style of analysis. First, the word order domains are very flat. There is not even an identifiable verb cluster domain in contrast with most assumptions about the constituent structure of German subordinate clauses. Coordination data suggests that verb clusters are constituents, and therefore, have continuous domains. However, there is a great deal of nonconstituent coordination evidence in the Mittelfeld which suggests that coordination is not a good metric for determining whether verb clusters are constituents or not. Furthermore, topicalisation of verb clusters or partial verb clusters is not necessarily an indication of constituency either as this can be explained in terms of raising and remnant topicalisation as discussed above. Neither is the fact that verb clusters cannot be interrupted by any other material. Dowty (1991) presents an analysis of English which contains *attachment operators* in addition to operations equivalent to sequence union. These attachment operators are just like sequence union except that they force the heads of the two sequences being unioned to be "attached", i.e., immediately adjacent and not interrupted by any other material in any domain. These operators could explain why verb clusters must not be interrupted and are prosodic phrases. That is, domain union may not only involve sequence union but also adjacency of the head verbs. The fact that verb clusters are prosodic phrases does not imply that a verb cluster must be a constituent in a VP or S domain though. So far, it has not been necessary to use an immediate precedence relation although its role in the treatment of clitics and clitic-like elements is of obvious utility.

A second reason that verb clusters contain no internal domain structure is based on empirical evidence. Typical verb raising analyses of verb clusters assume a nested $\overline{V}$ structure where each level is of the form $[_{\overline{V}}\ V\ \overline{V}]$ or $[_{\overline{V}}\ \overline{V}\ V]$. This covers the possible 1 – 2, 2 – 1 and 1 – 2 – 3 government orders of Dutch and all of the possible Standard German verb cluster orders (and many more). These can all be dealt with very easily within the current account since a verb can be lexically specified to occur to the right or left of the verbs it governs. This is equivalent to "direction of status government" in von Stechow's terms (1990). However, a government order of 4 – 1 – 3 – 2 could not be accounted for in terms of a verb raising analysis unless adjunction to the highest $\overline{V}$ was allowed and then movement of the V_4 to the adjoined position. Such orders can be found in nonstandard dialects of German. In Zürich German, there seems to be no restriction on the relative order of auxiliaries, modals, verbs of perception and the causative within a domain. In fact, these verbs need not even form a verb cluster (Cf. Cooper 1988). Furthermore, it can be shown that such instances are not examples of extraposition or verb projection raising. This dialect evidence suggests strongly that the verb cluster is not a constituent in word order domains.

4. An interpretation in HPSG

I will now present an interpretation of this account of word order in a variant of HPSG as described in (Pollard and Sag 1987; henceforth P&S).[8] The account presented here is reminiscent of certain categorial grammar analyses. As in standard HPSG, linguistic objects are *signs*. All signs are specified for the attributes PHON (PHONOLOGY), SYN (SYNTAX) and SEM (SEMANTICS) encoding the phonology, syntax and semantics respectively of a sign. PHON takes a sequence of atomic elements representing orthographic words as its value. SYN and SEM are to be interpreted precisely as in P&S. Phrasal signs are also specified for the DOM (DOMAIN) attribute. It encodes the word order domains discussed in section 1 and takes a sequence of signs as its value. Lexical signs are undefined for the DOM attribute. Whereas domains as labelled bracketed strings encode category information in the label, here domains are the value of the attribute within a sign. That is,

(24) $[_{VP} X_1, \ldots, X_n] \equiv \left[\text{SYN}|\text{LOC VP}[\text{DOM } \langle X_1, \ldots, X_n \rangle]\right]$

Phrasal signs are specified for the DTRS (DAUGHTERS) attribute. Its value can be of type *functor-argument-structure*. Functor-argument structures are defined for the attributes FUN-DTR (FUNCTOR-DAUGHTER), ARG-DTRS (ARGUMENT-DAUGHTERS) and HEAD-DTR (HEAD-DAUGHTER). HEAD-DTR is the same attribute as in P&S. FUN-DTR is the syntactic functor in a phrasal sign. It is either the head daughter (HEAD-DTR) in a *head-complement-structure* (cf. (25)) or the adjunct daughter in a *head-adjunct-structure* (cf. (26)). Both *head-complement-structure* and *head-adjunct-structure* are subtypes of *functor-argument-structure*.

(25) $[\text{DTRS }_{\textit{head-complement-structure}}[\,]] \Rightarrow \left[\text{DTRS} \begin{bmatrix} \text{HEAD-DTR } \boxed{1} \\ \text{FUN-DTR } \boxed{1} \end{bmatrix}\right]$

(26) $[\text{DTRS }_{\textit{head-adjunct-structure}}[\,]] \Rightarrow \left[\text{DTRS} \begin{bmatrix} \text{HEAD-DTR } \boxed{1} \\ \text{FUN-DTR}|\text{SYN}|\text{LOC}|\text{ARGS } \langle \boxed{1} \rangle \end{bmatrix}\right]$

ARGS (ARGUMENTS) takes a sequence of signs as its value representing the arguments of the functor. (It replaces the SUBCAT attribute of P&S.) ARG-DTRS is the subsequence of ARGS that have been syntactically saturated. (It replaces the COMP-DTRS attribute of P&S.) The *Head Feature Principle* guarantees that the HEAD features of the mother and head daughter are coindexed properly.

(27) $[\text{DTRS }_{\textit{headed-structure}}[\,]] \Rightarrow \begin{bmatrix} \text{SYN}|\text{LOC}|\text{HEAD } \boxed{1} \\ \text{DTRS}|\text{HEAD-DTR}|\text{SYN}|\text{LOC}|\text{HEAD } \boxed{1} \end{bmatrix}$

The *Functor-Argument Principle* replaces the *Subcategorisation Principle* of P&S and amends it in accordance with the changes to the feature system described above.[9]

(28) $[\text{DTRS }_{\textit{headed-structure}}[\,]] \Rightarrow \begin{bmatrix} \text{SYN}|\text{LOC}|\text{HEAD } \boxed{1} \\ \text{DTRS}|\text{HEAD-DTR}|\text{SYN}|\text{LOC}|\text{HEAD } \boxed{1} \end{bmatrix}$

In addition to the Functor-Argument Principle, there is also the *Domain Principle* (which does not occur in P&S).[10] Although it looks formidable, the intuition underlying it is quite simple. It states the relation between the DTRS attribute and the DOM attribute according to the domain construction rules given in section 1. Informally, it "maps" the syntactic structure onto the domain structure "nondeterministically". It references the UNIONED attribute which specifies whether a daughter can be sequence unioned into the word order domain DOM. (The value of UNIONED can either be specified by lexical functors of their arguments or by language specific principles. In German, nonverb projections are [UNIONED –] while verb projections are unspecified for UNIONED. Therefore they can either appear continuously or discontinuously in a domain.) Basically, the Domain Principle states that the functor (FUN-DTR) is an element of the domain DOM and that every argument daughter (element of ARG-DTRS) is either an element of DOM or its domain is domain unioned into DOM.

(29)

$$\left[\text{DTRS}\ {}_{\textit{functor-argument-structure}}[\,]\right] \Rightarrow$$

$$\begin{bmatrix} \text{DTRS} & \begin{bmatrix} \text{FUN-DTR} & \boxed{1} \\ \text{ARG-DTRS} & \langle \boxed{2}[\text{UNIONED} -], \ldots, \boxed{i}[\text{UNIONED} -]\rangle \bigcirc \\ & \langle [\text{UNIONED} +, \text{DOM}\ \boxed{i+1}], \ldots, [\text{UNIONED} +, \text{DOM}\ \boxed{n}]\rangle \end{bmatrix} \\ \text{DOM} & \langle \boxed{1}\rangle \bigcirc \langle\boxed{2}\rangle \bigcirc \ldots \bigcirc \langle\boxed{i}\rangle \bigcirc \boxed{i+1} \bigcirc \ldots \bigcirc \boxed{n} \end{bmatrix}$$

Given the definition of $\bigcirc$ in section 1, $\bigcirc$ is deterministic on a sequence *C* if every element of *C* is marked either F + or F – for some feature F. That is, there will exist unique sequences *A* and *B* such that $\bigcirc(A, B, C)$ and every element of *B* is marked F + and every element of is *C* marked F –. Therefore, $\bigcirc$ is deterministic in the definition of the Domain Principle since every element is either UNIONED + or UNIONED –. Therefore, there will be only one way of dividing a sequence into the set of unioned and nonunioned elements.

The HPSG *Constituent Ordering Principle* is amended so that it requires that the value of the PHON attribute be the concatenation of the values of the PHON attributes of the elements of the DOM sequence if it is specified. Lexical signs specify their phonologies lexically.

(30)

$$\textit{phrasal-sign}[\,] \Rightarrow \begin{bmatrix} \text{PHON} & \boxed{1} \circ \ldots \circ \boxed{n} \\ \text{DOM} & \langle [\text{PHON}\ \boxed{1}], \ldots, [\text{PHON}\ \boxed{n}]\rangle \end{bmatrix}$$

This concludes the modifications to the universal principles of P&S. We will now look at the three phrase structure rules and the language specific principles required for the fragment of German considered in section 3.

(31)–(33) replace Rules 1, 2 and 3 of P&S. They are all amended for the FUN-DTR , ARGS and ARG-DTRS attributes. Rule 4 is eliminated. Instead, Rules 1 and 2 generalise the syntax of head-complement signs and head-adjunct signs. Rule 1 lets nonlexical heads combine with a single remaining argument. It disallows VPs from combining with subjects (NP[NOM]) since the analysis assumes that there is no VP in a clause. This enforces the prohibition of [S NP[NOM] VP] syntactic structures in German.

(31) Rule 1

a
$$\begin{bmatrix} \text{SYN}|\text{LOC}|\text{ARGS} \ \langle\ \rangle \\ \text{DTRS} \begin{bmatrix} \text{FUN-DTR}|\text{SYN}|\text{LOC}|\text{LEX} \ - \\ \text{ARG-DTRS} \ \langle \neg\text{NP}[\text{NOM}] \rangle \end{bmatrix} \end{bmatrix}$$

b $[\text{ARGS}\langle\ \rangle] \rightarrow \text{F}[\text{LEX} -], \text{A}(\neg\text{NP}[\text{NOM}])$

((31b), (32b) and (33b) are the "schematic" form of the rules. F indicates the functor and A a complement in the schematic rules.)

Rule 2 is just like the corresponding rule for English and Dutch. It lets a lexical head combine with all but one of its complements. It specifies [INV –] to guarantee that VPs are head-final.

(32) Rule 2

a
$$\begin{bmatrix} \text{SYN}|\text{LOC}|\text{ARGS} \ \langle[\ ]\rangle \\ \text{DTRS}|\text{FUN-DTR}|\text{SYN}|\text{LOC} \begin{bmatrix} \text{HEAD}|\text{INV} & - \\ \text{LEX} & + \end{bmatrix} \end{bmatrix}$$

b $[\text{ARGS}\langle[\ ]\rangle] \rightarrow \text{F}[\text{INV} +, \text{LEX} +], \text{A}^{*}$

Rule 3 drops the [INV +] specification on the head and requires that the functor (the head verb) be a finite verb. This rule allows all of the complements of a verb to be combined with a finite verb at one time, thus allowing the subject to appear in the same domain as the nonsubject complements.

(33) Rule 3

a
$$\begin{bmatrix} \text{SYN}|\text{LOC}|\text{ARGS} \ \langle\ \rangle \\ \text{DTRS}|\text{FUN-DTR}|\text{SYN}|\text{LOC} \ \text{V}[\text{LEX} +] \end{bmatrix}$$

b $[\text{ARGS}\ \langle\ \rangle] \rightarrow \text{V}[\text{LEX} +], \text{A}^{*}$

Rules 1, 2 and 3, the Functor-Argument Principle and the Domain Principle determine the elements of a DOM sequence but only partially determine the *order* of the elements in a DOM sequence.

Assume the LP statements in (34) – (37).

(34) $[\text{DOM}] \Rightarrow [\text{DOM NP} \prec \text{V}]$

(35) $[\text{DTRS}|\text{HEAD-DTR } \boxed{1}\text{V}[\text{INV} -]] \Rightarrow [\text{DOM V} \preceq \boxed{1}]$

(36) $[\text{DTRS}|\text{HEAD-DTR } \boxed{1}\text{V}[\text{INV} +]] \Rightarrow [\text{DOM } \boxed{1} \prec [\,]]$

(37) $[\text{DOM}] \Rightarrow [\text{DOM } [\text{EXTRA} -] \prec [\text{EXTRA} +]]$

(34) requires that NPs precede verbs, (35) that noninverted (i.e., non-clause-initial) head daughter verbs are preceded by the verbs they govern, (36) that inverted (clause-initial) verbs precede everything and (37) that non-extraposed constituents precede extraposed constituents. (35) has the effect it does because it requires the head verb of a sign to be preceded by (or be equal to) all the verbs in the sign's domain. Since all the verbs in the sign's domain are governed by the head verb, they will remain in that order in any domain the domain is unioned into. So, in any domain, each verb will precede any verb that governs it. Inverted clauses occur in V1 and V2 clauses.

Let VP be notational shorthand for $\text{V}[\text{ARGS}\langle\text{NP}[\text{NOM}]\rangle]$ and S notational shorthand for $\text{V}[\text{ARGS}\langle\rangle]$. Then also assume the language specific principles (38) and (39).

(38) $[\text{EXTRA} +] \Rightarrow \text{VP}$

(39) $[\text{UNIONED} +] \Rightarrow \text{VP} \vee \text{S}$

(38) encodes the fact that only VPs can be extraposed. (39) encodes the fact that only VPs and Ss can be sequence unioned. The contrapositives (40) and (41) can also be derived since every sign is specified for EXTRA and UNIONED.

(40) $\neg\text{VP} \Rightarrow [\text{EXTRA} -]$

(41) $\neg\text{VP} \wedge \neg\text{S} \Rightarrow [\text{UNIONED} -]$

With these formal preliminaries in hand, we can now consider an example. Let the features NOM, DAT, ACC, FIN and PSP be exactly as in Pollard and Sag (1987). We also assume the VFORM features ZU for *zu*-infinitivals and INF for bare infinitivals. Then assume the following (schematic) German lexical entries.

(42) *jemand* : $\text{NP}[\text{NOM}]$

(43) *ihm* : NP[DAT]

(44) *es* : NP[ACC]

(45) *hat* : V[FIN, ARGS ⟨NP[NOM],VP[PSP]⟩]

(46) *versprochen* : V[PSP, ARGS ⟨NP[NOM],NP[DAT],VP[ZU]⟩]

(47) *zu lesen* : V[ZU, ARGS ⟨NP[NOM],NP[ACC]⟩]

Given these assumptions, we can give an analysis of (8), *es ihm jemand zu lesen versprochen hat* 'someone has promised him to read it'.

In (48), the sign labelled $\boxed{8}$, the NP *es* ($\boxed{1}$) has combined by Rule 2 with the *zu*-infinitival verb *zu lesen* ($\boxed{4}$) forming the VP[ZU] *es zu lesen* whose DOM sequence is ⟨$\boxed{1}$, $\boxed{4}$⟩. $\boxed{1}$ precedes $\boxed{4}$ as required by (34).

(48)

$$\boxed{8}\begin{bmatrix} \text{PHON} & \langle \text{es zu lesen}\rangle \\ \text{SYN|LOC} & \text{VP[ZU]} \\ \text{DTRS} & \begin{bmatrix} \text{HEAD-DTR} & \boxed{4}\begin{bmatrix}\text{PHON} & \langle\text{zu lesen}\rangle \\ \text{SYN|LOC} & \text{V[ZU,ARGS}\langle\text{NP[NOM]},\boxed{1}\rangle]\end{bmatrix} \\ \text{FUN-DTR} & \boxed{4} \\ \text{ARG-DTRS} & \left\langle \boxed{1}\begin{bmatrix}\text{PHON} & \langle\text{es}\rangle \\ \text{SYN|LOC|HEAD} & \text{NP}\end{bmatrix}\right\rangle \end{bmatrix} \\ \text{DOM} & \langle\boxed{1},\boxed{4}\rangle \end{bmatrix}$$

In (49), the sign labelled $\boxed{7}$, the NP *ihm* ($\boxed{2}$) and the VP *es zu lesen* ($\boxed{8}$) have combined by Rule 2 with the past participle *versprochen* ($\boxed{5}$) forming the VP[PSP] *es ihm zu lesen versprochen* whose DOM sequence is ⟨$\boxed{1}$, $\boxed{2}$, $\boxed{4}$, $\boxed{5}$⟩. This time, the domain of the VP *es zu lesen* has been unioned into the domain of $\boxed{7}$. Both NPs ($\boxed{1}$ and $\boxed{2}$) precede both verbs ($\boxed{4}$ and $\boxed{5}$) in the domain as required by (34). Furthermore, the governing verb *versprochen* ($\boxed{5}$) is preceded by the governed verb *zu lesen* ($\boxed{4}$) as required by (35). *es* and *ihm* are not restricted in order with respect to each other so they can come in either order.

(49)

$$\boxed{7}\begin{bmatrix} \text{PHON} & \langle \text{es ihm zu lesen versprochen} \rangle \\ \text{SYN|LOC} & \text{VP[PSP]} \\ \text{DTRS} & \begin{bmatrix} \text{HEAD-DTR} & \boxed{5}\begin{bmatrix}\text{PHON} & \langle\text{versprochen}\rangle \\ \text{SYN|LOC} & \text{V[PSP,ARGS}\langle \text{NP[NOM]},\boxed{2},\boxed{8}\rangle]\end{bmatrix} \\ \text{FUN-DTR} & \boxed{5} \\ \text{ARG-DTRS} & \left\langle \boxed{2}\begin{bmatrix}\text{PHON} & \langle\text{ihm}\rangle \\ \text{SYN|LOC|HEAD} & \text{NP[DAT]}\end{bmatrix}, \boxed{8}\right\rangle \end{bmatrix} \\ \text{DOM} & \langle \boxed{1},\boxed{2},\boxed{4},\boxed{5}\rangle \end{bmatrix}$$

Finally, in (50), the NP *jemand* ($\boxed{3}$) and the VP *es ihm zu lesen versprochen* ($\boxed{7}$) have combined by Rule 3 with the auxiliary *hat* ($\boxed{6}$) forming the S *es ihm jemand zu lesen versprochen hat* whose DOM sequence is $\langle \boxed{1},\boxed{2},\boxed{3},\boxed{4},\boxed{5},\boxed{6}\rangle$. The domain of the VP *es ihm zu lesen versprochen* has been unioned into the domain of the S. Again, all NPs precede all verbs and governing verbs precede governed verbs as required by (34) and (35).

(50)

$$\begin{bmatrix} \text{PHON} & \langle \text{es ihm jemand zu lesen versprochen hat} \rangle \\ \text{SYN|LOC} & \text{S} \\ \text{DTRS} & \begin{bmatrix} \text{HEAD-DTR} & \boxed{6}\begin{bmatrix}\text{PHON} & \langle\text{hat}\rangle \\ \text{SYN|LOC} & \text{V[ARGS}\langle \boxed{3},\boxed{7}\rangle]\end{bmatrix} \\ \text{FUN-DTR} & \boxed{6} \\ \text{ARG-DTRS} & \left\langle \boxed{3}\begin{bmatrix}\text{PHON} & \langle\text{jemand}\rangle \\ \text{SYN|LOC|HEAD} & \text{NP[NOM]}\end{bmatrix}, \boxed{7}\right\rangle \end{bmatrix} \\ \text{DOM} & \langle \boxed{1},\boxed{2},\boxed{3},\boxed{4},\boxed{5},\boxed{6}\rangle \end{bmatrix}$$

There are a few things which have not been dealt with in either the informal treatment in section 3 or in the formal treatment in this section. The first of these is the account of the complementiser *daß*. (51) is its lexical entry.

(51)

$$\begin{bmatrix} \text{PHON} & \text{daß} \\ \text{SYN|LOC} & \begin{bmatrix} \text{COMP} & + \\ \text{ARGS} & \left\langle \text{S}\begin{bmatrix} \text{SYN|LOC} & \begin{bmatrix} \text{HEAD} & \begin{bmatrix}\text{VFORM} & \text{FIN} \\ \text{INV} & - \end{bmatrix} \\ \text{COMP} & - \end{bmatrix}\end{bmatrix}\right\rangle \end{bmatrix} \end{bmatrix}_{\textit{lexical-sign}}$$

daß is a functor which takes a noninverted, finite clause as its argument.[11] The feature COMP (which is a SYN LOC feature) keeps track of whether or not a clause has combined with a complementiser to form a subordinate clause (which we abbreviate as S[COMP +]). Since *daß* requires an S[COMP −] argument but is itself an S[COMP +], it effectively allows only one complementizer to combine with a clause. (This is essentially the same as the GPSG analysis.) There is a small problem here in that the + value of COMP will not automatically be identified with the COMP value of the subordinate clause since it is not a head feature and the complementiser is not the head anyway. A purely technical solution is to add the implication (52) to the grammar.

(52) [DTRS|FUN-DTR|SYN|LOC|COMP +] ⇒ [SYN|LOC|COMP +]

We will also see momentarily that we could state the antecedent in terms of the type *head-complementiser-structure*.

(53) [DTRS $_{head\text{-}complementiser\text{-}structure}$[ ]] ⇒ [SYN|LOC|COMP +]

Both (52) and (53) require that if the sign is a subordinate clause then the value of SYN LOC COMP is +. This is reminiscent of the Head Feature Principle. An analysis which takes the complementiser to be the head would not suffer from this problem. An even more categorial style of analysis would solve this problem as well. I will leave the best way to handle this as an open question.

Another issue is the distribution of INV and COMP. Since both INV and COMP are binary valued, there are four possibilities. All four combinations are realised. They are summarised in (54).

(54)

[COMP +, INV +]	dialect subordinate clauses
[COMP +, INV −]	subordinate clauses
[COMP −, INV +]	conditional clauses, V1, constituent of V2 clauses
[COMP −, INV −]	constituent of subordinate clauses

In addition to head-adjunct structures, we need to allow other headed structures which are not head-complement structures. For example, specifiers are not adjuncts but enter into headed structures where the Head Feature Principle should apply. For the present purpose, we will assume that the value of the DTRS feature of a subordinate clause is a headed structure of type *head-complementiser-structure*. Since the complementiser specifies a head clause argument, it will combine with its argument by Rule 1. The Head Feature

Principle means that the head features of the head clause will be identified with the head features of the S[COMP +].

We also need to describe V2 clauses. As stated in section 3, V2 clauses consist of a topic followed by an inverted clause with a gap in it corresponding to the topic. This means that we will need a filler-gap rule which requires that the gapped clause be [INV +]. For the link between the filler and the gap we assume some trace-based account of unbounded dependencies. A trace has a null phonology. That is, the value of the PHON feature is ϵ, the empty sequence, so it will contribute nothing to the phonology of any sign whose domain contains it since the Constituent Ordering Principle will just concatenate ϵ with the other PHON values.

The filler-gap rule will create a headed structure with a FILLER-DTR and a HEAD-DTR. This structure will be of type *head-complementiser-structure*. Schematically, the *head-complementiser-structure* type is of the form [$_{CP}$ $\boxed{1}$, S[SLASH {$\boxed{1}$}, INV +]]. In detail, it is (55). Notice that the FILLER-DTR (the topic) is the only element in the SLASH set.

(55)

$$\begin{bmatrix} \text{DTRS} & \begin{bmatrix} \text{FILLER-DTR} & \boxed{1} \\ \text{HEAD-DTR} & \begin{bmatrix} \text{SYN} & \begin{bmatrix} \text{LOC}|\text{HEAD} & \text{s[INV +]} \\ \text{BIND}|\text{SLASH} & \{\boxed{1}\} \end{bmatrix} \end{bmatrix} \end{bmatrix} \end{bmatrix}_{\textit{head-complementiser-structure}}$$

The Head-Filler Rule (56) is the filler-gap rule.

(56) **Head-Filler Rule**

$$\begin{bmatrix} \text{SYN}|\text{BIND}|\text{SLASH} & \{\ \} \\ \text{DTRS} & \begin{bmatrix} \text{FILLER-DTR} & \boxed{1} \\ \text{HEAD-DTR} & \boxed{2} \begin{bmatrix} \text{SYN} & \begin{bmatrix} \text{LOC}|\text{HEAD} & \text{s[FIN,INV +]} \\ \text{BIND}|\text{SLASH} & \{\boxed{1}\} \end{bmatrix} \end{bmatrix} \end{bmatrix} \\ \text{DOM} & \langle \boxed{1},\boxed{2} \rangle \end{bmatrix}$$

Whquestions are just a subset of the V2 clauses. There is a [WH +] constituent in topic position which has been moved from the inverted, finite head clause. This is exactly the same in both Dutch and English. Inverted clauses with no topic, i.e., V1 clauses, also appear in German, Dutch and English as yes-no questions. In German, they are also used as conjunction-less conditional clauses. The same is true to a lesser degree of English. E.g., *Were I to win a million pounds, I would quit work tomorrow*. Of course in English, the inverted verb must be an auxiliary or a modal.

A further issue is the distribution of the specifications [INV +] and [INV –] with respect to VPs and Ss. The implication VP ⇒ [INV –] is sufficient. For verb projections, this is equivalent to the implication [INV +] ⇒ ¬ VP since INV is defined for all verb projections (although its value may be unspecified). Rule 3 (and its equivalent for Dutch and English) produces [INV +] for German, Dutch and English clauses. In German, the heads of subordinate clauses (without a subject NP-VP configuration) are [INV –]. In Dutch and English we will see that a clause can be [INV –] by virtue of the fact that there is a $[_S$ NP VP[INV –]] configuration available by the Dutch equivalent of Rule 2 which is unlicensed in German. An S[INV –] which is not of the form $[_S$ NP VP[INV –]] is impossible in Dutch and English because the Dutch equivalent of Rule 3 licenses VP-less clauses only if they are [INV +].

With respect to VPs, $[_S$ NP VP] is not licensed in German, so we need not consider the distribution of the values of INV. We already said above that Rule 2 licenses [INV –] VPs in Dutch and English. But furthermore, only Rule 2 licenses VPs so VP[INV +] is out.

One point which needs some elaboration is the scheme used to order verbs in a verb cluster. Earlier we saw that the LP constraint (35) (repeated here as (57)) was responsible for the characteristic 3 – 2 – 1 German verb government order.

(57) [DTRS|HEAD-DTR [1]V[INV –]] ⇒ [DOM V $\preceq$ [1]]

Of course, there are many other word orders available in German. For example, in the so-called *Ersatzinfinitiv* construction, the government order for verbs is 1 – 3 –2 where V_1 is a finite auxiliary or modal verb and both V_2 and V_3 are bare infinitives as in (58).

(58) weil er hat_1 $kommen_3$ $dürfen_3$
because he has come may
'because he was allowed to come'

Bech (1955) cites many other possible orders including 1 – 2 – 3 – 5 – 4 and 1 – 2 – 5 – 4 – 3. I will not bother to give a characterisation of the possible orders here. For a very good overview, see Evers (1975). However, all of these verb cluster orders have the property that, for a cluster of length *n*, V_{n-1} (where the subscript denotes depth of government) is (trivially) adjacent either to the left or right of V_n, V_{n-2} is adjacent to the left or right of the V_{n-1} sequence, V_{n-3} is adjacent to the left or right of the V_{n-2} sequence and so on for V_{n-m} for $m < n$. That is, the possible orders are a subset of (59).

(59)
V_1
$V_1\ V_2 \quad V_2\ V_1$
$V_1\ V_2\ V_3 \quad V_2\ V_3\ V_1 \quad V_3\ V_2\ V_1 \quad V_1\ V_3\ V_2$
...

That is, all of these orders can be explained in terms of a verb V_i appearing to the left or right of every verb V_{i+j} for $j > 0$ it governs. This suggests that direction of verb government should be specified in terms of a feature DIR (DIRECTION) for direction of "status government" or "verbal case" which takes only the values LEFT and RIGHT and a general ordering principle that says that if the value of DIR is LEFT then all verbs governed by the head verb precede it and if the value of DIR is RIGHT then all verbs governed by the head verb follow it. DIR should be an attribute of SYN|LOC. Then (60) is the *Direction of Status Government Principle* (in two parts).

(60) (a) [DTRS|HEAD-DTR [1][SYN|LOC|DIR|LEFT]] ⇒ [DOM V ⪯ [1]]

(b) [DTRS|HEAD-DTR [1][SYN|LOC|DIR|RIGHT]] ⇒ [DOM [1] ⪯ V]

The Ersatzinfinitiv (59) can then be explained as follows. The bare infinitive *dürfen* subcategorises for a bare infinitival VP and lexically specifies the value LEFT for the value of its DIR attribute. *kommen* is such a VP so the verb cluster *kommen dürfen* is well-formed since *kommen* is to the left of *dürfen* as required by the value of DIR. Next, the finite auxiliary *hat* subcategorises for a bare infinitive VP rather than a past participle as expected and lexically specifies the value RIGHT for the value of its DIR attribute. *kommen dürfen* is such a VP so the verb cluster *hat kommen dürfen* is well-formed since *kommen dürfen* is to the right of *hat* as required by the value of DIR. The more complicated patterns are just extensions of this scheme. Although every lexical verb is defined for the attribute DIR, its value need not be defined. This would allow other principles of the grammar to determine the direction of verbal government, for example. Another possibility is that a given verb might be capable of governing in either direction.

The types of government order that this treatment cannot account for are those like 4–1–3–2 which violate the left-right adjacency pattern. In that case, there are two ways out available. Either V_4 is considered to be raised directly to a higher domain where its governing verb has no effect on its position and it is positioned by a different type of ordering constraint for raised lexical heads or we can look for evidence that some or all of the verbs are unordered for direction of government. Then it might be the case that V_4 is unordered by V_3 and so is not ordered by any of V_1, V_2 or V_3 by transitivity. As mentioned before, the class of verbs which subcategorise for bare infinitival VPs in Zürich German seem to be of this type.

Finally, although we have said rather little about adjuncts and modifiers, we have not said anything about how the type of a headed structure is determined. For example, a VP or a PP can be an adjunct or a head, therefore it can occur in both head-adjunct and head-complement structures as the FUN-DTR. The reason that this is important is that the HEAD-DTR must be coindexed correctly with either the FUN-DTR in the case of head-complement structures or the single argument of the FUN-DTR in the case of head-adjunct structures for the Head Feature Principle to be effective. This is a rather deep issue which goes to the heart of the treatment of specifiers, modifiers, semantic interpretation and the role of maximal and nonmaximal projections in HPSG. A discussion of these topics is beyond the scope of this paper, unfortunately.

We will now briefly outline what changes are required to the language specific principles of the German grammar fragment above to capture a similar range of facts in Dutch and Zürich German.

5. An analysis of Dutch

To account for Dutch, we have to alter Rules 1–3 and change one of the LP statements. Perhaps surprisingly, Rules 1–3 are precisely of the form they take for English (modified of course for the changes to the feature system in P&S that we have adopted in this paper). I list them here for convenience.

(61) **Rule 1 (Dutch)**

a
$$\begin{bmatrix} \text{SYN|LOC|ARGS } \langle\,\rangle \\ \text{DTRS} \begin{bmatrix} \text{FUN-DTR|SYN|LOC|LEX } - \\ \text{ARG-DTRS } \langle[\,]\rangle \end{bmatrix} \end{bmatrix}$$

b $[\text{ARGS}\langle\,\rangle] \rightarrow \text{F}[\text{LEX } -], \text{A}$

(62) **Rule 2 (Dutch)**

a
$$\begin{bmatrix} \text{SYN|LOC|ARGS } \langle[\,]\rangle \\ \text{DTRS|FUN-DTR|SYN|LOC} \begin{bmatrix} \text{HEAD|INV } - \\ \text{LEX } + \end{bmatrix} \end{bmatrix}$$

b $[\text{ARGS}\langle[\,]\rangle] \rightarrow \text{F}[\text{INV} \quad ,\text{LEX } +], \text{A}^{*}$

(63) **Rule 3 (Dutch)**

a $$\left[\begin{array}{ll} \text{SYN}\mid\text{LOC}\mid\text{ARGS}\ \langle\,\rangle & \\ \text{DTRS}\mid\text{FUN-DTR}\mid\text{SYN}\mid\text{LOC} & \left[\begin{array}{l}\text{HEAD}\mid\text{INV}\ + \\ \text{LEX}\ + \end{array}\right]\end{array}\right]$$

b $[\text{ARGS}\ \langle\,\rangle] \rightarrow \text{F}[\text{INV}\ +, \text{LEX}\ +],\ \text{A}^*$

Before we consider the effect of Rules 1–3 we need to state the modification to (35) necessary for Dutch. We replace (35) with (64).

(64) $[\text{DTRS}\mid\text{HEAD-DTR}\ \boxed{1}\text{V}[\text{INV}\ -]] \Rightarrow [\text{DOM}\ \boxed{1} \preceq \text{V}]$

Here we assume that in Dutch, unlike German and like English, the structure [$_S$ NP[NOM] VP] is grammatical. Therefore, we need to explain the differences in the structure of V2 clauses and subordinate clauses. In German, we have assumed that in finite clauses, the finite verb is a sister of *all* of its complements in both V2 clauses and subordinate clauses. In Dutch, we assume that the finite verb can be a daughter of a finite VP as in English. Rule 1 allows a nonlexical head (e.g., a VP) to combine with its single unsaturated argument (e.g., the subject). Rule 2 allows a noninverted ([INV –]) lexical head (e.g., a verb) to combine with all of its complements except the first one (e.g., the subject). Rule 3 allows an inverted ([INV +]), lexical head to combine with all of its complements at one time creating an inverted phrase.

We will now explain subordinate clause order. Nonfinite, noninverted verbs combine with all of their complements except the first (the subject) by Rule 2 to form nonfinite VPs. Nonfinite, nonextraposed VPs are unioned into governing VPs (as in German). As in German, all verbs must be preceded by all NPs. However, Dutch serialises verbs in the opposite order to German. That is, governing verbs must precede governed verbs. (64) forces this order. Finally, subject NPs combine with finite VPs by Rule 1 to form Ss. (Noninverted, finite VPs are not unioned into S.) An LP statement similar to the one for English that requires that complements precede nonlexical heads seems to be required in Dutch as well to force the subject NP to precede the finite VP. This produces the characteristic facts about Dutch subordinate clause order, namely, that subject NPs may not be interchanged with object NPs (65), that objects can in fact sometimes interchange (66) and that the canonical order in the verb cluster is that governing verbs precede governed verbs (67).

(65) dat mijn vader mijn moeder zag
that my father my mother saw
(a) 'that my father saw my mother'
(b) *'that my mother saw my father'

(66) (a) dat hij alleen zijn vader zulke dingen durft te vertellen
that he only his father such things dares to tell
'that he only dares to tell his father such things'

(b) dat hij zulke dingen alleen zijn vader durft te vertellen

(67) dat Piet Jan Marie zag helpen zwemmen
that Pete John Marie saw help swim
'that Pete saw John help Marie swim'

Of course, there are exceptions to each of these three generalisations. First, passives of ditransitive verbs (as in (68)) and unaccusative clauses (as in (69) and (70)) sometimes allow subject inversion. This indicates that for this class of sentences without an agentive subject, finite subordinate clause structure is as it is in German.

(68) (a) dat het boek mijn vader geschonken is
that the book my father given is
'that the book has been given to my father'

(b) dat mijn vader het boek geschonken is
that my father the book given is
'that my father has been given the book'

(69) dat hem de fouten opgevallen zijn
that him the mistakes noticed are
'that he noticed the mistakes'

(70) dat hem de fouten geïrriteerd hebben
that him the mistakes irritated have
'that the mistakes irritated him'

Object swap seems to be limited to cases where the semantics or pragmatics of the sentence makes it clear which object fulfills which object role. This is evidence for LP constraints of precisely the same type as in German. If LP constraints are ordered with respect to preference along different dimensions, then pairs of constituents which are ambiguous with respect to preferential features will necessarily be given an interpretation that is consistent with the strongest LP constraint. Since Dutch lacks the rich case system of German, this is usually the case. Therefore, the word order appears to be very fixed.

However, pragmatic information can be sufficiently strong to allow semi-free order as in German. The consequence of this line of reasoning is that the characteristic "cross-serial" order of most Dutch serial clauses is not proof that Dutch is an indexed language or some other type of context-sensitive language.

We will now explain the post-topic structure of V2 clauses in Dutch. This structure is very similar to the structure of subject-auxiliary inversion clauses in English. Basically, an inverted ([INV +]), lexical head (only a verb) can combine with all of its complements at one time. Then, (36) requires that the finite verb be clause-initial. The other LP statements then apply as in subordinate clauses. The difference between English and Dutch is that, whereas in English only auxiliaries can be specified [INV +], in Dutch any finite verb can be so specified. The key difference between subordinate and V2 clauses in Dutch then is that in subordinate clauses there is a finite VP whereas in V2 clauses there is no finite VP.

As stated at the beginning, the syntax rules for Dutch are precisely the same as those for English. (A quick check of P&S will verify that this is true modulo the changes to the feature system.) There are six major differences between Dutch and English. First, verbs in English do not union their VP complements whereas those in Dutch do. Second, the ordering constraint (64) is eliminated for English. Head verbs never end up in the same domain with any of their governed verbs. Third, head verbs precede their NP complements in English unlike German and Dutch. English is head-initial whereas Dutch and German are head-final in [INV –] constructions. Fourth, only modals and auxiliaries can be INV + in English whereas any verb can be INV + in Dutch and German. Fifth, there is no process of NP complement raising as there is in Dutch and German. Sixth, main clauses in English are *usually* not V2. They are usually "SVO" clauses of the form [$_S$ NP[NOM] VP[FIN]]. This is just the same as Dutch subordinate clause structure however (modulo the differences noted here). However, English does have the V2 structure in *wh*-questions and "negative adverbial" sentences of the form "Never have I seen such a crazy linguist".

6. An analysis of Zürich German

6.1 Basic clause order

For Zürich German (henceforth Zh), Rules 1–3 for German are appropriate. However, (34) must be replaced. It appears that the correct generalisation for at least the Zürich dialect is that NP complements need only precede the verb that they depend on but are unordered with respect to all other verbs and follow the same ordering restrictions as German with respect to each other. In (71) (Cooper 1988: ex. 105), the two NPs *sini Chind* and *Mediziin* can appear in either order but *sini Chind* < *laat* and *Mediziin* < *schtudiere* as required by the generalisation. These are the only six possibilities (where *das er* is initial).

(71) (a) **das er sini Chind laat Mediziin schtudiere**
that he his kids lets medicine study
'that he lets his kids study medicine'

(b) **das er sini Chind Mediziin laat schtudiere**
(c) **das er sini Chind Mediziin schtudiere laat**
(d) **das er Mediziin sini Chind laat schtudiere**
(e) **das er Mediziin sini Chind schtudiere laat**
(f) **das er Mediziin schtudiere sini Chind laat**

Therefore, for Zh we must add the following LP constraint which requires that head verbs must be preceded by all their NP complements.

(72) $\forall \boxed{1}. [([\text{DTRS}|\text{HEAD-DTR } \boxed{3}\text{V}[\text{ARGS } \boxed{2}] \wedge \boxed{1} \in \boxed{2}) \Rightarrow [\text{DOM } \boxed{1} \prec \boxed{3}]]$

This statement should be read as "every element of a sign's head daughter verb's argument list must precede the verb in the sign's domain". Or, in other words, all NP arguments must precede their head verb.[12] Notice that the original LP constraint for German NP < V implies (72). In other words, the Zh constraint is more general.

To illustrate the point further, (73) Cooper (1988: App A, ex. 2) replaces *laat* 'lets' with *wil la* 'wants to let' and holds the order of the three verbs fixed as *wil* < *la* < *schtudiere*. There are only eight possibilities (with initial *das er*) if the constraint on NP-verb order is maintained and they are all acceptable.

(73) (a) das er sini Chind wil la Mediziin schtudiere
that he his kids wants let medicine study
'that he wants to let his kids study medicine'

(b) das er sini Chind wil Mediziin la schtudiere
(c) das er sini Chind Mediziin wil la schtudiere
(d) das er wil sini Chind la Mediziin schtudiere
(e) das er wil sini Chind Mediziin la schtudiere
(f) das er wil Mediziin sini Chind la schtudiere
(g) das er Mediziin sini Chind wil la schtudiere
(h) das er Mediziin wil sini Chind la schtudiere

Notice that in (71), the verbs may appear in both possible orders. This suggests that verbs are unordered with respect to each other in Zh. For the class of verbs that take a bare infinitival VP (with or without an additional NP object complement), this appears to be the correct generalisation. Cooper (1988) notes that there are 30 possible orderings of *wil sini Chind la Mediziin schtudiere* which follow the NP-verb generalisation and all but three of them are acceptable.[13] We should note that there are two forms of the causative. *la* is the unstressed "short" form and *laa* is the stressed citation form. The inescapable conclusion to be drawn from the data is that *la* is used if it precedes the verb it governs and *laa* is used if it follows the verb it governs. The "distance" from the NP complement it governs or the verb it governs does not seem to make any difference. This is clearly a case which motivates lexical specification of direction of government. In any case, the German verb ordering constraint (35) has to be dropped for Zh, or at the very least, weakened substantially. Cooper also notes that some speakers allow *la* to precede its NP object complement but apparently the stressed form *laa* does not.

6.2 *z*-VP Extraposition

In this section I will examine extraposition of so-called *z*-VPs in Zh. *z* plays the same role in Zh that *zu* does in German and *te* does in Dutch. This section is based on Cooper's (1990) account. I will present some basic data from her paper and suggest that there is a simple domain union treatment which accounts for the data in a straightforward way.

(75a) is an example of recursive VP extraposition in German and (75b) is the corresponding Zh translation where the German past participle *versprochen* governs the V[ZU] *zu probieren* which in turn governs the V[ZU] *zu erreichen* which are the heads of the two extraposed VP[ZU]s *zu probieren den Hans zu erreichen* and *den Hans zu erreichen* respectively. (75b) is the corresponding grammatical Zh word for word translation.

(75) (a) **Er hat versprochen zu probieren den Hans zu erreichen**
he has promised to try the Hans to reach
'He has promised to try to reach Hans'

(b) **Er hät verschproche z probiere de Hans z erreiche**

This data indicates that recursively extraposed VPs consisting of a head verb and its complements behave exactly as in German. However, there are two problems. *z* can be missing in some extraposed VPs when *zu* cannot be in the corresponding German examples. Cooper calls this the "missing *z*" problem. Compare (76) and (77).

(76) **Er hat versprochen [$_{VP}$ den Hans zu erreichen zu probieren]**
he has promised the Hans to reach to try
'He has promised to try to reach Hans'

(77) **Er hät verschproche [$_{VP}$ de Hans probiere z erreiche]**
he has promised the Hans try to reach

We know from (75) that *verschproche* takes a VP[Z] complement and so *probiere* should occur with *z*. However, this *z* is missing in (77). To consider this problem, we need to make some assumptions about domain structure. I assume that the structure of (76) is as indicated in the example. In particular, the syntactic VP *den Hans zu erreichen* is unioned with the domain of the indicated VP that *zu probieren* is the head of. I also assume that the structure of (77) is (78).[14]

(78) **[$_{CP}$ er [$_{S[FIN]}$ hät verschproche [$_{VP[ZU]}$ de Hans probiere z erreiche]]]**

er is the subject occurring in topic position, *hät* is the inverted finite auxiliary appearing clause-initially, *verschproche* is not extraposed and crucially, for the analysis, *de Hans probiere z erreiche* is an extraposed VP. Furthermore, the domain of the VP *de Hans (z) erreiche* is unioned into the domain of the VP headed by *(z) probiere*. This means that the syntactic structure and the domain structure of (76) and (77) are the same. The only difference is that a *z* is missing in the Zh example and *probiere* precedes *erreiche* unlike the German example where *zu probieren* governs to the left when its complement is not extraposed. (79a) shows that adding the missing *z* makes the example ungrammatical.

(79) (a) *Er hät verschproche de Hans z probiere z erreiche

(b) *Er hät verschproche de Hans erreiche z probiere

(c)?*Er hät verschproche de Hans z erreiche z probiere

Furthermore, swapping *erreiche* and *probiere* as in (79b) is ungrammatical. This appears to be due to an ordering constraint which requires that the verb governed by *probiere* follows it. Compare (80).

(80) (a) Er hät wele de Hans probiere z erreiche
he has wanted the Hans try to reach
'he wanted to try to reach Hans'

(b) *Er hät wele de Hans erreiche z probiere

Regardless of whether *probiere* is extraposed or not in (80a), it is ungrammatical for *erreiche* to precede *probiere* as in (80b). (79c) is similar to the German example (76). It is ungrammatical as well.[15] (79c) would be expected to be ungrammatical since *probiere* must govern to the right as indicated above.

The second problem is that *z* can appear on the "wrong" verb. Instead of occurring on the head of a VP[Z] it may occur on some verb that is governed by the head of the VP as in (81). (81a) is expected since *verschproche* governs *laa* and *verschproche* takes a VP[Z] which *laa* is the head of. We know that *schtudiere* may precede *laa* (as in (81a)) and that *la* may precede *schtudiere* (as in (81b)). However, in (81b), the *z* appears on the wrong verb *schtudiere*. Cooper calls this the "misplaced *z*" problem.

(81) a. Er hät verschproche d Chind schtudiere z laa
he has promised the kids study to let
'He promised to let the kids study'

b. Er hät verschproche d Chind la z schtudiere
he has promised the kids let to study
'He promised to let the kids study'

She also cites the examples in (82) taken from a Zürich radio station. The prepositions *um* in (82a) and *ohni* in (82b) and (82c) subcateogise for a VP[Z].

(82) (a) Um Gerächtigkeit chöne z haa, mues mer ...
for justice can to have must one ...
'in order to be able to have justice one must ...'

(b) ...ohni s Schtüürrad mit bedne Händ müese z verlaa chönd si rede
without the wheel with both hands must to leave can you talk
'you can phone without having to let go of the steering wheel with both hands'

(c) ...ohni de Telefonhörer i de Hand müese z haa
without the receiver in the hand must to have
'without having to hold the receiver in your hand'

In (82a), *z* appears on *haa* instead of *chüne* as it should, in (82b), on *verlaa* instead of *müese* and in (82c), on *haa* instead of *müese.*

Cooper also cites relevant examples in her thesis. She cites (83a) and (83b) from Haegeman and van Riemsdijk (1986) which they claim are grammatical.

(83) (a) das er wil aagää en Arie z chöne singe
that he will pretend an aria to can sing
'that he will pretend to be able to sing an aria'

(b) das er wil aagää, z chöne singe

Cooper claims that these sentences are completely ungrammatical because the *z* should appear on *singe* and not *chüne* in both cases. However, (84a) and (84b) where *z* appears on the final verb in the extraposed VPs are grammatical.

(84) (a) das er aagää wil, en Arie chöne z singe

(b) das er aagää wil, chöne en Arie z singe

(84b) shows that *z* marks the last verb in an extraposed VP and not necessarily the last verb in a continuous verb cluster. Cooper also gives examples (85).

(85) (a) das er en Arie wil aagää chöne z singe

(b) das er wil aagää, chöne en Arie z singe

(85a) should be analysed as the verb cluster *wil aagää* followed by the extraposed VP *chüne z singe* with *en Arie* raised to the finite clause. (85b) is just like (84b) except that *aagää* and *wil* have swapped positions.

The analysis that I would like to suggest theory-neutrally (which Cooper (1990) dismisses) is that if a verb subcategorises for a VP[Z] and the VP is extraposed then *z* marks the last V in the extraposed VP's domain. This means that if several VPs have been unioned together but the head of the extraposed VP is not the last verb in the domain then *z* will not occur on it. It also means that if domain union in an extraposed VP should give rise to more than one *z* in an extraposed VP (as in the German example (76)) then only one *z* will appear. However, if the extraposed VP itself governs a recursively extraposed *z*-VP, then *z* will appear on the last verb in its domain and so on as in (75b) which is assigned the domain structure (86).

(86) [$_{CP}$ er [$_{S}$ hät versproche [$_{VP[Z]}$ z probiere [$_{VP[Z]}$ de Hans z erreiche]]]]

This is sufficient to explain all of the data presented and much more but it does depend on (descriptively) distinguishing between cases of "verb raising", "verb projection raising" and extraposition very carefully. Making this distinction in Zh can be very difficult because of the amount of order freedom.

Although it would seem to be easy to explain this data in terms of a domain union account which says that the final verb in an extraposed VP is z-marked, it is rather difficult because of the construction rules. For a start, it is not the case that the occurrence of *z* is construction dependent, i.e., that it depends completely on the fact that the VP is realized in extraposed position. First, some verbs take nonextraposed VP[Z] complements (87) (Cooper 1990: ex. 8) and second, some verbs appear to extrapose VP[INF]s (88) (Cooper 1990: ex. 8).[16]

(87) (a) das er*hät vill z tue / vill z tue hät
that he has much to do much to do has
'that he has a lot to do'

(b) das er*isch z beduure / z beduure isch
that he is to pity to pity is
'that he is to be pitied'

(88) (a) **das er nöd wil [sini Chind schtudiere laa]**
that he not wants his kids study let
'that he doesn't want to let his kids study medicine'

(b) **das er sini Chind laat [Mediziin schtudiere]**
that he his kids lets medicine study
'that he lets his kids study medicine'

(c) **das er mich gseet [s Gschiir abwäsche]**
that he me sees the dishes up-wash
'that he sees me wash up the dishes'

(d) **das er em Vatter hilft [s Gschiir abwäsche]**
that he the father helps the dishes up-wash
'that he helps father wash up the dishes'

(e) **das er wird [schpöter aachoo]**
that he will later arrive
'that he will arrive later'

There are basically three options that I see. All of them depend on the idea that the *z* can "float off" of its lexical head to the last verb in an extraposed VP's domain. Thus the *z* will only appear in the domain of the VP[Z]. This requires a treatment of morphosyntax, which I am unprepared to give here, to explain how the *z* gets incorporated into separable prefix verbs like *biilegge* to give *biizlegge* when the account makes it clear that *biilegge* is what comes out of the lexicon. This in itself is enough to treat the "misplaced *z*" problem. However, it does not handle the "missing *z*" problem because multiple *z*'s may appear before the final verb. Barring deletion or identification of all these *z*'s (which would be in violation of the domain construction principles) this problem is irreparable.

The second option is an elaboration of the first. It says that the head verb of the extraposed VP does indeed come out of the lexicon with the *z* and that it floats off to the last V but in addition, every verb which is the head of a nonextraposed VP in the government chain is required not to be a V[Z]. Those which would be V[Z] if extraposed become V[INF]s instead. This option does cover both the missing and misplaced *z* problems. On face value, this appears to be descriptively necessary, since the verb forms of the missing *z* verbs which appear in the surface string are all V[INF]s when they would be V[Z]s if they appeared as the head of a topicalised VP.

A further, third refinement is possible which claims that the *z* is just like the English *to*, that is, it is a functor from VP[INF]s to VP[Z]s. However, *z* domain unions its complement VP[INF] and then floats to the last verb and enforces the government requirement above. This at least means that there is no need to explain how the *z* floats off of its head verb although we still have to explain how the *z* undergoes incorporation with separable prefix verbs.

Some account of morphosyntactic processes is required for the treatment of V2 given in German, Dutch and Zh. In all three cases, we assume that the finite verb appears clause-initially. Obviously, in the case of separable prefix verbs, this is insufficient. To take just one example, in (89) (Uszkoreit 1987: ex. 184), the separable prefix verb *anrufen* consists of a separable prefix *an* and an infinitival stem *rufen*. In V2 and V1 clauses ((89c) and (89d), respectively) the inflected stem appears in domain initial position. So something still needs to be said about the morphosyntax of separable prefix verbs at least.

(89) (a) **Peter wird Paul anrufen**
Peter will Paul up-call
'Peter will call Paul up'

(b) **weil Peter Paul anruft**
because Peter Paul up-calls
'because Peter calls up Paul'

(c) **Peter ruft Paul an**
Peter calls Paul up
'Peter calls Paul'

(d) **Ruft Peter Paul an?**
calls Peter Paul up
'Does Peter call Paul'

One possibility is to give lexical entries domains. Then the domain of *anruft* might consist of two elements, one for *an* and one for *ruft* (where arbitrary categorial information could be associated with each element). This two element domain could then either undergo domain union (in the case of V2 and V1 clauses) or appear as an element of its mothers domain continuously (i.e., nonunioned). Different LP constraints might then apply to the different elements of the lexical domains. This might help us explain the baffling placement of the prefix *aan* immediately before the verb cluster and after the negation *niet* in the Dutch example (90) and its effect on the scope of *niet* with respect to the three verbs.

(90) (a) **dat een lijfwacht de koningin niet moet kunnen aankijken**
that a bodyguard the queen not must can at-look
(i) 'that a bodyguard must not be able to look at the queen'
(ii)?'that a bodyguard must be unable to look at the queen'
(iii)*'that a bodyguard must be able not to look the queen'

(b) dat een lijfwacht de koningin niet aan moet kunnen kijken
that a bodyguard the queen not at must can look
(a) 'that a bodyguard must not be able to look at the queen'
(b) 'that a bodyguard must be unable to look at the queen'
(c) 'that a bodyguard must be able not to look the queen'

At this point, Dowty's (1991) use of *attachment* starts to look very attractive for explaining the "integrity" of morphologically complex lexical items in some positions and their discontinuity in other positions. All of this is really just an argument for sublexical structure which will have to be addressed anyway.

Finally, although a statement of the government requirement that all verbs which would normally be V[Z]s in the domain of an extraposed VP must be V[INF]s except for the head verb is easy to state, it is messy to formalise in the formalism of HPSG. It is certainly possible to "program" the features to make it work, but the results are not elegant. Rather, it seems preferrable to derive the phenomenon from more general principles, especially as their is relevant data (although impoverished) from German as in (91) (von Stechow and Sternefeld 1988: 380) and (92) (von Stechow and Sternefeld 1988: 444). See von Stechow and Sternefeld (1988) and Cooper (1990) for discussion.

(91) (a) ohne ihn haben sehen zu können
without him have see to can
'without having been able to see him'

(b) *ohne ihn zu haben sehen können

(92) Er scheint ihn haben sehen zu können
he seems him have see to can
'He seems to have been able to see him'

7. Comparative clause structure

In this section I will briefly indicate how the main clause and subordinate clause structures of German, Dutch and English compare and where the difference and similarities between them originate from the point of view of the account given in the preceding sections.

German main clauses are verb-second (V2) clauses (Figure 10). They consist of a topic position followed by an inverted head-initial clause. This inverted clause does not have an articulated $[_S$ NP[NOM] VP] structure. Instead, Rule 3 (German) creates an inverted clause which consists of the finite daughter and all of its complement. The topic can be filled by any major category (XP) by an unbounded dependency in the clause. German subordinate clauses (Figure 11) consist of a complementiser followed by a noninverted head-final clause. As in V2 clauses, there is no NP-VP structure.

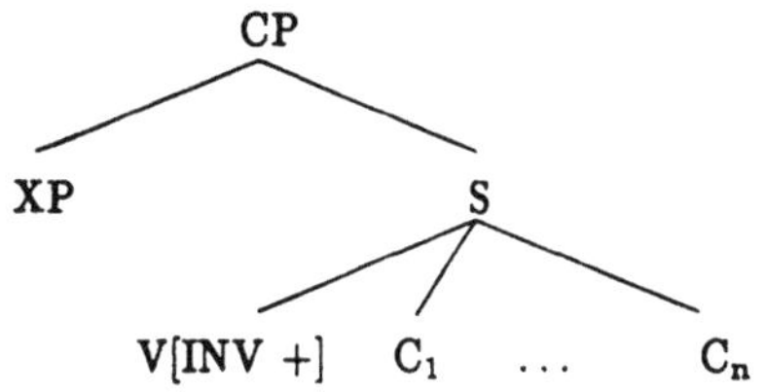

Figure 10. German V2 clauses

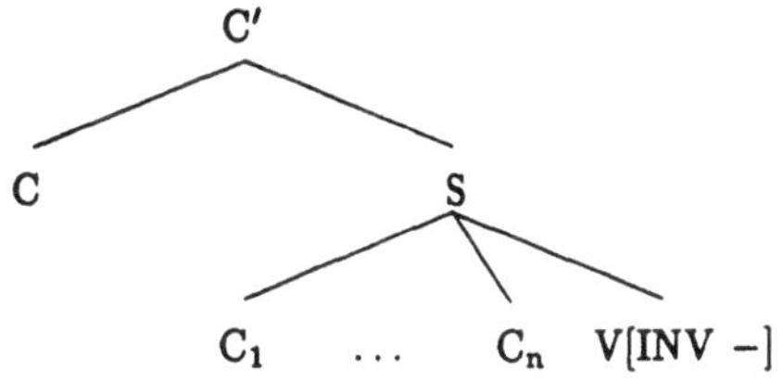

Figure 11. German subordinate clauses

Dutch V2 clauses (Figure 12) are exactly like German V2 clauses. Rule 3 (Dutch) allows the formation of an inverted head-initial clause without an NP-VP structure. However, Dutch subordinate clauses (Figure 13) do show an NP-VP structure. The VP is nevertheless noninverted and head-final.

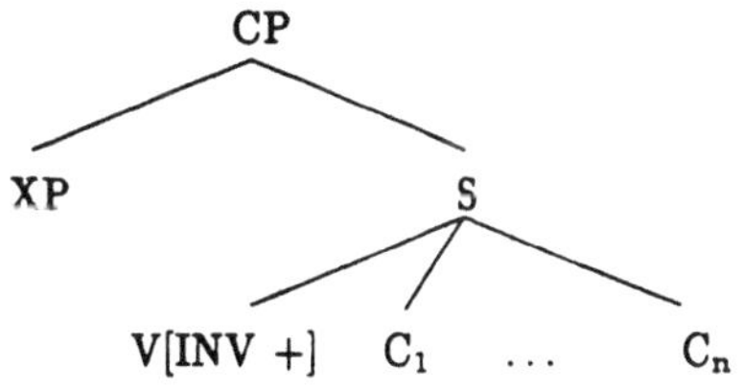

Figure 12. Dutch V2 clauses

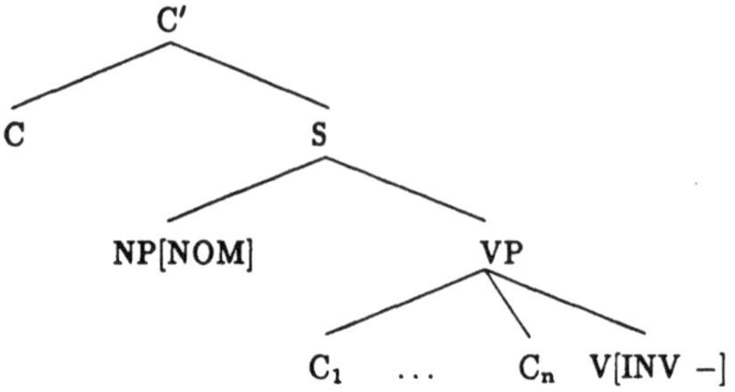

Figure 13. Dutch subordinate clauses

English so-called "subject-aux inversion" clauses (Figure 14) are just like the head-initial clauses of German and Dutch. They occur in yes-no questions (V1) and as constituents of V2 constructions. Although normally declarative sentences are not V2 clauses, V2 clauses do appear as *wh*-questions and negative adverbial sentences as mentioned earlier. Unlike German and Dutch, English main and subordinate clauses have the same structure. This so-called "SVO" structure (Figure 15) is exactly the same as the constituent clause in Dutch subordinate clauses except that noninverted VPs are head-initial in English unlike the head-final Dutch VPs.

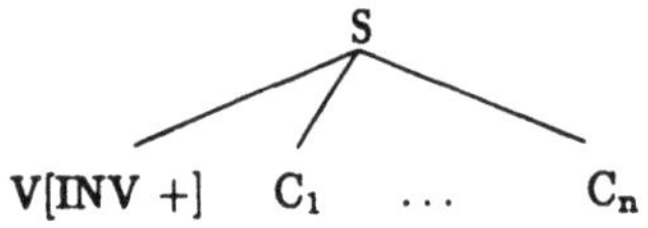

Figure 14. English subject-aux inversion clauses

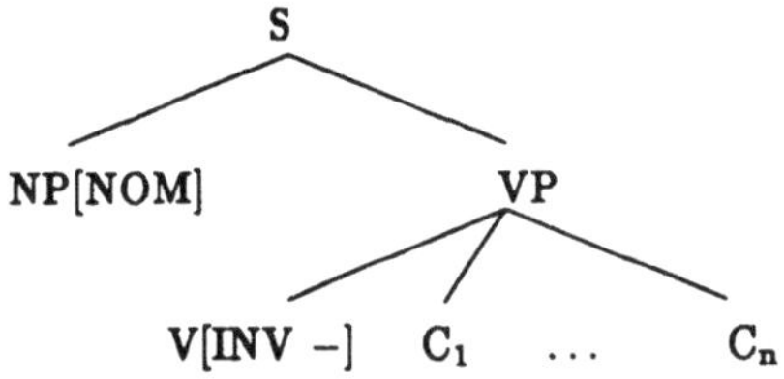

Figure 15. SVO clauses

Therefore, the same structures are available to both English and Dutch. Whereas Dutch employs V2 clauses as main clauses, English uses SVO clauses, which are constituents of Dutch subordinate clauses, for both main clauses and subordinate clauses. On the other hand, English only uses V2 clauses for *wh*-questions and negative adverbial clauses. Finally, the only major difference between Dutch and English on the one hand and German on the other is that the SVO structure is unavailable in German altogether. This is usually referred to by saying that German is "nonconfigurational" or that it has a "subject-inclusive VP."

Clearly, the outline of V2 clauses here is inspired by the standard GB analysis, namely that the topic fills the specifier of the CP (or complementiser phrase) position. In fact, the category label I have assigned to V2 clauses is CP since I essentially agree that the topic is in the [Spec, CP] position. Unlike GB analyses however, I do not assume that the finite verb fills COMP position. Rather, it is just initial in the constituent finite clause domain. I will simply say that the movement to COMP analysis is not justified by this approach and I am aware of convincing dialect data where both Spec and C(OMP) can be filled simultaneously. Therefore, COMP is either empty or not present in V2 clauses. Given the treatment of the complementiser as a functor, it is reasonable to assume that the COMP position is not "topologically obligatory". On the other hand, the Spec position is topologically obligatory in V2 clauses. This uncontroversial claim is based on contrasts such as the behaviour of impersonal passive constructions in German such as (93).

(93) (a) **daß wurde getanzt**
that was danced
'that there was dancing'

(b) **es wurde getanzt**
it (EXPL) was danced
'there was dancing'

By itself, *wurde getanzt* is a full-fledged finite clause and as such can appear as the argument of the complementiser *daß* in (93a). However, in (93b) there is nothing in *wurde getanzt* to fill the topic position so it is filled by the expletive pronoun *es*. That is, topic position must be filled. Given the analysis presented here, the only way that this can be the case is if it is topologically obligatory, or in other words, that it is assigned by a rule of syntax. The rule in question is the Head-Filler rule.

8. Conclusion

This approach to word order can be given several interpretations. First, it can be seen as an alternative version of representational GB which maintains *D*-structure and eliminates *S*-structure. This is exactly the opposite of other representational approaches which eliminate *D*-structure but maintain *S*-structure (cf. Koster 1987). Nonlexical word order domains are associated with *D*-structure phrasal projections and it is the *functor* of a phrasal projection which determines whether an *argument* daughter's domain is an element of the domain of the phrasal projection or whether its elements are elements of the phrasal projection's domain. (This allows the same approach to discontinuity to be applicable to head-adjunct structures.)

This allows two further refinements. First, domains can be (partially) ordered and *D*-structure can be unordered. *D*-structure is then (partially) 'linearised' in the projection to domains. As domains are incorporated into larger domains (via sequence union) additional (partial) constraints can be placed on them further constraining domain order. Therefore order is inherited *monotonically* "bottom-up". I.e., a partial order constraint, once imposed, can never be removed or changed. Intuitively, we incrementally get words *in order* by imposing partial constraints rather than get them *out of order* via movement or some other mechanism which relates canonical structures to noncanonical structures. This implements a kind of *vertical locality principle* which states that the order domain of a constituent is determined by its functor and the domains of its argument daughters but not the domains of the domains of its argument daughters, etc. In other words, functors can "look down one level" for domain elements but no further. In the second refinement, *D*-structure and domains are totally ordered and lexical functors impose well-formedness conditions on the order of their arguments and their arguments' domains. There is little difference between the two refinements.

The previous analyses are rather idealised and omit a fair amount of detail. However, even this simplified presentation illustrates quite clearly that very small changes to Rules 1–3 and the LP statements are responsible for the variation in Dutch, German and Zürich German word order.

Acknowledgments. I would like to thank Klaus Netter for helpful discussions about German data over a long period of time and for letting me adapt the name of his paper (Netter 1986). This paper would not have been possible without him. I would also like to thank Mark Hepple for reading an earlier draft of this paper.

Notes

1. His research and mine were developed independently without knowledge of the other's work.
2. Henceforth, we shall use the shorter terms *order domain* or simply *domain* to refer to *word order domain* since we will be referring to no other domains.
3. In the past I have used the symbol $\cup_{<>}$ for sequence union. I am abandoning it here for typographical reasons.
4. Although domains are just sequences of constituents we will usually subscript the opening bracket of the labelled bracketed string denoting the domain of constituent X with X itself for clarity. However, the subscript is purely to make the bracketed strings more legible. This notation runs the risk of confusing syntactic structures with domains since they are both represented by labelled bracketed strings, but we will be careful to indicate the difference in what follows.
5. This is basically the concept that Gunnar Bech (1955) calls "status government".
6. Actually one would want to develop a theory of 'weak' ordering constraints on NPs, as discussed by Uszkoreit (1987). I have developed a theory of such constraints which builds on Uszkoreit's work but a presentation of it is beyond the scope of this paper.
7. This example is not accepted by many speakers.
8. In this paper, we will have to assume familiarity with the development of HPSG in (Pollard and Sag 1987). For formal details of the semantics of a notational variant of the formalism used here, cf. Reape (1991).
9. Unlike P&S '87 and like P&S '94, less oblique arguments appear to the left and more oblique arguments appear to the right in the argument list.
10. For the technically inclined, the Domain Principle is really a schema.
11. This is probably too strict as inverted subordinate clauses are sometimes found in German and in many dialects.
12. The semantics of the relational dependency $\in$ and the universal quantifier $\forall$ is defined in Reape (1991). It is sufficient here to say that they are classically defined.
13. Cooper notes that in these three cases the subordinate clause ends in the sequence *sini Chind laa* which means that a well-formed subordinate clause can be formed if this sequence is dropped. On these grounds she argues quite reasonably that the hearer garden paths on these sentences and is unable to backtrack. She also provides the thirty admissible permutations of *das ich mues em Vatter hälfe s Gschiir abwäsche* (74) (Cooper 1988: App. B, ex. 0) and points out that all of them are acceptable except the three which end in the sequence *em Vatter hälfe*.

(74) das ich mues em Vatter hälfe s Gschiir abwäsche
that I must the father help the dishes wash-up
'that I must help father wash up the dishes'

Therefore, in these three cases the same problem arises, namely, that the subordinate clause without the sequence *em Vatter hälfe* is perfectly well-formed and the hearer garden paths. Thus, it does seem that the generalisations are correct.

14. A presentation of the justification of the structure in (78) is unfortunately beyond the scope of this paper.
15. Cooper found one speaker who accepted this example. She attributes this to interference from Standard German.
16. It is arguable that all of these cases involve domain union or perhaps verb projection raising. In any case, none of the German counterparts of these verbs allow extraposition. Furthermore, (88a) and (88e) seem like particularly convincing examples of extraposition. In fact, (88a) supports an optional intonation break before the putative extraposed VP which would be unexpected if *sini Chind schtudiere laa* was not an extraposed VP (Cooper, p.c.).

References

Bech, Gunnar
1955 *Studien über das Deutsche Verbum Infinitum*, Band I. Copenhagen.

den Besten, Hans and Gert Webelhuth
1988 *Stranding*. Manuscript, Universiteit van Amsterdam and University of Massachusetts, Amsterdam.

Bresnan, Joan (ed.)
1982 *The Mental Representation of Grammatical Relations*. Cambridge, Mass., MIT Press.

Bunt, Harry
1996 Formal tools for describing and processing discontinuous constituent structure. *This volume*, 63–85.

Chomsky, Noam
1957 *Syntactic Structures*. Mouton, den Haag.

Cooper, Kathrin
1988 Word Order in Bare Infinitival Complement Constructions in Swiss German. Master's Thesis, Centre for Cognitive Science, University of Edinburgh, Edinburgh.

Cooper, Kathrin
1990 Zürich "German Z and verb raising constructions". In: E. Engdahl, M. Reape, M. Mellor and R. Cooper (eds.), *Parametric Variation in Germanic and Romance: Proceedings from a Dyana Workshop*, 76 – 85. Centre for Cognitive Science, University of Edinburgh, Edinburgh.

Dowty, David
1996 Toward a minimalist theory of syntactic structure. *This volume*, 11–62.

Evers, Arnold
1975 *The Transformational Cycle in Dutch and German.* PhD Thesis, University of Utrecht, Utrecht.
Gazdar, G., E. Klein, G. K. Pullum and I.A. Sag
1985 *Generalised Phrase Structure Grammar.* Blackwell, Harvard University Press, Cambridge, England. Cambridge, MA.
Haegeman, Liliane and Henk van Riemsdijk
1986 Verb projection raising, scope, and the typology of rules affecting verbs. *Linguistic Inquiry,* 17(3), 417 – 466.
Hopcroft, John E. and Jeffrey D. Ullman
1979 *Introduction to Automata Theory, Languages and Computation.* Addison-Wesley, Menlo Park, Calif.
Koster, Jan
1987 *Domains and Dynasties.* Dordrecht, Foris.
Netter, Klaus
1986 Getting Things Out of Order. *Proceedings of the 11th International Conference on Computational Linguistics,* 494 – 496. Bonn University, Bonn.
Pollard, Carl and Ivan Sag
1987 *Information-based Syntax and Semantics.* CSLI, Stanford, California.
Pollard, Carl and Ivan Sag
1994 *Head-Driven Phrase Structure Grammar.* CSLI, Stanford, California, and The University of Chicago Press, Chicago.
Mike Reape
1990 A Theory of Word Order and Discontinuous Constituency in West Continental Germanic. In: E. Engdahl and M. Reape (eds.), *Parametric Variation in Germanic and Romance: Preliminary Investigations,* Dyana Deliverable R1.1.A, 25 – 40. Centre for Cognitive Science, University of Edinburgh.
Mike Reape
1991 *An Introduction to the Semantics of Unification-based Grammar Formalisms.* Dyana Deliverable R3.2.A, Centre for Cognitive Science, University of Edinburgh.
von Stechow, Arnim
1990 Status government and Coherence in German. In: G. Grewendorf and W. Sternefeld (eds.), *Scrambling and Barriers.* Amsterdam, Benjamin.
von Stechow, Arnim and Wolfgang Sternefeld
1988 *Bausteine Syntaktischen Wissens. Ein Lehrbuch der Generativen Grammatik.* Opladen, Westdeutscher Verlag.
Uszkoreit, Hans
1987 *Word Order and Constituent Structure in German.* CSLI, Stanford, California.
Zaenen, Annie
1990 *Unaccusativity in Dutch: an integrated approach.* Unpublished manuscript, Xerox-PARC and CSLI-Stanford, Stanford, California.

Grammatical relations and the Lambek calculus

Mark Hepple

Abstract. This paper addresses the treatment of phenomena that depend on grammatical relations and obliqueness within an extended version of the Lambek calculus. We consider an account of grammatical relations proposed within Montague Grammar, and discuss problems for adopting this account in frameworks that, like the Lambek calculus, employ only concatenative string forming operations. A new Lambek account of word order is then proposed which factors apart the specification of a head's position from the specification of the order of its complements, a move which allows a modified version of the Montague Grammar account of grammatical relations to be adopted. The resulting approach is illustrated with treatments of some phenomena that depend on grammatical relations and obliqueness.

1. Introduction

This paper is primarily concerned with the treatment of word order and obliqueness dependent phenomena in categorial grammar (CG), and specifically extensions of the Lambek calculus.[1] An account is proposed which factors apart the specification of a head's position from the specification of the order of its complements. This move has a number of advantages in relation to the treatment of word order and grammatical relations (GRs). Dowty (1982a) outlines a theory of GRs within Montague Grammar, a framework which uses distinct rules to allow different combinations of functors with arguments, with rule-specific stipulations as to how the string associated with the result of each combination is derived from those of the expressions combined. The string forming operations used go beyond just concatenation. This fact has presented problems for adapting Dowty's account to frameworks such as the Lambek calculus which restrict themselves to string concatenation. The treatment of word order to be proposed avoids these problems, allowing a modified version of Dowty's account to be adopted. The paper includes discussion of the relation that the new approach predicts between word order and obliqueness, and considers some treatments of phenomena that depend on GRs.

2. Montague Grammar and grammatical relations

Montague Grammar is a CG framework that originated primarily in concern with issues of natural language semantics, but which was later developed in application to broader linguistic questions by a number of authors (e.g. Partee 1976; Thomason 1976; Bach 1979; Dowty 1978). Types are formed using directionless slash connectives. Functions specify the type of their argument and the type of the phrase that results from combination, but do not specify the relative order in which the function and argument must occur. Instead, a different rule is provided for each possibility of combining functions and arguments and each rule is associated with an *operation* which specifies how the string associated with the result of the combination is derived from the strings associated with the phrases combined. These operations go beyond simple concatenation, and play a crucial role in the treatment of word order, as well as tense and case marking and the introduction of prepositions.

Dowty (1982a) points out that this approach provides a natural basis for a theory of GRs (i.e. notions such as *subject* and *direct object*). By this view, the syntactic rules used in all natural languages are largely the same, the primary focus of variation between languages being the rules' string operations. Dowty suggests that it is the language universal syntactic rules (aside from their language particular string operations) that define GRs. Thus, a *subject* is defined to be a complement which combines with an intransitive verb to give a sentence, a *direct object* a complement which combines with a transitive verb type to give an intransitive verb, and an *indirect object* a complement which combines with a ditransitive verb type to give a transitive verb. This approach unavoidably orders GRs (i.e. subcategorisation order), an ordering taken to correspond with that of the traditional notion of obliqueness. For a verb type of the form "(s/../x/../y/..)" (dots standing for possible further arguments), where x occurs later in argument order than y, x is a less oblique complement of the verb than y. Dowty's theory aims to give a universal characterisation of GRs without treating them as primitives and avoiding problems that arise when GRs are defined in terms of phrase structure configurations. Note that GRs as such play no direct role in this account. Rather, the apparent properties of, say, subjects are in fact properties of intransitive verbs, the combinations they participate in and the rules that they undergo.

The use of non-concatenative operations in the Montagovian approach is illustrated by the derivation (1). Each step shows the strings and types associated with two phrases and the result of their combination. (Standard

Montague Grammar notation is used, where sentences have type t, and where T, IV, TV and TV/T abbreviate the types of noun phrases, intransitive, transitive and ditransitive verbs, respectively.) Note in particular the combination TV + T $\Rightarrow$ IV which is associated with a non-concatenative operation *right wrap*, whereby the result string is derived by inserting the noun phrase string after the verb word in the transitive verb string. Clearly, the Montague approach assumes the existence of discontinuous constituents, e.g. *gave to Mary* is a discontinuous constituent within *gave a book to Mary*. This account of GRs has provided the basis for accounts of various phenomena, including relation changing (Bach 1980; Dowty 1982a; 1982b), control (Bach 1979), and binding (Bach — Partee 1980; Chierchia 1988).

(1) a. $[\text{gave}]_{TV/T}$ + $[\text{Mary}]_{T}$ $\Rightarrow$ $[\text{gave to Mary}]_{TV}$
b. $[\text{gave to Mary}]_{TV}$ + $[\text{a book}]_{T}$ $\Rightarrow$ $[\text{gave a book to Mary}]_{IV}$
c. $[\text{gave a book to Mary}]_{IV}$ + $[\text{John}]_{T}$ $\Rightarrow$ $[\text{John gave a book to Mary}]_{t}$

3. Concatenative CGs

An number of CGs attempt to provide a highly general system for stating possible combinations. The Lambek calculus is perhaps the most striking instance of this trend, with its free calculus of type combinations. Such CGs are obviously incompatible with Dowty's theory, based as it is on defining GRs in terms of *combination-specific* rules. However, such CGs are less obviously incompatible with a modified version of Dowty's theory in which the encoding of relative obliqueness by subcategorisation order is taken as basic, with GRs being defined in terms of subcategorisation order. For example, a *subject* may be defined as the least oblique complement of a verb (i.e. its last argument), a *direct object* (or sometimes *first object*) as a next-to-last subcategorised NP complement, and a *second object* (a term combining the Montagovian notions of indirect and oblique object) as a second-to-last subcategorised NP or PP complement.

CGs which attempt to provide highly general combination systems typically make an assumption, which we might call the *concatenative assumption*, requiring that the string associated with the result of a combination arises purely by concatenating the strings of the types combined. This assumption leads to difficulties for adopting even the modified version of Dowty's account, specifically because of problems that arise with the cases for which Montague Grammar uses wrapping. Consider the sentence *John gave a book to Mary*, in which *to Mary* is the verb's most oblique complement, and hence its first argument. But then, by the concatenative assumption, *to Mary* should appear next to the verb in the observed word order.

Some workers have attempted to adopt a version of Dowty's account of GRs in concatenative frameworks by using some kind of "wrap simulation" method (e.g. Szabolcsi 1987; Jacobson 1987; Kang 1988). The account of Jacobson (1987) is of particular interest here, since the Lambek account presented later draws upon its insights in several ways. Jacobson uses a synthesis of Montague Grammar and Generalized Phrase Structure Grammar (GPSG) (Gazdar et al. 1985), in which phrase structure-like rules are provided for combining what are essentially categorial types. Following GPSG, constituent order is determined by linear precedence rules. However, phrase structure rules are derived not from immediate dominance rules as in GPSG, but rather from highly schematic combination rules, which in the simplest case are closely analogous to (non-directional) application rules of CG. In the default case, such rules would give analyses in which the relative proximity of a verb to its complements would correlate with obliqueness, as for example in the analysis (2a) (where labels VP, TVP and V abbreviate functional types, much as in the Montagovian notation). The correct word order for English is obtained by what Jacobson terms *Verb Promotion*, under which the verb is extracted from the TVP to become a daughter of the VP node (as mediated by a gap-passing feature [DSL], for "double slash"). This yields the structure (2b) as the Verb Promotion variant of (2a). Verb Promotion effectively reconstructs wrapping within a context-free phrase structure approach. It is taken to be a marked option of language, with the grammars of individual languages stipulating the promotions that occur. It is interesting to note that a role for verb movement in English word order has also been suggested in non-categorial approaches (e.g. Larson 1988; Koster 1988), to some extent to avoid problems arising in the cases for which Montague Grammar uses wrapping.

(2) a. [$_{S}$ [$_{NP}$ Mary] [$_{VP}$ [$_{TVP}$ [$_{V}$ gave] [$_{NP}$ John] [$_{NP}$ vodka]]]]
b. [$_{S}$ [$_{NP}$ Mary] [$_{VP}$ [$_{NP}$ John] [$_{V}$ gave] [$_{TVP[DSL:V]}$ [$_{V[DSL:V]}$ e] [$_{NP}$ vodka]]]]

4. Extended Lambek calculus

I will next outline the CG framework in which the account of word order proposed in the next section is set. This is a version of the Lambek calculus (Lambek 1958; 1961) augmented with additional operators and inference rules.[2] I use a natural deduction formulation of the calculus (see Morrill et al. 1990; Barry et al. 1991). Proofs proceed from a number of initial assumptions, some of which may be "discharged" or "withdrawn" during the course of the proof. For the product-free Lambek calculus, we require the inference rules shown in Figure 1.

Hypothesis rule: $\mathrm{A}{:}x$

Elimination rules:

$$\frac{\begin{matrix}\vdots & \vdots\\ \mathrm{A/B}{:}f & \mathrm{B}{:}x\end{matrix}}{\mathrm{A}{:}fx}\,/\mathrm{E} \qquad \frac{\begin{matrix}\vdots & \vdots\\ \mathrm{B}{:}x & \mathrm{A\backslash B}{:}f\end{matrix}}{\mathrm{A}{:}fx}\,\backslash\mathrm{E}$$

Introduction rules:

$$\frac{\begin{matrix}[\mathrm{B}{:}x]^{i}\\ \vdots\\ \mathrm{A}{:}f\end{matrix}}{\mathrm{A/B}{:}\lambda x.f}\,/\mathrm{I}^{i}$$ where B is the rightmost undischarged assumption in the proof of A

$$\frac{\begin{matrix}[\mathrm{B}{:}x]^{i}\\ \vdots\\ \mathrm{A}{:}f\end{matrix}}{\mathrm{A\backslash B}{:}\lambda x.f}\,\backslash\mathrm{I}^{i}$$ where B is the leftmost undischarged assumption in the proof of A

Figure 1. Inference rules for (product-free) Lambek calculus

The notation of a type with dots above it is used to designate a proof of that type. Assumptions are simply individual types, as licensed by the hypothesis rule. Undischarged assumptions are termed *hypotheses*. Note that in this formulation, each type in a proof is associated with a lambda expression, its *proof term*, shown to the right of a colon. The elimination rule [/E] states that a proof of A/B and a proof of B may be combined as shown to construct a proof of A. The introduction rule [/I] states that given a proof of A, we may discharge some hypothesis B within the body of the proof to form a proof of A/B. Square brackets are used to indicate a discharged assumption. Note that there is a side condition on this rule, which relates to the constituent order significance of the directional slash. To demonstrate that some type combination $X_1, \ldots, X_n \Rightarrow X_0$ is possible, a proof of x_0 is given having hypotheses $X_1, \ldots, X_n$ (in that order) with zero or more discharged assumptions interspersed amongst them. The proof term for the conclusion of a proof expresses its meaning as a combination of the meanings of the proof's hyptheses, and the inference rules specify how this lambda expression is constructed. Each assumption has a unique variable for its proof term. The elimination and introduction rules correspond to semantic operations of functional application and abstraction, respectively. In general, proof terms are omitted to simplify presentation. The proof of the combination a/b, b/c ⇒ a/c ("simple forward composition") in Figure 2 illustrates this approach.

$$\cfrac{\cfrac{\mathrm{a/b}:x \qquad \cfrac{\mathrm{b/c}:y \qquad [\mathrm{c}:z]^{i}}{\mathrm{b}:y\,z}\,/E}{\mathrm{a}:x\,(y\,z)}\,/E}{\mathrm{a/c}:\lambda z.x\,(y\,z)}\,/I^{i}$$

Figure 2. Proof for simple forward composition

I require two extensions of the basic Lambek calculus. Firstly, following Morrill (1989; 1990), an operator □ for handling locality constraints (although our use of □ differs from Morrill's in certain details). This operator has the inference rules in Figure 3, which make it behave somewhat like necessity in the modal logic S4.

$$\cfrac{\vdots \\ \Box\mathrm{A}:x}{\mathrm{A}:x}\,\Box E \qquad\qquad \cfrac{\vdots \\ \mathrm{A}:x}{\Box\mathrm{A}:x}\,\Box I$$

where each path to an undischarged assumption in the proof of A leads to an independent subproof of a □-type

Figure 3. Inference rules for □

In this system, each lexical type is of the form □A, and additionally some functions may seek modal arguments, e.g. the sentence embedding verb *believe* has a type □(s\np/□s) (the □ on the complement making it a bounded domain, in a manner illustrated shortly). I assume a treatment of extraction (deriving ultimately from proposals by Ades — Steedman 1982) in which extracted items are given higher order types. For example, a relative pronoun might be rel/(s/np), a type which seeks a "sentence lacking a noun phrase", in effect "abstracting" over the missing NP in the extraction domain. Proofs of such examples involve an additional assumption which appears in the place of the missing element, and which is later discharged. In relation to the modal system, consider the case of extraction from an embedded clause derived in Figure 4.

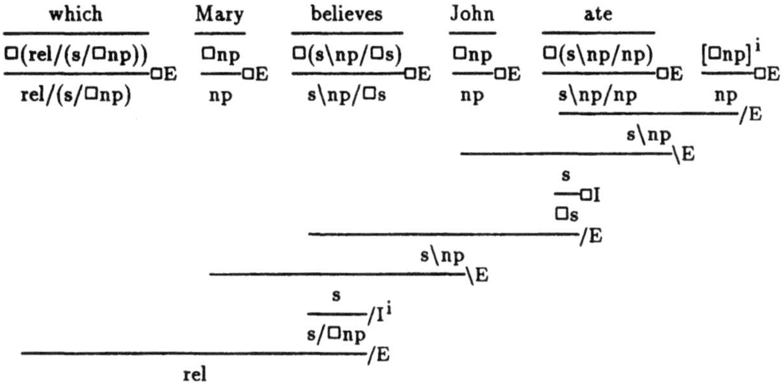

Figure 4.

The relative pronoun type □(rel/(s/□np)) seeks an argument (s/□np), i.e. a sentence lacking a modal NP, and the additional assumption appearing in the position of the missing item is □np, accordingly. At the stage when the [□I] inference is made in proving the embedded clause, the additional assumption is not yet discharged, but since it is □np the rule's side condition is met and the proof goes through. However, a relative pronoun □(rel/(s/np)) would require a non-modal np assumption, so that the side condition on [□I] rule would not be met, preventing completion of the proof. Hence this latter relative pronoun type would only allow bounded extraction in this system.[3]

The second extension of the basic calculus is a *structural modality*, an idea borrowed from linear logic. Structural modalities allow controlled involvement of *structural rules*, in this case permutation (see Morrill et al. 1990 and Barry et al. 1991) for discussion, and linguistic proposals). The *permutor* operator has the inference rules in Figure 5.

$$\frac{\begin{array}{c}\vdots\\ \triangle A{:}x\end{array}}{A{:}x}\,\triangle E \qquad \frac{\begin{array}{c}\vdots\\ A{:}x\end{array}}{\triangle A{:}x}\,\triangle I$$

where each path to an undischarged assumption in the proof of A leads to an independent subproof of a △-type

$$\frac{A{:}x \quad B{:}y}{B{:}y \quad A{:}x}\,\triangle P$$

where A or B is a △-type

(derived rule)

$$\frac{\begin{array}{c}[\triangle B{:}x]^i\\ \vdots\\ A{:}f\end{array}}{A/\triangle B{:}\lambda x.f}\,(/\triangle)I^i$$

Figure 5. Inference rules for △

Note that it has the same introduction and elimination rules as □, and so is another (S4-like) necessity operator. The third rule in Figure 5 is a permutation rule, which has the effect of undermining the ordering of permutor-marked types relative to other types in a proof. It is convenient to use a "derived" inference rule, also shown in Figure 5, which is similar to [/I] but lacks its side condition (since a permutor-marked assumption can always "move" to right peripheral position within a subproof to meet [/I]'s side condition). The relative pronoun type used in Figure 6 allows for extraction from non-peripheral positions, as the proof illustrates.

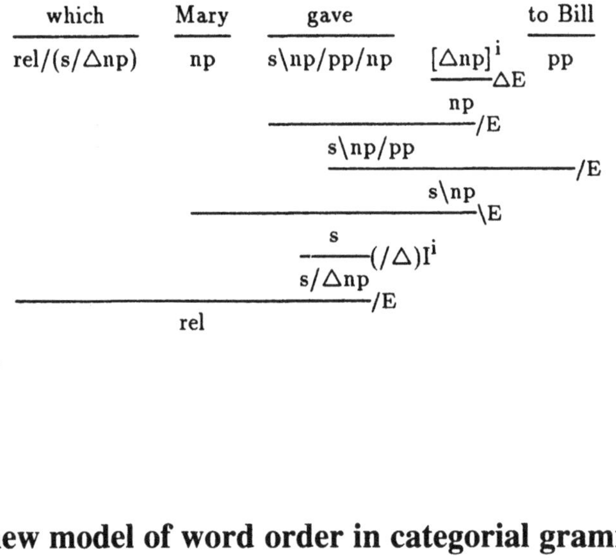

Figure 6.

5. A new model of word order in categorial grammar

In this section a new approach for handling word order within the Lambek framework is outlined. This approach factors apart the specification of a head's position from the specification of the order of its complements. Certain phenomena suggest the appropriateness of this separation, for example the Verb-Second behaviour of Germanic languages, exemplified by the Dutch sentences in (3). (3a) shows a simple embedded clause exhibiting characteristic verb-final order. Corresponding main clause examples (a declarative and a yes/no question) are shown in (3b,c), where the finite verb appears following the clause's first major constituent (here the subject) or in initial position. Such examples pose a problem for standard categorial treatments, particularly in explaining what the different cases have in common in their constituent order. Simply providing a different verb type for each word order would not explain why, when the verb's position changes, everything else stays the same. In the new model of word order, the position of heads is in general determined separately from the order of their complements, allowing a fairly natural treatment of Verb-Second.

(3) a. ... *omdat Jan de appels aan Marie gaf*
because Jan the apples to Marie gave
'... because Jan gave the apples to Marie'

b. *Jan gaf de appels aan Marie*
Jan gave the apples to Marie

c. *gaf Jan de appels aan Marie?*
gave Jan the apples to Marie
'Did Jan give the apples to Marie?'

Rather than develop the new account in relation to Germanic Verb-Second (a task addressed in Hepple 1990b), I will focus here on a different consequence of the new account, namely that it allows the incorporation of an account of GRs. We noted earlier that combining Dowty's theory of GRs with the concatenative assumption leads to some predictions about the relation between complement order and obliqueness which are not borne out empirically. The separation of the specification of complement order and head position in the new account avoids this problem. In what follows, I will develop the account in relation to English assuming a modified version of Dowty's theory. We begin, however, by considering a problem that arises specifically for flexible CGs in adopting Dowty's approach.

5.1 Primitive subcategorisation

The Lambek calculus is a highly flexible system, and allows type transformations which may radically alter the structure of types, e.g. $x/y\backslash z \Rightarrow x\backslash z/y$ where two counterdirectional arguments of a function are commuted. Such flexibility clearly threatens the use of Dowty's account, at least for syntactic treatments of GR dependent phenomena, since the argument order of lexical functors plays a crucial role in encoding information of GRs. This problem can be avoided by adopting two additional slash connectives, which are used to specify *primitive subcategorisation*, i.e. lexically given functional structure, where argument order encodes obliqueness. These connectives have the elimination rules shown in Figure 7 (which are just like those for / and \), but have no corresponding introduction rules, with the consequence that occurrences of these connectives must originate lexically, and functions constructed with them must exhibit lexically given argument order.

Elimination rules:

$$\dfrac{\begin{matrix}\vdots & \vdots \\ \mathrm{A}\not/\mathrm{B}{:}f & \mathrm{B}{:}x\end{matrix}}{\mathrm{A}{:}fx}\not/\mathrm{E} \qquad\qquad \dfrac{\begin{matrix}\vdots & \vdots \\ \mathrm{B}{:}x & \mathrm{A}\not\backslash\mathrm{B}{:}f\end{matrix}}{\mathrm{A}{:}fx}\not\backslash\mathrm{E}$$

Derivations:

$$\dfrac{\dfrac{\mathrm{x}\not/\mathrm{y} \quad [\mathrm{y}]^{i}}{\mathrm{x}}\not/\mathrm{E}}{\mathrm{x/y}}/\mathrm{I}^{i} \qquad\qquad \dfrac{\dfrac{\mathrm{x/y} \quad \mathrm{y}}{\mathrm{x}}/\mathrm{E}}{\mathrm{x}\not/\mathrm{y}}{**}\ \textit{(no introduction rule)}$$

Figure 7. Inference rules for $\not/$ and $\not\backslash$, with two derivations

The two derivations in Figure 7 show that whilst it is possible to "convert" a primitive subcategorisation slash into a standard slash (i.e. change the principal connective of a functor from the former to the latter), the converse is not possible.

5.2 The factors that determine word order

Under the new approach, word order results from the interaction of three factors: (i) the order of subcategorisation by a head for its complements (corresponding to obliqueness), (ii) the directionality of each argument, (iii) a lexical process of *Head Location*, implemented as a lexical rule, which determines the position of the head relative to its complements. Factors (i) and (ii) together determine the linear order of a head's complements, and would also determine the position of the head were it not for the involvement of factor (iii). The types which form input to the Head Location rule are called *prelocation* head types, and the rule's operation gives rise to *located* head types. For English, Head Location causes verbs to appear following their subject (if present) and preceding their non-subject complements. Since we require that prelocation types are not available to syntax, this approach requires a slightly more complicated model of the lexicon than that generally assumed in categorial work, about which I will briefly comment.

5.3 A note on the structure of the lexicon

A standard view in categorial work is that the lexicon consists of little more than a set of type assignments to words. Lexical rules may be allowed, giving further type assignments. It is assumed that all assignments are available to syntax as lexical categorisations. In contrast, I assume that lexical assignments are built up over several stages. This notion of "stages in construction" is handled by allowing the lexicon to consist of a number of distinct "compartments" or subdomains, where the types assigned to any word may differ in different compartments. A designated "final" compartment specifies the type assignments that are made available to syntax, all other compartments being invisible to syntax. Type assignments in different compartments are related by lexical rules. Certain compartments specify initial type assignments (i.e. ones not resulting from the operation of a lexical rule).

Consider, for example, the lexical rule "Box Addition" in (4), that adds a single □ to lexical types as the final step in their construction (ensuring type assignments made available to syntax are of the form □A). The rule specifies its input and output compartments (here "named" by letters). This rule's output domain is the lexicon's "final" compartment. In what follows, details of input/output domains will be suppressed to simplify presentation.

(4) $\mathrm{A}{:}x \Rightarrow \Box\mathrm{A}{:}x$
(Input domains: {e, g, k}, Output domain: z)

5.4 Complement order

The relation between subcategorisation and the linear order of a head's complements is determined by the head's prelocation type (Head Location affecting only the head's position). Consider the four functional types (differing only in directionality) shown in (5) together with the linear order that follows for the function's arguments. Notice that the linear order of the arguments appears to depend solely on the directionality of the argument A. This is because A occurs later than B in the function's argument order. In general, given two arguments of a function A and B (not necessarily successive), where A occurs later than B in subcategorisation order, if A is leftward directional it precedes B, and if A is rightward directional it follows B. Generalising this relation gives the observation that a leftward or rightward directional argument will uniformly precede or follow all earlier arguments of the function. In respect of Dowty's theory of GRs, this observation becomes a claim linking relative obliqueness to constituent order, and since argument order and directionality are the basic means for specifying constituent order for concatenative CGs, this observation becomes a prediction of a universal constraint on canonical constituent order, stated in (6), which rules out certain orders as possible canonical orders. For example, it is predicted that no language may exhibit a canonical constituent order in which a verb's subject occurs between its first and second objects. As far as I'm aware, the predictions of this constraint are borne out, i.e. no "configurational" language exhibits such an order as canonical. Of course, we can expect to see cases which appear to violate the constraint in languages that exhibit some extent of free word order, or where other processes apply to give non-canonical orders.

(5)	X/A/B	B A
	X/A\B	B A
	X\A/B	A B
	X\A\B	A B

(6) *Obliqueness Constraint on Constituent Order:*
A complement must uniformly precede or follow all the more oblique complements of its head.

(7) *Complement Ordering Principles of English:*

complement:	directionality:
subject	leftward
direct object	leftward
second object	rightward
non-subject VP	rightward

I assume the conditions (7) on directionality assignment for arguments of English prelocation verb types. These "ordering principles" are largely determined by the Obliqueness Constraint on Constituent Order and the facts of English word order. Since subjects linearly precede a verb's more oblique complements, they must be leftward directional in prelocation types, as must direct objects, since they precede second objects. The directional requirement for second objects can be argued for on the basis of facts about the ordering of particles (see Jacobson 1987; Hepple 1990b). Concerning verbal complements, Bach (1979; 1980) argues that the VP complement of subject control verbs is less oblique than the object NP (when present). Given this, the VP argument must be rightward directional as it follows the object (e.g. *Mary promised John to go*). These ordering conditions give prelocation types for English verbs such as those in Figure 8.[4]

run:	s⍀np
eat:	s⍀np⍀np
give:	s⍀np⍀npøpp
will:	s⍀npø(s⍀np)
want:	s⍀npø□(s⍀np)
believe:	s⍀npø□sp
tell:	s⍀np⍀npø□sp
persuade:	s⍀np⍀npø□(s⍀np)
promise:	s⍀npø□(s⍀np)ønp

Figure 8. Example prelocation verb types

5.5 Head Location

Head Location can be handled by adapting the general approach to extraction outlined above. A head having prelocation type H can be allowed to occur left peripherally in phrases of type X by giving it an "extracting" raised lexical type, generated by a lexical rule of the general form shown in Figure 9.

Head Location: $\mathrm{H}{:}f \Rightarrow \mathrm{X}/(\mathrm{X}/\triangle\mathrm{H}){:}\lambda g.gf$

English Verb Location: $\mathrm{vp}\phi{:}f \Rightarrow \mathrm{vp}/(\mathrm{vp}/\triangle(\mathrm{vp}\phi)){:}\lambda g.gf$

Figure 9. Head Location rules

This rule is essentially an instance of type-raising (as its semantics reveals). To ensure that the head appears at some position *amongst* its own complements, X must be a "natural projection" of the head, i.e. a type that could be gained by combining the head with some of its complements in order of decreasing obliqueness. The Head Location rule for English verbs, also shown in Figure 9, causes them to appear to the left of their own VP projection. In this rule, vp abbreviates possible English VP types (i.e. leftward directional 'primitive' functions from English subject types to the sentence type), and vpø stands for any type vp or function into vp. The located types produced by the rule only allow the verb to appear to the left of its own

VP projection, not those of any dominating verbs. This is because firstly, the "movement" effected by the rule may not cross any modal boundaries (i.e. is bounded), and secondly, the verb must appear left peripherally to some VP projection bearing the same features for tense etc. as the verb's prelocation type (since the three occurrences of vp in the rule's output are all copies of the vp subtype in the rule's input). These conditions can only be satisfied when the verb appears beside its own VP projection (i.e. since a boundary will always intervene between any VP and a dominating VP which bears the same feature markings). The types produced by the Verb Location rule require only a final step of "Box Addition" for their completion (see rule stated earlier).

In addition to the types produced under Verb Location, we might choose to allow "located status" for all prelocation types which already specify an appropriate constituent order for English (i.e. where the only argument preceding the verb is the subject), allowing simpler proofs than are needed when using the raised located types. This could be achieved with a lexical rule of the form $vp\phi \Rightarrow vp\phi$, where ϕ is forbidden to stand in place of any leftward directional arguments, and which assigns its output to the compartment for located verb types. Figure 10 shows some final verb types, resulting after Verb Location (or its non-raising counterpart), Box Addition and other lexical processes have applied.

run:	$\Box(s \obslash np)$
run:	$\Box(s \obslash np/(s \obslash np/\triangle(s \obslash np)))$
eat:	$\Box(s \obslash np/(s \obslash np/\triangle(s \obslash np \obslash np)))$
give:	$\Box(s \obslash np/(s \obslash np/\triangle(s \obslash np \obslash np \phi pp)))$
will:	$\Box(s \obslash np \phi (s \obslash np))$
want:	$\Box(s \obslash np \phi \Box(s \obslash np))$
believe:	$\Box(s \obslash np \phi \Box sp)$
tell:	$\Box(s \obslash np/(s \obslash np/\triangle(s \obslash np \obslash np \phi \Box sp)))$
persuade:	$\Box(s \obslash np/(s \obslash np/\triangle(s \obslash np \obslash np \phi \Box(s \obslash np))))$
promise:	$\Box(s \obslash np/(s \obslash np/\triangle(s \obslash np \phi \Box(s \obslash np) \phi np)))$

Figure 10. Example final verb type assignments (located)

Note that both raised and unraised types are shown for the intransive verb *run*. The raised type for *run* might seem unusual since its "extraction domain" does not "contain" any arguments of the verb. In general, a raised extractor type's extraction domain must contain some lexical material (because the calculus does not allow the assignment of any type to the empty string), and so the raised type for *run* does not allow for simple clauses such as *John runs* (although this case is covered by the verb's unraised type). However, uses for the raised type do arise, e.g. when the extraction domain contains an adverbial. The derivation in Figure 11 illustrates this treatment of word order.

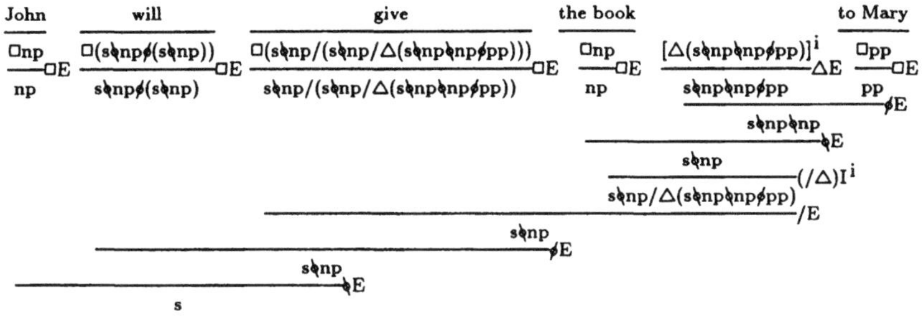

Figure 11.

6. Lexical treatments of relation changing phenomena

The new treatment of word order should provide a basis for handling a range of phenomena which depend on grammatical relations and obliqueness. Relevant cases can be subdivided as to whether they require a lexically or syntactically based account. A case requiring a syntactic account is considered in the next section. In this section, we look at some lexical treatments of relation changing phenomena, which can be handled by what Dowty calls "category changing rules", i.e. rules which modify the functional types of verbal constituents.

Passivisation can be handled using a modified version of the account of Bach (1980), one change being to base the account in the lexicon since it is easier to state the required rules as applying to prelocation types and since this move avoids various problems for handling passive morphology in syntax. The Agentless Passive rule, which takes prelocation verb types as input and yields further prelocation types as output, is shown in Figure 12.

Agentless Passive (lexical):

$$(\mathrm{s}\backslash\!\!\!\phi\,\mathrm{np}\backslash\!\!\!\phi\,\mathrm{np})\phi^{n}{:}f \Rightarrow (\mathrm{s}\backslash\!\!\!\phi\,\mathrm{np})\phi^{n}{:}\lambda x_1 \ldots x_n.\lambda y.\exists z.(f x_1 \ldots x_n\, y\, z)$$

e.g. *give* $\qquad\qquad$ *given*

$$(\mathrm{s}\backslash\!\!\!\phi\,\mathrm{np}\backslash\!\!\!\phi\,\mathrm{np}\oslash\mathrm{pp}){:}\mathrm{give}' \Rightarrow (\mathrm{s}\backslash\!\!\!\phi\,\mathrm{np}\oslash\mathrm{pp}){:}\lambda x.\lambda y.\exists z.(\mathrm{give}'\, x\, y\, z)$$

Figure 12. Agentless Passive rule, with example

The notation X^n is schematic for functions requiring n arguments ($n \geq 0$) to give X (e.g. X is of the form $X\oslash^0$, X/A/B of the form $X\oslash^2$). The two occurrences of $\oslash^n$ in the rule indicate that its input and output types require identical sequences of arguments to give their respective values. The rule takes as input functions into (prelocation) transitive verb types and yields functions requiring the same arguments to give an intransitive verb type. The rule's semantics abstracts over the verb's non-subject arguments and existentially quantifies over its subject, so that the subject of the output type corresponds semantically to the first object of the input. Some details of the rule have been suppressed to simplify, e.g. the rule marks the type as [+passive] , and is accompanied by a change to the verb's lexical morpology. This lexical treatment of passive is reminiscent of that suggested for Head-driven Phrase Structure Grammar (Pollard — Sag 1987). Figure 12 illustrates the rule's use in deriving the prelocation type for the passive participle of *give*.

Adapting the account of Dowty (1982a), dative shift can be handled using the lexical rule shown in Figure 13, which again creates additional prelocation verb types. The rule's semantics abstracts over the two object arguments so as to reverse their semantic order. Thus, the first object of the output type corresponds semantically to the second object of the input and vice versa. The rule's use is illustrated in Figure 13, deriving an additional (prelocation) type for *give*.

Dative Shift (lexical):

$$(\mathrm{vp}\backslash\!\!\!\phi\,\mathrm{np}\oslash\mathrm{pp})\phi^{n}{:}f \Rightarrow (\mathrm{vp}\backslash\!\!\!\phi\,\mathrm{np}\oslash\mathrm{np})\oslash^{n}{:}\lambda x_1 \ldots x_n.\lambda y.\lambda z.(f x_1 \ldots x_n\, z\, y)$$

e.g. *give* $\qquad\qquad$ *give*

$$(\mathrm{s}\backslash\!\!\!\phi\,\mathrm{np}\backslash\!\!\!\phi\,\mathrm{np}\oslash\mathrm{pp}){:}\mathrm{give}' \Rightarrow (\mathrm{s}\backslash\!\!\!\phi\,\mathrm{np}\backslash\!\!\!\phi\,\mathrm{np}\oslash\mathrm{np}){:}\lambda y.\lambda z.(\mathrm{give}'\, z\, y)$$

Figure 13. Dative Shift rule, with example

7. Obliqueness and binding

We will next consider binding as an instance of an obliqueness dependent phenomenon requiring a syntactically based treatment. I treat reflexives as being simple functions of the form □(np/@np) (whose operator @ will be explained shortly), which serve to introduce an argument position which can be co-bound with some other argument position). Reflexives have identity semantics (i.e. $\lambda x.x$) so that binding the reflexive's argument is equivalent to binding the argument position that the reflexive itself occupies (making this account somewhat like others that treat reflexives as variables which may be bound to some argument position. The operator @ is required to identify the reflexive's argument as belonging to a reflexive and hence available for binding, and also to prevent the reflexive incorrectly taking a lexical NP as argument (giving e.g. *himself John* as NP). In Hepple (1990b), @ is a permutor structural modality (though having different modal behaviour from □ or the permutor used in extraction). It is sufficient here to provide no inference rules for @, making it effectively a "dead" operator. By either view, @ cannot be introduced in syntax, and so @ occurrences must originate lexically with anaphor types. Binding is effected by the Reflexive Interpretation Rule (RIR), shown in Figure 14.

$$\frac{\begin{array}{c}[@\mathrm{B}:x]^{\mathrm{i}}\\ \vdots \\ \mathrm{C}:f\end{array}}{\mathrm{C}:\lambda x.fx}\,\mathrm{RIR}^{\mathrm{i}} \qquad \text{where C is } \mathrm{A}\backslash\!\!\!\circ\mathrm{B} \text{ or } \mathrm{A}/\!\!\!\circ\mathrm{B}$$

Figure 14. Reflexive Interpretation Rule (RIR)

The RIR discharges a hypothesis @B (which must correspond to an anaphor's argument since only anaphors introduce @ operators) within the proof, but does not change the proof's conclusion type. The link between the types of the discharged assumption and the argument sought by the proof's conclusion type (which are B and @B) allows an anaphor to determine the type of its binding argument (e.g an anaphor □(np/@np) requires a NP binder). In the semantics of the result constituent, the lambda operator binds two instances of the variable x (since x already appears as a subterm of f) and so co-binds the reflexive's argument with the first argument sought by the main functor of the proof.

The proof in Figure 15 illustrates the rule's use. This proof assigns the meaning (10a) (where *loves* has meaning ($\lambda f.f$ loves′), with loves′ the meaning of the verb's prelocation type), which reduces to (10b) (since himself′ = $\lambda x.x$). Note that since the assumption @np in this proof is not □-modal, a reflexive appearing within an embedded clause must be bound within it (i.e. the RIR must apply to discharge the assumption, c.f. the earlier discussion of boundedness and relativisation), and so examples like **John$_i$ thinks Mary loves himself$_i$* cannot be derived.

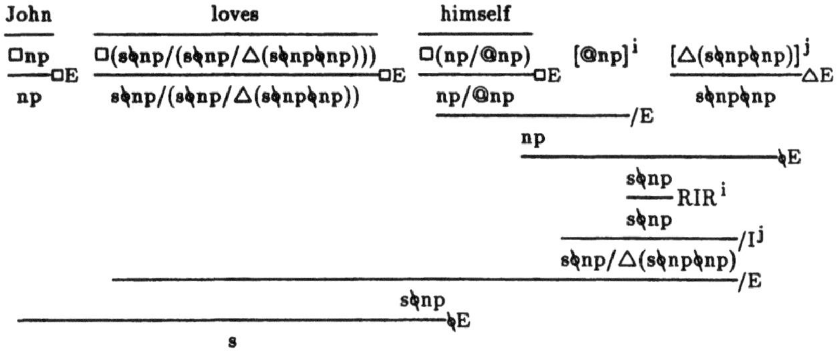

Figure 15.

(10) a. ($\lambda f.f$ loves′) ($\lambda g.\lambda v.(g$ (himself′ v) v)) john′
b. (loves′ john′ john′)

Certain asymmetries in the possibilities for binding, for example that subjects may bind objects and first objects second objects but not vice versa, have been explained in terms of *command* relations. Goverment and Binding work has used *c-command*, a condition on phrase-structure configurations. Montague Grammar has used an *F-command* relation (e.g. Bach — Partee 1980; Chierchia 1988), where an argument F-commands the "earlier" (and hence less oblique) arguments of the same functor and their subconstituents, e.g. in the type (((X/A)/B)/C), A F-commands B and C, whilst B F-commands only C. In Head-driven Phrase Structure Grammar (Pollard — Sag 1987; 1990), where heads, though not strictly functional, display explicit ordered subcategorisation which encodes obliqueness, an *o-command* relation is employed, which is similar to F-command but stated purely in terms of order of subcategorization and obliqueness, rather than function-argument structure.

Returning to the Lambek treatment of binding described above, note that the RIR applies only to proofs of functional types whose principal connective is a primitive subcategorisation slash. It follows from this that binding is subject to an obliqueness based command restriction, because such a type must be a projection of a lexical functor, and its argument B must be less oblique than any argument with which the functor has already combined. Hence the anaphor must appear as (or as a subpart of) a more oblique complement of the functor. Note that this obliqueness requirement applies even though it is the prelocation verb type, which appears embedded within a raised located verb type, that has the relevant functional structure. The approach is further illustrated in Figure 16, which shows a derivation for the VP *showed Mary*$_i$ *herself*$_i$, with binding between first and second objects.

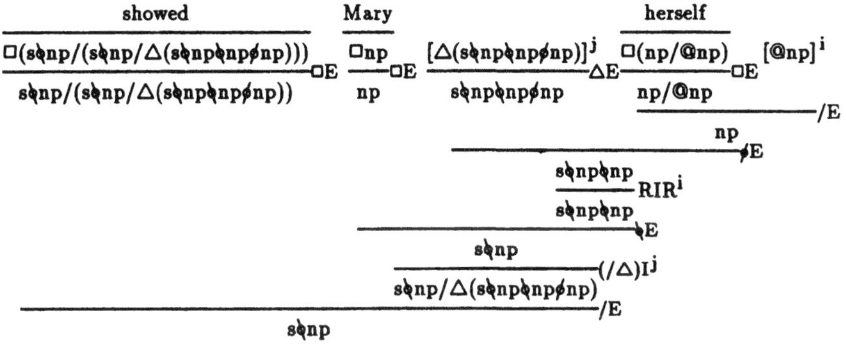

Figure 16.

No proof is possible for the converse binding **showed herself*$_i$ *Mary*$_i$. Unlike Pollard and Sag's account, where o-command is stipulated as a constraint on well-formed binding relations, the o-command property of binding relations in the present approach simply emerges from the fact that verb types encode obliqueness information and from the statement of the RIR. Although final verb type assignments may seem to be quite complicated in this approach, the fact that the obliqueness information encoded by their lexical precursors is still available to play a role in syntax suggests that this complexity is not superfluous.

8. Conclusion

I have presented an acount of word order within an extended version of the Lambek calculus which factors apart the specification of a head's position from the specification of the order of its complements. This move allows the incorporation of a modified version of the account of GRs outlined in Dowty (1982a), allowing various phenomena to be handled which depend on GRs and obliqueness. The approach has been illustrated in relation to lexical treatments of relation changing phenomena, and a syntactic treatment of binding.

Notes

1. I would like to thank the following people for discussion, comments and suggestions: Guy Barry, Elisabet Engdahl, Glyn Morrill, Mike Reape, Mark Steedman, Anna Szabolcsi. Earlier versions appear as Hepple (1990a) and Hepple (1990c). The work was carried out at the Centre for Cognitive Science, Edinburgh, with the support of ESRC Research Studentship C00428722003, and the final version of the paper prepared at the Cambridge University Computer Laboratory.
2. In the notation used here, types x/y and $x\backslash y$ are both functions *from* y *to* x. I assume a convention of left association for binary connectives, so that e.g. $a/b/(c/d)$ is the same as $((a/b)/(c/d))$, and that unary operators bind "more tightly" than binary connectives, so that $\Box x/y$ is the same as $((\Box x)/y)$.
3. Hepple (1990b) extends Morrill's proposals by adopting a *polymodal* system, which allows an approach in which there are many different notions of "linguistic boundary" and where the sensitivity of different syntactic processes to different boundaries can be directly addressed within the grammar. This system is applied to a range of locality phenomena involving extraction and binding.
4. Note that the type for *give* in Figure 8 would yield word order as in *John a book gave to Mary*. Of course, this type is not available to syntax, and so this word order is never realised, but some readers may feel that the approach would lack plausibility if it was not a possible word order of any language. It is interesting to note then that Travis (1989) reports precisely this order for the language Kpelle (i.e. subject < object < verb < (argument) PP).

References

Ades, A. and M. Steedman
1982 On the order of words. *Linguistics and Philosophy* 4, 517–558.

Bach, E.
1979 Control in Montague grammar. *Linguistic Inquiry* 10, 515–531.

Bach, E.
1980 In defense of passive. *Linguistics and Philosophy* 3, 297–341.

Bach, E. and B. Partee
1980 Anaphora and semantic structure. In: K. Kreiman and A. Ojeda (eds.), *Papers from the Parasession on Pronouns and Anaphora*. Chicago Linguistic Society, Chicago.

Barry, G., M. Hepple, N. Leslie and Glyn Morrill
1992 Proof Figures and Structural Operators for Categorial Grammar. *Proceedings of the European ACL*, Berlin.

Chierchia, G.
1988 Aspects of a categorial theory of binding. In: R. Oehrle, E. Bach and D. Wheeler (eds.), *Categorial Grammars and Natural Language Structures*. Dordrecht, D. Reidel, 125 and 151.

Dowty, D.
1978 Governed transformations as lexical rules in a Montague Grammar. *Linguistic Inquiry*, 393–426.

Dowty, D.
1982a Grammatical relations and Montague grammar. In: P. Jacobson and G. Pullum (eds.)*The Nature of Syntactic Representation*. Dordrecht, D. Reidel, 79–130.

Dowty, D.
1982b More on the categorial analysis of grammatical relations. In: A. Zaenen (ed.), *Subjects and Other Subjects: Proceedings of the Harvard Conference on Grammatical Relations*. Indiana, Bloomington. Also in *Ohio State University Working Papers in Linguistics* 26: 102–133.

Gazdar, G., E. Klein, G. Pullum and Ivan Sag
1985 *Generalized Phrase Structure Grammar*. London, Basil Blackwell.

Hepple, M.
1996 Grammatical relations and Lambek calculus. *This volume*, 225–277.

Hepple, M.
1990b *The Grammar and Processing of Order and Dependency: a categorial approach*. Unpublished Ph.D. thesis. Centre for Cognitive Science, University of Edinburgh, Edinburgh.

Hepple, M.
1990c Word Order and Obliqueness in Categorial Grammar, In: G. Barry and G. Morrill (eds.), *Studies in Categorial Grammar*. Edinburgh Working Papers in Cognitive Science 5. Centre for Cognitive Science, University of Edinburgh, Edinburgh.

Jacobson, P.
1987 Phrase Structure, Grammatical Relations and Discontinuous Constituents. In: G. Huck and A. Ojeda (eds.), *Syntax and Semantics 20. Discontinuous Constituency*. New York, Academic Press, 27–69.

Kang, Beom-mo
1988 *Functional Inheritance, Anaphora and Semantic Interpretation in a Generalized Categorial Grammar*. Ph.D. Thesis, Brown University, Providence RI..

Koster, J.
1988 The residual SOV structure of English, *Groningen Papers in Theoretical Linguistics* 5, University of Groningen, Groningen.

Lambek, J.
1958 The mathematics of sentence structure. *American Mathematical Monthly* 65, 154–170.

Lambek, J.
1961 On the calculus of syntactic types. *Structure of Language and its Mathematical Aspects, Proceedings of the Symposia in Applied Mathematics* XII. American Mathematical Society, Providence.

Larson, R.
1988 On the double object construction. *Linguistic Inquiry* 19, 335–391.

Moortgat, M.
1996 Generalized quantifiers and discontinuous type constructors. *This volume*, 181–207.

Morrill, G.
1989 *Intensionality, boundedness, and modal logic, Research Paper EUCCS/RP–32*, Centre for Cognitive Science, University of Edinburgh., Edinburgh.

Morrill, G.
1990 Intensionality and boundedness. *Linguistics and Philosophy* 13.

Morrill, G., N. Leslie, M. Hepple and G. Barry
1990 Categorial deductions and structural operations. In: G. Barry and G. Morrill (eds.), *Studies in Categorial Grammar*. Edinburgh Working Papers in Cognitive Science 5, Centre for Cognitive Science, University of Edinburgh, Edinburgh.

Partee, B.
1976 Some transformational extensions of Montague Grammar. In: B. Partee (ed.), *Montague Grammar*. New York, Academic Press.

Pollard, C. and I. Sag
1987 *An Information-Based Approach to Syntax and Semantics 1: Fundamentals.* CSLI Lecture Notes, Number 13, Center for the Study of Language and Information, Stanford.

Pollard, C. and I. Sag
1990 "Anaphors in English and the Scope of Binding Theory". Unpublished manuscript, Stanford University, CA.

Szabolcsi, A.
1987a Bound variables in syntax (are there any?), In: J. Groenendijk, M. Stokhof and F. Veltman (eds.), *Sixth Amsterdam Colloquium.* Institute for Language, Logic and Information, University of Amsterdam, Amsterdam.

Thomason, R.
1976 Some Extensions of Montague Grammar. In: B. Partee (ed.), *Montague Grammar.* New York, Academic Press, 77–117.

Travis, Lisa
1989 Parameters of Phrase Structure. In: M. Baltin and A. Kroch (eds.), *Alternative Conceptions of Phrase Structure.* University of Chicago Press, Chicago, 263–279.

On head non-movement

Carl J. Pollard

1. Introduction

In recent years the phenomenon called verb-second (or V2) has received a great deal of attention in the syntactic literature. In the government-binding community in particular, it has become standard to analyze V2 as a subspecies of *head movement*. On this account, which is originally due to den Besten (1983), the finite verb or auxiliary undergoes movement into the COMP position, while some phrasal constituent moves into the position to its left. In accordance with the analysis of clause structure proposed by Chomsky (1986), that pre-COMP position is usually taken to be the specifier of CP. Among head movement analyses of V2, there are some differences of opinion, for example as to the status of INFL, or whether subject-initial clauses also involve movement to COMP. But glossing over such differences, we can take the analyses shown in (1) as more or less standard:

(1a)

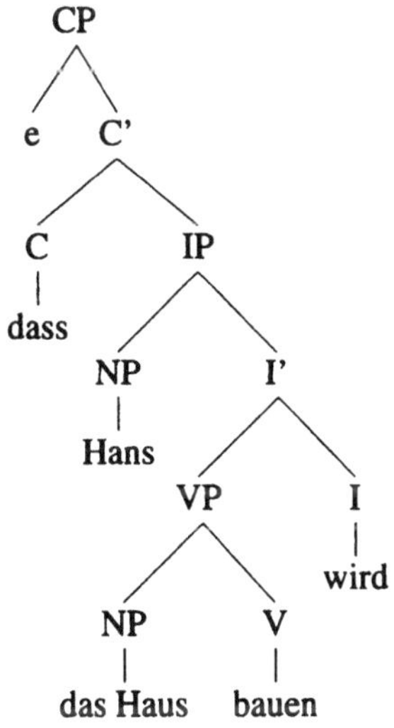

Here (1a) is the structure for a subordinate *daß*-clause, which does not involve movement. And (1b) shows how a typical V2 s-structure is derived by two instances of move-alpha from a d-structure similar to (1a).

(1b)

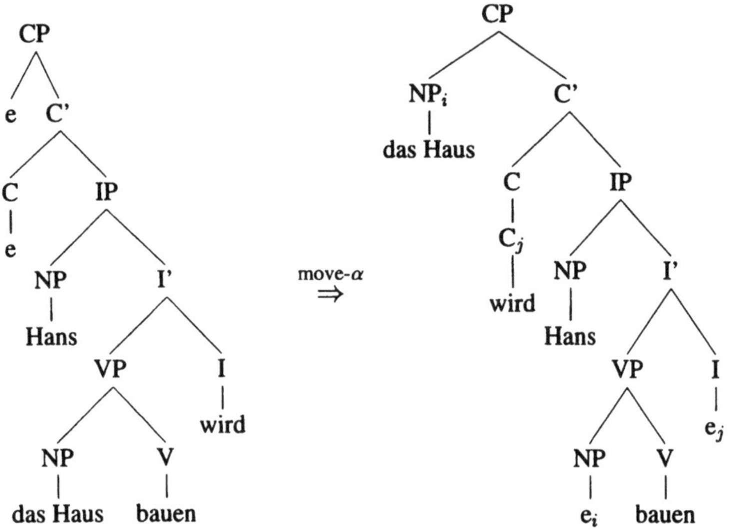

The apparent discontinuity between the finite auxiliary and its VP sister in such sentences might be thought to be problematic for non-transformational theories.

My immediate goal in this paper is to discuss some recent work directed at providing an account of V2 and related phenomena within a phrase-structural framework that does not employ any notion of movement. But in passing, I will consider some facts about German word order that do not appear to submit easily to a satisfactory phrase-structural account.

2. HPSG: a brief overview

The framework I will employ as the basis for the analysis is a version of the head-driven phrase structure grammar (HPSG) that Ivan Sag and I have been developing over the past several years (Pollard – Sag 1987, 1994).

HPSG is a framework for syntactic and semantic theorization that is influenced by a number of other research traditions, including categorial grammar, GPSG, GB, LFG, and situation semantics.

In HPSG, linguistic objects are modelled by graphs of a certain kind called sorted feature structures. For example, omitting some irrelevant details, the English pronoun *she* is modelled by the sorted feature structure shown in (2):

(2)
$$\left[\begin{array}{ll} \text{PHONOLOGY} & \langle \textit{she} \rangle \\ \text{SYNTAX} & \left[\begin{array}{ll} \text{LOCAL} & \left[\begin{array}{ll} \text{CATEGORY} & \left[\begin{array}{ll} \text{HEAD} & \left[\text{CASE} \quad \text{NOM}\right]_{\textit{noun}} \\ \text{SUBCAT} & \langle\ \rangle \end{array}\right]_{\textit{category}} \\ \text{CONTENT} & \left[\begin{array}{ll} \text{PER} & \text{3RD} \\ \text{NUM} & \text{SNG} \\ \text{GEND} & \text{FEM} \end{array}\right]_{\textit{parameter}} \end{array}\right]_{\textit{local}} \\ \text{SLASH} & \{\ \} \end{array}\right]_{\textit{syntax}} \end{array}\right]_{\textit{word}}$$

The main idea here is that different kinds of linguistic object are modelled by different *sorts* of feature structures, and each sort of feature structure has different *features*. For example, *she* is a word, so it is modelled by a feature structure of sort *word*: that is indicated by the left outermost subscript.

Now we think of a word as a complex of phonological and syntactic information, so this feature structure has the features PHONOLOGY and SYNTAX. Here the value of the PHONOLOGY feature is just a list of phonological words, represented by their standard orthographics, in this case a list of length one, with just the single phonological word *she*.

The SYNTAX value is more interesting. This is another feature structure, this time with the sort *syntax*. This sort of feature structure in turn has features of its own called SLASH and LOCAL. In general the value of the SLASH feature for an expression is a set that describes the unfilled gaps in the expression (thus generalizing the SLASH feature in GPSG, which does not allow set values). In this case the SLASH value is the empty set, denoted by { }, since words do not contain gaps.

The LOCAL value is still another feature structure, this one of sort *local*. This sort of feature structure has the features CATEGORY and CONTENT. Let us consider the values of those two features in turn.

First, the CATEGORY value, of sort *category*, has the features HEAD and SUBCATEGORIZATION. HEAD is roughly analogous to the head features of GPSG. In this case the HEAD value has sort *noun*, which in turn has the feature

CASE. Of course the value of the CASE feature is *nominative*. In general the SUBCAT feature is a list that describes the valence of an expression; that is, it gives information about the complements, such as subjects and objects, that the expression has to combine with in order to become *saturated* or grammatically complete.[1] In this case, since *she* is an NP and NPs are already saturated, the SUBCAT value is just the empty list, denoted by $< >$.

The last piece of information we have to consider here is the CONTENT value. Roughly, the CONTENT value of an expression contains syntactic information that bears more or less directly on semantic interpetation. In the case of an NP, the CONTENT value is a thing called a *parameter*, which plays a role in the theory analogous to that of referential indices in GB theory or reference markers in discourse representation theory. Note that the agreement features PERSON, NUMBER, and GENDER are treated as part of the internal structure of the parameter, not as part of the category. This way of structuring the information plays an important role in the HPSG theory of agreement, because it entails that expressions that share the same parameter agree with each other.

More generally, the way the different pieces of linguistic information are arranged within a feature structure are not arbitrary, but instead reflect natural groupings based on shared behavior. For example, SYNTAX information is information that can be subcategorized for by another expression; it is also the kind of information that undergoes *raising*, of which we will encounter numerous instances in due course. LOCAL information is the kind of information that is shared between a gap and its filler in an unbounded dependency construction. And HEAD information is the kind of information that is shared between an expression and its phrasal projections.

Sorted feature structures are well-suited for representing structured linguistic information, but they are a little unwieldy. To lighten the notation, I need to introduce some abbreviatory conventions, as shown in (3).

(3) $$\text{NP} = \begin{bmatrix} \text{LOCAL} & \begin{bmatrix} \text{CAT} & \begin{bmatrix} \text{HEAD } \textit{noun} \\ \text{SUBCAT } \langle \, \rangle \end{bmatrix} \end{bmatrix} \end{bmatrix} \qquad \text{S} = \begin{bmatrix} \text{LOCAL} & \begin{bmatrix} \text{CAT} & \begin{bmatrix} \text{HEAD } \textit{verb} \\ \text{SUBCAT } \langle \, \rangle \end{bmatrix} \end{bmatrix} \end{bmatrix}$$

$$\text{VP} = \begin{bmatrix} \text{LOCAL} & \begin{bmatrix} \text{CAT} & \begin{bmatrix} \text{HEAD } \textit{verb} \\ \text{SUBCAT } \langle \text{ NP } \rangle \end{bmatrix} \end{bmatrix} \end{bmatrix}$$

This just says that an NP is a saturated nominal, while an S is a saturated verbal. And a VP is a verbal phrase that is saturated except for one NP, namely its subject. We can add other feature values to our abbreviations if necessary; for example, the notation in (4) abbreviates much of the information contained in the structure for *she* given in (2):

(4) NP[nom]:[3rd,sng,fem]

Note that in abbreviations of this kind, CONTENT information (if given) comes after the colon. For an NP, this will just be the parameter, which in the present example contains the agreement specification [3rd,sng,fem].

Let us consider another example of a lexical entry, and then I will turn to the question of phrase structure. The LOCAL value for one form of the verb *gives* is shown in (5):

(5)
$$\left[\begin{array}{ll} \text{CATEGORY} & {}_{category}\left[\begin{array}{ll}\text{HEAD} & {}_{verb}\left[\text{VFORM}\quad \text{FIN}\right] \\ \text{SUBCAT} & \langle \text{NP[NOM]:}\boxed{1}\text{[3RD,SNG]}, \text{NP[ACC]:}\boxed{2}, \text{NP[ACC]:}\boxed{3}\rangle \end{array}\right] \\ \text{CONTENT} & {}_{soa}\left[\begin{array}{ll}\text{RELATION} & \text{GIVE}\\ \text{AGENT} & \boxed{1} \\ \text{GOAL} & \boxed{2}\\ \text{THEME} & \boxed{3}\end{array}\right]\end{array}\right]$$

Here we see that *gives* subcategorizes for a third-singular nominative subject, an accusative primary object, and an accusative secondary object. Note that the CONTENT value of the verb is a state-of-affairs, or *soa*, which specifies a certain relation, the relation of giving, together with values for its argument roles, in this case AGENT, GOAL, and THEME. Note also that the values assigned to the argument roles are just the parameters of the corresponding subcategorized complements. For example, the parameter of the subject NP, which is indicated by the tag $\boxed{1}$, also appears as the value of the AGENT role. Another way of saying the same thing is that the AGENT value of the verb's CONTENT and the CONTENT value of the verb's subject are *token-identical* or *structure-shared*. This means that in the graph structure represented by the diagram (5), these two values correspond to the same node in the graph.

We now consider how phrases are formed. In GB, of course, phrases are licensed by schematic immediate dominance rules like the two $\overline{X}$ schemata shown in (6):

(6) a. $X'' \rightarrow Y''\ X'$
(specifier or subject)
b. $X' \rightarrow X\ Y''$ (complement)

In HPSG, there is no notion of bar level. Instead, the immediate dominance schemata (or ID schemata) are formulated in terms of degree of saturation. To be completely formal about it, ID schemata in HPSG should be represented as feature structure constraints written in a formal feature logic. But informally they can be represented by tree diagrams as in (7).

(7)

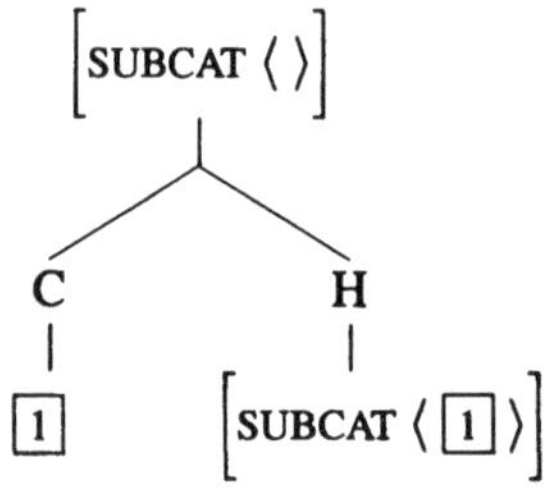

Figure 1. Schema A

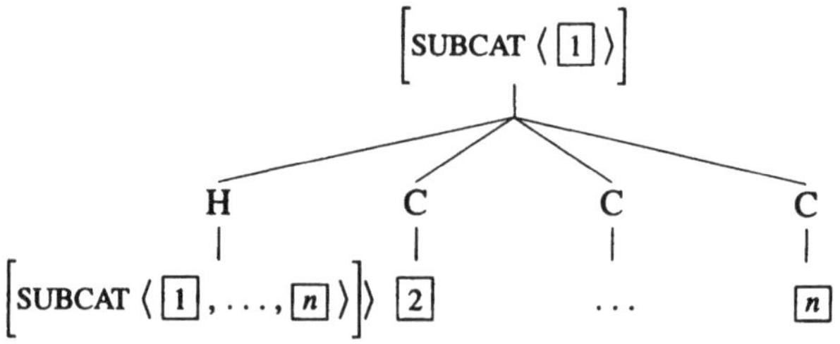

Figure 2. Schema B

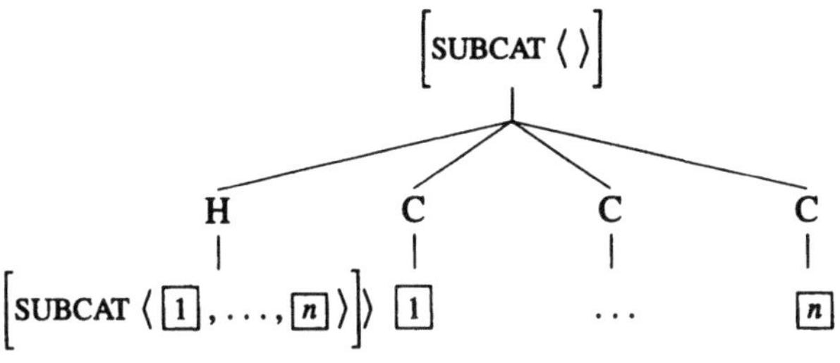

Figure 3. Schema C

Here the labels on the tree branches stand for HEAD-DAUGHTER and COM-PLEMENT-DAUGHTER, two of the kinds of daughters in HPSG. Schema A is the HPSG analog of the $\overline{X}$ schema (6a). It says that one of the options for a phrase is to consist of two daughters, a head daughter and a complement daughter. The two occurrences of the tag [1] indicate that the SYNTAX value of the complement daughter has to be token-identical with the SUBCAT specification on the head daughter.

Schema B is the analog of $\overline{X}$ schema (6b). This schema says that another option for a phrase is to have a head daughter and n-1 complement daughters, where n is the number of complements that the head daughter subcategorizes for. In this case, each of the complement daughters has to be token-identical with one of the SUBCAT specifications on the head daughter.

In (7), I have rendered the schemata informally in such a way as to reflect the facts of English consituent ordering. Of course in their most general form, the schemata should be interpeted only as immediate dominance schemata, with the particular orderings of the daughters being a matter of cross-linguistic parametrization.

Schema C does not have any analog in $\overline{X}$ theory, and I will return to this point presently. Before that, though, let us consider an example that illustrates schemata A and B. This is given in (8):

(8)

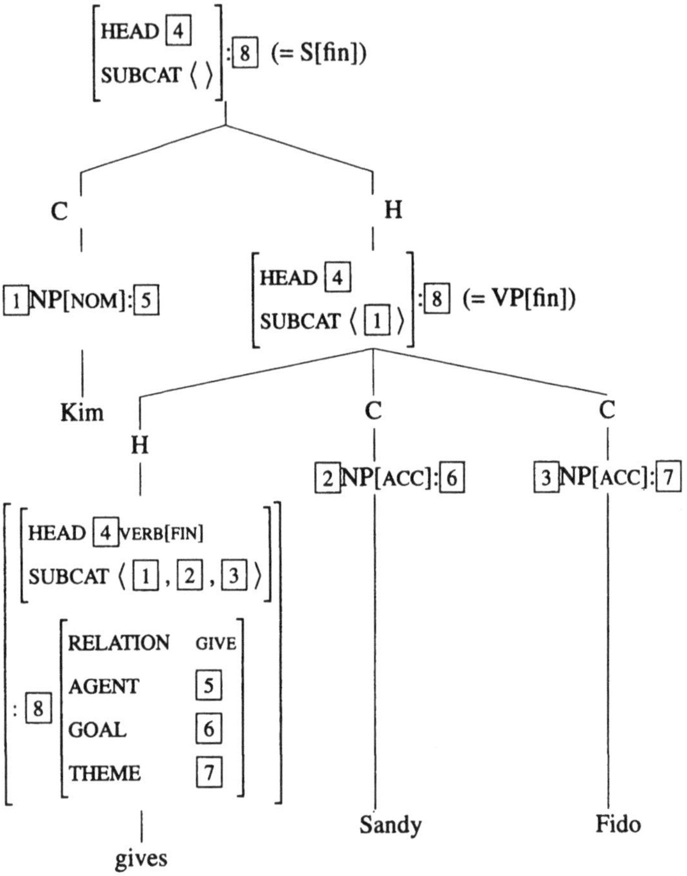

This sentence is headed by the verb *gives*, whose lexical entry was given in (5). Using Schema B, we combine this verb with the two non-subject complements *Sandy* and *Fido* to form the VP node. There are three points to note about the VP node.

First, the SUBCAT value on the VP has had the elements 2 and 3 removed, since these subcategorization requirements have already been satisfied. This is an example of one of HPSG's universal principles, called the Subcategorization Principle, which is stated in (9a).

(9) Three Principles of Universal Grammar

a. (Subcategorization Principle) In a phrase, the SUBCAT value of the head daughter is the concatenation of the phrase's SUBCAT value with the list of the complement daughters.

b. (Head Feature Principle) The HEAD value of a phrase is token-idenitical with the HEAD value of the head daughter.
c. (Content Principle) The CONTENT value of a phrase is token-identical with the CONTENT value of the head daughter.

HPSG's Subcategorization Principle is similar to cancellation in categorial grammar. The effect is just to check the subcategorization requirements off the list as they become satisfied. At the same time, the actual complement daughters have their SYNTAX values unified with the corresponding SUBCAT values on the head daughter.

A second point to note here is that the HEAD value of the VP is the same as the HEAD value verb[fin] on the head daughter, indicated by the tag [4]. This illustrates a second universal principle, called the Head Feature Principle, stated in (9b).

And third, note that the CONTENT of the VP, indicated by the tag [8], is the same as the head daughter's CONTENT, namely the state-of-affairs that [5] gives [6] to [7]. This is an example of a third universal principle, called the Content Principle, which is stated in (9c).

Actually this is a simplification, since it does not take quantifiers and adjuncts into consideration, but it will suffice for present purposes. It is important to be aware that there is no functional application, as in standard categorial grammar, since the arguments are built right into the head's CONTENT. In a sense, the effect of functional application is obtained by structure sharing.

Finally, we consider the S node at the top of (8). Here we have used Schema A to combine the VP with a complement that satisfies its one remaining subcategorization requirement. By the Subcategorization Principle, the SUBCAT value on the mother now becomes empty, and the other two principles take care of passing the HEAD and CONTENT values from the VP up to the S. It is important to keep in mind that, unlike GB theory, we do not posit a separate category INFL that serves as a repository of tense and agreement information. Instead, the finiteness and subject agreement information are present in the verb's lexical entry, and the sentence is projected directly from the verb.

We turn now to the subject of head movement. For a simple example, consider first a GB analysis of the simple sentence *she can go* shown on the left side of (10):

(10)

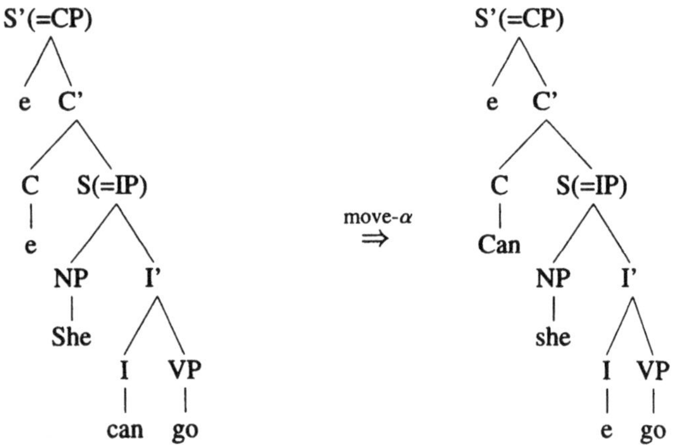

For this sentence, the structure on the left does duty as both d-structure and s-structure, since no movement is involved. The s-structure for the inverted sentence *can she go* is then derived from this structure by an instance of move-alpha that takes the INFL *can* into COMP. We next consider how HPSG analyzes the same sentence. The heart of our analysis is the lexical entry for the auxiliary, which is shown in (11):

(11)

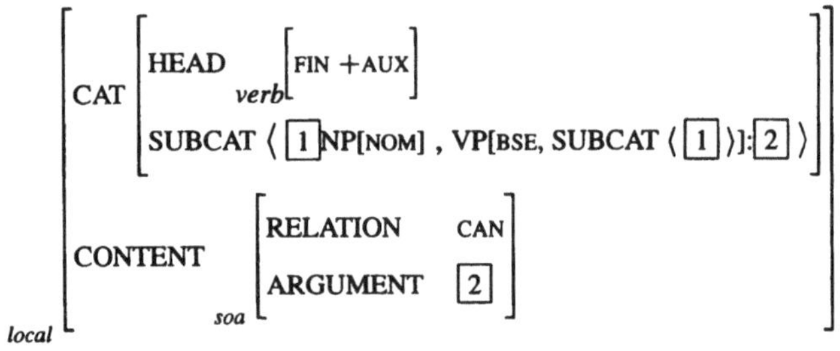

First, the HEAD value tells us that *can* is a finite verb which is further specified positively for the binary feature AUX. That is, auxiliaries are distinguished from other verbs by a feature, essentially as in GPSG.

Second, let us examine the SUBCAT value. It shows that *can* subcategorizes for a nominative NP subject, indicated by the tag [1], and a base-form VP complement. Of course since this complement is a VP, it subcategorizes for an NP subject itself. One crucial point to notice here is that this complement subject also bears the tag [1], that is, it is token-identical with the subject of *can*. In HPSG, this property is characteristic of raising-to-subject verbs. The verb *seem* would be analyzed in the same way, except that the form of the VP complement would be specified as infinitive instead of base, and *seem* is -AUX.

Finally, the CONTENT value is just a state-of-affairs whose relation is *can* and whose argument is some other state-of-affairs, [3], which in turn comes from the CONTENT of the VP complement. Of course the subject of *can* does not have its CONTENT value assigned to any role, because raising controllers are never thematic.

The HPSG analysis of *she can go* is given in (12):

(12)

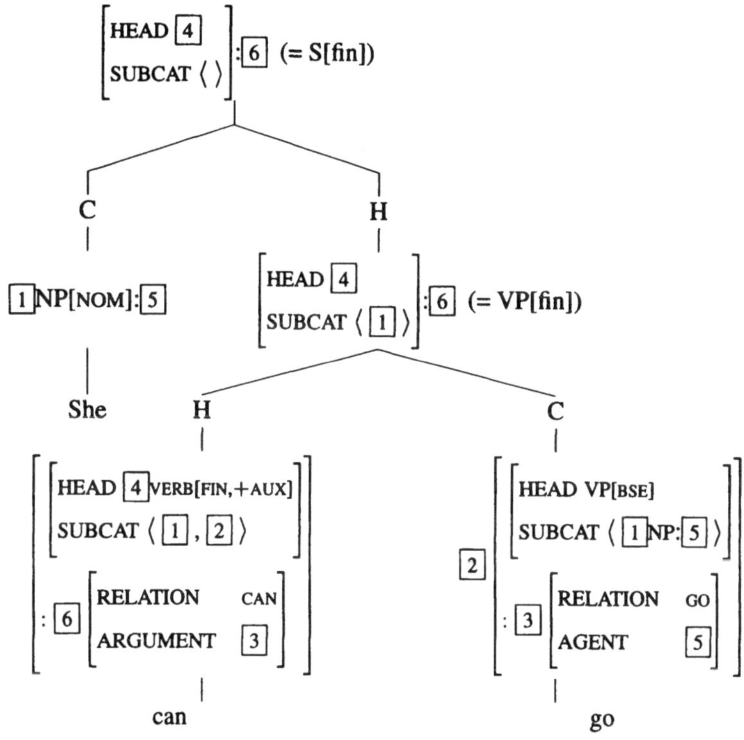

Syntactically, there is nothing new here: the finite head verb combines with its non-subject complement using Schema B to form a finite VP. Then the VP combines with its subject by Schema A to form a finite S. All this is pretty much the same as with the example in (8).

The interesting thing about (12) is the way raising works semantically. Recall that the CONTENT value of *can*, indicated by the tag [6], specifies that the argument of the *can* relation is the CONTENT of the VP complement, indicated by the tag [3]. In the present case, this complement CONTENT value is the state-of-affairs of $\boxed{5}$ going, where $\boxed{5}$ is the parameter corresponding to the complement subject. But the complement subject is also lexically specified to be token-identical with the matrix subject, so the goer $\boxed{5}$ must in fact be identified with the parameter of the matrix subject *she*. And by the Content Principle, the CONTENT of the whole sentence must be token-identical with the CONTENT of the head verb, which is shown in (13):

(13)
$$\begin{bmatrix} \text{RELATION} & \text{CAN} \\ \text{ARGUMENT} & \begin{bmatrix} \text{RELATION} & \text{GO} \\ \text{AGENT} & \boxed{5} \end{bmatrix} \end{bmatrix}$$

This completes the analysis of *she can go*. But what about the inverted sentence *can she go*? This is where the third ID schema presented in (7), Schema C, comes in. Recall that this schema had no analog in $\overline{\text{X}}$ theory. In essence, all this schema does is allow a head to combine with *all* its complements, including the subject, to form a saturated phrase. In particular, we can use this schema to combine *can* with both its complements to produce the flat structure shown in (14):

(14)

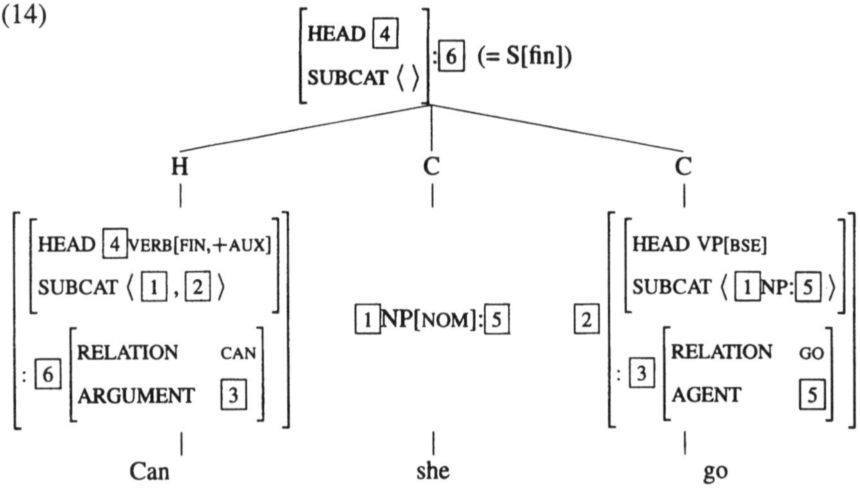

Here the CONTENT values $\boxed{3}$, $\boxed{5}$, and $\boxed{6}$ are all the same as in the uninverted example, so the inverted example comes out with the same CONTENT value as the uninverted one. The only difference is that all the relevant structure-sharings take place at one phrasal projection of the head instead of two.

There is still one syntactic detail to take care of. What stops us from using Schema C to produce non-sentences like *saw she Fred*? The answer, of course, is that in English only finite auxiliaries can invert. To capture this generalization, we borrow from GPSG the binary head feature INVERTED (INV). The basic idea is that all lexical entries except finite auxiliaries are specified as -INVERTED. But finite auxiliaries in general are unspecified for this feature, which means that either instantiation is possible. All that remains now is to stipulate that in English, the head daughter in Schema C is specified +INVERTED, while the head daughters in the other two schemata are specified -INVERTED. These should be thought of as language-specific parametrizations of universal schemata. The upshot of all this is that the analyses of the two examples we have been discussing are essentially as shown in (15):

(15a)

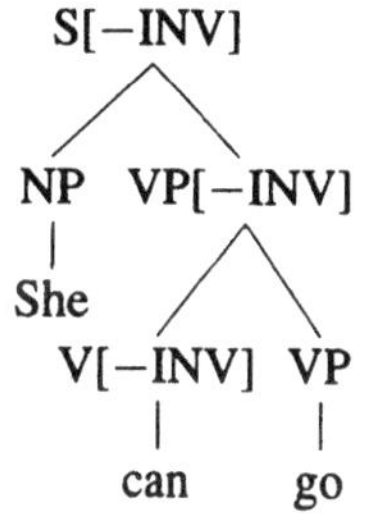

(15b)

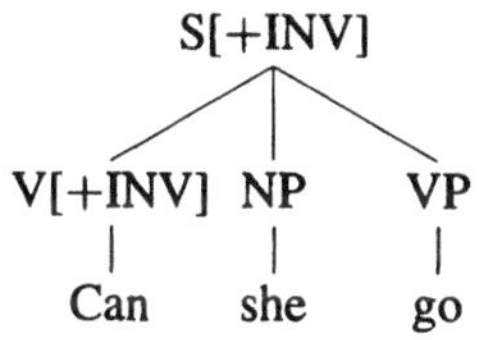

In particular, (15b) should be compared with the much more complicated GB analysis of the same sentence, which was given in (10). Incidentally, these examples show that the connection between ID schemata and grammatical relations are very different in HPSG than they are in GB. As shown in (6), in GB the schemata *define* grammatical relations like subject and object configurationally. But in HPSG, the grammatical relations are defined lexically, in terms of the ordering of the SUBCAT list, at least in languages like English. Our ID schemata do not define grammatical relations, but only specify the options for how they can be realized configurationally. In this respect, HPSG resembles LFG and categorial grammar.

Of course Schema C is not limited in its application to English. For example, we also assume that Schema C is responsible for VSO order in finite clauses in languages like Welsh. In this respect, what distinguishes Welsh typologically from English is that in Welsh, all finite verbs (not just inverted auxiliaries) project flat structures. Similarly, we assume that in Japanese, all clauses are licensed by schema C; but in Japanese, there is a linear precedence constraint that makes all heads phrase-final.

3. An HPSG analysis of German clause structure

In the remainder of this paper, I want to explore the extent to which this model of phrase structure can be adapted to the case of German. I will sketch the overall plan first, and then see how far we can get carrying the plan out. The first move is simply to introduce the same head feature INVERTED that we used for the analysis of inversion in English. Second, we posit linear precedence constraints for German to the effect that +INVERTED verbs are clause-initial while, to simplify slightly, -INVERTED verbs are clause-final. Finally, following Uzskoreit (1982), we obtain V2 structures by extracting a constituent from a +INVERTED clause. So without going into any detail yet about the internal structure of the clauses, our top-level analysis for the two sentences in (1) is assumed to be as in (16):

(16) a.

b.

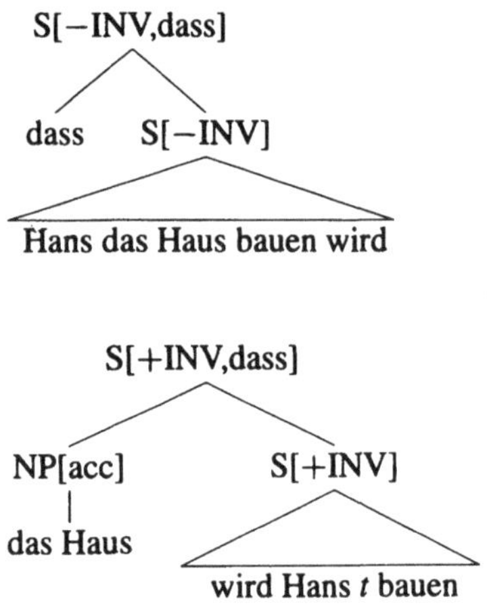

One thing I have to make clear at the outset is that this analysis presupposes two ID schemata that I have not introduced yet. The first of these, which is used at the top node of (16a), is a schema which allows certain kinds of particles, such as complementizers, to attach to phrases of the appropriate category and mark them with a feature, in the case the feature DAß. Unlike GB, we assume that the marked phrase is the head, not the particle. More interesting is the schema for extraction given in (17), called Schema D.

(17)

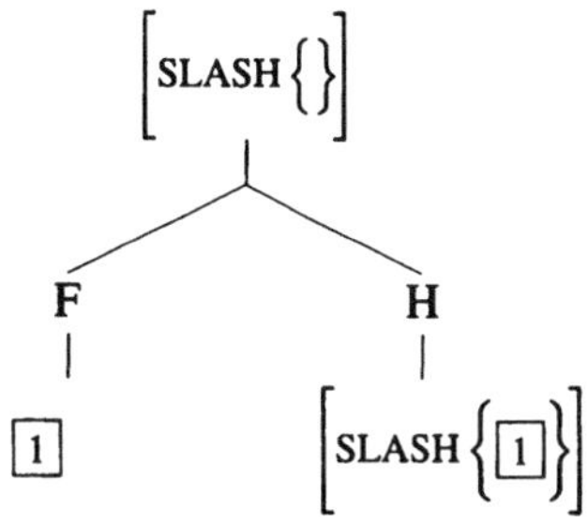

Schema D licenses phrases with a head daughter and a daughter of a new kind called a *filler* daughter. Here the head daughter has to be a finite sentence whose SLASH value set contains an element that is structure-shared with the filler daughter. This schema is an analog of Gazdar's (1981) linking rule for unbounded dependencies. The basic idea is that the SLASH value reflects the presence of a gap somewhere down inside the sentence. For this to work, we need some additional constraints to introduce SLASH values and pass them up, but the precise details of how this works will be passed over here (for detailed discussion, see Pollard – Sag 1994: chapter 4).

The question is now: can we use the schemata A, B, and C to analyze the internal structure of German clauses? If so, which ones? If not, what else do we need? We begin by observing that data like those in (18) (Uszkoreit 1987) argue strongly that inverted clauses have flat structure:

(18) a. Der Doktor gibt die Pille dem Patienten.
'The doctor-nom gives the pills-acc the patient-dat'
b. Die Pille gibt der Doktor dem Patienten.
c. Dem Patienten gibt die Pille der Doktor.

And as the examples in (19) show, there is good reason to assume that the structure of non-inverted clauses is also flat:

(19) a. ... daß der Doktor die Pille dem Patienten gibt.
b. ... daß die Pille der Doktor dem Patienten gibt.
c. ... daß dem Patienten die Pille der Doktor gibt.

If German only had finite verbs, evidently we could get by on Schema C alone. Of course, as I mentioned before we would need constituent-ordering principles to make +INVERTED verbs clause-initial and -INVERTED verbs clause-final, with the non-head sisters otherwise being freely ordered modulo further linear precedence constraints. In particular, it looks as if we can manage without finite VPs.

The difficulty with this simple plan is that the finite verb might govern a non-finite verb or VP complement, and then things get more complicated. For example, let us return to sentence (1a), repeated here as (20a).

(20) a. ... daß Hans das Haus bauen wird.

If we imitate our strategy with English, the most obvious thing to do here is assume that the auxiliary is a raising-to-subject verb that takes an NP subject and a base-form VP complement. In that case, the structure for (20a) would be as shown in (20b):

(20) b.

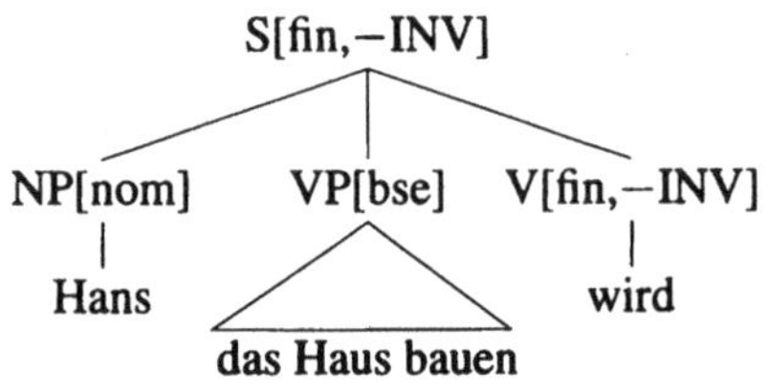

This is just like the analysis of the English sentence *will John build the house*, except that the verbs are phrase-final.

What I am proposing here is that, even though German lacks finite VPs, it does have non-finite VPs. This is similar to a proposal that Borsley (1989) has made in connection with Welsh. A solid piece of evidence that German does indeed have non-finite VPs is provided by the example in (21a). Under the assumptions I have been making here, this would have the analysis given in (21b):

(21) a. Das Haus bauen wird Hans.

b.

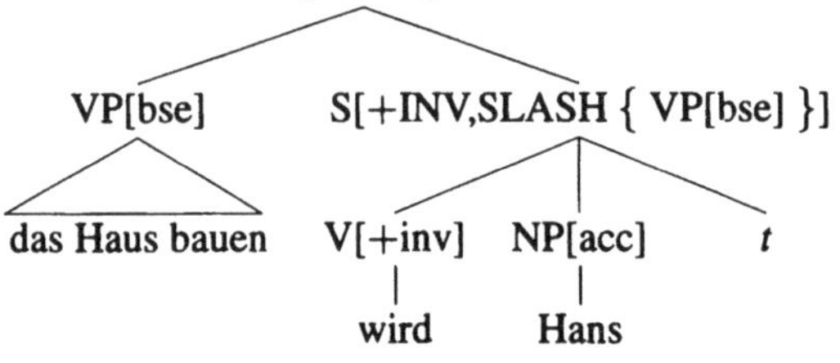

Here the non-finite VP complement has been fronted using Schema D, leaving behind a VP trace. Here I am adopting the standard assumption that what appears in the pre-verbal position is always a constituent.

Assuming that this analysis is on the right track, we now ask: where do non-finite VPs come from? The most obvious thing to try is the same schema, Schema B, that we used to construct VPs in English. Recall that this is the schema that makes all non-subject complements sister to the verb. Before jumping to conclusions, though, let us look at more data. The sentences in (22-24) are from Uszkoreit (1987):

(22) a. ??Den Brief nachher sollte der Kurier einem Spion zustecken.
The letter later should the courier a spy slip
"The courier was later supposed to slip a spy the note."

b. ??Den Brief einem Spion sollte der Kurier nachher zustecken.

(23) a. Zustecken sollte der Kurier den Brief nachher einem Spion.
b. Den Brief zustecken sollte der Kurier nachher einem Spion.
c. Einem Spion zustecken sollte der Kurier nachher den Brief.
d. Nachher einem Spion zustecken sollte der Kurier den Brief.

(24) a. ??Der Kurier zustecken sollte den Brief nachher einem Spion.
b. ??Der Kurier den Brief zustecken sollte nachher einem Spion.

The examples in (22) show that two complements, or a complement and an adjunct, cannot be fronted together. This is expected, since the fronted material must form a constituent. The examples in (23) illustrate the phenomenon of partial VP fronting. They show that a non-finite verb, together with zero or more of its non-subject complements or adjuncts, can form a constituent. On the other hand, the examples in (24) show that these partial VPs may not include subjects.

As it stands, Schema B is too weak to produce these partial VPs, since the only option it provides is to combine the verb with all its non-subject complements. To deal with this situation, I propose to borrow an idea that was originally proposed by Borsley (1989) for Welsh. Borsley's idea is that, at least in some languages, subjects of non-finite verbs should be selected by a distinct SUBJECT feature, reserving the SUBCAT feature only for selection of non-subject complements. If we define the term "complement" to mean dependent element selected via the SUBCAT feature, another way to express Borsley's idea is to say that subjects of finite verbs are complements but subjects of non-finite verbs are not. The effect in German is illustrated in (25):

(25) a.

$$\text{gibt} = \begin{bmatrix} \text{HEAD} & {}_{verb}\begin{bmatrix}\text{VFORM FIN}\end{bmatrix} \\ \text{SUBCAT} & \left\{\text{NP[NOM] NP[DAT] NP[ACC]}\right\} \end{bmatrix}$$

b.

$$\text{geben} = \begin{bmatrix} \text{HEAD} & {}_{verb}\begin{bmatrix}\text{VFORM FIN}\end{bmatrix} \\ \text{SUBCAT} & \left\{\text{NP}\right\} \\ \text{SUBCAT} & \left\{\text{NP[DAT] NP[ACC]}\right\} \end{bmatrix}$$

By the way, there are two technical points I should mention here. First, note that in these lexical entries, the SUBCAT value is given as a set, not a list as in English. This is adopting an idea originally proposed for Japanese by Gunji (1986). The basic intuition behind Gunji's proposal is that in languages where the different NP complements are distinguished by case inflections or postpositions, there is no need to distinguish them by position on a list.

The second point is that the subject of the non-finite verb is assumed to have no case assigned to it. This is in accordance with the standard assumption, within both GB and GPSG, that nominative case is assigned only by the finite verb.

The main point of (25), though, is that subjects are treated as complements for finite verbs, but not for non-finite verbs.

Now in place of Schema B, I propose the more general Schema B′ in (26):

(26)

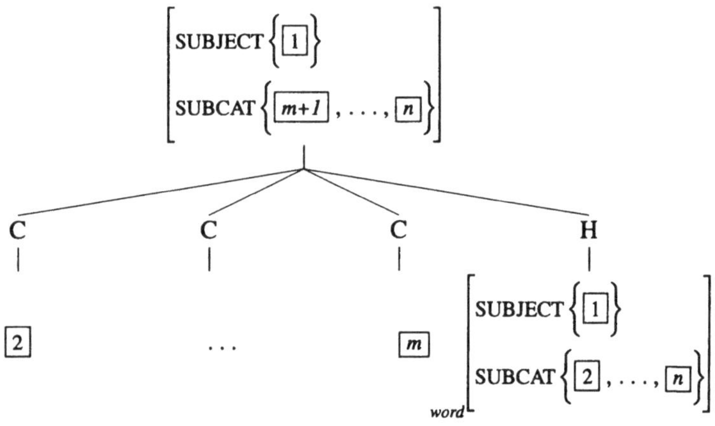

Figure 5. Schema B′ ($m < n+1$)

This schema is largely coextensive with the output of Nerbonne's (1986) Flat Adding of Complements Metarule. It says that any word that selects a subject can form a phrase in combination with some subset of its complements. In fact, we can regard the old schema B as a parametrization of Schema B′ where *m* is set equal to *n*. Unlike Nerbonne's analysis, though, on the account I am proposing there is no alternative analysis of VPs as binary-branching.

Using Schema B′, we can now generate partial VPs like the fronted constituents in (23). There is still some work to do in explaining the extractions, though, since under fairly standard assumptions about unbounded dependencies, the fronted constituent should be capable of appearing *in situ*, that is as an unextracted complement daughter within a clause. But as yet, we have no way of licensing partial VPs as complements, so there is no place to extract them from. To understand this problem a little more clearly, let us look at the example in (27a). According to our analysis of extraction, the top-level structure must be as in (27b):

(27) a. Das Buch gebegeben hat Peter dem Jungen.
the book given has Peter the boy.
"Peter has given the boy the book."

b.

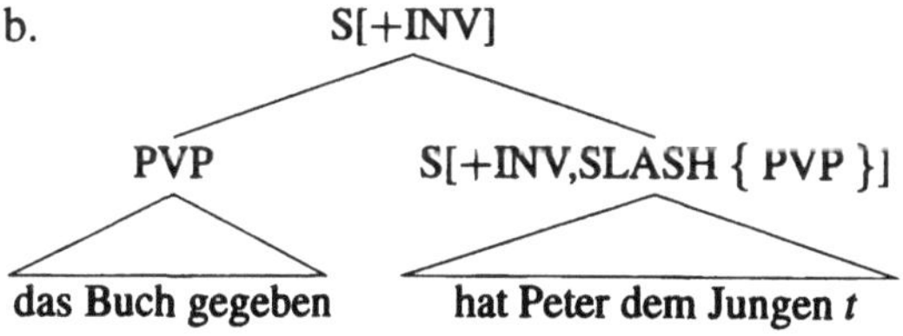

The question is: what is the phrase structure of the lower S containing the partial VP trace? Before dealing with this problem, let us look at another, seemingly unrelated problem. Consider the example in (28a), from Uszkoreit (1984); Uszkoreit took the structure of this sentence to be the one given in (28b). Of course, this analysis is unavailable to us since we have been assuming finite clauses are flat and that base-form clauses do not exist. In addition, Uszkoreit's analysis is inconsistent with our assumption that nominative case is assigned by the finite verb. What I would like to suggest as an alternative is the structure in (28c):

(28) a. Wird dem Patienten die Pille der Doktor geben?
Will the patient the pill the doctor give?
"Will the doctor give the patient the pill?"

b.

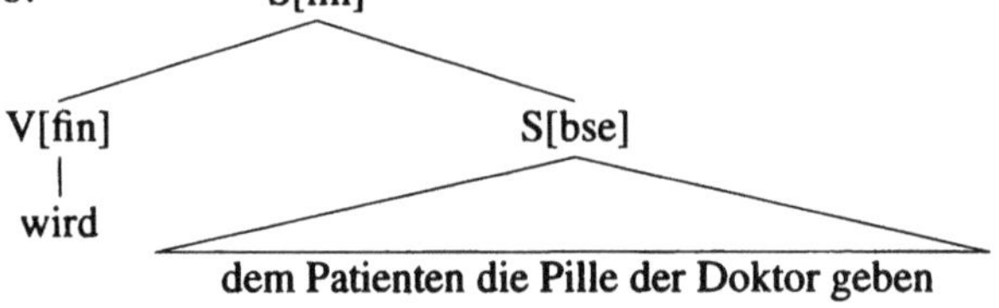

c.

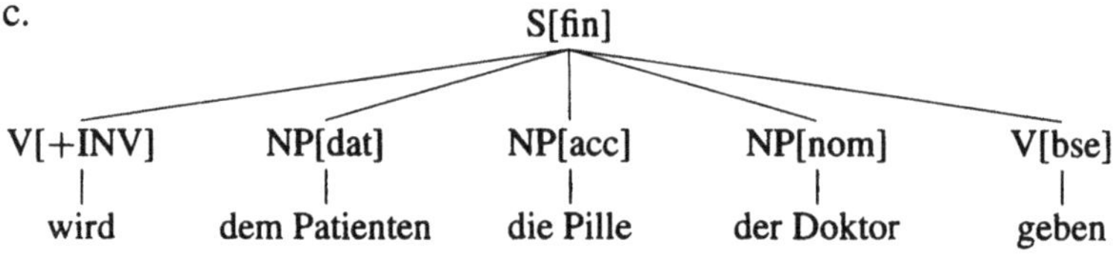

The idea that underlies this structure is one that had been proposed in various forms by Johnson (1986) and Hinrichs – Nakazawa (1994), namely that the arguments of a verb which is governed by an auxiliary can be raised to become arguments of the auxiliary. In fact, this is really the same idea we used in the analysis of English auxiliaries, for example the auxiliary *can* whose lexical entry was given in (11). There the idea was that the auxilary subcategorized for a base-form VP complement, and also for the raised subject of that VP complement.

What I am proposing is that in German auxiliaries work exactly the same way, except that the VP complement of the auxiliary is allowed to be partial. To put it another way, we assume that, universally, auxilaries select a non-finite verbal projection; the only reason these are always full VPs in English is that in English, Schema B′ is parametrized in such a way to license only non-finite VPs that contain all their non-subject complements. Of course in languages like German, if the VP complement is only partial, then its remaining arguments should be raised along with the subject to become arguments of the governing auxilary. To put this idea in practice, all we need is lexical entries for finite auxiliaries like the one for *wird* in (29):

(29)

$$\text{wird: } \begin{bmatrix} \text{HEAD} & {}_{verb}\begin{bmatrix}\text{FIN} + \text{AUX}\end{bmatrix} \\ \text{SUBCAT} & \left\{ \boxed{1}\text{NP[NOM]}, \text{VP[BSE}, \begin{bmatrix}\text{SUBJECT} & \{\boxed{1}\} \\ \text{SUBCAT} & \boxed{2}\end{bmatrix}] \right\} \cup \boxed{2} \end{bmatrix}$$

The important thing to notice here is the SUBCAT value. This tells us that an auxiliary subcategorizes for the following things: first, the raised subject of the possibly partial VP, indicated by the tag $\boxed{1}$; second, the VP itself; and finally, the set indicated by the tag $\boxed{2}$ consisting of all the complement requirements that were not satisfied within the VP. Of course in English, which lacks partial VPs, the set $\boxed{2}$ will always be empty, so that the lexical entry in (29) reduces to the form given in (11).

With this analysis of auxiliaries, the structure (28c) now becomes legitimate. Since the subject is now subcategorized for by the finite auxiliary, there is no question about where its nominative case came from.

But that is not all. We now have a solution to the partial VP extraction problem as well. For example, let us return to the example (27a), whose partial analysis was given in (27b). We can now complete this analysis as in (30):

(30)

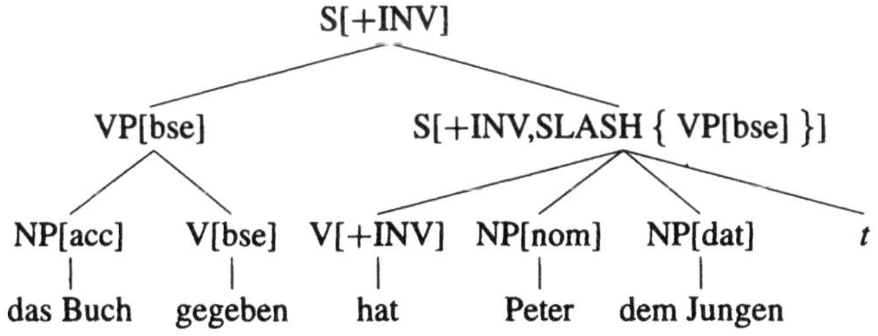

Here the accusative complement of the main verb is in the fronted partial VP, while the subject and the dative complement have been raised to become complements of the finite auxilary.

This analysis also explains why it is possible to front the main verb together with a non-finite modal. Consider the examples in (31) from Hinrichs – Nakazawa (1994):

(31) a. Verkauft haben wird Peter das Auto.
sold have will Peter the car
"Peter will have sold the car."
b. Verkauft haben müssen wird Peter das Auto.
sold have have-to will Peter the car
"Peter will have had to sell the car."

What drives the analysis here is the lexical entry for base-form *haben* given in (32):

(32)
$$\text{haben: } \begin{bmatrix} \text{HEAD} & _{verb}\begin{bmatrix}\text{BSE} & +\text{AUX}\end{bmatrix} \\ \text{SUBJECT} & \{\boxed{1}\} \\ \text{SUBCAT} & \left\{ \text{(P)VP[PSP]}\begin{bmatrix}\text{SUBJECT} & \{\boxed{1}\}\\ \text{SUBCAT} & \boxed{2}\end{bmatrix}\right\} \cup \boxed{2}\end{bmatrix}$$

This is similar to the entry for finite auxiliaries given in (29) except for the fact that the subject of the non-finite auxiliary has to be handled by the SUBJECT feature and the VP complement of *haben* is specified as a past participle. Now sentence (31a) receives the analysis in (33):

(33)
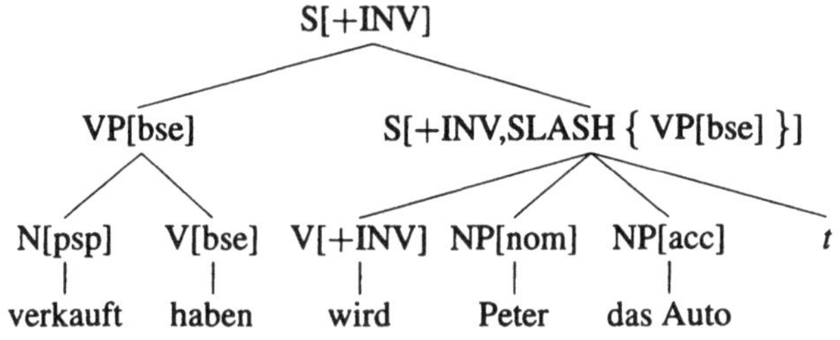

This is similar to (30), except that in this case the arguments of the main verb are raised twice, first to *haben* and then to *wird* where they become satisfied. The analysis of (31b) would be similar except that the main verb arguments get raised three times.

Let me summarize this analysis of German constituent structure and word order, and then I will conclude by pointing out two problems, one perhaps not so serious but the other potentially disastrous. I assume that the main facts of German clause structure arise from three universal schemata. The first one, Schema B′ given in (26), licenses possibly partial VPs with flat structures, which are always non-finite.

The second one, Schema C given in (7), licenses clauses with flat structures, which are always finite. Separate linear precedence constraints ensure that verbs are ordered phrase-initially just in case they are +INVERTED, which is an option only for finite verbs. In particular, in German as with other languages we have examined, there is no need to posit a mechanism of head movement.

The third schema, Schema D given in (17), licenses extraction of a traced constituent to the left of the inverted clause.

4. Problems for the proposed analysis; conclusions

Now for the problems. First, consider the question (34a):

(34) a. Wird Hans gehen können?

b.

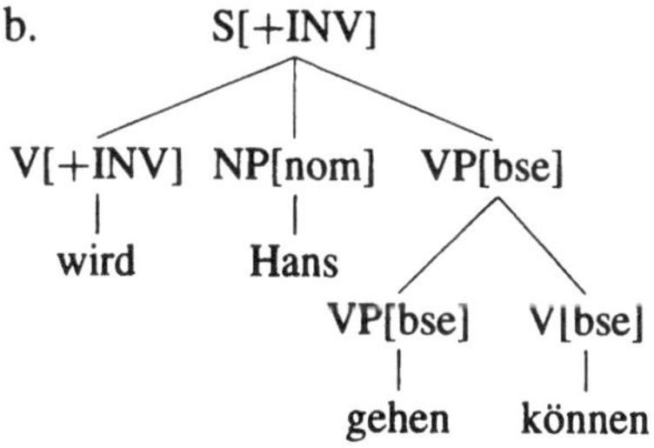

c.

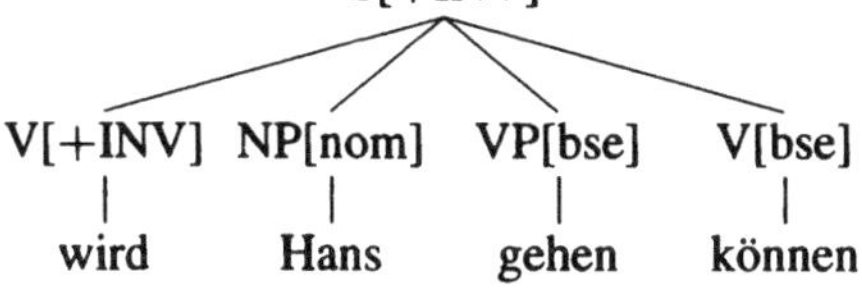

Recall that according to the lexical entry (29), the finite auxiliary *wird* can take as its verbal complement either the complete VP *gehen können* or the partial VP *können*. In the first case, we get the double subject-raising analysis shown in (34b). In the second case, the VP complement *gehen* has to be raised along with the subject, which gives the analysis shown in (34c).

The first problem is this. Given our analysis of fronting as extraction of a nonhead constituent, all the frontings in (35) should be possible:

(35) a. Hans wird gehen können.
b. Gehen können wird Hans.
c. Gehen wird Hans können.
d. *Können wird Hans gehen.

Unfortunately, in German a modal cannot be fronted unless it is accompanied by the verb it governs, as (35d) shows. To solve this problem, we need to somehow disallow VP complements from undergoing raising. Various technical solutions are available here.

The second problem, the potentially disastrous one, is that of spurious ambiguity. Even if we can eliminate the structural ambiguity of (34) by blocking the raising of VP complements, the problem resurfaces if we consider transitive main verbs. For example, sentence (36a) has the two analyses (36b) and (36c):

(36) a. Wird Hans das Haus bauen?

b.

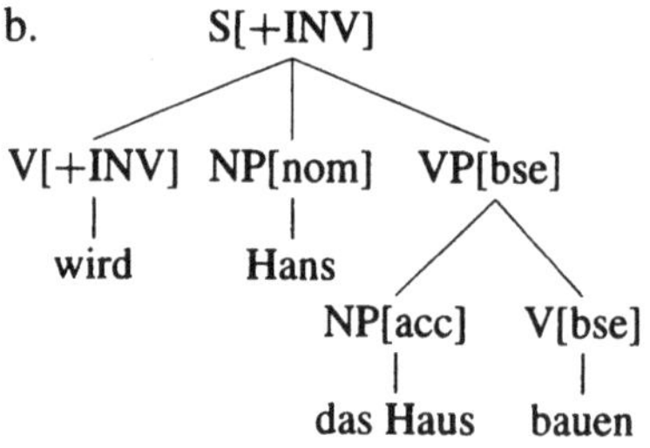

c.

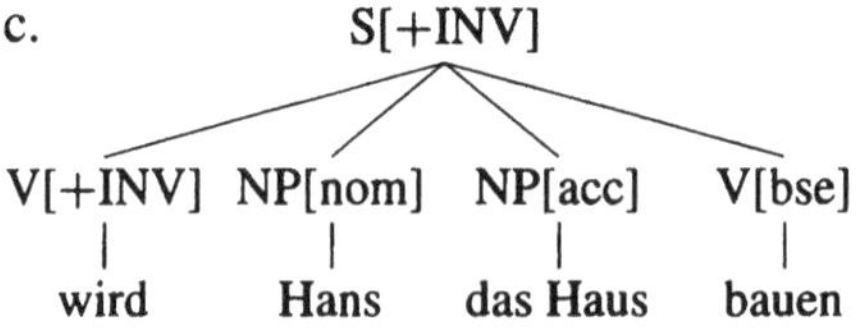

Given the semantic analysis of raising sketched above, there is certainly no semantic difference between the two structures, and as far as I know there are are no phonological or pragmatic correlates of the structural difference either. The problem becomes worse as the number of embedded governed verbs increases, since each complement has several potential attachment sites.

For example, assuming that we have figured out how to block raising of VP complements, the innocent question (37) has 6 distinct structural analyses:

(37) Hat er seiner Tochter ein Märchen erzählen können?
Has he his daughter a fairy-tale tell be able
"Has he been able to tell his daughter a fairy tale?"

Now it is a premise of phrase structure grammar, perhaps the fundamental premise, that consituent structure is linguistically significant. This is true not just of frameworks like GPSG and HPSG that call themselves phrase structure theories, but also of theories like GB and LFG that posit levels of linguistic representation such as s-structure and c-structure. But according to the analysis I have just sketched, German sentences like the one in (36) exhibit multiple structural ambiguities that do not have any demonstrable linguistic significance. It seems to follow from these considerations that my analysis of German is not really phrase structure grammar at all but something else. Somehow, between generalizing Schema B to license partial VPs and relaxing auxiliary subcategorizations to allow raising of non-subject complements, we have passed beyond the frontier of phrase structure grammar into the territory of something more like categorial unification grammar.

Of course calling what I am doing by a different name does not make the problem go away. Even categorial grammarians acknowledge spurious structural ambiguity as a problem, and they have devoted considerable effort over the past several years to wrestling with it. The way I think about the problem goes something like this. The kind of structural analysis that I have been doing here, or that is done within the recent "flexible" varieties of categorial grammar, is too fine-grained, in the sense that it produces distinct structures like those in (36) that do not reflect genuine linguistic differences. What is needed then, is a coarser-grained level of representation than phrase structure, some canonical method of dividing phrase-structural analyses into equivalence classes such that (36b) and (36c) end up in the same equivalence class.

There are a number of ways one might go about this. A logical approach would be to formalize the grammar as a kind of equational calculus, treating the ID schemata as equivalences between category sequences. Then the appropriate notion of equivalence would simply be provable equality. This has a lot in common with work in flexible categorial grammar like that of Moortgat (1988), where grammars are formalized as sequent calculi. A more structural approach is suggested by Dowty (this volume), in which the tectogrammatic constituency reflected in phrase-structure trees takes a back seat to a coarser-grained notion of phenogrammatic constituency. For the time being, I leave the resolution of this issue to future study.

Notes

1. In the final chapter of Pollard – Sag (1994), it has been suggested to replace the SUBCAT feature by two features (SUBJ and COMPS) for representing the valence aspects corresponding to subjects and nonsubject complements (retaining the SUBCAT list for purposes of binding theory only). In fact, the phenomena discussed here support such a move; see below, section 3.

References

den Besten, H.
1983 On the Interaction of Root Transformations and Lexical Deletive Rules. In W. Abraham (ed.), *On the Formal Syntax of the Westgermania. Papers from the Third Groningen Grammar Talks,* Groningen, January 1981, 47-138. Amsterdam and Philadelphia: Benjamins.

Borsley, R.
1989 An HPSG Approach to Welsh. *Journal of Linguistics* 25: 333-354.

Chomsky, N.
1986 *Barriers.* Cambridge, MA: MIT Press.

Dowty, D.
1992 Toward a minimalist theory of syntactic structure. *This volume* , 11–62.

Gazdar, G.
1981 Unbounded Dependencies and Coordinate Structure. *Linguistic Inquiry* 12: 155-184

Gazdar, G., E. Klein, G. Pullum, and I. Sag
1985 *Generalized Phrase Structure Grammar.* Cambridge, MA: Harvard University Press.

Gunji, T
1986 *Japanese Phrase Structure Grammar.* Dordrecht: Reidel.

Hinrichs, E. and T. Nakazawa
1989 Flipped Out: AUX in German. In *Proceedings of the 25th Regional Meeting of the Chicago Linguistic Society.* Chicago: Chicago Linguistics Society.

Hinrichs, E. and T. Nakazawa
1994 Subcategorization and VP Structure in German. In *Proceedings of the Third Symposium on Germanic Linguistics*. Philadelphia: Benjamins.

Johnson, M.
1986 A GPSG Account of VP Structure in German. *Linguistics* 24: 871-882.

Kathol, K.
1990 A Uniform Approach to V2. *NELS* 1989.

Moortgat, M.
1988 *Categorial Investigations: Logical and Linguistic Aspects of the Lambek Calculus*. Dordrecht: Foris.

Nerbonne, J.
1986 'Phantoms' and German Fronting: Poltergeist Constituents? *Linguistics* 24:857-870.

Pollard, C. and I. Sag
1987 *Information-Based Syntax and Semantics. Vol. 1: Fundamentals*, CSLI Lecture Notes Series No. 13. Stanford: CSLI.

Pollard, C. and I. Sag
1994 *Head-Driven Phrase Structure Grammar*. Chicago: University of Chicago Press.

Uszkoreit, H.
1982 German Word Order in GPSG. In D. Flickinger, M. Macken, and N. Weigand (eds.), *Proceedings of the First West Coast Conference on Formal Linguistics*, 137-138. Stanford: Stanford Linguistics Department.

Uszkoreit, H.
1984 *Word Order and Constituent Structure in German*. CSLI Lecture Notes Series No. 8. Stanford: CSLI.

Uszkoreit, H.
1987 Linear Precedence in Discontinuous Constituents: Complex Fronting in German. In Huck, G. and A. Ojeda (eds.), *Syntax and Semantics, Vol. 20: Discontinuous Constituents*. London: Academic Press.

Discontinuity and the Binding theory*

Eric Hoekstra

Abstract. In this paper an approach to binding phenomena is proposed that makes use of paths and chains, in the spirit of Kayne (1984), Barss (1986), Everaert (1986), and others. Two types of binding relationships are distinguished, the stronger of which is subject to a strict locality requirement. The resulting analysis accounts for a long-standing problem involving the effect of discontinuity created by movement on condition C and a recently discovered but analogous problem involving the effect of movement on the binding of negative polarity items.

1. Introduction

In this paper I will propose a new way of dealing with connectivity phenomena. Facts involving condition V and negative polarity provide a useful testing ground for my theory. In this section I will limit myself to cases in which a subject is coreferential with part of a preposed constituent. Furthermore, I will only be concerned with coreference, not with bound variable binding.

Let me first give a brief idea of how our view of grammar and language has changed. It has often been thought that principles of Universal Grammar (UG) should receive what I prefer to call "an absolute interpretation". Recent developments have shown, for instance, that it is not quite correct to operate on the assumption that a given category is always a bounding node or never. Instead, the notion bounding node has become relativised, relativisation depending crucially on other principles like government, L-marking, etc. Principles influencing the choice of bounding node are always local, which can now be looked upon as a consequence of minimality (Rizzi 1990).

The example given here typically concerns movement, but the same holds for the determination of bounding nodes for Binding theory. It was thought that binding domains are constant. Huang (1982) showed that binding domains should be relativised depending on whether a possible antecedent is present. This tendency towards relativisation is also clear from Barss (1986) who shows, in reaction to earlier work by van Riemsdijk – Williams (1981), that movement may affect choice of binding domain for anaphors. I will broadly refer to (questions concerning) the effect of movement on Binding theory as connectivity.

Connectivity is typically known in connection with facts about condition A. The crucial question is always whether a movement process does or does not affect possibilities for binding anaphors, apparently a simple question. Here I would like to focus on the question to what extent condition C and negative polarity are sensitive to connectivity. Learning from recent developments, we are aware that the question is not whether condition C exhibits connectivity or not. As we will see, it sometimes shows connectivity and sometimes not. The question is therefore: how to relativise connectivity?

2. The problem

The facts have been obscured by the assumption that either there is or there is not connectivity. Let us first consider cases without movement, where a pronoun c-commands a coreferential[1] R-expression:

(1) * *She smokes pot in Mary's apartment.*

(2) * Pronoun ... [... R-expression ...], where the pronoun c-commands a coreferential R-expression.

Italics are used to indicate coreference. An R-expression cannot be coreferential with a c-commanding pronoun.

What happens if a constituent containing the R-expression is preposed to the beginning of the sentence, over the coreferential subject pronoun? My claim is that connectivity effects will typically show up in case the subject is contained in the binding domain of the R-expression. If the subject pronoun is outside this binding domain, no connectivity is expected. The binding domain of an R-expression is assumed to be the same as the binding domain of an anaphor, that is, a Complete Functional Complex (CFC) (Chomsky 1986a). In this way, connectivity is relativised, depending on the CFC of the R-expression.

The following sentences illustrate the connectivity problem with respect to condition C (Lakoff 1968; Jackendoff 1972; and others):

(3) * She smokes pot in Mary's apartment.

(4) ?* In Mary's apartment, she smokes pot.

(5) * She smokes pot in the apartment Mary rents.

(6) In the apartment Mary rents, she smokes pot.

(3) and (4) have the same D-structure. Both are ungrammatical. (3) is a plain violation of condition C. (4) might thus be ungrammatical because the VP contains a trace: the pronoun c-commands the trace, hence it c-commands the R-expression. But this same line of reasoning leads to a problem in the case of (5) and (6). The pair (5,6) is directly analogous to the pair (3,4). The question is: how can we account for the fact that (6) is grammatical whereas (4) is not?

The problem is actually more complex because we must also take into acoount that (4), although ungrammatical, is much better than the related sentence (3). It is therefore incorrect to assume that the cause of ungrammaticality is some condition applying to the D-structure that (3) and (4) have in common. The same conclusion is, of course, enforced by the pair (5,6).

Within transformational grammar, this problem leads to an ordering paradox (Postal 1971: 18). The pair (3,4) supports the conclusion that the transformation of pronominalisation should be ordered before preposing, whereas the pair (5,6) supports the contrary ordering. It is only fair to say that Government & Binding theory faces the same problem. Chomsky's (1986a) analysis explains that (6) is grammatical, since the R-expression is free, having been moved away out of the c-command domain of the pronoun. By the same token, (4) should be grammatical as well. Equivalently, it might be claimed that condition C applies to D-structure, in a Hellan (1980) or van Riemsdijk – Williams (1981) type of analysis. But this leaves unanswered why (6) is grammatical, as pointed out by Everaert (1983).

3. A solution without connectivity

A syntactic solution to this problem was attempted in Reinhart (1983). Reinhart's heuristic, neither implicitly nor explicitly questioned, is that coreference facts such as noted above should be dealt with by a condition operating on

S-structure. Traces play no role. The issue of connectivity (or reconstruction) does therefore not arise. Reinhart's analysis goes like this. The landing site of preposed XP's is still in the c-command domain of the subject, in case the XP originates in the VP. The landing site of other XP's that are preposed is outside the c-command domain of the subject. The definition of c-command is revised (Reinhart 1983: 23), just to take this case into account:

(7) Node A c(onstituent)-commands node B iff (i) or (ii)
 (i) the branching node most immediately dominating A (C) dominates B
 (ii) (a) and (b)
  (a) C is immediately dominated by another node (D) which dominates B
  (b) C and D are of the same category type.

Thus there are two landing sites for preposed XP's, in addition to the possibility of left-dislocation. The resulting definition is a disjunction. The second disjunct is motivated solely by the stipulation that preposed constituents originating in VP must land in the c-command domain of the subject.

Reconsider now the facts in (3-6). Reinhart predicts that it should not make any difference how deep an R-expression is embedded in a preposed constituent. It will anyhow be in the c-command domain of the subject, provided the preposed constituent originates in VP. However, we have already seen that depth of embedding does play a role. Consider the relevant examples repeated here for convenience as (8-9):

(8) ?* *In Mary's apartment, she smokes pot.*

(9) *In the apartment Mary rents, she smokes pot.*

The contrast between these two sentences cannot be captured by Reinhart. For her, both cases should be ungrammatical. Both cases involve extraction of a PP out of the VP. The PP is an obligatory complement of the verb so that it cannot be argued that the PP originates in IP. But even if the PP originates in IP, the facts cannot be accounted for. In that case, both sentences should be grammatical, for Reinhart's theory.[2] Hence Reinhart's theory faces the same paradox as standard GB-theory and transformational grammar.

The following sentences illustrate the same paradox. This time the preposed constituent is a direct object:

(10) * *John's mother, he doesn't like.*

(11) *The women whom John is talking with, he doesn't like.*

There can be no doubt that the preposed constituent originates within the VP since it is a direct object. These facts are also problematic for Chomsky (1981). Chomsky (1981) is not explicit about the way in which movement may or may not affect the operation of grammatical principles. The tacit assumption seems to be that movement causes circumvention of various principles. Thus it would be expected that (10,11) are both grammatical since the pronoun does not (directly) c-command the R-expression at S-structure.

4. A solution without syntax

It might be thought that the problem cannot receive a syntactic explanation. Reinhart (1986) claims that coreference is not a syntactic phenomenon.[3] Instead, coreference is a pragmatic phenomenon. I will not discuss her specific proposal, but present a counter-argument. The view that pragmatics is involved might have some plausibility if the connectivity problem were restricted to R-expressions. However, we encounter exactly the same problem with negative polarity (see Ladusaw 1980; Zwarts 1981). Consider the following sentences:

(12) *Niemand heeft ook maar iets gezien.*
nobody has anything seen
'Nobody saw anything.'

(13) *Ook maar iets heeft niemand gezien.*
anything has nobody seen
'Anything, nobody saw.'

(14) *Ook maar iets gezien heeft niemand.*
anything seen has nobody
'Anything seen, nobody has.'

The negative NP *niemand* triggers the occurrence of the negative polarity item *ook maar iemand*. Hence (12) becomes ungrammatical if we replace *niemand* with a non-negative NP like *Jan*. Preposing the negative polarity element over the trigger leads to ungrammaticality, as the paradigm shows.

As in the case of condition C, not all discontinuities are created equal. In the case of condition C, ungrammaticality can be avoided if the R-expression is embedded deep enough in the preposed constituent. Now we will see that ungrammaticality can similarly be avoided if the negative polarity item is embedded deep enough in the preposed constituent:

(15) *Niemand had verwacht dat er ook maar iets zou gebeuren.*
nobody had expected that there anything would happen,
'Nobody had expected that anything would happen.'

(16) *Dat er ook maar iets zou gebeuren had niemand verwacht.*
that there anything would happen had nobody expected
'That anything would happen, nobody had expected.'

The contrast between (14) and (16) is identical to the contrast between (7) and (8). In two different fields of the grammar, we find the same generalisation about the effect of discontinuity. It is very unlikely that negative polarity has anything to do with pragmatics. The striking similarity between negative polarity and condition C with respect to preposing suggests that there is an underlying principle applying to both.

Methodology will be as follows. Condition C as it stands is too weak since it cannot explain why sentences like (4) are ungrammatical. Hence I will formulate an additional constraint. The same will be done for negative polarity. After that the question is discussed of how to unify the additional constraints with the original formulation of the Binding theory.

5. Relativising connectivity

To account for the full paradigm, depth of embedding must be taken into account. I will make the standard assumption that the subject does not c-command the landing site of preposed elements. Traces must be taken into account in order to be able to relate pronoun and R-expression to each other by means of a path. Furthermore, c-command itself relies explicitly on the notion path, because it relies on the path-theoretic notion dominance. In addition, I will take into account the notion chain, since chains impose unity on discontinuous elements.

C-command is viewed as describing a path between two elements (cf. Kayne 1984). How does discontinuity (or a trace) affect a path? To give some concrete examples, consider the following:

(17) *John would never talk about himself.*

(18) *Himself, John would never talk about.*

(19) *About himself, John would never talk.*

The path from *John* to *himself* is not erupted by discontinuity in (17), whereas it is in (18-19). For anaphors, this does not make any difference, but for R-expressions it does. Let us hypothesize that there are two kinds of paths: paths that include discontinuities and paths that do not. This boils down to a distinction between paths containing traces, and paths that do not contain traces. I will refer to the former as weak paths, and to the latter as strong paths. Two types of binding naturally correspond to the two types of paths:

(20) A strongly binds B iff the c-command path from A to B does not include a trace.

(21) A weakly binds B iff there is a c-command path from A to B.

Similarly, there are two types of disjoint reference:

(22) B is strongly free from A iff there is no c-command path from A to B.

(23) B is weakly free from A iff the c-command path from A to B includes a trace.

It is assumed that an R-expression has a CFC, just as an anaphor, a domain in which it must be free or bound. The constraint needed to supplement condition C can now make reference to depth of embedding, as follows:

(24) An R-expression is strongly free in its CFC and weakly free outside.

Disjointness is relativised depending on the presence of a coreferential element in the CFC of the R-expression.

Let us now go through the problematic cases again to show how it works. Reconsider the pair (5,6), repeated as (25,26):

(25) * *She smokes pot in the apartment Mary rents.*

(26) *In the apartment Mary rents, she smokes pot.*

In both cases, the pronoun is outside the CFC of the R-expression. Hence weak disjointness is sufficient. Weak disjointness is not met in (25), since the path from *she* to *Mary* does not include a trace. Weak disjointness is met in (26), where the path from pronoun to R-expression includes the trace of the preposed PP. In this way, the effect of discontinuity on Binding theory is accomodated.

Reconsider next the pair (3,4), repeated as (27,28):

(27) * *She smokes pot in Mary's apartment.*

(28) ?* *In Mary's apartment, she smokes pot.*

In both cases, the pronoun occurs in the CFC of the R-expression. Hence strong disjointness is required. This requirement is not met, since in either sentence there is a path from pronoun to R-expression. This path is strong in (27) and weak in (28). Hence both are ungrammatical, but (27) more than (28).

Further support for the proposed analysis comes from well-known examples like the following (Postal 1971:19):

(29) * *He left town after Jake robbed the bank.*

(30) *After Jake robbed the bank, he left town.*

The pronoun does not occur in the CFC of the R-expression in either sentence. Hence weak disjointness is sufficient, that is, either there is no path from pronoun to R-expression, or if there is, it must include a trace. In (29) there is a path but it does not include a trace. Hence condition C is violated. In (30), the path includes the trace of the preposed sentence; hence the sentence is grammatical.[4]

The following sentences make clear that the trace must be part of the path:

(31) * *He knows that Mary saw a car of John.*

(32) * *He knows [which car of John] Mary saw.*

Here a discontinuity is created but it does not affect binding possibilities. The reason is simple: the trace is not part of the path from pronoun to R-expression. Both sentences are correctly ruled out, since the path from pronoun to R-expression does not contain a trace.

A different problem concerns psych-verbs (Postal 1971). It is illustrated below:

(33) * *It disappointed him that John flunked.*

(34) *That John flunked disappointed him.*

The pronoun c-commands the following S' in (33), as shown in Hoekstra (1991a,b). The pronoun does not occur in the CFC of the R-expression. Hence the path must include a trace, which it does not. In (34) the path does include a trace, and, correspondingly, the sentence is grammatical. To sum up, the proposed analysis solves a number of long-standing puzzles.

6. What is the local domain?

The local domain of an R-expression is its CFC.[5] Hence it is predicted that embedding an R-expression in a NP should make a difference depending on whether the NP is a CFC for the R-expression or not. Consider the following sentences:

(35) * *Rosa's confrontatie met de koning heeft ze goed beschreven.*
Rosa's confrontation with the king has she well described
'Rosa's talk with the king, she described accurately.'

(36) *Mijn confrontatie van de koning met Rosa heeft ze goed*
My confrontation of the king with Rosa has she well
beschreven.
described
'My confrontation of the king with Rosa, she described accurately.'

The preposed constituent does not function as a CFC in (35). The pronoun occurs in the CFC of the R-expression. Condition C is violated because there is a path from pronoun to R-expression. In (36), the preposed constituent is a CFC for the R-expression. Pronoun and R-expression do not occur in the same CFC. Hence a path is allowed if it includes a trace. In (36), the path includes a trace, and the sentence is grammatical.[6] The contrast (35,36) supports the claim that the binding domain of an R-expression is its CFC, and that the type of disjointness that is required depends on whether the pronoun occurs in the CFC of the R-expression or not.

Independent evidence comes from sentences in which constituents containing infinitivals are preposed. Preposing an infinitival over the offending pronoun should make it possible to obviate a condition C violation, just as was the case with relative clauses. Consider now the following facts:

(37) * *Hij stelt mij nietsvermoedend [haar schriftelijk verzoek*
he puts me unsuspecting her written request
om Jan uit de club te verwijderen] ter hand.
for Jan from the club to remove in hand
'He gives me without suspicion her written request
to remove John from the club.'

(38) *[Haar schriftelijk verzoek om Jan uit de club te*
her written request for Jan from the club to
verwijderen]$_i$ *stelt hij mij nietsvermoedend* t_i *ter hand.*
remove puts he me unsuspecting in hand
'Her written request to remove John from the club,
he gives me without suspicion.'

Preposing the NP containing the infinitival results in a considerable increase in acceptability. The NP itself is not a CFC since it does not contain a possessor. Thus it is the infinitival clause which counts as a CFC. These facts support the idea that the local domain is a CFC.

7. Negative polarity

The statement necessary to account for negative polarity is remarkably similar to the one needed for condition C. It is presented below:

(39) A negative polarity item is strongly bound in its CFC or weakly bound outside.

Reconsider (12,13) repeated as (40,41):

(40) *Niemand heeft ook maar iets gezien.*
nobody has anything seen
'Nobody saw anything.'

(41) * *Ook maar iets heeft niemand gezien.*
anything has nobody seen
'Anything, nobody saw.'

In both sentences, the trigger occurs in the CFC of the negative polarity item. Hence strong binding is required, i.e., the path may not include traces. This requirement is met in (40) but not in (41). Next reconsider (15,16) repeated as (42,43):

(42) *Niemand had verwacht dat er ook maar iets zou gebeuren.*
nobody had expected that there anything would happen
'Nobody had expected that anything would happen.'

(43) *Dat er ook maar iets zou gebeuren had niemand verwacht.*
that there anything would happen had nobody expected
'That anything would happen, nobody had expected.'

In both sentences, the triggers occurs outside the CFC of the negative polarity item. Hence weak binding is sufficient, i.e. the c-command path may or may not include a trace. This requirement is met in both sentences. Hence both are grammatical.

8. Remaining problems

Attention has been restricted to cases in which the antecedent is a subject. If we turn to non-subjects, a different paradigm is observed (cf. Lakoff (1968:8)):

(44) * *Ben z'n problemen wil hij niet bespreken.*
Ben his problems wants he not discuss
'Ben's problems, he does not want to discuss.'

(45) *Ben z'n problemen wil ik niet met hem bespreken.*
Ben his problems wants I not with him discuss
'Ben's problems, I don't want to discuss with him.'

These facts are problematic if the trace of the preposed PP must occur in the c-command domain of the PP *met hem*, as in (46) below:[7]

(46) * *Ik wil niet met hem Ben z'n problemen bespreken.*
I want not with him Ben his problems discuss
'I do not want to discuss with him Ben's problems.'

However, I would like to suggest that the trace of the preposed PP does not necessarily occur within the c-command domain of the PP *met hem*, as in (47) below:

(47) *Ik wil niet Ben z'n problemen met* hem *bespreken*
I want not Ben his problems with him discuss
'I do not want to discuss Ben's problems with him'

Generally, then, the possibility of sentences like (45) is explained by the absence of any necessity to postulate traces in the c-command domain of the VP-internal pronoun. Another problem is discussed by Yusa (1989). It is illustrated below:

(48) *[Which claim that John had made]$_i$ did he deny t_i.*

(49) * *[Which claim that John had made a mistake] did he deny t_i.*

(48) is a familiar case of non-local weak disjointness, which is allowed. But why is (49) ungrammatical? I would claim that R-expression and pronoun occur in the same local domain in (49). Hence weak disjointness is not allowed here. This idea is confirmed by the fact that (49) improves if a possessor is plugged in:

(50) *[Which of Mary's claims that John had made a mistake]$_i$ did he deny t_i.*

(51) *[Whose claim that John had made a mistake]$_i$ did he deny t_i.*

The possessor closes off a CFC, so that the pronoun does not occur in the CFC of the R-expression. If this line of reasoning is correct then the problematic paradigm supports the proposed analysis rather than disconfirming it.

An interesting question is why anaphors rely on weak binding rather than on strong binding, seeing that it is possible to prepose an anaphor over its antecedent (for example in (18,19) above). Of course, this can simply be stipulated but then the connection between strong binding and locality would have to be given up.[8]

9. Unification

The proposed reformulation of condition C is remarkably similar to the constraint imposed on negative polarity. The two are repeated below, as (52,53):

(52) An R-expression is strongly free in its CFC and weakly free outside.

(53) A negative polarity item is strongly bound in its CFC or weakly bound outside.

In both cases, the stronger requirement is limited to the local domain, the CFC. The connectivity problem has thus been solved by distinguishing between two paths: paths including traces and paths not including traces. Which type of path is required depends on whether the pronoun (trigger) occurs in the CFC of the R-expression (negative polarity item). The question of unification will have to focus on the role and interpretation of the concept of locality.

Notes

* I would like to thank Ale de Boer, Hans Broekhuis, Martin Everaert, Jan Koster, Eric Reuland, Noriaki Yusa and Jan-Wouter Zwart for comments and suggestions. The research reported in this paper was supported by the Foundation for Linguistic Research, which is funded by the Netherlands organisation for the advancement of pure research (NWO), project number 300-171-003, which is gratefully acknowledged.

1. Following Reinhart (1983) I make a distinction between coreference and binding. However, I do not believe that the fact of such a distinction should lead to the position that coreference is a pragmatic phenomenon (cf. Lasnik 1989). Pending further research, I therefore use the term binding to also refer to coreference under c-command.
2. Certain grammatical cases are treated as left-dislocation. However, it is unclear why the ungrammatical cases cannot be saved by left-dislocation either.
3. See Lasnik (1989) for arguments against this position.
4. Koster (1987) discusses cases like (i) below:

   (i) *<u>Hij</u>* *kende* *Eline* *al* *vele* *jaren* *toen*
   he knew Eline already many years when
   <u>Osewoudt</u> *plots* *besloot* *haar* *te* *huwen.*
   Osewoudt suddenly decided her to marry
   'He had already known Eline for many years when Osewoudt suddenly decided to marry her

   Koster argues that such cases are grammatical only if the adjunct clause has scope over the matrix clause. The adjunct clause may therefore be assumed to be outside the c-command domain of the subject pronoun.
5. Chomsky (1986a) has an unnecessarily complex definition of condition C for R-expressions due to his assumption that traces are R-expressions.
6. Vat (1981) perceives subtle contrasts depending on the presence or absence of resumptive pronouns, which I will not attempt to deal with here.
7. I assume that the c-command domain of the prepositional complement of *met* ("with") is identical to the c-command domain of the PP as a whole. Correspondingly, the prepositional complement can be the antecedent for an anaphor outside this PP (Postal 1971):

   (i) *I talked with <u>the boys</u> about <u>themselves</u>*
8. See Reinhart – Reuland (1990) on certain problems with condition A.

References

Barss, A.
1986 *Chains and Anaphoric Dependence: on Reconstruction and its Implications*, Unpublished Ph.D. dissertation, Massachusetts Institute of Technology, Cambridge, MA.

Chomsky, N.
1981 *Lectures on Government and Binding*, Dordrecht, Foris.

Chomsky, N.
1986a *Knowledge of Language: its Nature, Origin and Use*, New York, Praeger.

Chomsky, N.
1986b *Barriers*, MIT Press, Cambridge MA.

Everaert, M.
1983 *The interpretatie van pronominale elementen in een NP-structure model*, The Hague, ZWO.

Everaert, M.
1986 *The Syntax of Reflexivisation*, Unpublished Ph.D. dissertation, University of Utrecht, Utrecht.

Hellan, L.
1980 On Anaphora in Norwegian, *Chicago Linguistic Society 16*, 166–183.

Hoekstra, E.
1991a On the Relation between Arguments and Heads, *GLOW Newsletter 26*, 26–27.

Hoekstra, E.
1991b *Licensing Conditions on Phrase Structure*, Unpublished Ph.D. dissertation, University of Groningen, Groningen.

Huang, J.
1982 *Logical Relations in Chinese and the Theory of Grammar*, Unpublished Ph.D. dissertation, Massachusetts Institute of Technology, Cambridge, MA.

Jackendoff, R.
1972 *Semantic Interpretation in Generative Grammar*, Cambridge MA, MIT Press.

Kayne, R.
1984 *Connectedness and Binary Branching*, Dordrecht, Foris.

Koster, J.
1987 *Domains and Dynasties*, Dordrecht, Foris.

Ladusaw, W.
1980 *Polarity Sensitivity as Inherent Scope Relations*, Bloomington, Indiana University Linguistics Club.

Lakoff, G.
1968 *Pronouns and Reference*, Bloomington, Indiana University Linguistics Club.

Lust, B.
1986 *Studies in the Acquisition of Anaphora*, Dordrecht, Reidel.

Postal, P.
1971 *Cross-Over Phenomena*, New York, Holt, Rinehart and Winston.

Reinhart, T.
1983 *Anaphora and Semantic Interpretation*, London, Croom Helm.

Reinhart, T.
1986 Center and Periphery in the Grammar of Anaphora, In: B. Lust (ed.), *Studies in the Acquisition of Anaphora*, Dordrecht, Reidel.
Reinhart, T. and E. Reuland
1990 *Anaphoric Territories*, Unpublished MS, University of Tel Aviv, University of Groningen, Groningen.
Riemsdijk, H. van and E. Williams
1981 NP-Structure, *The Linguistic Review 1*, 171–217.
Rizzi, L.
1990 *Relativised Minimality*, Cambridge MA, MIT Press.
Vat, J.
1981 *Left-dislocation, Connectedness and Reconstruction*, Unpublished MS, University of Amsterdam, Amsterdam.
Zwarts, F.
1981 Negatief Polaire Uitdrukkingen I, *GLOT 4*, 35–132.

Thematic accessibility in discontinuous dependencies

Antonio Sanfilippo

1. Introduction

It is well-known that discontinuity in VP constituency in Italian is largely due to the possibility of rearranging the order of complements within a sentence through left or right clitic dislocation (henceforth CLD).[1] For example, left CLD allows either the direct or indirect object of a verb to be realized in sentence-initial position to yield OSV ordering as shown in (1) and (2).

(1) a. *Maria vedrá Carlo domani*
Maria will see Carlo tomorrow
'Maria will see Carlo tomorrow'

b. *Carlo, Maria lo vedrà domani*
Carlo, Maria him(CLITIC) will see tomorrow
'Carlo, Maria will see him tomorrow'

(2) a. *Carlo non ha ancora scritto a Gianni*
Carlo not has already written to Gianni
'Carlo has not written to Gianni yet'

b. *A Gianni, Carlo non gli ha ancora scritto*
to Gianni Carlo not to-him(CLITIC) has already written
*'To Gianni, Carlo has not written to him yet'

Prima facie, CLD does not seem to differ from canonical *wh*-movement insofar as it obeys island restrictions such as the Complex NP Constraint (Cinque 1977; 1990), as illustrated in (3).

However, the fact that CLD does not license parasitic gaps and is insensitive to weak crossover effects places serious doubts on the possibility of assimilating CLD to *wh*-movement (Cinque 1990). *Wh*-movement does in fact exhibit exactly the opposite distribution: parasitic gaps are licensed, while weak crossover leads to ungrammaticality. The sets of contrasts in (4) and (5) exemplify this issue.

(3) **Carlo, Maria ha conosciuto il giornalista che l'*
Carlo, Maria has met the reporter who him(CLITIC)
ha intervistato
has interviewed
'Carlo, Maria met the reporter who interviewed him'

(4) *wh*-MOVEMENT

a. *Chi*$_1$ *ama sua*$_1$ *madre?*
who loves his mother
*'Who$_1$ does his$_1$ mother love?'

b. *Qual articolo hai archiviato senza leggere?*
which article have-you filed without read-INF
'Which article did you file without reading?'

(5) CLD

a. *Carlo*$_1$, *l' ha sempre viziato sua*$_1$ *madre*
Carlo, him(CLITIC) has always spoiled his mother
'Carlo$_1$, his$_1$ mother has always spoiled him'

b. **Quell' articolo, l' ho archiviato senza leggere*
that article it(CLITIC) have-I filed without read-INF
*'That article, I filed it without reading'

Indeed, CLD differs from extraction processes which can be characterized in terms of *wh*-movement (e.g. *wh*-questions, topicalization and relativization) in that it can relate a verb and one of its arguments across two *wh*-islands as shown in (6), and it allows for multiple displacements and crossed dependencies as indicated in (7).

(6) a. *Carlo, chi sa chi l' ha visto?*
Carlo, who knows who him(CLITIC) has seen
Carlo, who knows who saw him?'

b. *Questo problema, chi ti ha chiesto come*
this problem, who to-you(CLITIC) has asked how

si faccia a risolverlo?
IMPERSONAL makes to solve-INF-it(CLITIC)
'This problem, who asked of you how to solve it?'

(7) a. *A Gianni, Carlo, gliel' ha presentato Maria*
to Gianni, Carlo, to-him(CLITIC)–him(CLITIC) has introduced Maria
*'To Gianni, Carlo, Maria introduced him to him'

b. Carlo$_1$, a Gianni$_2$, gliel'ha presentato Maria $_{-1}$ $_{-2}$

Moreover, an extraction analysis of CLD is deemed to assume that the pronominal clitics which are associated with dislocation sites (e.g. *gli* and *lo/l'* in the examples above) may function as agreement markers which do not saturate the valency of a verb. This assumption is at variance with the behaviour that pronominal clitics exhibit in environments other than dislocation: a clitic is in complementary distribution with a concordant object phrase whether the phrase is *in situ* as in (8), or displaced through *wh*-movement as in (9).

(8) a. **Maria lo vedrà Carlo domani*
Maria him(CLITIC) will see Carlo tomorrow

b. **Carlo gli scrive a Luigi ogni mese*
Carlo to-him(CLITIC) writes to Luigi every month

(9) a. *Chi (*l') hai incontrato ieri?*
who him(CLITIC) have-you met yesterday?
*'Who did you meet him yesterday?'

b. *CARLO Luigi (*l') ha incontrato ieri*
Carlo Luigi him(CLITIC) has met yesterday
'CARLO Luigi met him yesterday'

c. *L'uomo il quale Gianni (*l') ha incontrato ieri ...*
the man whom Gianni him(CLITIC) has met yesterday
'The man whom Gianni met him yesterday ... '

Were we to generalize the restrictions which hold for canonical extraction operations to CLD, we would be at a loss to explain the different behaviour which these two types of long distance dependencies exhibit with respect to the *wh*-island constraint, the occurrence of multiple displacements and crossed dependencies, as well as the co-occurrence of clitics with concordant object phrases. It would then be advisable to consider alternative treatments where obedience to some island constraints (e.g. the Complex NP Constraint) does not imply an extraction analysis of dislocation.

In keeping with the data discussed above, a version of the Unification Categorial Grammar framework developed in Zeevat – Klein – Calder (1987) is presented in section 1 according to which CLD dependencies can be accounted for in terms of thematic assignment properties of verbs arising from lexical entailments within a *neo-Davidsonian* approach to verb semantics (Parsons 1980; Carlson 1984; Dowty 1989). In section 2, we show how such an account can be derived by making some minimal assumptions about the nature of cliticization. Dislocated phrases are analyzed as sentential adjuncts which saturate a thematic role in the domain of active entailments of verb meanings associated with a sentence, and integrate the instantiated role with the semantics of the sentence. The resulting approach provides a syntactic treatment of discontinuous VP constituency in Italian that integrates a semantic analysis and has a clear computational interpretation.

2. Unification Categorial Grammar

Unification Categorial Grammar (UCG) partakes of recent trends in theoretical and computational linguistics that have characterized the surge of unification-based grammar frameworks throughout the last decade. More specifically, UCG combines general properties of sign-based and categorial grammar formalisms with a typed system of unification. The interaction of these formal tools for grammar development forms the basis for a model of natural language understanding which provides a novel and sophisticated integration of syntax and semantics within a computationally efficient system of linguistic description.

As in the HPSG framework of Pollard – Sag (1987; 1994), a lexical item or phrase in UCG is described as a feature structure where phonological, categorial (syntactic) and semantic information is simultaneously represented as a conjunction of attribute-value pairs forming a *sign*. The structure of a sign is established in an axiomatic fashion through "type declarations". Type declarations express global restrictions on the range of possible instantiations which can be assigned to both a sign and its attributes (Moens et al. 1989). The type declaration in Figure 1, for example, expresses the generalization that any legal instantiation for a structure of type *sign* must contain a specification for the three attributes *phonology*, *category*, and *semantics*.

$$sign \Rightarrow \begin{bmatrix} \texttt{phon} = \textit{atomic-phon} \sqcup \textit{complex-phon} \\ \texttt{cat} = \textit{basic-cat} \sqcup \textit{complex-cat} \\ \texttt{sem} = \textit{formula} \end{bmatrix}$$

Figure 1. Declaration for the type *sign*

Each attribute of a sign is likewise associated with a type declaration indicating restrictions on the range of values that the attribute may take. For example, the types *atomic-phon* and *complex-phon* in Figure 1 specify the value for the phonology attribute to be either a single word, or the concatenation of two phonological structures each taking either an atomic or a complex value:

$$\textit{complex-phon} \Rightarrow [\,\textit{atomic-phon} \sqcup \textit{complex-phon}\,]^\frown[\,\textit{atomic-phon} \sqcup \textit{complex-phon}\,]$$

Figure 2. Type declaration for *complex-phon*

In keeping with the insights of a categorial calculus, the type restrictions relative to the second attribute of the sign structure in Figure 1 state that the category of a sign can be either basic or complex. Basic categories are binary structures consisting of a category name, and a series of attribute value pairs encoding morphosyntactic features inherent to these category names:

$$\textit{basic-cat} \Rightarrow \begin{bmatrix} \texttt{name} = \textit{noun} \sqcup \textit{np} \sqcup \textit{sent} \\ \texttt{m-feats} = \textit{noun-or-np-feats} \sqcup \textit{sent-feats} \end{bmatrix}$$

Figure 3. Type declaration for basic categories

Complex categories are recursively defined by letting the category attribute of a sign to be of the form *result* $_{dir}/$ *active* where *result* can instantiate either a basic or complex category, *active* is of type *sign*, and *dir* encodes directionality relative to the active part of the sign (*f* for "forward" and *b* for "backward"):

$$\textit{complex-cat} \Rightarrow \textit{basic-cat} \sqcup \textit{complex-cat} \;{}_{f \sqcup b}/\; \textit{sign}$$

Figure 4. Declaration for the type *complex-cat*

The semantic attribute of a sign takes a value of type *formula*. A UCG formula is defined as a tripartite feature structure consisting of an index, a predicate and a list of its arguments:

$$\mathit{formula} \Rightarrow \begin{bmatrix} \texttt{ind} = \mathit{variable} \\ \texttt{pred} = \mathit{predicate} \\ \texttt{args} = \mathit{arg\text{-}list} \end{bmatrix} \qquad \mathit{arg\text{-}list} \Rightarrow \begin{bmatrix} \texttt{arg-first} = \mathit{variable} \sqcup \mathit{formula} \\ \texttt{arg-rest} = \mathit{empty\text{-}arg\text{-}list} \sqcup \mathit{arg\text{-}list} \end{bmatrix}$$

Figure 5. Declaration for the types *formula* and *arg-list*

The index of a formula is a sorted variable which provides information about the ontological type denoted by the formula. Sorted variables are defined as partial descriptions of semantic entities relative to a given set of defining properties and co-occurrence restrictions regimenting their distribution. These partial descriptions correspond to formulae of propositional logic, and form a subsumption ordering where the unification of two sorts is computed as the logical conjunction of their defining formulae (Moens et al. 1989).

Phonological, syntactic and semantic relations among signs are captured through rules of functional application. Functional application allows a functor sign to combine with an adjacent argument sign just in case the information contained in the active sign of the functor is compatible with the information encoded in the argument sign. The result is a sign whose phonology is the concatenation of the functor and argument phonologies, semantics correspond to the semantics of the functor, and category is equal to the category of the functor with its active sign removed. This is shown in Figures 6–7 where structure sharing is indicated by repeated occurrence of PATR-boxes, e.g. $\boxed{1} \ldots \boxed{1}$.

$$\begin{bmatrix} \texttt{phon} = \boxed{1} \\ \texttt{cat} = \boxed{2} \;{}_f/\; \boxed{3} \\ \texttt{sem} = \boxed{4} \end{bmatrix}, \; \boxed{3}\begin{bmatrix} \texttt{phon} = \boxed{5} \\ \texttt{cat} \\ \texttt{sem} \end{bmatrix} \rightarrow \begin{bmatrix} \texttt{phon} = \boxed{1} \frown \boxed{5} \\ \texttt{cat} = \boxed{2} \\ \texttt{sem} = \boxed{4} \end{bmatrix}$$

Figure 6. Forward functional application

$$\boxed{3}\begin{bmatrix}\texttt{phon} & = & \boxed{5}\\ \texttt{cat} & & \\ \texttt{sem} & & \end{bmatrix}, \begin{bmatrix}\texttt{phon} & = & \boxed{1} & & \\ \texttt{cat} & = & \boxed{2} & /_{b} & \boxed{3}\\ \texttt{sem} & = & \boxed{4} & & \end{bmatrix} \rightarrow \begin{bmatrix}\texttt{phon} & = & \boxed{5}\frown\boxed{1}\\ \texttt{cat} & = & \boxed{2}\\ \texttt{sem} & = & \boxed{4}\end{bmatrix}$$

Figure 7. Backward functional application

2.1 Thematic roles and verb semantics

It is now often recognized that the elaboration of Davidson's approach to verb semantics proposed by Parsons (1980) provides a natural encoding of thematic information within a model-theoretic framework. The naturalness of such encoding results from the central role which thematic relations play in the association of a verb with its arguments during sentence formation. In the light of Parsons' approach, verbs denote properties of eventualities, and thematic roles are relations between eventualities and individuals; the logical form of a sentence involves event quantification over these two types of eventuality-denoting expressions, e.g.

(10) ∃e[walk(e) & agent(e,john)]

Thematic relations thus provide an indispensable layer of semantic interpretation to combine verb and noun phrase meanings into sentence meanings. A UCG specification of this approach to verb semantics and predicate-argument association can be provided easily, as indicated in Figure 8 where `arg1` and `arg2` abbreviate the feature paths `args:arg-first` and `args:arg-rest:arg-first` respectively.

$$\begin{bmatrix}\texttt{ind} & = & \boxed{1}\\ \texttt{pred} & = & \textit{and}\\ \texttt{arg1} & = & \begin{bmatrix}\texttt{ind} & = & \boxed{1}\\ \texttt{pred} & = & \textit{walk}\\ \texttt{arg1} & = & \boxed{1}\,e\end{bmatrix}\\ \texttt{arg2} & = & \begin{bmatrix}\texttt{ind} & = & \boxed{1}\\ \texttt{pred} & = & \textit{agent}\\ \texttt{arg1} & = & \boxed{1}\\ \texttt{arg2} & = & \textit{john}\end{bmatrix}\end{bmatrix}$$

Figure 8. Neo-Davidsonian semantics for the sentence *John walks*

Within a system of this kind, properties of verbs regarding thematic assignment and subcategorization are derived from a model-theoretic characterization of verb meanings in terms of necessary thematic entailments (Carlson 1984; Dowty 1989). More precisely, the participant roles assigned by a verb are identified as roles which the verb necessarily entails, and subcategorization is derived as a projection from these entailments. Clearly, not all roles which are necessarily entailed by a verb are syntactically realized as arguments of the verb. For example, an event of selling necessarily entails the existence of a seller, a buyer, and an object on sale, as well as a location where the transaction takes place and the price (to be) paid. Yet, only the first three roles correspond to subcategorized arguments (i.e. subject, object and indirect object of *sell*). Therefore, this account of subcategorization requires a specific indication of which thematic entailments of a verb must be realized syntactically. For ease of reference the set of thematic entailments which results from this selection will henceforth be referred to as the *thematic domain* of the verb (θ-DOM).

The thematic entailments contained in the θ-DOM of a verb encode expectations about possible extensions of the verb's semantics, as well as restrictions on the eventuality argument variable of the verb. For example, the agent and theme roles which forms the θ-DOM of *drink* confine the referential scope of the index variable of the verb to some eventuality in which there are two individuals, one functioning as the agent participant and the other as theme. This can be expressed in terms of restricted event quantification as shown below.

(11) (∃e: ∃x [agent(e,x)] & ∃y [theme(e,y)])walk(e)

To accommodate this characterization of argument roles, the index attribute of a UCG formula is allowed to be a complex structure consisting of a sorted variable and a θ-DOM as shown in Figure 9.

$$ind \Rightarrow \begin{bmatrix} \texttt{var} & = & \mathit{sort} \\ \theta\text{-DOM} & = & \theta\textit{-sequence} \end{bmatrix}$$

Figure 9. Type declaration for complex indexes

The θ-DOM is encoded as a string sequence of thematic formulae which is constructed with the associative operator $\circ$ as specified in (12), and for which the identity axiom in (13) holds.[2]

(12) a. If A is a feature structure, a variable, or the empty string Λ then $\langle A \rangle$ is a string.

b. If $\langle A \rangle$ and $\langle B \rangle$ are strings, then $\langle A \circ B \rangle$ is also a string.

(13) The symbol Λ is a string (i.e. the empty string), such that $\Lambda \circ \sigma = \sigma = \sigma \circ \Lambda$ for any element σ of a sequence.

In light of this approach, the semantics of a verb such as *drink* is represented by the UCG formula in Figure 10.

$$\begin{bmatrix} \texttt{ind} = \begin{bmatrix} \texttt{var} = \boxed{1} \\ \theta\texttt{-dom} = \left\langle \begin{bmatrix} \texttt{ind} = \boxed{1} \\ \texttt{pred} = \textit{theme} \\ \texttt{arg1} = \boxed{1} \\ \texttt{arg2} = y \end{bmatrix} \circ \begin{bmatrix} \texttt{ind} = \boxed{1} \\ \texttt{pred} = \textit{agent} \\ \texttt{arg1} = \boxed{1} \\ \texttt{arg2} = x \end{bmatrix} \right\rangle \end{bmatrix} \\ \texttt{pred} = \textit{drink} \\ \texttt{arg1} = \boxed{1}\, e \end{bmatrix}$$

Figure 10. Verbs semantics for *drink*

The use of string sequences in this context makes it possible to select a thematic formula out of a θ-DOM structure without having to specify its exact position in the θ-DOM. In the next section, we will show how this encoding can be made to provide appropriate means to characterize the degree of freedom in VP constituency which is found in CLD dependencies.

Grammatical relations are encoded by coinstantiating the thematic formulae of the verb θ-DOM with the values for the semantic attribute of subcategorized signs (Sanfilippo 1991). An illustrative example is given in Figure 11 where x3 is a sorted variable for third person individual objects and `catn` abbreviates the feature path `cat:name`.[3]

The association of a verb with one of its subcategorized arguments involves saturation of the active sign in the category structure of the verb, and removal of the outermost thematic entailment from the verb θ-DOM. The removed thematic entailment is integrated with the semantics of the verb to form a complex formula which is the semantic representation of the newly formed phrasal sign. In addition, the current verb θ-DOM (i.e. the original θ-DOM minus the removed thematic entailment) becomes the θ-DOM of this complex formula. This process as a whole is induced through a single step of functional application by structuring subject and object phrases as polymorphic type-raised complements (i.e. signs with category type X/(X/np) where X is a variable over categories), as shown in Figure 12. (The PATR-box $\boxed{5}$ in Figure 12 allows additional elements within the θ-DOM of the active sign

$$\begin{bmatrix} \mathtt{phon} = \textit{walks} \\ \mathtt{catn} = \textit{sent} \;{}_{f}\!/ \begin{bmatrix} \mathtt{catn} = \textit{np} \\ \mathtt{sem} = \boxed{1} \end{bmatrix} \\ \mathtt{sem} = \begin{bmatrix} \mathtt{ind} = \begin{bmatrix} \mathtt{var} = \boxed{2} \\ \theta\text{-}\mathtt{dom} = \left\langle \boxed{1} \begin{bmatrix} \mathtt{ind} = \boxed{2} \\ \mathtt{pred} = \textit{agent} \\ \mathtt{arg1} = \boxed{2} \\ \mathtt{arg2} = x3 \end{bmatrix} \right\rangle \end{bmatrix} \\ \mathtt{pred} = \textit{walk} \\ \mathtt{arg1} = \boxed{2}\, e \end{bmatrix} \end{bmatrix}$$

Figure 11. Sample sign for intransitive verbs; the coindexation of the active semantics with the agent role in the verb θ-DOM encodes the subject relation

(e.g. a verb or verb phrase) to be transmitted to the θ-DOM of the resulting sign; if there are no additional thematic entailments, $\boxed{5}$ instantiates the empty sequence and it is merged with the preceding formula according to the identity axiom in (13).)

$$\begin{bmatrix} \mathtt{phon} = \textit{John} \\ \mathtt{cat} = \boxed{1} \;{}_{\boxed{2}}\!/ \begin{bmatrix} \mathtt{cat} = \boxed{1} \;{}_{\boxed{2}}\!/ \begin{bmatrix} \mathtt{catn} = \textit{np} \\ \mathtt{sem} = \boxed{3} \end{bmatrix} \\ \mathtt{sem} = \begin{bmatrix} \mathtt{ind} = \begin{bmatrix} \mathtt{var} = \boxed{4} \\ \theta\text{-}\mathtt{dom} = \langle \boxed{3} \circ \boxed{5} \rangle \end{bmatrix} \\ \mathtt{pred} = \boxed{6} \\ \mathtt{args} = \boxed{7} \end{bmatrix} \end{bmatrix} \\ \mathtt{sem} = \begin{bmatrix} \mathtt{ind} = \begin{bmatrix} \mathtt{var} = \boxed{4} \\ \theta\text{-}\mathtt{dom} = \langle \boxed{5} \rangle \end{bmatrix} \\ \mathtt{pred} = \textit{and} \\ \mathtt{arg1} = \begin{bmatrix} \mathtt{ind} = \boxed{4} \\ \mathtt{pred} = \boxed{6} \\ \mathtt{args} = \boxed{7} \end{bmatrix} \\ \mathtt{arg2} = \boxed{3} \begin{bmatrix} \mathtt{ind} = \boxed{4} \\ \mathtt{pred} = \textit{predicate} \\ \mathtt{arg1} = \boxed{4} \\ \mathtt{arg2} = \textit{john} \end{bmatrix} \end{bmatrix} \end{bmatrix}$$

Figure 12. Sample sign for argument NPs

For example, the result of combining the verb sign in Figure 11 with the type-raised NP above is the sentential sign shown in Figure 13. In this case the θ-DOM of the resulting sign is empty since the original verb θ-DOM contained a single thematic entailment.

$$
\begin{bmatrix}
\texttt{phon} = \textit{John}^\frown\textit{walks} \\
\texttt{catn} = \textit{sent} \\
\texttt{sem} = \begin{bmatrix}
\texttt{ind} = \begin{bmatrix} \texttt{var} = \boxed{4} \\ \theta\texttt{-dom} = \langle\,\rangle \end{bmatrix} \\
\texttt{pred} = \textit{and} \\
\texttt{arg1} = \begin{bmatrix} \texttt{ind} = \boxed{4} \\ \texttt{pred} = \textit{walk} \\ \texttt{arg1} = \boxed{4}\,e \end{bmatrix} \\
\texttt{arg2} = \begin{bmatrix} \texttt{ind} = \boxed{4} \\ \texttt{pred} = \textit{agent} \\ \texttt{arg1} = \boxed{4} \\ \texttt{arg2} = \textit{john} \end{bmatrix}
\end{bmatrix}
\end{bmatrix}
$$

Figure 13. Sentential sign derived from the NP and verb signs in Figures 11–12

This treatment of predicate-argument association can be briefly summarized by saying that argument phrases have the following properties:

1. they satisfy the subcategorization requirements of a verb,
2. instantiate participant roles in the thematic domain of the verb,
3. integrate the instantiated roles with the semantics of the verb, and
4. reduce the domain of thematic entailments of the verb through removal of the instantiated roles.

Thematic instantiation is computed on the basis of four basic types of thematic roles: *proto-agent*, *proto-patient*, *prepositional* and *propositional* roles. Prototypical (*p-agt, p-pat*) and prepositional roles are defined in terms of entailments of verb meanings and lexical semantic defaults which qualify the agentivity potential of argument roles for each choice of predicate. This specification reproduces the basic insights of Dowty's treatment of thematic information (Dowty 1987) within a neo-Davidsonian approach to verb semantics (Sanfilippo 1990: 91–94, 149–169). Prepositional roles are chosen from the set of contentful prepositions (e.g. *to, in, from*), while the propositional role (*prop*) encodes the thematic relation between a matrix verb and its sentential complement as a relation between eventualities and propositions (e.g. *prop(e, formula)*).

3. Clitics as *Quasi-Arguments*, Dislocated Phrases as Thematically Bound Adjuncts

Our first step in providing an analysis of clitic dislocation is to give a characterization of clitics as *quasi-arguments*. More precisely, we are going to assume that a pronominal clitic saturates a subcategorized argument of the verb with which it combines and instantiates a participant role in the verb θ-DOM, but may neither reduce the thematic domain of the verb nor integrate the instantiated role with the verb semantics. The basic idea behind this assumption is that, syntactically, clitics behave exactly as argument phrases do, while with respect to semantic interpretation they may only provide further specification (e.g. agreement information) relative to the thematic entailments they instantiate, and postpone the discharge of such entailments. For example, the UCG representation for the sentence in (14) where both direct and indirect objects are realized as pronominal clitics will be a sentential sign where the object thematic entailments of the verb are still encoded in the verb θ-DOM as shown in Figure 14; the individual argument variable of such roles will nevertheless carry the agreement information contributed by the object clitics (*m3* is a sorted variable for third person objects which are both male and singular).

(14) *gliel' ha presentato Maria*
to-3rd(CLITIC)-him(CLITIC) has introduced Maria
'Maria introduced him to her/him'

The complementary distribution between clitics and concordant argument phrases noted earlier for the sentences in (8) and (9) can thus be made to follow from the fact that both pronominal clitics and argument phrases seek to remove the active sign from the complex category of a verb.

Consider next the behaviour of dislocated phrases. Prima facie, the ungrammaticality of sentences such as the one in (15) where the same argument position is shared by a dislocated phrase and an object NP *in situ* might lead us to conclude that dislocated phrases are arguments.

(15) **Carlo, Maria vedrà lui domani*
Carlo, Maria will see him tomorrow
'Carlo, Maria will see him tomorrow'

$$\left[\begin{array}{lll}
\texttt{phon} & = & \textit{gliel'ha}^\frown\textit{presentato}^\frown\textit{Maria}\\
\texttt{catn} & = & \textit{sent}\\
\texttt{sem} & = & \left[\begin{array}{lll}
\texttt{ind} & = & \left[\begin{array}{lll}
\texttt{var} & = & \boxed{1}\\
\theta\texttt{-dom} & = & \left\langle \left[\begin{array}{lll}\texttt{ind} & = & \boxed{1}\\ \texttt{pred} & = & \textit{p-pat}\\ \texttt{arg1} & = & \boxed{1}\\ \texttt{arg2} & = & \textit{m3}\end{array}\right] \circ \left[\begin{array}{lll}\texttt{ind} & = & \boxed{1}\\ \texttt{pred} & = & \textit{to}\\ \texttt{arg1} & = & \boxed{1}\\ \texttt{arg2} & = & \textit{x3}\end{array}\right]\right\rangle
\end{array}\right]\\
\texttt{pred} & = & \textit{and}\\
\texttt{arg1} & = & \left[\begin{array}{lll}\texttt{ind} & = & \boxed{1}\\ \texttt{pred} & = & \textit{introduce}\\ \texttt{arg1} & = & \boxed{1}\,\textit{e}\end{array}\right]\\
\texttt{arg2} & = & \left[\begin{array}{lll}\texttt{ind} & = & \boxed{1}\\ \texttt{pred} & = & \textit{p-agt}\\ \texttt{arg1} & = & \boxed{1}\\ \texttt{arg2} & = & \textit{maria}\end{array}\right]
\end{array}\right]
\end{array}\right]$$

Figure 14. UCG representation for a sentence where the direct and indirect objects are realized as clitics

However, this conclusion is at variance with the fact that dislocated phrases typically occur in association with concordant pronominal clitics (see (1b), (2b), (6) and (7)) since clitics and concordant argument phrases are not allowed in environments other than dislocation (see (8) and (9)). Moreover, at least with dislocated direct objects the occurrence of pronominal clitics is mandatory, e.g. compare (16) with (1b).

(16) **Carlo, Maria vedrà domani*

In short, dislocated phrases exhibit only some of the distributional properties of true arguments in that they can freely co-occur with concordant clitics within the same sentential domain. This fact can be formally captured by treating dislocated phrases as syntactic adjuncts whose semantic properties are nevertheless akin to those of argument phrases as specified in (17).

(17) A dislocated phrase instantiates a thematic role in the thematic domain of a sentence, removes the instantiated role, and integrates it with the semantics of the sentence without saturating a syntactic argument.

The sign for the dislocated object *Carlo* below provides a concrete example of how the basic insights of this treatment can be expressed within our UCG framework.[4]

$$\begin{bmatrix} \texttt{phon} = \textit{Carlo} & \\ \texttt{catn} = \textit{sent} \; /_{f \sqcup b} & \begin{bmatrix} \texttt{catn} = \textit{sent} & \\ \texttt{sem} = & \begin{bmatrix} \texttt{ind} = \begin{bmatrix} \texttt{var} = \boxed{1} \\ \theta\texttt{-dom} = \langle \boxed{2} \circ \boxed{3} \rangle \end{bmatrix} \\ \texttt{pred} = \boxed{4} \\ \texttt{args} = \boxed{5} \end{bmatrix} \end{bmatrix} \\ \texttt{sem} = & \begin{bmatrix} \texttt{ind} = \begin{bmatrix} \texttt{var} = \boxed{1} \\ \theta\texttt{-dom} = \langle \boxed{3} \rangle \end{bmatrix} \\ \texttt{pred} = \textit{and} \\ \texttt{arg1} = \begin{bmatrix} \texttt{ind} = \boxed{1} \\ \texttt{pred} = \boxed{4} \\ \texttt{args} = \boxed{5} \end{bmatrix} \\ \texttt{arg2} = \boxed{2} \begin{bmatrix} \texttt{ind} = \boxed{1} \\ \texttt{pred} = \textit{p-pat} \\ \texttt{arg1} = \boxed{1} \\ \texttt{arg2} = \textit{carlo} \end{bmatrix} \end{bmatrix} \end{bmatrix}$$

Figure 15. Sign for clitic dislocated direct object

The association of dislocated phrases and sentences will essentially involve the same semantic operations which characterize the association of a verb with its subject and object arguments, while syntactically it will proceed in terms of sentential modification. For example, the sentential and dislocated NP signs in Figures 14–15 can combine through forward application yielding a sentential sign whose semantics results from removing the top thematic entailment from the θ-DOM of the input sentential sign and conjoining it with the semantics of the verb and its subject argument, as indicated in Figure 16 (to enhance readability the index of subformulae is omitted).

More generally, the association of a dislocated phrase and a sentence will succeed whenever the role introduced by the dislocated phrase has access to a compatible role within the thematic domain of the sentence. Provided this condition is satisfied, there are no restrictions as to how many dislocated phrases can be combined with a sentence. The occurrence of multiple displacements in dislocated sentences such as the one in (7a) will therefore follow from the possibility of combining the sentential sign in Figure 16 with an additional dislocated phrase (i.e. a dislocated indirect object introducing

$$
\left[\begin{array}{lll}
\texttt{phon} & = & \textit{Carlo,}^\frown\textit{gliel'ha}\,^\frown\textit{presentato}^\frown\textit{Maria} \\
\texttt{catn} & = & \textit{sent} \\
\texttt{sem} & = & \left[\begin{array}{lll}
\texttt{ind} & = & \left[\begin{array}{lll}
\texttt{var} & = & \boxed{1} \\
\theta\texttt{-dom} & = & \left\langle \left[\begin{array}{lll} \texttt{pred} & = & \textit{to} \\ \texttt{arg1} & = & \boxed{1} \\ \texttt{arg2} & = & \textit{x3} \end{array}\right] \right\rangle
\end{array}\right] \\
\texttt{pred} & = & \textit{and} \\
\texttt{arg1} & = & \left[\begin{array}{lll}
\texttt{pred} & = & \textit{and} \\
\texttt{arg1} & = & \left[\begin{array}{lll} \texttt{pred} & = & \textit{introduce} \\ \texttt{arg1} & = & \boxed{1}\,\textit{e} \end{array}\right] \\
\texttt{arg2} & = & \left[\begin{array}{lll} \texttt{pred} & = & \textit{p-agt} \\ \texttt{arg1} & = & \boxed{1} \\ \texttt{arg2} & = & \textit{maria} \end{array}\right]
\end{array}\right] \\
\texttt{arg2} & = & \left[\begin{array}{lll} \texttt{pred} & = & \textit{p-pat} \\ \texttt{arg1} & = & \boxed{1} \\ \texttt{arg2} & = & \textit{carlo} \end{array}\right]
\end{array}\right]
\end{array}\right]
$$

Figure 16. Sentential sign derived from the dislocated NP and sentential signs in Figures 14–15

the prepositional role *to*, whose individual object argument is third person). Such a possibility is granted by the presence of an accessible role entailment in the thematic domain of the sentential sign. Moreover, the notion of thematic accessibility adopted hitherto can be minimally extended so as to provide an account of crossed dislocation dependencies (see (7b)). The extension needed consists in weakening the requirement that the role which a dislocated phrase seeks to instantiate be the outermost thematic formula of the argument θ-DOM. This weaker notion of thematic accessibility can be implemented by adding a variable as the outermost member of the active and result θ DOMs in the sign for dislocated phrases, as indicated in the sign below by $\boxed{3}$ with reference to clitic dislocated indirect objects.

$$
\left[\begin{array}{lll}
\texttt{phon} & = & \textit{a Gianni} \\
\texttt{catn} & = & \textit{sent}_{f \sqcup b} \Big/ \left[\begin{array}{lll}
\texttt{catn} & = & \textit{sent} \\
\texttt{sem:ind:}\theta\texttt{-dom} & = & \left\langle \boxed{3} \circ \left[\begin{array}{lll} \texttt{pred} & = & \textit{to} \\ \texttt{arg1} & = & \textit{e} \\ \texttt{arg2} & = & \textit{gianni} \end{array}\right] \circ \boxed{4} \right\rangle
\end{array}\right] \\
\texttt{sem:ind:}\theta\texttt{-dom} & = & \langle \boxed{3} \circ \boxed{4} \rangle
\end{array}\right]
$$

Figure 17. Dislocated NP sign for crossed CLD dependencies

This addition will allow the dislocated oblique NP sign in Figure 17 to combine with either one of the sentential signs in Figures 14 and 16, i.e. before or after the proto-patient entailment has been removed from the θ-DOM of the sentence. The option of delaying the removal of the first entailment from the sentence θ-DOM will give rise to a sentence structure with crossed CLD dependencies (see (7b)).

3.1 Island constraints and θ-DOM inheritance

In the introductory section, we saw that dislocation may give rise to violations of the *wh*-island constraint, although it generally obeys the Complex NP Constraint. Within the present framework, this behaviour can be made to follow from a regime of θ-DOM inheritance according to which the unsaturated entailments of a complement are included in the thematic domain of its subcategorizing expression as indicated in (18b) and Figure 18. The rationale underlying such regime of inheritance is a natural consequence of the transitive nature of entailment relations, and can therefore be derived as a corollary of the notion of thematic domain developed earlier, here briefly summarized in (18a).

(18) a. θ-DOM
The θ-DOM of a lexical sign consists of participant roles which the lexical sign necessarily entails.
b. θ-DOM *Inheritance Corollary*
The θ-DOM of a lexical sign includes all the elements contained in the θ-DOM of its thematic entailments.

$$\begin{bmatrix} \texttt{phon} = \ldots \\ \texttt{cat} = \ldots \\ \texttt{sem:ind:}\theta\texttt{-dom} = \left\langle \begin{bmatrix} \texttt{ind} = \begin{bmatrix} \texttt{var} = \\ \theta\texttt{-dom} = \langle \boxed{1} \rangle \end{bmatrix} \\ \texttt{pred} = \textit{predicate} \\ \texttt{args} = \textit{arg-list} \end{bmatrix} \circ \ldots \circ \boxed{1} \right\rangle \end{bmatrix}$$

Figure 18. Sample instance of the θ-DOM Inheritance Corollary

Consider, for example, the case of a sentence such as (19).

(19) *Chi sa chi l' ha visto?*
who knows who him(CLITIC) has seen
'Who knows who saw him?'

Because the object of the complement verb *ha visto* is realized as a clitic, the θ-DOM of the complement sentence in (19) will encode the proto-patient role associated with that object as shown in Figure 19.[5,6]

$$\left[\begin{array}{l}\texttt{phon} = \textit{chi}^\frown \textit{l'ha}^\frown \textit{visto}\\ \texttt{cat} = \boxed{1}\ {}_{\boxed{2}}/\left[\begin{array}{l}\texttt{cat} = \boxed{1}\ {}_{\boxed{2}}/\left[\begin{array}{l}\texttt{catn} = \textit{sent}\\ \texttt{sem} = \boxed{3}\end{array}\right]\\ \texttt{sem:ind:}\theta\texttt{-dom} = \left\langle \boxed{3}\left[\begin{array}{l}\texttt{ind:}\theta\texttt{-dom} = \left\langle\left[\begin{array}{l}\texttt{pred} = \textit{p-pat}\\ \texttt{arg1} = e\\ \texttt{arg2} = m3\end{array}\right]\right\rangle\\ \texttt{pred} = \textit{prop}\\ \texttt{arg1} = e\\ \texttt{arg2} = \ldots\end{array}\right] \circ \boxed{4}\right\rangle\end{array}\right]\\ \texttt{sem:ind:}\theta\texttt{-dom} = \langle\boxed{4}\rangle\end{array}\right]$$

Figure 19. UCG representation for sentential complements with an unsaturated thematic entailment

Given the θ-DOM Inheritance Corollary in (18b), the θ-DOM of the matrix verb *sa* in (19) will include any role entailment which the complement θ-DOM might have. This result is obtained by entering the elements of the complement θ-DOM in the matrix verb θ-DOM as indicated in Figure 20 by $\boxed{4}$.

$$\left[\begin{array}{l}\texttt{phon} = \textit{sa}\\ \texttt{catn} = \textit{sent}\ {}_{f}/\left[\begin{array}{l}\texttt{catn} = \textit{np}\\ \texttt{sem} = \boxed{1}\end{array}\right]{}_{b}/\left[\begin{array}{l}\texttt{catn} = \textit{sent}\\ \texttt{sem} = \boxed{3}\end{array}\right]\\ \texttt{sem:ind:}\theta\texttt{-dom} = \left\langle \boxed{3}\left[\begin{array}{l}\texttt{ind:}\theta\texttt{-dom} = \langle\boxed{4}\rangle\\ \texttt{pred} = \textit{prop}\\ \texttt{arg1} = \boxed{2}\\ \texttt{arg2} = \textit{formula}\end{array}\right] \circ \boxed{1}\left[\begin{array}{l}\texttt{pred} = \textit{p-agt}\\ \texttt{arg1} = \boxed{2}\,e\\ \texttt{arg2} = x3\end{array}\right] \circ \boxed{4}\right\rangle\end{array}\right]$$

Figure 20. UCG representation for verbs taking a sentential complement

The fact that the complement object is inside a *wh*-island will have no effect on the inheritance of the role entailment associated with it. Notice in fact that according to the θ-DOM *Inheritance Corollary* the only prerequisite for entailment inheritance is that the expression from which the entailment is inherited be contained within the θ-DOM of the inheriting expression. This condition holds of a verb and its sentential complement regardless of whether the complement is a *wh*-island or not. The unsaturated thematic entailment of the complement sentence in (19) will therefore be transmitted to the θ-DOM of the entire sentence as shown in Figure 21, so that the sentence as a whole will be amenable to combination with a dislocated object giving rise to a sentence structure such as the one in (6a) here repeated as (20).

$$\begin{bmatrix} \texttt{phon} = \textit{chi}^\frown \textit{sa}^\frown \textit{chi}^\frown \textit{l'ha}^\frown \textit{visto} \\ \texttt{catn} = \textit{sent} \\ \texttt{sem:ind:}\theta\texttt{-dom} = \left\langle \begin{bmatrix} \texttt{pred} = \textit{p-pat} \\ \texttt{arg1} = e \\ \texttt{arg2} = m3 \end{bmatrix} \right\rangle \end{bmatrix}$$

Figure 21. UCG sign for *wh*-question with an active θ-DOM

(20) *Carlo, chi sa chi l'ha visto?*

Because the relation of role inheritance can essentially be established only between a functor expression and its complements, it follows that unsaturated entailments of adjuncts cannot be transmitted to the θ-DOM of the phrase which they modify. For example, the object entailment of the relative clause in Figure 22 will not be inherited by the θ-DOM of its head noun because the relative clause is not a subcategorized complement of the noun, and therefore its semantics is not an element of the noun θ-DOM.

$$\text{il} \left[_{\langle\,\rangle}\ \textit{giornalista} \left[_{\langle [e]p\text{-}pat(e,\,m3)\rangle}\ \textit{che l'ha intervistato}\right]\right]$$

'the reporter who interviewed him(CLITIC)'

Figure 22. Complex NP containing a nominal adjunct which has an unsaturated role entailment

The θ-DOM of the noun will therefore act as a barrier with respect to the inheritance of the complement object role. Consequently, the θ-DOM of the (complex) noun phrase in Figure 22 will be empty, and the matrix verb in Figure 23 will not be in a position to inherit the unsaturated entailment of the relative clause; ultimately, the sentence as a whole will not have an accessible thematic entailment in its θ-DOM.

$$\left[_{\langle\,\rangle}\ \textit{Maria} \left[_{\langle [e]p\text{-}agt(e,\,x3)\rangle}\ \textit{ha conosciuto} \left[_{\langle\,\rangle}\ \textit{il giornalista che l'ha intervistato}\right]\right]\right]$$

'Maria met the reporter who interviewed him(CLITIC)'

Figure 23. Sentence whose object NP contains a nominal adjunct with an unsaturated role entailment

Insofar as dislocated phrases require the presence of an accessible role within the θ-DOM of the sentence with which they combine, the occurrence of a dislocated object in this case is ruled out even though somewhere inside the sentence there is an unsaturated role entailment. The sensitivity of CLD dependencies to the Complex NP Constraint (see, for example, (3)) can therefore be made to follow from the θ-DOM Inheritance Corollary which effectively disallows the transmittance of thematic entailments across adjuncts. This treatment is corroborated by the ungrammaticality of sentences such as (21) where a dislocated object is related to the unsaturated role entailment of a sentence across a VP/sentential adjunct clause.

(21) **A Giorgio, Grazia si è preoccupata perchè/quando*
to Giorgio, Grazia got worried because/when
gliel' hanno detto
to-him(CLITIC)-it(CLITIC) have-they told
*'To Giorgio, Grazia got worried because/when they told it to him'

4. Conclusion

The basic idea developed in this paper is that the relevant constraints on discontinuous verb-object dependencies which arise in Italian through clitic dislocation can be expressed in terms of access to the thematic domain of a sentence as indicated in (22).

(22) A dislocated phrase must have access to a compatible participant role within the domain of unsaturated thematic entailments of the sentence with which it combines.

This generalization was shown to have a precise syntactic, semantic and computational interpretation within a UCG framework augmented with a neo-Davidsonian treatment of verb semantics and predicate-argument association. The resulting approach also provides an account of the co-occurrence of pronominal clitics and concordant NPs found in CLD, and can be easily extended to yield a treatment of dislocated subjects by adopting an analysis of subject agreement morphemes which reproduces the basic insights of the analysis of pronominal clitics as quasi-arguments, e.g. assuming that tensed verbs do not subcategorize for a subject phrase (Sanfilippo 1990: 315–316). This extension is empirically motivated by the fact that dislocated subject and object phrases exhibit identical distributional properties with respect to island constraints, e.g. obedience to the Complex NP constraint, and violation of the *wh*-island constraint:

(23) a. *Carlo, chi sa dov' è andato?*
Carlo, who knows-he(AGR) where is-he(AGR) gone
'Carlo, who knows where he has gone?'

b. **Sciascia, Maria ha letto tutti i libri che*
Sciascia, Maria has-she(AGR) read all the books which
ha scritto
has-he(AGR) written
'Sciascia, Maria has read all the books which he wrote'

Our treatment of clitic dislocation will therefore have interesting consequences with respect to discontinuous subject-VP dependencies as well.

Acknowledgements. I am indebted to John Beaven, Steven Bird, Jo Calder, Elisabet Engdahl, Ewan Klein, Pete Whitelock, Henk Zeevat, and the participants of the DYANA workshop on Parametric Variation for helpful comments.

Notes

1. Clitic dislocation is restricted to constituents which convey given information; for example, a questioned object NP is not amenable to CLD:

   **Quale giornale, l' hai letto?*
   which newspaper it(CLITIC) have-you read
   'Which newspaper, have you read it(CLITIC)?'

   The displaced constituent is followed by a short intonational break which is orthographically rendered as a comma. A pronominal clitic (*l'* in the example above) is usually found which marks the position of canonical occurrence for the dislocated phrase. See Cinque (1977, 1990) and Duranti – Ochs (1979).
2. The unification of θ-DOM sequences is computed in terms of *string unification* – i.e. unification augmented with associativity (Siekmann 1975). Although in the general case, the unification of two string forms presents computational com-

plexities with respect to both completeness and termination, it is well known that where the occurrence of repeated variables is limited to only one of the two string forms string unification is decidable and yields a unique result (Siekmann 1975, 1984; Calder 1990). The treatment of clitic dislocation proposed in this paper is in keeping with this restriction.

3. The specification for direction relative to the subject is "forward" because verbs combine with type raised NPs whose category inherits directionality from the outermost categorial slash of the verb, as indicated in Figure 12 by [2].
4. The underspecification of directionality encoded by the disjunction f $\sqcup$ b in Figure 15 makes it possible to use the same sign for both right and left clitic dislocation.
5. In keeping with our treatment of subject and object phrases, a sentential complement is treated as a type-raised argument (e.g. a sign with category of type X/(X/sent) where X is a variable over categories) which reduces the subcategorization list and θ-DOM of its matrix verb, and conjoins the semantics of the matrix verb with a propositional role. The first argument of this propositional role is the eventuality variable of the matrix verb, while the second argument corresponds to the semantics of the complement verb including its dependents. For example, the semantic representation for a sentence like *John heard that Mary arrived* will correspond to the first order formula below. (See Sanfilippo (1990: 157–161) for further details, and Klein (1987) for a similar proposal within a different treatment of verb semantics.)
   ∃ e [hear(e) & prop(e, ∃ e'[arrive(e') & p-agt(e', mary)]) & p-agt(e, john)]
6. The PATR-box [4] in Figure 19 allows thematic entailments of the argument θ-DOM other than the propositional role introduced by the sentential complement (i.e. the formula indexed by [3]) to be transmitted to the result θ-DOM.

References

Calder, Jonathan
1990 *An Interpretation of Paradigmatic Morphology*, PhD thesis, Centre for Cognitive Science, University of Edinburgh, Scotland.

Carlson, Greg
1984 On the Role of Thematic Roles in Linguistic Theory, *Linguistics* 22, 259–279.

Cinque, Guglielmo
1977 The Movement Nature of Left-Dislocation, *Linguistic Inquiry* 8, 397–412.

Cinque, Guglielmo
1990 *Types of A' Dependencies*, MIT Press, Cambridge, Massachusetts.

Dowty, David
1987 Thematic Proto Roles, Subject Selection, and Lexical Semantic Defaults, *LSA Colloquium paper.*

Dowty, David
1989 On the Semantic Content of the Notion 'Thematic & Role', In: Chierchia, Gennaro – Barbara Partee – Ray Turner (eds.), *Property Theory, Type Theory and & Natural Language Semantics*, D. Reidel, Dordrecht.

Klein, Ewan
1987 *Control and Binding in Unification Categorial Grammar,* ms, Centre for Cognitive Science, University of Edinburgh.

Moens, Mark, Jo Calder, Ewan Klein, Mike Reape and Henk Zeevat
1989 Expressing Generalizations in Unification-Based Grammar Formalisms, *Proceedings of the Fourth Conference of the European Chapter of the Association for Computational Linguistics*, Manchester.

Parsons, Terence
1980 Modifiers and Quantifiers in Natural Language, *Canadian Journal of Philosophy*, supplementary Volume VI, 29–60.

Pollard, Carl – Ivan Sag
1987 *An Information-Based Approach to Syntax and Semantics: Volume 1 Fundamenals*, CSLI Lecture Notes 13, Stanford CA.

Pollard, Carl – Ivan Sag
1994 *Head-Driven Phrase Structure Grammar*, Center for the Study of Language and Information, Stanford, and University of Chicago Press, Chicago and London.

Sanfilippo, Antonio
1990 *Grammatical Relations, Thematic Roles and Verb Semantics*, PhD thesis, Centre for Cognitive Science, University of Edinburgh, Scotland.

Sanfilippo, Antonio
1991 Argument Selection and Selection Change: An Integrated Approach, *Proceedings of the 27th Regional Meeting of the Chicago Linguistic Society.*

Siekmann, Jürg
1975 *String-unification, Part 1,* ms., University of Essex.

Siekmann, Jürg
1984 Universal Unification, In: R. H. Shostak (ed.), *Proceedings of the Seventh International Conference on Automated Deduction*, Napa, California, 1–42, (Lecture Notes in Computer Science), Springer-Verlag.

Zeevat, Henk, Ewan Klein and Jo Calder
1987 An Introduction to Unification Categorial Grammar, In: Haddock, J. Nick, Ewan Klein and Glyn Morrill (eds.), *Edinburgh Working Papers in Cognitive Science, Volume 1: Categorial Grammar, Unification Grammar, and Parsing*, Centre for Cognitive Science, University of Edinburgh, Scotland.

Index

Bei Fragen zur Produktsicherheit wenden Sie sich bitte an:
If you have any questions regarding product safety,
please contact:

Walter de Gruyter GmbH
Genthiner Straße 13
10785 Berlin
productsafety@degruyterbrill.com